Running the World's Markets

Running the World's Markets

THE GOVERNANCE
OF FINANCIAL INFRASTRUCTURE

Ruben Lee

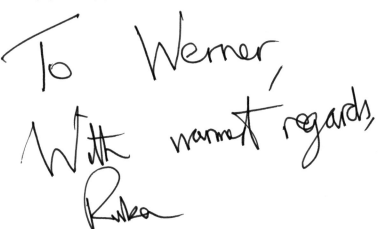

To Werner,
With warmest regards,
Ruben

Ruben Lee
22/1/2014
London

PRINCETON UNIVERSITY PRESS

PRINCETON AND OXFORD

Library of Congress Cataloging-in-Publication

Lee, Ruben.
Running the world's markets : the governance of financial infrastructure /
Ruben Lee.
p.   cm.
ISBN: 978-0-691-13353-9 (hardcover : alk. paper)
Includes bibliographical references and index.
I. Definitions—II. Market power—III. The allocation of regulatory powers over
securities markets—IV. Regulation and governance of market infrastructure
institutions : global perspective—V. Governance of market infrastructure institutions :
a snapshot—VI. Exchanges—VII. CCPs and CSDs—VIII. What is the most efficien
governance structure?—IX. Who should regulate what?—X. How should market
infrastructure institution governance be regulated?
HG4551 .L343 2011
332.64 22—dc   2010025764

British Library Cataloging-in-Publication Data is available

This book has been composed in Sabon

Printed on acid-free paper. ∞

Printed in the United States of America

10 9 8 7 6 5 4 3 2 1

To Swee-Kheng, Tian-Mei, and Tian-Long
To Mom and Dad

Contents

Foreword and Acknowledgments

This book is the result of a project analyzing the governance of infrastructure institutions in the financial markets led by Ruben Lee. He initiated the project, formulated its goals, designed its structure, raised the sponsorship for the project, and commissioned and managed a large team of experts to contribute papers on specified topics for the project. Lee then wrote the book, incorporating those elements of the experts' contributions into the text as he saw fit. The book is not an edited collection of essays written by the different contributors. Rather, Lee's goal was to produce an authoritative, coherent, and well-argued document that represented his views, but that also drew on the knowledge, wisdom, and expertise of a wide range of specialists.

Twenty-eight experts provided input to the book. These contributors, together with the chapters to which they contributed are as follows: James Angel (chap. 2), Sonya Branch (chap. 1), John Carson (chaps. 9 and 10), Andrea Corcoran (chap. 10), Jennifer Elliot (chap. 4), Allen Ferrell (chap. 2), Andreas Fleckner (chap. 10), Stavros Gadinis (chap. 3), Mark Griffiths (chap. 1), Pamela Hughes (chap. 10), Howell Jackson (chap. 3), Huw Jones (chaps. 6 and 7), Cally Jordan (chap. 10), Roberta Karmel (chaps. 9 and 10), C. K. Low (chap. 6), Alistair Milne (chaps. 1 and 2), Sadakazu Osaki (chap. 6), Onenne Partsch (chap. 1), Duo Qin (chap. 8), Reinhard Harry Schmidt (chap. 8), Baris Serifsoy (chap. 2), Herbie Skeete (chaps. 6 and 7), and Stephen Wells (chap. 5). Brandon Becker, Geoffrey Horton, Alix Prentice, Catherine Waddams, and Cherie Weldon provided additional research for the book.

The project was sponsored by a group of major institutions operating and interested in financial markets. The aim was to obtain a broad diversity of sponsors, both in terms of type and location, in order to ensure that the project would be independent of them. The sponsors include the Autorité des Marchés Financiers, BNP Paribas Securities Services, The Canadian Depository for Securities, Clearstream International, Euroclear, the International Capital Market Association, and SIX Swiss Exchange. Some other sponsors chose to remain anonymous.

Many individuals and institutions provided valuable ideas and comments in the preparation of the book—all on a nonattributable basis. The sponsors, some of the case study institutions, and many other individuals and organizations commented on selected draft sections. Over

600 people from over 150 institutions were also interviewed in order to obtain information for the project.

The author would like to express enormous gratitude to everybody who helped in the preparation of the book. Given their number and the confidential nature of their help, it is not possible to thank them all by name. To the sponsors who made the project possible, to the contributors for their text and comments, to the many interviewees for their time and insights, to the many people who provided valuable comments on the document, to Richard Britton, Diana Chan, Ian Dalton, Mark Gem, Heinrich Henckel, Christian Katz, Antoinette Maginness, Stefan Mai, Toomas Marley, Richard Meier, Jürg Spillmann, Paul Symons, Jeffrey Tessler, Ingrid Vogel, and to Werner Vogt—thank you all very much.

Finally, the author would also like to give a big thank you to the people who brought the book into existence: Annabel Gregory, who helped prepare the references and bibliography; Maria denBoer, who prepared the index; Richard Isomaki, who copyedited the book; and everybody at Princeton University Press—Richard Baggaley, Seth Ditchik, Peter Dougherty, Theresa Liu, Heath Renfroe, Jennifer Roth, Deborah Tegarden, and Kimberley Williams.

Acronyms

AEMS	Atos Euronext Market Solutions
AG	Aktiengesellschaft (stock corporation) (Germany)
AMEX	American Stock Exchange (United States)
AMF	Autorité des Marchés Financiers (Financial Markets Authority) (France)
APCIMS	Association of Private Client Investment Managers and Stockbrokers
ASE	Alberta Stock Exchange (Canada)
ASIC	Australian Securities and Investments Commission
ASX	Australian Stock Exchange
ATS	alternative trading system
BAWe	Bundesaufsichtsamt für den Wertpapierhandel (Federal Securities Supervisory Office) (Germany)
BBA	British Bankers Association
BIS	Bank for International Settlements
BME	Bolsas y Mercados Españoles (Spanish exchanges)
BSE	Bombay Stock Exchange
CalPERS	California Public Employees' Retirement System
CalSTRS	California State Teachers' Retirement System
CARR	Centre for the Analysis of Risk and Regulation
CB	Commission Bancaire (Banking Commission) (France)
CBOE	Chicago Board Options Exchange (United States)
CBOT	Chicago Board of Trade (United States)
CC&G	Cassa di Compensazione e Garanzia (Italy)
CCP	central counterparty
CDS	Canadian Depository for Securities Ltd.
CDS	credit default swap
CEBS	Committee of European Banking Supervisors
CECEI	Comité des Établissements de Crédit et des Entreprises d'Investissements (Credit Institutions and Investment Firms Committee) (France)
CEO	Chief Executive Officer
CESAME	Clearing and Settlement Advisory and Monitoring Expert group
CGE lished	Committee on the Governance of the Exchanges (established by the Monetary Authority of Singapore)
CME	Chicago Mercantile Exchange (United States)

CMVM	Comissão do Mercado de Valores Mobiliários (Securities Market Commission) (Portugal)
CONSOB	Commissione Nazionale per la Società e la Borsa (Companies and Stock Exchange Commission) (Italy)
CPSS	Committee on Payment and Settlement Systems
CSD	Central Securities Depository
DG	Directorate General
DIFX	Dubai International Financial Exchange
DOJ	Department of Justice (United States)
DSDA	Danish Securities Dealers Association
DTB	Deutsche Terminbörse (German Futures Exchange)
DTC	Depository Trust Corporation (United States)
DTCC	Depository Trust and Clearing Corporation (United States)
DTI	Department of Trade and Industry (UK)
DVP	delivery versus payment
EACH	European Association of Central Counterparty Clearing Houses
EASD	European Association of Securities Dealers
EBIT	earnings before interest and taxes
ECB	European Central Bank
ECCU	Eastern Caribbean Currency Union
ECH	European Clearing House
ECN	electronic communication network
ECS	Euroclear Clearance System plc
ECSDA	European Central Securities Depositories Association
EFP	exchange for physicals
EMCF	European Multilateral Clearing Facility
ESA	Euroclear SA/NV
ESF	European Securities Forum
ESIUG	European Securities Industry Users' Group
EuroCCP	European Central Counterparty Limited
FBF	French Banking Federation
FFI	Fidessa Fragmentation Index
FIA	Futures Industry Association (United States)
FIBV	Fédération Internationale des Bourses Valeurs (now WFE)
FICC	Fixed Income Clearing Corporation
FINRA	Financial Industry Regulatory Authority (United States)
FOA	Futures and Options Association
FRC	Financial Reporting Council (UK)
FSA	Financial sector assessment
FSA	Financial Services Authority (UK)
FSAP	Financial Services Action Plan (EU)
FSAP	Financial Sector Assessment Program

FSSA	Financial System Stability Assessment
G30	Group of Thirty
HKEx	Hong Kong Exchanges and Clearing Ltd.
HKSAR	Hong Kong Special Administrative Region
HMT	Her Majesty's Treasury (UK)
ICA	International Co-operative Alliance
ICMA	International Capital Market Association
ICSA	International Council of Securities Associations
ICSD	international central securities depository
(I)CSDs	ICSDs and CSDs
IDA	Investment Dealers Association of Canada
IFES	International Foundation for Electoral Systems
IIROC	Investment Industry Regulatory Organization of Canada
IMF	International Monetary Fund
IOSCO	International Organization of Securities Commissions
IPMA	International Primary Market Association
IPO	Initial Public Offering
IPR	Intellectual Property Rights
ISC	International Securities Consultancy Ltd (Singapore)
ISDA	International Swaps and Derivatives Association
ISE	International Securities Exchange
ISE	Irish Stock Exchange
ISMA	International Securities Market Association
ISSA	International Securities Services Association
JFSA	Japan Financial Services Agency
LCH	London Clearing House (UK)
LIBA	London Investment Banking Association
LIFFE	London International Financial Futures and Options Exchange (UK)
LLC	Limited Liability Corporation
LSE	London Stock Exchange (UK)
LSE	Luxembourg Stock Exchange
LSEG	London Stock Exchange Group
MAD	Market Abuse Directive (EU)
ME	Montreal Exchange (Canada)
MiFID	Markets in Financial Instruments Directive
MONSTER	Market Oriented New System for Terrifying Exchanges and Regulators
MOS	Mutual Offset System
MOU	Memorandum of understanding
MTF	Multilateral trading facility
MTS	Societa per il Mercato dei Titoli di Stato S.p.A. (market for government bonds) (Italy)

NASD	National Association of Securities Dealers (United States)
NASDAQ	The NASDAQ Stock Market Inc. (United States)
NCSD	Nordic Central Securities Depository
NERA	National Economic Research Associates
NMS	National Market System (United States)
NOG	NASDAQ OMX Group Inc.
NSCC	National Securities Clearing Corporation (United States)
NSE	National Stock Exchange (India)
NV	Naamloze Vennootschap (public limited company) (Netherlands)
NYSE	New York Stock Exchange Inc. (United States)
OECD	Organisation for Economic Co-operation and Development
OFG	Oxford Finance Group (UK)
OFT	Office of Fair Trading (UK),
OSE	Osaka Securities Exchange
OTC	Over-the-Counter
OXERA	Oxford Economic Research Associates
PD	Prospectus Directive (EU)
Pellervo	Confederation of Finnish Cooperatives
Plc	Public limited company (UK)
PSE	Philippines Stock Exchange
QIA	Qatari Investment Authority
RCH	Recognised Clearing House (UK)
RIE	Recognised Investment Exchange (UK)
RCPS	Redeemable Convertible Preference Shares
ROC	Regulatory Oversight Committee
ROSC	Report on Observance of Standards and Codes
RS	Market Regulation Services Inc. (Canada)
SA	Sociedade Anonima (limited liability company) (Portugal)
SA	Société Anonyme (public limited company) (Belgium/France)
SBF	Société des Bourses Françaises (French Stock Exchanges Company) (France)
SEA	Securities Exchange Act (United States)
SEBI	Securities and Exchange Board of India
SEC	Securities and Exchange Commission (United States)
SEHK	Stock Exchange of Hong Kong
SEL	Securities and Exchange Law (Japan)
SFC	Securities and Futures Commission (Hong Kong)
SGO	Self-Governing Organization
SGX	Singapore Stock Exchange
SIA	Securities Industry Association (United States)

SIX	SIX Group
SRO	self-regulatory organization
SSS	securities settlement system
STP	straight-through processing
SUGEVAL	Superintendencia General de Valores (General Authority for Securities) (Costa Rica)
SWX	Swiss Exchanges Group (Switzerland)
T2S	TARGET2-Securities
TD	Transparency Directive (EU)
TSE	Tokyo Stock Exchange (Japan)
TSE	Toronto Stock Exchange (Canada) (new TSX)
TSX	Toronto Stock Exchange (Canada) (previously TSE)
VSE	Vancouver Stock Exchange (Canada)
WB	Wiener Börse (Austria)
WCCC	West Canada Clearing Corporation
WCDTC	West Canada Depository Trust Company
WFE	World Federation of Exchanges (previously FIBV)

Running the World's Markets

Introduction

THE GOVERNANCE of infrastructure institutions in the financial markets has become a matter of significant commercial, regulatory, legislative, and even political concern. These institutions include exchanges (such as Istanbul Stock Exchange, NYSE Euronext, and Stock Exchange of Thailand), central counterparties (CCPs) (such as EuroCCP, Japan Securities Clearing Corporation, and LCH.Clearnet in the UK), and central securities depositories (CSDs) (such as The Canadian Depository for Securities, Indeval in Mexico, and Strate in South Africa). They play a fundamental role in ensuring the efficiency, safety, and soundness of financial markets globally, and more generally in furthering economic development. The manner in which market infrastructure institutions are governed critically affects their performance. There is great debate, however, both about how they are governed and about how they should be governed.

NATURE OF GOVERNANCE

Governance is about power, and three questions are critical in understanding the governance of market infrastructure institutions: Who has what power at such institutions? How and why do they obtain it? and, How and why do they exercise it? Answers to these questions for any particular market infrastructure institution are determined in large part by the formal, legal, and regulatory constructs within which it operates. These include the institution's constitution and associated corporate governance attributes, namely its corporate status and mandate, its ownership structure, the composition and role of its board, the role of its management, the rights of its shareholders and other stakeholders, and the relationships between board, management, owners, and other stakeholders. Other legal and regulatory factors also influence the exercise of power at a market infrastructure institution, including key contractual arrangements, its regulatory status, and any regulatory powers or duties it is allocated. In addition, a range of informal, nonconstitutional, and noncontractual factors may affect an institution's governance, such as the historical, cultural, and political framework within which it operates.

CONCERNS

There are many reasons why the governance of financial market infra-structure institutions is now seen as critically important. The financial crisis that began in 2007, as with past such crises, has led to public and political interest in the workings of financial markets, and in particular in the infrastructure institutions that seek to guarantee their safe operation and protect investors. Extreme volatility in the markets has both increased worries that the market infrastructure institutions central to the operation of financial systems may fail, and also increased pressures for trading, clearing, and settlement to be centralized on precisely such institutions. Notwithstanding the current high level of anxiety about market infrastructure institutions as a result of the present financial crisis, at some stage this apprehension may diminish as the severity of the crisis recedes. Concern about market infrastructure governance will, however, remain for many other reasons.

There is controversy about what is the most efficient way of governing market infrastructure institutions. Market practitioners now realize that the manner in which these institutions are governed may affect both the fees they pay and more generally the viability of their business models. There are also concerns about whether the pursuit of private interests at market infrastructure institutions is leading to anticompetitive behavior, and conversely about whether the pursuit of public interests at such institutions is adversely affecting efficiency.

There is mounting anxiety about the presence of conflicts of interests at market infrastructure institutions, and about whether governance mechanisms should be put in place to minimize the occurrence of such conflicts, or to facilitate the management of them when they do arise. Concern about conflicts of interest has become particularly acute where market infrastructure institutions have been allocated regulatory powers or duties.

The global focus on corporate governance, following various major corporate scandals, and the development of various international codes on corporate governance, such as from the Organisation for Economic Co-operation and Development (OECD), has brought to the fore questions concerning the governance of market infrastructure institutions. A range of mechanisms have been proposed globally with the prime aim of protecting shareholder interests, such as the adoption of independent directors on corporate boards. Whether these mechanisms are appropriate for market infrastructure institutions has, however, been controversial.

Consolidation among market infrastructures at both a national level (such as the creation of SGX in Singapore) and at an international level (such as the merger between the NASDAQ and OMX), and the perceived growing market power of such institutions, has led to disagreement about whether there should be greater regulatory, legislative, and even political intervention in their governance. This debate has been complicated by differences of opinion about regulatory goals, and also by the pursuit of national interests by various jurisdictions.

Not only has no global consensus developed for the optimal way of governing market infrastructure institutions, no framework for deciding what governance model is appropriate in different circumstances has been developed either. Very distinct governance models are currently being implemented across the globe and across different types of market infrastructure institutions, with demutualization, user governance, and public ownership and control, for example, all being actively promoted.

ISSUES

This book analyses the two fundamental issues of how market infrastructure institutions are governed, and how they should be governed. In order to assess how market infrastructure institutions *are* governed, four broad topics are examined:

- The key types of governance models market infrastructure institutions adopt
- The manner in which market infrastructure institutions are governed in practice;
- The way in which regulatory powers are allocated to market infrastructure institutions;
- The way in which market infrastructure institutions' governance is regulated.

In order to evaluate how market infrastructure institutions *should* be governed, three central policy questions are evaluated and answered:

- What is the most efficient form of governance for market infrastructure institutions?
- What regulatory powers, if any, should be allocated to market infrastructure institutions?
- What regulatory intervention in the governance of market infrastructure institutions, if any, is desirable?

APPROACH

A central thesis presented here is that there is no single global answer either to the question of how market infrastructure institutions are governed, or to the question of how market infrastructure institutions should be governed. Instead, the answers to these questions are specific to the contexts in which they are raised. This argument contradicts the notion promoted in many other analyses of financial markets, that standardization, harmonization, and the creation of an international consensus are critical. A key aim of the book is to provide insight into the governance of market infrastructure institutions for a wide range of situations globally. Much of the analysis is therefore presented in an abstract and general way so as to be useful across different types of institutions, jurisdictions, and contexts. Rather than offering any specific recommendations to address the key policy questions examined here, a series of general propositions are articulated in order both to capture the wide range of arguments discussed here in a simple and accessible manner, and to encapsulate the main lessons of the analysis. The book does not present answers to how market infrastructure institutions should be governed in any particular jurisdiction or context, nor does it provide simple or single conclusions.

In order to understand the complexity inherent in the topic of the governance of market infrastructure institutions, different types of analyses are necessary. In particular, it is vital to assess a broad range of both conceptual and specific issues, and also to appreciate that the two types of issues are inextricably linked. Although answers to conceptual questions concerning governance frequently transcend national, temporal, and physical, boundaries, no understanding of the conceptual is possible without a foundation of knowledge and information about specific instances and contexts to which the abstract is applicable. Conversely, a conceptual framework is required in order to describe and categorize any specific context under consideration. In seeking to understand the governance of market infrastructure institutions, it is also essential to draw on the knowledge and experience available from a wide spectrum of academic and practical fields, including business, economics, finance, law, regulation, and politics. Three broad methodologies are used in the book. Some analytical exegesis is employed to examine various conceptual issues, a range of survey evidence is presented to describe key aspects of how market infrastructure institutions are governed and regulated globally, and various case studies detail the particularities of specific situations and decisions at different market infrastructure institutions.

STRUCTURE

The book is composed of 10 main chapters in addition to the introduction, grouped into four parts. Part I contains two chapters that provide key background information and analyses necessary for an understanding of how market infrastructure institutions are, and should be, governed. Chapter 1 provides some insights into the definitions and nature of an "infrastructure," an "exchange," a "CCP," and a "CSD," and explores the reasons why these concepts are sometimes ambiguous and controversial. Chapter 2 analyses a key determinant of whether exchanges, CCPs, and CSDs should be considered infrastructure institutions, namely whether they have market power.

Part II contains three chapters that survey different aspects of how market infrastructure institutions were governed and regulated throughout the world as of the end of 2006. Chapter 3 compares how different jurisdictions allocated regulatory powers over their securities markets. Three surveys on the topic, covering various jurisdictions and institutions, are described and evaluated. Chapter 4 examines a unique set of assessments of securities markets and of their regulation from countries around the world, undertaken jointly by the International Monetary Fund (IMF) and the World Bank, in order to provide a global perspective on policymakers' viewpoints about the regulation and governance of market infrastructure institutions. Chapter 5 provides an overview of how market infrastructure institutions around the world were governed in the cash equities markets.

Part III contains two chapters that present a series of case studies illustrating how some particular market infrastructure institutions have been governed in practice in specific contexts. Chapter 6 presents case studies for various exchanges, and chapter 7 does the same for various CCPs and CSDs. A few brief general lessons from each case study are also identified.

Part IV contains three chapters that analyze, and make recommendations about, how market infrastructure institutions should be governed, and how their governance should be regulated. Chapter 8 analyzes the optimal governance model for market infrastructure institutions using the broad goal of efficiency as the main yardstick to compare different models. Three fundamental elements of governance are examined: ownership structure, mandate, and board composition. Chapter 9 discusses what regulatory authority over securities markets, if any, should be assigned to exchanges, CCPs, and CSDs. The question is analyzed in the broader context of examining how regulatory powers should be allocated between government regulators, self-regulatory organizations (SROs), and other types of regulatory institutions. Chapter 10 explores what regulatory intervention in the governance of market infrastructure institutions, if any, is optimal. Attention is focused on how such intervention can enhance the realization of three core objectives of securities markets regulation: the protection of investors; ensuring that markets are fair, efficient, and transparent; and the reduction of systemic risk.

PART ONE

Background Information and Analyses

CHAPTER ONE

Definitions

To MANY PEOPLE it is clear what are the "infrastructure institutions" in financial markets. They are the exchanges, CCPs, and CSDs that provide the trading, clearing, settlement, and sometimes other, core functions for cash and derivative markets.[1] These institutions are indeed the focus of attention here. There are, however, also many reasons why the definitions of an infrastructure, an exchange, a CCP, and a CSD are all quite opaque. This is important, as the identification of a particular organization as one of these types of institutions can have significant commercial, regulatory, and policy consequences. This chapter aims to provide some basic insights into the definitions and nature of an infrastructure, an exchange, a CCP, and a CSD; and to explore the reasons why these concepts are sometimes ambiguous and controversial. A comprehensive examination of each of these different concepts would require a series of complex and broad analyses, and is not undertaken here.[2]

The chapter is composed of three sections. In the first, the meaning and nature of what is an infrastructure is explored. Some comments on the definitions and nature of exchanges, CCPs, and CSDs, and on the functions they deliver, are provided in the second section. Brief conclusions are offered in the last section.

INFRASTRUCTURE

Understanding how the term "infrastructure" has generally been employed and the key factors relevant for determining whether an institution is an infrastructure illuminates how the term may be used regarding institutions in financial markets, and the implications of doing so.

Meaning and Use of the Term

An examination of a broad range of definitions and uses of the term "infrastructure" highlights eight key nonexclusive factors and attributes that contribute towards identifying an institution as an infrastructure:

1. An infrastructure may be, or provide, the *basic* equipment, facility, foundation, framework, installation, system, or services that *support* or *underly* some form of structure, system, or activity, defined quite broadly. Such a structure, system, or activity may include a corporation, an organization, a productive process, a community, a city, an economy, a society, a nation, or a group of nations.[3] The goods or services provided by an infrastructure are often both consumed directly and also used as inputs for a wide range of goods or services produced by users of the infrastructure institution. In this context, an infrastructure is often referred to as a "utility"—although this term, itself, is not easy to define.[4]

2. An infrastructure may be *critical, essential,* or *necessary,* to support commerce, economic activity and development, or whatever other activities are facilitated by the system it operates.[5] Given the critical nature of the basic goods or services that an infrastructure provides, there are frequently concerns about access to these goods or services.[6]

3. An infrastructure may be, or provide, a *network.*[7] In the economic sphere, such a network typically facilitates the delivery of goods and services, or links together the participants in a market, and is thus part of the structure underlying a market. The relationship between relevant producers and consumers takes place on, or via, the shared facilities or single medium provided by the infrastructure. A network is typically composed of both the physical structure linking market participants, and the associated commercial arrangements and rules for using this structure.

4. An infrastructure may exhibit *economies of scale.*[8]

5. An infrastructure may require *large, long-term, immobile,* and *sunk investments.*[9]

6. An infrastructure may be, or operate, a *natural monopoly.*[10]

7. An infrastructure may provide beneficial *public goods* or *services*, in addition to the specific goods and services it delivers directly.[11] There are two key attributes of a pure public good or service: it is nonrivalrous, so that its consumption by one person does not prevent other people from consuming it; and it is nonexcludable, so that it is not possible to stop somebody from consuming it. An often-cited example of a public good is good health, as facilitated by water and sanitation infrastructures.

8. An infrastructure may have some form of *government* or *public sector involvement*, defined very broadly.[12] For this reason, the term "public works" is sometimes used interchangeably for the term "infrastructure." The role of government or public sector involvement in infrastructures has been quite diverse. As Waller and Frischmann (2007, 12) note:

> The government has played and continues to play a significant and widely-accepted role in ensuring the provision of many infrastructure resources. While private parties and markets play an increasingly im-

portant role in providing many types of traditional infrastructure due to a wave of privatization as well as cooperative ventures between industry and government, the government's position as provider, coordinator, subsidizer, and/or regulator of traditional infrastructure provision remains intact in most communities throughout the world.

Several implications and aspects of this list of factors and attributes that contribute towards identifying an institution as being an infrastructure are noteworthy:

1. There are close links between many of them. For example, the presence of economies of scale is often associated both with a natural monopoly and with a network industry.

2. The presence of any one of the identified factors and attributes is not sufficient to determine that an institution is an infrastructure.

3. None of them are exclusive to infrastructure institutions.

4. The term "infrastructure" has been used in different contexts for different reasons. Unsurprisingly, therefore, different meanings have been assigned to the term.

5. A central aspect of an infrastructure is its importance, however this quality is defined. This importance may arise, in legal terms, because it is, or runs, an essential facility; in economic terms, because it is a monopoly; or its importance may lie in other directions, affecting social, political, or other factors.

6. The classification of an institution as an infrastructure, or not, may change. For example, technological changes and market developments may mean that an institution that was historically thought to be, and defined as, an infrastructure, given its importance, may no longer be so considered, if it becomes subject to competition.

7. It may be difficult to define an institution as an infrastructure if it undertakes multiple functions. In particular, if a single institution undertakes some functions that are recognized as infrastructure functions, and some others that are not, perhaps because they are provided in competitive markets, then it may be unclear how to characterize the institution. Should it be classified as an infrastructure institution, even though some of its functions are typically provided by non-infrastructure institutions? Or is it more useful to define activities as being associated with infrastructure provision rather than institutions?

8. The presence of these factors and attributes may have important policy implications.

A range of assets, services, organizations, and industries have typically been identified as infrastructure.[13] They include the basic physical systems of a nation, particularly its transport (airports, air traffic control, bridges, buses, rail, roads, ports, and public transit), communications (post, telephone, and sometimes the Internet), energy (electricity and gas supply and distribution facilities, and sometimes oil), and water and sanitation systems. In addition, infrastructure may include public and social facilities, such as police, fire, and emergency services, schools, hospitals, recreation facilities, prisons, and government systems, such as courts, ministries, and parliaments.

In financial markets, the term "infrastructure" has been widely used to refer to exchanges, CCPs, and CSDs as providers of trading, clearing, and settlement services,[14] and also to payment systems.[15] It has also infrequently been used to refer to other providers of trading, clearing, and settlement services.

A range of examples illustrate how the term has been used. The UK's Financial Services Authority (FSA) defined "infrastructure providers" to be

> entities whose business is organising and supporting the functioning of markets. Infrastructure providers include exchanges, non-exchange (or "alternative") trading systems, clearing houses and market service providers generally.[16]

More informally, Oleg Vyugin, a Russian regulator from the Federal Service for Financial Markets, noted that "double the infrastructure is madness," when discussing why Russia's two major exchanges should consider merging to improve their competitiveness against overseas exchanges.[17]

The Committee on Payment and Settlement Systems (CPSS) of the Bank for International Settlements (BIS) and the Technical Committee of IOSCO have jointly developed recommendations for Securities Settlement Systems (SSS), the first sentence of which notes that such entities "are a critical component of the infrastructure of global financial markets."[18] The committees have also developed recommendations for CCPs, and in doing so noted,

> Although a CCP has the potential to reduce risks to market participants significantly, it also concentrates risks and responsibilities for risk management. Therefore, the effectiveness of a CCP's risk control and the adequacy of its financial resources are critical aspects of the infrastructure of the markets it serves.[19]

Similarly, a paper prepared for the International Monetary Fund (IMF) noted that

> the smooth functioning of and confidence in the securities market depend on the efficiency and reliability of its infrastructure. In particular, it is crucial that the transfer of ownership from the seller to the buyer in exchange for payment takes place in a safe and efficient manner.[20]

The European Central Bank (ECB) has established a Contact Group on Euro Securities Infrastructures, which "addresses issues and developments which are relevant for the euro securities settlement industry and which are of common interest for the Eurosystem, market infrastructures and market participants."[21]

When describing clearing and settlement as the infrastructure underpinning financial markets, one metaphor that is very commonly used is that of plumbing.[22] The European Commission, for example, used this metaphor in explaining that such institutions are "vital, but unglamorous and forgotten until something goes wrong."[23] A report from the European Parliament used the same metaphor, similarly noting that clearing and settlement is "largely invisible, seldom understood and frequently overlooked but causes really unpleasant problems for everyone if it goes wrong."[24] As well as equating clearing and settlement systems with sanitation systems, which are typically themselves accepted as infrastructure, the metaphor also implies that clearing and settlement systems provide a public good in preventing things from "going wrong."

Key Attributes of an Infrastructure Institution

Five of the key factors relevant for determining whether an institution is an "infrastructure" are briefly examined here.

ESSENTIAL FACILITY DOCTRINE

A commonly accepted attribute of infrastructure institutions is that the goods or services they produce are *essential* in some manner. This characteristic has in some contexts brought them within the purview of a legal doctrine, initially developed under US antitrust law, called the "essential facility" doctrine.[25] The key thrust of the doctrine is that a monopolistic operator of an essential facility may be obliged to provide access to it to a competitor. In the past, four main criteria have needed to be satisfied under US law for such a possibility to arise:[26] (1) the monopolist must control access to an essential facility, (2) the facility cannot practically or reasonably be duplicated by the competitor, (3) the monopolist must deny access to the competitor, and (4) it is feasible for the monopolist to grant access to the competitor.

The essential facility doctrine has been applied by US courts to secure the access of competitors to various institutions that could be considered infrastructures, including a terminal railroad,[27] an information network for the press,[28] an electricity network,[29] a telecommunications network,[30] and ski facilities.[31]

As discussed by Waller and Frischmann (2006), however, the continued applicability of the essential facility doctrine has come into question and been subject to criticism from a range of different sources. In 2004 the US Supreme Court expressed a strong reservation as to the pertinence of the doctrine due to its drawbacks on competition policy, noting,

> Compelling such firms [i.e., with an essential facility] to share their advantage is in some tension with the underlying principles of antitrust law, since it may lessen the incentive for the monopolist, the rival or both to invest in those economically beneficial facilities. Enforced sharing also requires antitrust courts to act as a central planner identifying the proper price, quantity and other terms of dealings—a role for which they are ill-suited. Moreover, compelling negotiations between competitors may facilitate the supreme evil of antitrust: collusion.[32]

The Supreme Court stressed that "we have never recognized such a doctrine [i.e., the essential facility doctrine], and we find no need either to recognize it or to repudiate it here." A range of US commissions and enquiries, and analyses by antitrust enforcement agencies from the United States and other countries, and by academic scholars, have also found fault with the essential facility doctrine.[33]

Though not formally recognized under EU law, the essential facility doctrine has influenced the creation, implementation, and enforcement of EU law.[34] EU competition law does not forbid the creation or the maintenance of monopolies per se, but does regulate the actions of companies in dominant positions that abuse such positions, under Article 82 of the Treaty of Rome. One type of behavior that may constitute an abuse is the unfair denial of access. The European Commission has referred to the essential facility doctrine in order to demonstrate the existence of an infringement against Article 82 in cases where

> [an] undertaking, which occupies a dominant position in the provision of an essential facility and itself uses that facility, refuses other companies access to that facility without objective justification or grants access to competitors only on terms less favourable than those which it gives its own services.[35]

The Commission has also specifically defined an essential facility on its website as a

> facility or infrastructure which is necessary for reaching customers and/ or enabling competitors to carry on their business. A facility is essential if its duplication is impossible or extremely difficult due to physical, geographical, legal or economic constraints. Take for example a national electricity power grid used by various electricity producers to reach the final consumers: Since it would not be viable for these producers to build their own distribution network, they depend on access

to the existing infrastructure. Denying access to an essential facility may be considered an abuse of a dominant position by the entity controlling it, in particular where it prevents competition in a downstream market.[36]

In addition, the European Commission has adopted several items of sector-specific legislation regarding the nondiscriminatory access of competitors to what could be considered essential facilities, such as in the electricity and telecommunication sectors.[37]

Under the Merger Control Regulation, the European Commission has ruled on several occasions that entering into an agreement or a merger could create the equivalent of an essential facility, access to which by competitors should be granted as a preventative measure in order to avoid the possibility that the newly integrated business become the source of an undue restriction of competition.[38]

The European Court of Justice has not formally recognized the essential facility doctrine. Nevertheless, it has influenced the court's jurisprudence under Article 82, according to which access to an essential facility may be sanctioned if all of the following conditions are met:[39] (1) there must be an undertaking holding a dominant position in a market (sometimes called an upstream market), access to which is indispensable for the performance of services or the supply of goods in a downstream market; (2) this undertaking must refuse access to the goods or services supplied in the upstream market to its competitors in the downstream market; (3) the undertaking that requests access to the essential facility must intend to supply new goods or services not offered by the owner/operator of the essential facility for which there is a potential consumer demand; (4) the refusal is not justified by objective considerations; and (5) the refusal is such as to reserve to the owner of the essential facility the downstream market for the supply of goods or services by eliminating all competition on that market.

In the *Bronner* case,[40] Advocate General Jacobs noted the existence of the decisions of the European Commission referring to the essential facility doctrine, and also acknowledged that some commentators had seen an endorsement of the doctrine in some decisions by the European Court of Justice.[41] In the decision itself, however, the court analyzed the case in light of Article 82 and did not refer to the essential facility doctrine. It used a similar strategy in the *IMS* case.[42]

NETWORKS: EXTERNALITIES, SWITCHING COSTS, AND STANDARDS

An infrastructure institution is frequently thought to be, or to provide, a *network*. Defining a network is, however, itself difficult. Shy (2001) identifies four key characteristics of network industries that distinguish them from other types of markets: (1) consumption externalities; (2) switching costs and lock-in; (3) complementarity, compatibility, and standards; and (4) significant economies of scale in production. Brief comments on the first three of these characteristics are provided in this section, and the nature of economies of scale is discussed in the next.

Infrastructure institutions may enjoy market power as a result of different network effects. A distinction may be made between one-sided "$N \times 1$" and two-sided "$N \times M$" network industries.[43] A standard $N \times 1$ or one-way network industry typically delivers services to households through a physical network, such as gas or water piping, although non-physical delivery mechanisms are also possible. In such an industry, there is normally only one company or one delivery system for N customers. As in most other industries, the demand of the individual consumer does not depend on the decisions of other consumers. The network effect arises from an access bottleneck in the delivery system restricting, or preventing, other firms from reaching customers.

Consumer entertainment industries, including DVDs, music CDs, and video games, are typical examples of two-sided $N \times M$ networks. Here the network is not a physical network, but rather a technical standard or other "platform," linking M supplying firms with N customers. In such industries, the purchase decisions of individual customers depend upon the decisions of other customers, so the M suppliers are in a sense competing for the custom of the N customers simultaneously, rather than for each customer individually. This dependence of customer demand on the choices of other customers is known as a "participation," "consumption," or sometimes "network," externality. A positive consumption externality is an advantage that an incumbent firm providing a network has over potential competitors, and also a benefit that accrues to the users of such a network, which is dependent on the fact that other participants are already using the same network.

Such externalities may occur for several reasons. Consumers may value the consumption of the same good or service that is being consumed by other consumers. For example, in the case of differentiated products supplied over one network, such as computer games played on a specified type of games console, consumers may value the variety of products available over the network. The number of products provided will, however, depend upon the number of customers using the network. Participation externalities create coordination problems and a critical role for expectations. Customers' choices of which network to use depend on their beliefs about which networks other customers will use. They will prefer to use a network they believe will have many other customers, as such a network is likely to have a high number of products provided for it.

Differentiation in the prices charged to different buyers or different sellers can play an important role in "two-sided markets" or "two-sided platforms" with participation externalities.[44] There are many examples of this pattern, including trading arenas such as eBay, payment instruments such as credit cards, and social venues such as nightclubs. The willingness of one side of the market (in the nightclub example, men) to participate depends upon the number of participants on the other side of the market (in this case women). Overall participation in the market may thus be increased by setting different prices for the two types of participant (so the women may get free or discounted entry to the nightclub). Pricing structures may differentiate between the two sides using either differential membership charges, or differential per-transaction charges, or both.

Switching costs and product standards can also affect the economics of networks. As Shy explains:

> Switching costs affect price competition in two opposing ways. First, if consumers are already locked-in using a specific product, firms may raise prices knowing that consumers will not switch unless the price difference exceeds the switching cost to a competing brand. Second, if consumers are not locked in, brand-producing firms will compete intensively by offering discounts and free complimentary products and services in order to attract consumers who later on will be locked in the technology.[45]

The presence of switching costs is generally thought to reduce competition and increase market power.[46] In many consumer markets there are substantial costs, including both monetary costs and the time and effort of adapting to a new product, associated with switching to a new producer. Switching costs are also present in many business-to-business services. Even when there are several competing suppliers, substantial costs may be involved in terminating a contract with one supplier and initiating a new one. They may include the costs of negotiating appropriate contracts, or training and learning. The presence of switching costs in a market does not mean that there is no competition, as relevant business service contracts are regularly put out to tender, but that an incumbent firm may have a competitive advantage over new entrants, and may accordingly charge higher prices and make supernormal profits.

Both switching costs and participation externalities are affected by compatibility standards. Three main types of compatibility standards may typically be established. A single producer may develop a *proprietary* standard that is either implemented only through its own products, or for which other producers must pay a substantial license fee. A number of firms may together develop a *shared* standard that is licensed to many producers. Finally there are examples of *open* standards for which no license fee is paid and which can be used by any producer.

Proprietary standards are used by firms as a means of taking advantage of participation externalities and hence establishing a competitive advantage. Not all proprietary standards succeed in being adopted, however. In order to encourage adoption a proprietary standard may often be made available either for free or for a relatively low license fee. Participation externalities encourage customers to migrate to a single compatibility standard, but occasionally two competing standards may coexist. Open or widely available proprietary compatibility standards, such as shared communication protocols, help reduce switching costs in both business and consumer markets. In many markets compatibility goes beyond simply messaging and communication standards, and involves underlying business processes.

The adoption and availability of technical compatibility standards can have substantial effects on economic welfare. The adoption of a new standard may be excessively slow, for example, exhibiting so-called excess inertia, thus reducing economic welfare. This slowness can happen for several reasons: a new standard may not be available to all market participants; incumbent firms may prefer existing standards that discourage new market entry or lead to high switching costs; and coordination problems among market participants may hinder the adoption of a new standard. It is also conceivable, however, that standards may be replaced too quickly, and this too can be economically inefficient because of the resulting loss of standard-specific investments.[47]

ECONOMIES OF SCALE

Infrastructure institutions often exhibit *economies of scale*. They occur when the average cost of producing a good or service declines with the number of units produced. More formally, economies of scale exist if, over the relevant range of demand, the cost function is subadditive. Strict subadditivity means that the cost of producing a specified amount of output by a single firm is less than the cost of having two or more firms produce the same joint level of output. Global subadditivity means that the subadditivity condition applies to the entire cost function from the origin up to the entire market demand. An incumbent firm with a dominant market share that exhibits economies of scale will have an advantage over potential new entrants.

A common reason for the existence of economies of scale is the presence of fixed costs of production or marketing. If such fixed costs are high relative to the size of a market, then only a small number of firms will be able to supply the market while still covering their costs. If, in addition, there are barriers to entry in the market, then these firms may enjoy market power, and thus be able to raise prices above long-run average costs of production.

High fixed costs can complicate the achievement of allocative efficiency, where the resources in an economy are allocated to their most productive uses. In order for a market to be allocatively efficient, the price of a good or service should equal its marginal cost. When there are high fixed costs, however, marginal cost pricing may not generate sufficient surplus to cover fixed costs, as the marginal cost may be less than the average cost. In such circumstances, competitive efficiency may be approximately achieved if prices are set equal to long-run average costs of production, so that there are no economic rents.

In theory, the presence of high fixed costs of production may make it impossible for any firm to be able to supply a market and cover its long-run average costs. This is not a common outcome, but such circumstances have occurred in transport infrastructure.[48] Other outcomes are more common with high fixed costs of production. One is a scale monopoly, in which a single incumbent firm is able to cover its costs but is not threatened by the possibility of new entry because the market is too small to support two firms supplying the market. Another is a concentrated or oligopolistic market, where the market is able to support two or three firms.

It is sometimes argued that a combination of high fixed costs and low variable costs of production may lead to competitive efficiency even in a concentrated market. This argument is relevant to the case of a scale oligopoly, where two or three firms supply most of the market, and where firms are able to price discriminate, that is, set different prices for different customers. It is not, however, relevant to a monopoly where there is no competition, or to markets where four or more firms supply most of the market, as this situation is likely to lead to a competitive outcome.

The key claim is that low variable costs, and hence high marginal customer profits, will give firms a strong incentive to reduce prices to individual customers in order to capture them from their competitors. This in turn will pressure firms to reduce their average pricing to their long-run average costs. Such an outcome is, however, unlikely if firms cannot price discriminate, and in particular if they have to set a single price for all customers, and not just new "marginal" ones. In such circumstances, firms will be able to recognize the impact of their price-setting on their profitability, and the presence of low marginal costs will not greatly alter their competitive interaction. Even with price discrimination, the outcome will not be competitively efficient if firms compete strongly for only a relatively few footloose customers, but are still able to continue exploiting the bulk of their existing customer base through high charges.

If firms can price discriminate between customers, and also are in a position to compete actively across much of the market, then competition may be present even in a context with economies of scale. If such competition really is effective, however, it may still drive average pricing below long-run average costs, leading to one or more firms exiting the market. The eventual outcome may thus still be competitively inefficient, as the continuing exit of firms may in the end result in a monopoly. In general, while it is possible that industries with high fixed costs and low variable costs may be competitively efficient even if there are only two or three competing firms, competitive inefficiency is still the most likely outcome.

SUNK COSTS

An infrastructure is often characterized by the presence of large *sunk costs*. Such costs are expenses that a firm needs to incur to enter a market, but cannot recover if it leaves the market. The key importance of sunk costs is that their existence stops a market from being contestable.[49]

A contestable market is one in which if a new entrant comes into the market and offers goods or services at a marginally lower price than incumbents, customers will respond quickly to such price changes and switch to the new provider. If there are no switching costs, new entrants can take advantage of above-competitive profits or inefficient cost structures, and so-called hit-and-run entry is possible. This occurs when a new firm enters a market to exploit any inefficiencies present, and then leaves the market when such efficiencies have been exploited. For such competition to be possible, however, several key criteria must be satisfied. First, barriers to entry must be low. If they are not, potential new entrants will need to incur substantial costs to overcome these barriers, and this will restrict entry. Second, barriers to exit must be low, and in particular, new entrants to the market must face no sunk costs. If they did, then hit-and-run entry would not be profitable, because a new entrant would lose the sunk costs it had to incur to enter the market, if it decided to exit the market. Third, consumers must face no costs for switching to a new provider. If they did, then even if a new entrant were able to offer its goods or services at a marginally cheaper price than the incumbent, consumers would not immediately switch to the new provider, as they would need to pay the switching costs to do so.

"NATURAL" MONOPOLY

Infrastructure institutions are frequently referred to as being, or operating, *natural monopolies*. This term has historically been used to describe situations where it was believed that only one firm was able to operate in a specific market, with the implication that any such firm should be subject to special regulatory arrangements.[50] The commonest reason for the perceived existence of a natural monopoly was that it was uneconomic to replicate expensive infrastructure, given the presence of economies of scale. The presence of legal restrictions, access bottlenecks, or network externalities has also been used as a justification for the existence of so-called natural monopolies.

The word "natural" in the phrase "natural monopoly" is misleading, however, in that it implies that the structure of the relevant industry is inevitable. This has frequently been shown not to be true. Monopolies arising as a result of economies of scale are not inevitable. A competitor may be able to enter the relevant market and force the incumbent firm to exit, and even the threat of potential entry can be a significant competitive discipline. Such entry is more feasible when there are relatively few buyers. In the extreme case with a single buyer facing a single seller and other potential sellers, bargaining or tendering procedures can restore something close to competitive efficiency.

Bottleneck monopolies in $N \times 1$ network industries might more reasonably be characterized as "natural" monopolies, given that access to individual consumers is limited by physical constraints. Even in such contexts, however, it is important to distinguish the actual bottleneck itself (the "upstream" service), from any associated (or "downstream") products or services that rely on the bottleneck activity as an input. Technological developments have also allowed competition to threaten many monopolies previously considered "natural," whether their monopolistic status derived from economies of scale, the control of access bottlenecks, or network externalities.

EXCHANGES, CENTRAL COUNTERPARTIES, AND CENTRAL SECURITIES DEPOSITORIES

The meaning of the terms "exchange," "CCP," and "CSD," and the nature of what such institutions, do are briefly explored in this section.

Basic Meanings

There are many institutions around the world that it is easy to identify as an exchange, a CCP, or a CSD. They typically advertise themselves as being such an institution, and may also be a member of a trade association of similar bodies, such as the World Federation of Exchanges (WFE), the European Association of Central Counterparty Clearing Houses (EACH), and the America's Central Securities Depositories Association

(ACSDA).[51] The definition of each of the three types of institutions is also at first sight relatively clear.

The central element in almost all definitions of an exchange is that such an institution operates a trading system, and through this activity provides a market. Two core functions delivered by a trading system are data dissemination and order execution.[52] Data dissemination is the publication of pre- and post-trade data, about quotes (or orders) and trades respectively. Order execution is the process whereby orders can be transformed into trades. A market's structure or architecture is the full set of rules governing these components. This description of a trading system places no restrictions on the types of items that may be traded on such a mechanism, which may include securities, derivatives, futures, options, commodities, foreign exchange, or other types of assets or contracts.

Official definitions of an exchange are frequently provided in a legal or regulatory context. The US definition of a securities exchange, for example, illustrates the standard focus both on trading and markets:

> The term "exchange" means any organization, association, or group of persons, whether incorporated or unincorporated, which constitutes, maintains, or provides a market place or facilities for bringing together purchasers and sellers of securities or for otherwise performing with respect to securities the functions commonly performed by a stock exchange as that term is generally understood, and includes the market place and the market facilities maintained by such exchange.[53]

An organization is deemed to provide "a market place or market facilities," if it

> brings together the orders for securities of multiple buyers and sellers; and uses established, non-discretionary methods (whether by providing a trading facility or by setting rules) under which such orders interact with each other, and the buyers and sellers entering such orders agree to the terms of a trade.[54]

The widely accepted definition of a CCP is that it is an entity that interposes itself between counterparties to contracts in one or more financial markets, becoming the seller to every buyer and the buyer to every seller.[55] A CCP often also nets the obligations of the market participants for whom it clears, namely its members. On the cash side, the CCP does this by summing the total amount each member owes for its purchases, and the total amount each member is owed from its sales. The CCP also calculates for each member the net amount of each security, or other asset being traded, the member should receive or hand over.

CCPs have their origins in nineteenth-century futures exchanges.[56] Originally members cleared and settled bilaterally, with the loss of membership being the only marketwide disincentive to default. They then developed "clearing rings," with joint acceptance of contracts used as a means of promoting liquidity. This acceptance of mutual liability led to the introduction of more sophisticated risk management within such rings and, by the end of the nineteenth century, the emergence of loss default funds. A clearinghouse using novation of contracts—in order to become the buyer to all sellers and the seller to all buyers for every trade on the exchange—was first established with the founding of the Chicago Board of Trade Clearing Corporation in 1925. Derivatives clearinghouses are now all CCPs, but because of this history it is still common to refer to CCPs operating for derivatives exchanges as "clearinghouses."

The key difference between CCP-clearing for cash and for derivatives instruments is that a CCP's guarantee in a securities market lasts typically for only a few days, namely the period during which a securities settlement default might occur, whereas a CCP's guarantee may last for years in a derivatives market, until the relevant contracts are liquidated, exercised, or mature.[57] Derivatives CCPs thus typically have more complex risk management, margining, and collateral management systems than do securities CCPs.

Although there is significant variation in the definition of a CSD, two aspects are commonly believed critical. First, a CSD is an entity that holds securities centrally either in certificated or dematerialized form.[58] Second, a CSD enables the central transfer of ownership of securities, namely settlement, typically by means of book-entry transfer between securities accounts maintained on an electronic accounting system.[59]

Usually a CSD ensures that a record of title to securities is maintained on a central register that it operates, and it effects changes to entitlement on this central register. This record is called, and constitutes, the "ultimate root of title." As Kauko (2005, 7) notes,

> Many countries have a so-called "tiered" book-entry system in which there is a central securities register at the ... CSD. Individual investors normally cannot have accounts at the CSD. The central register consists of settlement system members' accounts. Many, if not most, accounts are omnibus accounts. An omnibus account is an account in which a member holds pooled securities owned by its own customers. The CSD may know the total amounts of securities owned by the customers of each member, but may have no detailed information on individual investors' holdings. The [member] ... keeps detailed accounts on the holdings of individual customers in its own system.

Three further aspects of a typical CSD are notable. First, the number of securities on the central register must always equal the number of securities issued. Second, it is possible that the book-entry register and the settlement system in a particular market are operated by different institutions. Third, although a CSD may facilitate the transfer of funds on its own internal accounts, in many contexts accounts at a central bank or at private commercial banks are employed.

One type of institution that is frequently discussed in the context of CSDs is that of an international central securities depository (ICSD). Historically, two institutions have been referred to as ICSDs: Clearstream and Euroclear. They were founded to provide settlement services for trading in Eurobonds in the 1960s. Such instruments were viewed as international instruments with no natural domestic base. Since then, the activities of the two ICSDs have expanded significantly, to include the provision of settlement services for many types of securities that are traded internationally, including both bonds and equities. Both Clearstream and Euroclear also now operate the domestic CSDs for various jurisdictions, and both also provide different types of banking services. The term "ICSD" is employed here to refer jointly to Euroclear and Clearstream.

Notwithstanding the perceived simplicity of the above definitions of an exchange, a CCP, and a CSD, various factors have led to disagreement and uncertainty about the definitions, and also to some confusion about which organizations should be classified as which of these types of institutions. This decision can be important for various reasons, including because the classification of an institution as an exchange, a CCP, or a CSD may bring with it substantive regulatory obligations or powers.

Historically, the identification of whether an institution was an exchange, a CCP, or a CSD was based on an assumption that an institution could be identified by what it does. The functions that an organization undertook were therefore thought critical in assessing what it was. There has, however, been growing confusion about the terms used to refer to different functions. If there is disagreement about how to define key functions in the financial markets, and the definition of an exchange, a CCP, or a CSD is dependent on such definitions, there will be disagreement about what constitutes each of these types of institutions.

Another problem with using functional definitions is that there is less and less commonality in the functions undertaken by institutions previously thought of as exchanges, CCPs, and CSDs. In the clearing and settlement industry, for example, a survey prepared by the European Central Securities Depositories Association (ECSDA) (2005, 2) noted that

> the services offered by (I)CSDs [where "(I)CSDs" stands for both ICSDs and CSDs] across Europe are extremely diverse. They are based on the provisions of each country's law, tax requirements and market practices and must be regarded very much as a reflection and result of this framework within which the (I)CSD operates. Services naturally also

differ between types of securities driven by the characteristics of each of these types.

If different institutions do different things, then it becomes less feasible to classify them according to what they do.

Another factor that has led to uncertainty about definitions is that technological changes and market developments have meant that institutions that were historically not thought to be exchanges, CCPs, or CSDs have begun to undertake functions previously thought the sole domain of these types of institutions.

In the trading arena, some brokers and other types of institutions have established electronic trading systems that appear similar to exchanges. These have been called different names in different contexts, including proprietary trading systems, electronic communication networks (ECNs), alternative trading systems (ATSs), and multilateral trading facilities (MTFs).[60] A central regulatory question has been whether to classify such systems, or the organizations that run them, as exchanges—and if so, whether they should be subject to the same regulatory requirements as other exchanges.[61] Among the criteria that have been employed to determine whether a trading system should be classified as an exchange are whether it provides two-sided quotes, liquidity, and volume; whether it provides trade execution and price discovery; whether its access is open to all types of market participants, subject to appropriate entry requirements; and also how its ownership and management are structured.

There has also been debate about the distinction between (I)CSDs and custodian banks, particularly in the EU. It has been argued that there is no difference between the settlement that custodians effect between clients on their own books, and that taking place at the (I)CSD level.[62] This purported functional equivalence has been taken to imply that both types of institutions should be regulated, and also classified, in the same manner. The claim that ICSDs and custodians are functionally similar has been challenged, however, using several counterarguments. First, custodians must hold their clients' securities in (I)CSDs, so they are users of, and not competitors to, (I)CSDs. Second, the legal rights associated with holding securities at a custodian and at (I)CSDs are different: (I)CSDs can effect ultimate change of ownership on the transfer of a security, while custodian banks cannot do so. Third, the systemic risks associated with the operations of (I)CSDs are different in kind and degree from the risks associated with the typical settlement-related activities undertaken by custodian banks. Fourth, (I)CSDs operate de facto monopolies, providing a "public utility" function, while custodian banks compete among themselves. Finally, it is argued that it is not within the power of a custodian bank to choose to internalize both purchase and sale transactions for settlement purposes: such activity arises only as a result of the independent and incidental decisions of both purchasers and sellers in the same transactions to use the same custodian bank.

Functions

The key functions that exchanges, CCPs, and CSDs undertake are listing, trading, information dissemination, and various post-trade services, including clearing and settlement. The nature and importance of these functions for different institutions are briefly reviewed here.

LISTING

At a general level, "listing" is the process of taking a privately owned company public so that its shares may be traded on a stock exchange. The term is, however, used in different ways in different jurisdictions, and indeed different exchanges undertake different activities associated with listing. An exchange normally has the power to decide whether to admit a security to trading on its trading platform, and may charge a company for this right. This process is sometimes called listing. In order for a company to be admitted to trading on an exchange, the exchange typically requires that the company have a minimum number of shares outstanding, a minimum market capitalization, and a minimum annual income or profitability.[63] When issuing a public security, a company is normally also required to satisfy a series of initial and ongoing regulatory obligations concerning the publication of relevant information. Sometimes this process is also referred to as obtaining a listing. Typically the company is required both to issue an initial prospectus with material information about its financial and business performance, and to disclose such information on an ongoing basis. Frequently, though not always, information disclosure requirements are established and enforced by a regulator distinct from an exchange.

There are many goals that a company may seek to achieve by listing—that is, having its shares publicly traded on an exchange. These include (1) to raise capital more cheaply than by alternative means; (2) to improve the liquidity of its shares; (3) to enhance the visibility of the company and its products; (4) to provide a stable environment for its stock; (5) to strengthen the company's image and gain the prestige of an exchange listing; (6) to improve access to brokers; (7) to gain more analyst research and newspaper coverage; (8) to obtain high standards of regulation—which might include better market surveillance, disclosure requirements, accounting standards, and shareholder rights' protection; (9) to access a diversity of investors; (10) to support the implementation of corporate strategies, for example by raising capital for mergers and acquisitions, or by using a listed security as an acquisition currency; and (11) to reduce political risk. Different companies seek different combinations of these benefits, and different exchanges have different relative strengths in delivering them.[64]

Issuers incur costs in listing.[65] These typically comprise one-off charges, such as underwriting fees for employing the financial intermediaries necessary to complete the listing process, and initial listing fees for stock exchanges, as well as ongoing costs, such as annual listing fees and the costs of an increased regulatory burden associated with listing, such as corporate governance rules and disclosure requirements. Given these costs, a public listing may not be economically viable for all companies. In response, stock exchanges have tried to accommodate the disparate needs of different types of firms, by introducing tailored market segments, with varying success.[66] Such segments may focus on start-up or high-technology companies. Listing requirements and fees vary considerably both across exchanges and across market segments.

The "listing" of a contract on a derivatives exchange is somewhat similar to the decision by a stock exchange to admit a security to trading on the exchange without the consent of the issuer. A derivatives exchange decides itself which contracts it wants to trade.[67] As a consequence, a derivatives exchange normally receives no listing fees for this activity, and in some contexts may even be required to pay fees to trade a particular contract, for example if the contract is based on an index owned by another institution.

TRADING

There is a broad range of types of trading systems and market structures that exchanges may employ. An analysis of this diversity is not presented here.[68] Instead, brief comments are provided on three key ways in which trading systems and market structures vary: whether they operate on a continuous or batch basis, the extent to which trading mechanisms are automated, and whether market-makers play a role in trading systems.

A market may operate on a "call," or a "continuous" basis. Call (or batch) markets organize the trading of securities only at certain points in time, and are thus discontinuous in nature. When the market "calls," all traders interested in dealing in a certain security can submit their orders to the order book. An execution system matches these orders, and executes all trades at the same time and at the same price, usually according to an algorithm that maximizes trading volume. The advantage of a call market is that it pools the orders of market participants, and therefore provides a focal point at which investors can trade a certain security, with potentially a relatively high degree of liquidity, relatively low volatility, and low search costs. Exchanges frequently use call markets to open trading, when resuming the trading of securities after a trading halt, and at a market's closing.

In contrast, continuous markets allow for the trading of securities at any time during a trading session. This can be attractive to investors if they do not want to wait until a certain time to execute their orders. The informational efficiency of a continuous market is also likely to be higher, as prices will reflect all publicly available information more quickly than in a discontinuous call market.

Historically, trading on exchanges took place at a central meeting point where traders physically met to exchange assets. These trading floors and pits, at stock and derivatives exchanges respectively, have now virtually ceased to exist.[69] Decentralized trading facilities using computer terminals have taken over the trading both at exchanges and at off-exchange trading mechanisms.[70]

This trend can be explained by the impact new technologies have had on the transaction costs of traders. Previously, meeting physically was economically indispensable for securities trading, as it minimized search, price discovery, and liquidity-related costs for traders by pooling buyers and sellers at one location. Nowadays, however, one of the major advantages of floor-trading, namely the almost cost-free communication between traders, can be replicated on automated trading systems. The necessity for a trader to be located at a central dealing location has thus been weakened with the proliferation of affordable information technology. Despite this trend, some authors find that execution costs on a trading floor are not necessarily higher than in automated markets.[71] Harris (2003, 552) notes that floor trading systems and automated trading systems have different relative strengths and weaknesses, comparing them along 11 dimensions: speed, information exchange, potential for order exposure strategies, trader convenience, buy-side access, scalability, initial costs, communications costs, labor costs, fairness, and audit trails.

There are two main types of execution system that facilitate the matching of orders between buyers and sellers. "Quote-driven" execution systems employ dealers that act as counterparties to every trade. A dealer sets bid and ask quotes with accompanying quantities for a certain security, depending on the perceived demand and supply for the security, and on its own inventory level in the security.[72] Dealers are usually required to provide liquidity to buyers and sellers at all times during the trading session. They often also trade with each other to adjust temporary imbalances in their inventories.

"Order-driven" execution systems usually do not employ an intermediary. Instead, buyers and sellers submit their orders directly to an order book. The market structure algorithm then determines which buyers trade with which sellers, and the price at which they trade. These trading rules, usually corresponding to a double auction market, induce a price discovery process for the traded securities. Historically, order-driven markets were employed for small orders, while quote-driven systems were used to facilitate block trades outside the order book, and sometimes to support less liquid stocks. Order-driven markets have, however, become progressively more popular with stock and derivatives exchanges globally, and also for trading other assets such as debt and foreign exchange. This shift has occurred for a range of reasons: dealers have become less willing to commit capital to market-making, order-driven markets are better equipped to handle computerized trading than dealer markets, and the growth in algorithmic trading has led to a large increase in the proportion of smaller orders. Pure order-driven or pure quote-driven markets are rarely observed.

INFORMATION DISSEMINATION

Exchanges collect and sell data about the orders (or quotes) and trades that occur on their markets.[73] There are substantial differences between the types of such data that exchanges both can, and choose, to release. Among the data that may be disseminated are[74]

1. price of last trade;
2. quantity of last trade;
3. time of last trade;
4. identities of parties to last trade;
5. high, low, open, and close trade prices;
6. aggregate price data and price indices;
7. cumulative trade volume;
8. best bid and ask prices;
9. quantities at best bid and ask prices;
10. identities of parties who placed those orders;
11. bid and ask prices behind the best prices;
12. quantities at those prices;
13. identities of parties who placed those orders;
14. high, low, open, and close midquote prices;
15. requests for quotes;
16. identities of parties who requested quotes;
17. number of individuals logged onto system;
18. identities of those individuals.

No trading system publishes all these categories of price and quote information, and indeed exchanges always have to decide about the optimal level of transparency they wish to support. Typically this decision involves answering the following key questions: *Who* can have access to *what* information, *when*, and at *what price*? These are highly complex, interrelated questions.[75]

For some categories of information, exchanges choose not to release relevant information as a matter of confidentiality. In most markets, for example, traders are unwilling to countenance releasing information about what their trading policies have been or will be, and thus exchanges do not disclose traders' identities. Some trading systems do, however, allow the practice of "sunshine" trading, whereby traders are offered the choice to release information about the trades they want to undertake, what type of trader they are, and even their identity. An uninformed trader may wish to provide this information both to attract the other side of the trade and to convince other market participants that it does not have any inside knowledge about the stocks to be traded. By releasing information about his identity, the trader hopes to lower his costs of trading, by not having to pay a premium either for immediacy or for the possibility that he might be an informed trader.

Generally, it is assumed that retail investors are the least informed traders, and that institutional investors are on average better informed.[76] Block holders in a security may have even more access to valuable information concerning the company in which they have invested. Thus, from a less informed trader's perspective, the knowledge that an order is submitted by an institutional investor or block holder may convey a valuable signal about the future development of the security price. Conversely, a better informed investor will seek to avoid the disclosure of its identity, as doing so may make it harder for the investor to trade without adversely affecting the price level.

Many electronic trading mechanisms allow hidden or "iceberg" orders, which conceal the order size of block trades in order to protect traders from adverse price movements. Increased transparency may reduce market participants' willingness to submit orders to a trading system. Some trading systems, sometimes called "dark pools," publish very little information about the quotes and trades executed on their systems. Some trading systems differentiate between the information they disseminate to their members and that which they publish more widely.

The manner in which quote and trade information is collected varies according to the technology used in the trading process. If an exchange uses an electronic trading system, the collection of market data is relatively easy, as the information is readily available in a digital format that can be processed and disseminated cheaply. If trading occurs nonelectronically, for example via traditional floor or telephone trading, the information needs to be obtained manually and is therefore more costly to collect. In telephone-based OTC markets, traders need to be induced to share relevant information. This may be accomplished by sharing the collected information with these traders, or by paying them for this task. Typically exchanges collect relevant price and quote data, and disseminate these to data vendors, which in turn repackage the information for their own customers, including intermediaries and institutional and retail investors.

A key decision regarding post-trade transparency of transactions is whether such information should be released in real time or with a delay. Some exchanges offer real-time information on a free basis to their members or direct users, whereas the public receives only delayed information, or has to pay a fee to obtain real-time information.

POST-TRADE PROCESSES

At the broadest level, CCPs and CSDs provide clearing and settlement services. The general way in which the processes of clearing and settlement are organized are well understood. Several key steps are involved.

If a trade is executed on an exchange or another form of organized market, it typically requires:[77] (1) confirmation of the terms of the trade between two direct trading members of an organized market;[78] (2) the possible interposition of a CCP between both sides of the trade; (3) calculation of the obligations of the trading members; (4) the possible netting of obligations; (5) communication of settlement instructions to the CSD, usually directly by the organized market or the central counterparty; and (6) transfer of securities in exchange for funds in order to settle the contractual obligations arising from a trade, either between the central counterparty and the trading firms, or between the trading firms directly if there was no central counterparty.

If a trade is between a broker and an investor client, the following broad steps are typically required: (1) confirmation by the broker with the client of the details of the order and the price; (2) communication of settlement instructions to the CSD, by the broker and by the custodian upon instruction by its investor client; (3) matching of the settlement instructions from the broker and the custodian; and (4) transfer of securities in exchange for funds between the broker and the custodian.

Despite the generally accepted understanding of how clearing, settlement, and other post-trade activities are organized, there are substantial difficulties in classifying the processes of clearing and settlement. Many of the relevant terms are used in different ways by market participants.[79] The precise way in which any particular trade is processed also varies a great deal, depending upon what security or derivative is traded, the particular market in which the trade takes place, the institutions that support post-trade processing, and the different parties to the trade. In addition, the procedures for post-trade processing have changed as market participants have sought to reduce its risks, to apply information technology, to accommodate growth in trading volumes, to reduce post-trade costs, and to lower their commitment of liquidity and collateral to post-trade activities. Together, these factors make it difficult to establish universal definitions for many post-trade processes.

The generally accepted meanings of some key terms, and also the difficulties in agreeing definitions, are well illustrated by discussions in the EU. On July 16, 2004, the European Commission established a Clearing and Settlement Advisory and Monitoring Expert group (CESAME) to advise and assist the Commission in the integration of EU securities clearing and settlement systems. CESAME established a subgroup on definitions that made a concerted effort to develop a standard "functional' terminology for post-trade processing.[80] The aim was to agree on definitions for the different post-trade processes applied to trading flows and associated "stock-related" activities, in order that these definitions might help clarify how regulation or other policy measures could usefully be applied to post-trade markets. In practice, there were many different views on these definitions. While there was general agreement about the range of activities involved, it was difficult to achieve consensus on whether some activities should be included in the definitions and whether activities typically performed by central institutions should be identified as such. Although progress was made towards agreement, it was not possible to achieve a complete consensus.

The CESAME subgroup discussed a set of broad headings for the various activities undertaken in the processing of a financial trade, and sought to establish clear definitions of precisely what activities should fall under each heading, taking account of a large number of policy and practitioner studies of the industry. Five headings were identified: verification, clearing, central counterparty clearing, settlement, and stock-related activities.

Verification: This was proposed as an umbrella term to cover the operational processes that ensure that different parties are agreed on trade details, and on how a trade is to be settled. It was intended to include affirmation by clients, confirmation of trade details between market participants, and also possibly confirmation of settlement arrangements and obligations. Several issues gave rise to controversy concerning the term "verification": the term itself, given that it was not in common use among market participants; whether the relevant activities should be considered post-trade at all, given that in many exchanges, trade confirmation was an automated process built into the trading system; and whether verification should include or exclude confirmation of settlement details, as well as of trade details.

Clearing: There was much discussion about this term. It was agreed that it was necessary to distinguish separately the services provided by a central counterparty, so that the general definition of clearing should exclude central counterparty clearing. Even with this restriction, however, there was still a great deal of variation in the use of the term. The subgroup proposed a definition that was intended to cover all the post-trade processing activities between verification and settlement other than central counterparty clearing is "the process of establishing settlement positions, possibly including the calculation of net positions, and the process of checking that securities, cash, or both are available."[81] This definition was consistent with that used in a report on clearing and settlement adopted by the European Parliament, but much broader than many practitioners' use of the term.[82]

Central Counterparty Clearing: There was a greater consensus on the role of a CCP as a third party interposed between the two sides of a trade, assuming their obligations, and thus becoming the buyer to every seller and the seller to every buyer. However, two issues complicated the discussions about this function. Some members of the CESAME subgroup sought to have the definition broadened to include the economic function of providing a guarantee on the fulfillment of the obligations of both buyers and sellers.[83] In addition, in order to cover other situations where one market participant assumes obligations on behalf of another—such as a general clearing member of a CCP acquiring an obligation to deliver a security on behalf of a client—two different definitions were put forward, distinguishing counterparty clearing, namely a transfer of an obligation not involving a central counterparty, from central counterparty clearing.

Settlement: Book-entry settlement was defined as "the act of crediting and debiting the tranferee's and tranferor's accounts respectively, with the aim of completing a transaction in securities."[84] This proposed definition covers only the very final act of transfers between securities accounts to fulfill the contractual obligations arising from a trade. The definition was strongly opposed by some market participants, who believed that CSD settlement, just as central counterparty clearing, should be separately defined. Besides the role of the CSD as the central place of settlement, there are various processes undertaken uniquely by CSDs in order to settle the largest number of transactions. These mechanisms include the algorithms used for prioritizing settlement instructions, multilateral netting, and many possible interventions in the handling of settlement obligations following predefined rules, such as a partial settlement of a particular obligation with the remainder of the obligation postponed to a later processing cycle.

Stock-Related Activities: Some of the greatest difficulties in the sub-committee discussions were in establishing agreed definitions to cover the range of services associated with the holding of securities, rather than the provision of transaction services. This diversity of opinion reflects both the wide range of such services and also differences in practices between different national markets. While all modern settlement arrangements require the creation of centralized book-entry accounts, with the issue itself either deposited or dematerialized within a depository, securities accounts are also provided by several institutions other than the depository. It is difficult to define these accounts in a standard way, clearly distinguishing their functions. For example, there was disagreement on whether the term "custody" is best restricted to the provision of accounts to institutional and other investors, with an emphasis on associated services, such as portfolio reporting and processing of corporate actions, or whether it should be applied generally to all investor accounts other than those located in the central depository, namely for accounts held for transaction as well as for stock-holding purposes. There were also differences of opinion about the definition of various issuer services, such as ensuring the integrity of an issue, namely that the number of securities held always exactly equals the number issued, and that the issuer has information about the owners of the security.

FINANCIAL IMPORTANCE

The importance to exchanges, CCPs, and CSDs of the key functions that they undertake, in terms of the relative proportions of revenues received for these different functions, varies greatly across institutions and over time. There are few publicly available data specifically about CCPs and CSDs. The WFE has, however, presented some very aggregated data about the sources of revenues received by its member exchanges. The WFE categorized such revenues into five broad sources: "Listing," "Trading," "Services," "Financial Income," and "Other." Consolidated data about these five sources of revenues for all the WFE member exchanges for the years 1995, 2000, 2005, and 2007, are illustrated in figure 1, based on data presented in table 1.[85] The "Services" category was very broad and included the provision of clearing, settlement, other post-trade services, market data, and IT sales. The WFE provided some more detailed information about three of the five categories of revenue sources, as illustrated in table 2 for 2007.

Several broad implications of figure 1 are evident. First, "Trading" has for the most part been exchanges' most important source of revenues, yielding 34% of total revenues in 1995, 43% in 2000, 37% in 2005, and 58% in 2007. Second, revenues from "Listing" have been declining relatively, providing 18% of total revenues in 1995, 15% in 2000, 10% in 2005, and 8% in 2007. Finally, the importance of the "Other" sources of

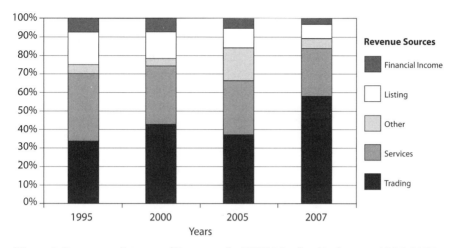

Figure 1: Percentage Sources of Revenues for WFE Member Exchanges, 1995–2007
Source: World Federation of Exchanges (2006) and (2008).

revenue to exchanges has varied significantly, tripling from 5% to 18% of total revenues from 1995 to 2005, then falling back to 5% in 2007.

The general decline in the importance of "Listing" revenues for exchanges has coincided with technological advances that have facilitated the unbundling of trading from listing services.[86] As a result, progressively less trading in certain shares takes place on exchanges where the shares were originally issued.[87] This reduces the economic justification for high listing fees, as stock exchanges providing listing cannot automatically guarantee that they will also provide the highest liquidity, and thus the lowest cost of capital, for their customers.[88] Another effect of unbundling is that exchanges can no longer subsidize their trading fees with revenues from their listing fees.

The importance to different exchanges of the various functions they undertake varies greatly. This may be illustrated by considering the percentages of revenues received by 10 selected European exchanges in 2008, as illustrated in figure 2, based on data presented in table 3.

Each column shows information for a specific exchange, as identified below the column. The percentages of the different sources of revenues received by an exchange are represented by the heights of the variously shaded parts of the exchange's column, with each shade representing a different revenue source. Although the data across exchanges are not fully comparable, several aspects of the figure are noteworthy. Two exchanges specialized in providing listing services—namely the Irish Stock Exchange and the Luxembourg Stock Exchange—with 74% and 75%

TABLE 1
Percentage Sources of Revenue for WFE Member Exchanges, 1995, 2000, 2005, 2007

Year	1995	2000	2005	2007
Listing	18%	15%	10%	8%
Trading	34%	43%	37%	58%
Services	36%	31%	30%	26%
Financial Income	7%	7%	5%	3%
Other	5%	4%	18%	5%
Totals	100%	100%	100%	100%

Source: World Federation of Exchanges (2006) and (2008).

TABLE 2
Subdivision of Revenue Categories from WFE Data for 2007

Listing	Share	Trading	Share	Services	Share
Annual listing fees	52%	Transaction fees	96%	Clearing	22%
Initial listing fees	24%	Other fees	4%	Settlement	4%
Other listing fees	24%			Other post-trade services	25%
				Market data	32%
				IT sales	17%
Totals	100%		100%		100%

of their respective revenues coming solely from this function. Percentage revenues from providing trading services—for cash products, derivatives products, or both—were over 50% for six of the other exchanges, and over 40% for the other two exchanges. Percentage revenues from information services and products varied from 0% for some exchanges to 27% for the London Stock Exchange Group. Deutsche Börse was unique in receiving 23% of its revenues from custody and banking, with the London Stock Exchange Group being the only other exchange to receive revenues from this function.

CONCLUSIONS

This chapter has two key goals: to provide some basic insights into the definitions and nature of an "infrastructure," an "exchange," a "CCP,"

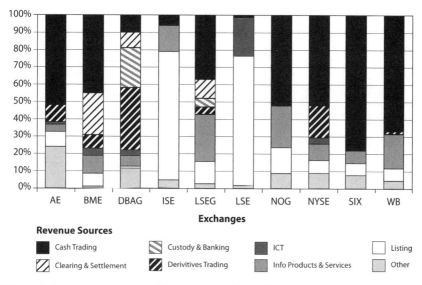

Figure 2: Percentage Sources of Revenue for Selected European Exchanges in 2008

Exchanges: AE: Athens Exchange: BME: Bolsas y Mercados Españoles: DBAG: Deutsche Börse Group: ISE: Irish Stock Exchange: LSEG: London Stock Exchange Group; LSE: Luxembourg Stock Exchange; NOG: NASDAQ OMX Group Inc.; NYSE: NYSE Euronext; SIX: SIX Group; WB: Wiener Börse.

Source: Federation of European Securities Exchanges (2009).

and a CSD; and to explore the reasons why these concepts are sometimes ambiguous and controversial.

An examination of a broad range of definitions and uses of the term "infrastructure" highlights eight key factors and attributes that contribute towards identifying an institution as an infrastructure. In particular, an infrastructure often (1) is, or provides, the *basic* framework that *supports* or *underlies* a system, defined quite broadly; (2) is *essential* to support commerce, economic activity and development, or whatever other activities are facilitated by the system it operates; (3) is, or operates, a *network*, which in the economic sphere facilitates the delivery of goods and services; (4) exhibits *economies of scale*; (5) requires *large, long-term,* and *sunk investments*; (6) is, or operates, a *natural monopoly*; (7) provides beneficial *public goods* or *services*, in addition to the specific goods and services it delivers directly; and (8) has some form of *government* or *public sector involvement*, defined very broadly. It is noteworthy that the term "infrastructure" has been used in different contexts for different reasons, and therefore, unsurprisingly, has been given many different meanings.

TABLE 3
Percentage Sources of Revenue for Selected European Exchanges in 2008

Exchange	AE	BME	DBAG	ISE	LSEG	LSE	NOG	NYSE	SIX	WB
Listing	9%	8%	1%	74%	13%	75%	15%	8%	7%	7%
Cash trading	52%*	45%	10%	6%	37%	0.2%	52%***	52%	78%***	67%**
Derivatives trading	10%*	8%***	36%**	0%	4%	0%	—	19%	—	1%**
Clearing & settlement	0%	24%	9%	0%	11%	0%	0%	0%	0%	0%
Custody & banking	0%	0%	23%	0%	5%	0%	0%	0%	0%	0%
Info products & services	4%	10%	6%	15%	27%	0%	24%	9%	7%	20%
ICT services	1%	4%	3%	0%	0%	23%	0%	3%	0%	0%
Other	24%	1%	12%	5%	3%	2%	9%	9%	8%	5%
Totals	100%	100%	100%	100%	100%	100%	100%	100%	100%	100%

Source: Federation of European Securities Exchanges (2009).

Legend: * includes clearing and settlement, ** includes clearing, *** includes derivatives trading,

AE = Athens Exchange, BME = Bolsas y Mercados Españoles, DBAG = Deutsche Börse Group, ISE = Irish Stock Exchange, LSEG = London Stock Exchange Group, LSE = Luxembourg Stock Exchange, NOG = NASDAQ OMX Group Inc., NYSE = NYSE Euronext, SIX = SIX Group, WB = Wiener Börse

The nature of five of the factors that contribute to identifying an institution as an infrastructure are briefly examined. These are whether an institution is an "essential facility," whether it operates a "network," whether it exhibits economies of scale, whether it requires the investment of large sunk costs, and whether it is a "natural monopoly." All five of these factors suggest that infrastructure institutions may have some form of market power.

A range of assets, services, organizations, and industries have typically been identified as "infrastructure." These include the basic physical systems of a nation, particularly its transport, communications, energy, and water and sanitation systems. In addition, infrastructure may include public and social facilities and government systems. In financial markets, the term has been widely used to refer to exchanges, CCPs, and CSDs.

The definitions of the terms "exchange," "CCP," and "CSD" are at first sight relatively clear. The central element in almost all definitions of an exchange is that such an institution operates a trading system, and through this provides a market. Two core functions delivered by a trading system are data dissemination and order execution. Data dissemination is the publication of pre- and post-trade data, about quotes and trades respectively, to market participants. Order execution is the process whereby orders can be transformed into trades. The widely accepted definition of a CCP is that it is an entity that interposes itself between counterparties to contracts in one or more financial markets, becoming the seller to every buyer and the buyer to every seller. Although there is significant variation in the definition of a CSD, two aspects are commonly believed critical. First, a CSD is an entity that holds securities centrally either in certificated or in dematerialized form. Second, it is an entity that enables the central transfer of ownership of securities, typically by means of book-entry transfer, usually on an electronic accounting system.

Notwithstanding the perceived simplicity of these definitions, a wide range of factors have led to disagreement and uncertainty about whether they are correct, and also to some confusion about which organizations should be classified as an exchange, a CCP, or a CSD. Despite the generally accepted understanding of how clearing, settlement and other post-trade activities are organized, there are particular difficulties in classifying the processes of clearing and settlement.

The key functions that exchanges, CCPs, and CSDs undertake are listing, trading, information dissemination, and various post-trade services, including clearing and settlement. The importance of these functions to different exchanges, as measured by the share of revenues they receive from each function, varies widely.

CHAPTER TWO

Market Power

A CRITICAL DETERMINANT of whether exchanges, CCPs, and CSDs should be considered infrastructure institutions is whether they have market power. This chapter explores whether they do. It is composed of five sections. Some introductory comments are presented first. The extent to which exchanges, CCPs, and CSDs may each have market power is discussed, respectively, in the next three sections. Conclusions are provided in the last section.

PRELIMINARY COMMENTS

The question of whether exchanges, CCPs, and CSDs have market power turns primarily on whether there is competition in the provision of trading, clearing, central register, and settlement services. The broad factors that lead towards consolidation of market power in the provision of these services, and also those that tend to promote competition and reduce market power, are identified and analyzed here. The discussion is illustrated with descriptions of particular markets, institutions, and relevant industry experience. It is not intended, however, to offer a definitive assessment of whether any particular institutions do or do not have market power. To do so would require a full specification of the relevant markets and institutions in question, access to pertinent nonpublic information, and a more concentrated approach than is possible here.[1] Some generic propositions about the competitive structure of the industry in each of the exchange, CCP, and CSD sectors are articulated. They seek to capture and summarize the accumulated knowledge and experience on the topic in a simple manner. It is accepted, however, that by their nature they cannot be comprehensive and may also oversimplify a complex reality.

Market power is not important per se, but rather for its economic implications. The UK Office of Fair Trading (OFT) suggests that market power may be thought of as

> the ability profitably to sustain prices above competitive levels or restrict output or quality below competitive levels. An undertaking with market power might also have the ability and incentive to harm the

process of competition in other ways; for example, by weakening existing competition, raising entry barriers or slowing innovation.[2]

A firm operating in a monopolistic or consolidated industry may have an ability to undertake such anticompetitive or abusive actions. Market share does not always, however, bring market power. If, for example, a firm operates in a contestable market, it will face a credible threat of new entry into the market, which will mean it cannot act anticompetitively even if it is a monopolist. In a perfectly contestable market, even a monopolist will be forced to be efficient, faced with the threat of potential new entrants. There will thus be no need to worry about anticompetitive behavior on the part of incumbents. The key goal of regulators of contestable markets is to ensure that entry and exit costs to and from the markets remain low.

One context in which consolidation may reduce the problems typically associated with market power can arise when two suppliers of a joint good or service each enjoy market power, and can each impose its own anticompetitive markups on customers. This is often referred to as the "double marginalization" problem. Vertical integration may enhance efficiency in such circumstances. As Kobayashi (2005, 714) explains,

> Two monopolists, setting prices independently, will set the prices at an inefficiently high level when the goods are complements. This effect occurs because the individual firms do not take into account the negative effect an increase in the price of one good has on the demand for the complementary good. As a result, both sellers and consumers can be better off if both prices were lowered. Having the two firms agree to bundle their individual products allow the firms to internalize this pricing externality.[3]

The consequence is a reduction in final prices and an efficiency gain, following integration of both firms. The outcome is not as efficient as would be the case were there competition in all markets, but if markets are not competitive, integration may alleviate some of the efficiency losses arising from market power.

The determination of whether an institution has market power, and the closely related issues of whether competition or contestability is effective in the relevant market, cannot simply be made by following a mechanical algorithm. Judgment is required, and differences of opinion are possible. There has in fact been great debate about the elemental question of whether competition exists at all in the provision of each of the key activities examined here—namely trading, clearing, and settlement. Opposing views have arisen for many reasons, including differences of interpretation as to the precise definitions of the markets in question, confusion about terminology, and disagreements about both the importance and the merits of assorted conceptual arguments and empirical evidence. Different parties have also argued either for or against the existence of market power or competition in various regulatory and policy contexts, so as to best promote their own interests.

The OFT states that market power is "not absolute, but a matter of degree." Although recognizing that an assessment of whether, and to what extent, a firm has market power will depend on the circumstances of each case under examination, the OFT identifies five key factors as being important in making such a determination: the presence of existing competitors, potential competition, buyer power, economic regulation, and the firm's behavior and financial performance. The nature and importance of these factors is as follows:[4]

> *Existing competitors* are undertakings already in the relevant market. If an undertaking . . . attempts to sustain prices above competitive levels, this might not be profitable because customers would switch their purchases to existing competitors. The market shares of competitors in the relevant market are one measure of the competitive constraint from existing competitors. It can also be important to consider how the market shares of undertakings in the market have moved over time.
>
> *Potential competition*—This refers to the scope for new entry. Where entry barriers are low, it might not be profitable for one or more undertakings in a market to sustain prices above competitive levels because this would attract new entry which would then drive the price down.
>
> *Buyer power* exists where buyers have a strong negotiating position with their suppliers, which weakens the potential market power of a seller.
>
> *Economic regulation* is a further relevant factor when assessing market power in industry sectors where, for example, prices and/or service levels are subject to controls by the government or an industry sector regulator. While economic regulation is not a competitive constraint in itself, it can limit the extent to which undertakings can exploit their market power.
>
> *Evidence about the behaviour and financial performance of undertakings* is also relevant. Where there is direct evidence that, over the long term, prices substantially exceed relevant costs or profits substantially exceed competitive levels, this may point to market power.

Of these five factors that might be indicative of market power, the first three—namely those relating to existing competitors, potential competition, and buyer power—are examined in some detail in the context of exchanges, CCPs, and CSDs. There has been relatively little direct *economic* regulation, namely regulation seeking to control prices or service levels, of these types of institutions. Exchanges, CCPs, and CSDs are, however, subject to a broad array of other forms of regulation, some of which does affect their market power, and some relevant examples of such regulation are noted in the discussion. Finally, there has been very little analysis of whether the prices of trading, clearing, and settlement services are competitive or not, and the analysis that has been undertaken has been highly controversial.[5] Only brief comments are provided on this topic.

One other crucial factor affecting whether an exchange, a CCP, or a CSD can exploit any market power it has, is its governance structure. Governance is defined here in its broadest sense, encompassing the ownership, control, board, management, and other aspects of an institution, affecting the exercise of power at the institution. There are many ways in which governance can be important in responding to the existence of market power. Two of the most critical and controversial are whether a mutually owned institution, be it an exchange, a CCP, or a CSD, can mitigate some of the problems that arise from market power, and whether vertical integration between an exchange, a CCP, and a CSD can do the same. These and other relevant issues relating to governance are referred to only briefly in this chapter, but are examined in subsequent chapters.

Many factors make assessing whether exchanges, CCPs, and CSDs have market power, and the implications of such market power, extremely complicated. While some of these factors are explored below, it is not possible here to investigate their ramifications in full. The first such complication is that the ways in which trading, clearing, and settlement services are provided have evolved significantly over the recent past, and given current market, technological, regulatory, and policy developments, may do so again in the future. Such changes can affect the market power that exchanges, CCPs, or CSDs have.[6]

Another complication arises because the provision of trading, clearing, and settlement services are not independent of each other. Trading and post-trade services together form a composite good. Failure to recognize this interconnection has led to confusion surrounding the application of the terminology of vertical and horizontal differentiation to trading and post-trade services. The term "vertical silo" has been used to describe a situation where an exchange owns a CCP and a CSD. Such ownership arrangements are in fact not vertically integrated in the standard sense applied in industrial organization economics. Neither clearing nor settlement services are inputs required by an exchange in order to offer a trading system. Rather, trading, clearing, and settlement services together are components of a composite or bundled good, all of which, typically, must be consumed by market participants, or their agents, to complete a trade. If market power can be exploited in providing one of these services, and it is not possible to unbundle the provision of this service from the provision of the other services, then it may be possible for such market power to be exploited in the other bundled services.

Assessing the market power of exchanges, CCPs, or CSDs is also difficult because the presence of network effects in the provision of all three types of service—trading, clearing, and settlement—may mean that these markets are "tippy." In particular, while it may be difficult for a new competitor to compete against an incumbent provider, if a new competitor does start being successful, then the whole market may tip rapidly from the incumbent provider to the new entrant. This tendency may reinforce the possibility of using market power in providing one service to exploit market power in the provision of another service. As noted by Cruickshank (2002b),

> The dynamics of these types of "tippy" markets are extremely complex and, for producers, having the best, or most efficient, system is not sufficient to ensure success. Indeed, given the apparent economies of scope across different demand-defined markets (eg clearing, settlement and netting across bond and equity markets) and likely different speeds of demand integration within these markets, there is considerable scope for an astute, but relatively inefficient, operator to end up as the main supplier. By sequentially setting prices at marginal costs for the precise product/service in competitive transition the relatively inefficient operator is always price competitive and reaps the economies of scale without having to meet the other operators' level of technical efficiency.

Seven further aspects and limitations of the discussion presented in this chapter are noteworthy. First, although attention is focused on the provision of trading, clearing, and settlement services, a few comments are made on listing and information dissemination services.[7] Second, while most of the analysis relates to the equity markets, issues and examples from other types of markets, including bond and derivatives markets, are also explored. Third, the analysis is based on the publicly available data and literature—no primary research has been undertaken. While competition between exchanges has been widely scrutinized empirically, there is little empirical evidence about whether CCPs or CSDs have market power. Fourth, where possible, the balance of opinion on relevant questions, such as whether market power is present or not, is assessed. Whatever is determined to be the balance of opinion on a particular issue, however, is not necessarily accepted as true here. Fifth, the legal question of whether exchanges, CCPs, or CSDs might be, or operate, essential facilities is not addressed.[8] Sixth, no assessment is made of the intensities of competition in the relevant sectors in individual countries, nor are the levels of competition compared across jurisdictions or regions. Given that competition in the provision of trading, clearing, and settlement services has been more prevalent in the EU and the United States than elsewhere, however, much of the analysis draws on experience from these jurisdictions. Finally, the aim is to *describe* the industry structures in trading, clearing, and settlement, not to *prescribe* an optimal structure for any of these industry sectors.

EXCHANGES

The extent to which exchanges have market power is explored in this section. It is composed of four parts. The key factors that lead towards consolidation of market power, and those that tend to promote competition and reduce market power, are examined in turn. Brief comments on the industry structure in practice, for both the securities and the derivatives markets, are presented. Some generic propositions about the exchange industry's structure are then articulated.

Factors Amplifying Market Power

Order Flow Network Externality: A powerful factor limiting competition to an incumbent exchange arises from the positive order flow network externality from which all trading systems benefit: the likelihood of a trader receiving an execution of its order on a trading system is higher if other traders already send their orders to the same system.[9] Order flow attracts order flow; liquidity attracts liquidity. This gives an incumbent trading system an advantage over new competing systems, whatever asset or contract is being traded.

Economies of Scale: Trading systems have historically been thought to exhibit economies of scale. Malkamäki (1999) examined whether there were economies of scale in 1997 for trading, listing, and other associated activities involving company-specific information, for 37 stock exchanges from four continents. Trading exhibited clear economies of scale, while listing showed less returns to scale, although the biggest stock exchanges did exhibit very significant returns to scale in the provision of listing services. Hasan and Malkamäki (2001) similarly studied whether expansions are cost effective for stock exchanges over the period 1989–98. They found that activities related to both trading and firm-specific information processing possessed economies of scale, although there were both geographic and size-related variations. The North American and European exchanges exhibited substantially higher economies of scale than the Asian-Pacific exchanges. The largest exchanges also appeared to benefit from the most returns to scale. Schaper (2009) also found that large exchanges provide trading services at lower costs per trade than smaller ones, examining a group of 26 exchanges over the period 2005–7.

Automation appears to have opposing effects on the importance of economies of scale. On the one hand, as advances in technology lower the costs of building trading systems, a smaller amount of fixed costs will need to be spent to enter the market. This may make it easier for new entrants, as the minimum scale necessary to achieve the lowest cost per unit of production may be reduced. On the other hand, as automation has led to a decline in the marginal cost of executing a trade on a digital platform to such an extent that it is now effectively zero, the ratio of fixed to variable costs of operating a trading system has increased. This will enhance the importance of economies of scale.

Law/Regulation: Competition between trading systems may be restricted by law or regulation. At the extreme, the law may require that all trading be concentrated on a particular exchange. Less direct forms of anticompetitive regulation are also possible. For example, in certain government bond markets, a financial intermediary may need to trade a specified volume on an incumbent trading system in order to obtain primary dealer status.[10] This requirement may restrict the development of rival trading platforms, if being a primary dealer is valuable to financial intermediaries.

All regulators of exchanges are concerned that such institutions operate in a safe and sound manner, and that the risks inherent in trading are appropriately managed. In order to ensure this safe operation, regulatory requirements are typically imposed on exchanges, which by their nature restrict entry into the exchange business only to those institutions able to satisfy the requirements. In the UK, for example, an exchange is required to have sufficient financial resources; to be a suitable institution to be an exchange; to have proper monitoring and enforcement processes; to promote and maintain high standards of integrity, fair dealing, and safeguards for investors; to have appropriate rules and a proper consultation process; to have an appropriate complaints procedure; and have rules regarding defaults in the contracts traded on the exchange.[11]

The issue of whether the law sanctions competition between exchanges and trading systems in an international context is often complicated. In order for an exchange to compete for customers on a cross-border basis, it needs to be granted the right to operate in a foreign country. However, the conditions necessary for cross-border recognition, which are likely to include regulatory standards that define minimum standards for exchanges, currently exist in very few sets of jurisdictions.[12] The most prominent instance where a legal and regulatory basis exists for competition between exchanges and trading systems on a cross-border basis is in the EU, which passed the Markets in Financial Instruments Directive (MiFID) to sanction such competition.[13] A policy discussion about allowing international exchanges access to the United States began in 2006.[14]

Transparency: The amount and quality of prices and quotes a dominant trading system disseminates affects the extent to which other systems can compete against it. The less transparent a dominant trading system is, the more difficult it is for other systems to compete against it, because participants only using the other trading systems will not receive the information about the prices and quotes on the dominant trading system. They may therefore be at an informational disadvantage compared to traders who do have access to the dominant trading system, and may accordingly be less willing to trade on the new trading systems. As Harris (2003, 535) notes, however,

> In very active markets, information usually is quite cheap relative to the volume of trade, and the competition among arbitrageurs to profit from trading opportunities ensures that they provide cheap and efficient service. The benefits of complete consolidation in such markets therefore are small relative to the benefits of market diversity. Active markets therefore can support more diverse market structures than less active markets can.

The fact that by being less transparent, an exchange may be able to reduce the competition it faces from other trading systems does not necessarily mean that an exchange, or any other type of trading system, has an incentive not to disseminate information. Many factors affect this decision, not least that in order to attract trading some price and quote dissemination is typically necessary.[15]

Access to Clearing/Settlement: Competition between exchanges may be foreclosed if potential new entrant exchanges and trading systems do not have the same access to clearing and settlement facilities as incumbent exchanges.[16] This may occur if competition for the provision of clearing or settlement services is limited or nonexistent, and if an incumbent exchange operates a vertical silo, thus owning the CCP and CSD.[17] If an incumbent exchange operates a vertical silo, but competition at both the clearing and settlement level is viable, then a new entrant exchange could simply seek clearing and settlement services from a CCP and a CSD other than those owned by the incumbent exchange. The new exchange could also create its own CCP or CSD. If an incumbent exchange operates a vertical silo and the provision of clearing and settlement services is not competitive, however, the incumbent may choose to restrict access to its CCP and CSD in order to hinder competition at the trading level.

Whether an exchange will seek to restrict access to its CCP if it is vertically integrated is a controversial question. Pirrong (2007a, 34) argues that a vertically integrated exchange will not seek to restrict access to its CCP in order to restrict competition in the trading arena, if it has market power in clearing, if it is profit-maximizing, and if the market for exchanges is competitive:

> If trade execution is potentially highly competitive, foreclosure is not a profitable strategy; the clearing monopolist can extract all the rent by pricing clearing services appropriately, and actually has an incentive to encourage entry by a more efficient execution venue.

Competition between exchanges may be constrained, however, even if there is competition in the provision of clearing services but there are switching costs for market participants to use a new CCP. If a new exchange enters the market and decides to use a new CCP, it might cost market participants more to trade on the new exchange, given that they would have to pay the switching costs to use the new CCP, as compared to using the existing one. This again could limit new entry for the provision of trading services.

Intellectual Property Rights: Unlike securities exchanges, which standardly do not own any intellectual property rights (IPR) in the securities they trade, derivatives exchanges typically design and create the contracts they trade, thereby obtaining IPR in them. Such rights, which are sometimes also recognized in relevant law governing derivatives markets, mean that derivatives exchanges are often able to stop other exchanges from trading identical contracts, and financial intermediaries from trading their contracts off-exchange.[18]

The existence of such IPR has, however, been argued as providing a positive incentive for an exchange to create new products. An exchange will be able to exploit the financial benefits of such innovation, in the knowledge that other exchanges will not be able to free-ride off the investments it made by trading similar products.[19]

Listing: There has been debate about whether the ability to compete to provide trading services may be affected by competition in the listing market. The central reason why the two have been thought to be separate markets, as for example was concluded by the UK Competition Commission (2005, 31), is that it is not necessary for a company wishing to provide trading services also to provide listing services, and many companies have indeed sought to provide just trading services. In addition, there is little evidence to suggest that listing and trading fees are jointly determined.

In contrast, it has been suggested that the ability to compete to provide trading services may be affected by competition in the listing market. Pagano and Padilla (2005, 26–27) argue, for example,

> The listing decisions of companies can ... generate network effects ... listed companies benefit from the presence of investors and stock analysts; and investors and stock analysts benefit from the presence of listed companies. Each new listing makes the market more attractive for investors and analysts, since they prefer to operate on exchanges where many securities are listed. In turn, companies are more likely to list in a market where more investors trade stocks and more analysts collect and analyse data about them.

Listing takes place predominantly in an issuer's home market, and even when a security is listed simultaneously in more than one market, trading tends to be concentrated almost entirely in the home market. This has been explained largely by informational biases that favor domestic trading platforms. Issuers find it cheaper to provide information to their domestic markets. Informed traders have faster and cheaper access to local information, and can process it better than foreign-originated information; thus, these traders have an advantage in the trading and underwriting of local securities. Such a process in turn attracts domestic issuers seeking to target those investors. Pagano and Padilla (2005, 4) claim that, as a result, domestic trading platforms have an advantage over foreign platforms in the listing and trading of domestic securities. This home bias does not, however, limit competition between domestic trading platforms.

Factors Enhancing Competition and Reducing Market Power

Lower Prices and Better Services: Advances in technology have meant that it is much cheaper than before to build and operate a trading system, and also to distribute and receive relevant information—concerning prices, quotes, orders, and trades—over wide-area computer networks, including on a cross-border basis.[20] This has allowed new entrants to offer lower prices than incumbent exchanges for the provision of trading services.

Advances in technology have also led to the growth of algorithmic trading that in turn has increased the sensitivity of traders to the price of trading services. Algorithmic trading allows market participants to examine different pools of liquidity around a market, determine an optimum execution strategy, in terms of where and how orders should be routed to different execution systems, and then execute that strategy. Such strategies frequently involve breaking up large block orders into small orders, and delivering them over time to different trading platforms. The growth in algorithmic trading has thus led to a large growth in the number of trades and a reduction in the size of trades. This, in turn, has meant that in some jurisdictions the price of execution per trade has become a more important factor in the competition between trading systems than previously.

New technology has also facilitated the creation of trading systems that satisfy a diversity of preferences among market participants with different trading objectives. There are many objectives that traders may wish fulfilled when executing their orders, including, among others, best price, the minimization of indirect trading costs such as market impact, speed of execution, low transaction costs, anonymity, and the ability to execute contingent orders. Different trading systems have been developed to satisfy each of these preferences.

Enhanced Access: Technological developments have enhanced competition by increasing access to markets in several important ways. They have allowed some trading systems to compete with incumbent exchanges by providing access to the market to a new group of customers who previously did not have such access. Reductions in the cost of routing orders to new trading systems has increased traders' willingness to use such systems, and thus to support competition between them.

Advances in order-routing technology have also made it possible for market participants to route their orders to new trading systems, without losing the benefits of the order flow network externality associated with incumbent dominant trading systems. For example, improvements in the ease of submitting contingent orders to many markets may mean that the switching costs to traders of diverting their order flow away from an incumbent market to a newly developed one become lower. As it has become easier to submit the same order to several markets, on condition that if one of the orders submitted is executed all the orders on the other markets are cancelled, so the likelihood of using different markets increases.

Another order routing strategy that can deliver an equivalent effect is for a new trading system to assess whether any particular order routed to it can be best executed on its system, or would obtain a better execution by being routed to an alternative system, and potentially a dominant incumbent exchange. Such an order-routing strategy means that market participants do not lose the benefits of any network externality offered by an incumbent and dominant trading system, by sending their orders to a new trading system that cannot offer such benefits but may still be cheaper to use.[21]

New technology has also meant that speed of access and execution has become an important factor affecting competition between exchanges.

This speed has become so crucial to some electronic traders that they have sought to co-locate their trade engines in the data centers of exchanges, in order to execute their orders faster than their competitors.

The combination of enhanced order flow technology and speed of execution may, however, have complicated and unanticipated effects, and may not always be pro-competitive. As Harris (2003, 528) notes:

> The exposure of a limit order in two markets at once puts the order in *double jeopardy* of executing twice. The problem is especially serious if either market has slow execution, quotation, order-routing, or trade reporting systems. In that case, both markets may try to execute the order before either market can cancel an order or adjust a quote.

A trader may not wish to submit orders to a new trading system, if the new trading system agrees to route the orders to an incumbent market and the incumbent market is slow. This is because information about whether orders sent to the slow market are executed or not will be slow in coming, and during the period when such information is unavailable, alternative options for executing the order may disappear. A dominant exchange may thus be rewarded for having *slower* execution facilities than its more innovative new competitors with advanced order-routing facilities, because traders will not risk sending their orders to the new trading systems for fear that they will not be executed on the dominant exchange, where the likelihood of execution is higher.

Incentives: New trading systems can attract order flow from incumbent exchanges by offering incentives to market participants to increase their use of the new systems. Such incentives may include paying for order flow, subsidizing market making on a new system, sharing revenues—for example from trading fees or information sales—or giving users ownership stakes in the new trading system.

Coordination of Customers and Bargaining Power: The existence of a powerful, concentrated customer group, which is dissatisfied with an incumbent provider, and which has the ability to switch its trading business from an existing venue to a new provider in a coordinated fashion, can enhance competition between trading systems. The UK Competition Commission (2005, 5) has explained this effect as follows:

> Trading on LSE [London Stock Exchange], as on other exchanges in Europe, is concentrated in a small number of large trading firms. This degree of concentration has facilitated a higher degree of actual head-to-head competition between exchanges in recent years than would otherwise have been the case. There are two important consequences of this concentration of trading firms. First, the actions of a relatively small number of trading firms in transferring their trading activities

from one platform to another would facilitate a shift in liquidity. Second, an exchange wishing to compete head-to-head with LSE could readily identify key trading firms and, more importantly, would need to gain the commitment of only a small number of them.

There have indeed been occasions when a small group of powerful customers has moved in a coordinated manner from one trading system to another.[22] Nevertheless, although a large share of the order flow in many markets frequently passes through a small number of financial intermediaries, there is often confusion about what power such financial intermediaries have.

Most financial intermediaries do not control most of the orders that pass through their books, in the sense that they are not in a position to decide where the orders should be routed.[23] Either the customers of the financial intermediaries, who initiated the orders, decide where they should be routed, or best-execution obligations imposed on the financial intermediaries mean that they can only divert trading volumes to a new trading system if it offers quotes the same as or better than any incumbent systems. The threat of a small group of relatively powerful intermediaries acting in a coordinated manner is therefore sometimes overestimated.

If there is a single monopolistic exchange in a market that operates without the threat of new entrants, its ability to exploit its market power could, however, be circumscribed by the bargaining power of the users of the exchange. A small group of major financial intermediaries could, for example, act as a monopsonistic buyer to bargain with the monopolistic exchange. Instances of such bargaining are hard to verify. In the context of the UK Competition Commission's inquiry into the potential takeover of the LSE, Euronext told the commission that users had successfully negotiated lower fees at several major exchanges.[24] Several other respondents to the commission stated, however, "that collective action only had limited success in terms of fee negotiations." The London Investment Banking Association (LIBA), in particular, noted that market participants are held back from taking collective action in response to obstacles to competition in trading by a number of factors, including "a fear of retaliation by exchanges, particularly those with a degree of regulatory control."

Expectations: Traders' perceptions of the likely liquidity on a new trading system affect the probability of success of the system.[25] Such expectations may be determined by many factors, including the identities of the sponsors and financial backers of a new trading system, its management, its technology, its order execution algorithm, and even advertising about its likely success.

Avoiding Clearing Restrictions: Competition between exchanges is possible even if each exchange has its own CCP, and there is no interoperability between the two CCPs.[26] If the benefits of netting and collateral management across exchanges are relatively low, then a lack of interoperability between the two CCPs will not be seen as an obstacle to trading on both exchanges at the same time.

Even without a formal linkage between the CCPs, it may be possible to deliver the same effects as would occur with full interoperability. One way in which this might be implemented between derivatives exchanges involves the use of a form of settlement called an exchange for physicals (EFP). An EFP is a transaction negotiated off-market in which one party buys physical assets and sells futures contracts, while another party sells the physical market products and buys the futures contracts. EFPs provide a mechanism to swap from a futures to a physical asset, or vice versa. Appropriate use of EFPs might allow fungibility between the two exchanges' contracts, without the need for any linkage between their two CCPs. Consider an environment with two derivatives exchanges that trade substantially similar contracts, each of which has a CCP, but that do not have any form of linkage allowing offsetting of exposures between the two CCPs. In such a context, it would not be possible to take a long position on one exchange, and a corresponding short position on the other exchange, and offset them against each other. If EFPs are sanctioned on both markets, however, it would be possible to exchange a position in one market for a position in the physical market, and then exchange that same physical position for a corresponding position on the other market. This would effectively deliver fungibility between the exchanges' contracts.

Law/Regulation: There are many laws and regulations in different jurisdictions that have sought to promote, or at least eliminate restrictions to, competition between trading systems, both domestically and internationally. It is not feasible to list, describe, or assess any of them here. Of critical importance are national laws that allow any organization wishing to operate a trading system or exchange to do so. The way in which competition between trading systems is managed has also been the subject to much regulatory intervention. Two relatively recent and important initiatives attempting to promote such competition are Regulation NMS in the United States and MiFID in the EU.[27]

Industry Structure in Practice

There are various potential sources of competition to an exchange for the provision of trading services, including:[28]

1. other domestic and international exchanges;
2. nonexchange trading systems;
3. financial intermediaries, including dealers and brokers, who can deal with each other over the counter (OTC), or internalize trades on their own books, thus disintermediating exchanges;
4. investors who can deal directly with each other, or, if they are institutional investors, can internalize trades on their own books, thus disintermediating both exchanges and financial intermediaries; and,[29]
5. trading in contracts that have similar risk characteristics.

The manner in which competition to exchanges for the provision of trading services has evolved varies widely across jurisdictions, and in several jurisdictions has also been very complex. Several common themes in how such competition has developed are, however, noteworthy.

In many countries there is only one, or at least only one dominant, securities exchange. The historical development of such national exchanges has often followed a similar path, with multiple exchanges being created in different major cities of the country, and then over time gradually being consolidated into a single national exchange.[30]

Progressively the regulatory restrictions on establishing new exchanges and other types of trading systems are being relaxed around the world, although such restrictions remain in many countries. The creation of ATSs is a relatively modern phenomenon. The first trading system that might reasonably be classified as an ATS, namely Instinet, was founded in the United States in 1969. It was only in the late 1990s, however, that many such systems—at that stage referred to as ECNs—were established, again primarily in the United States, and this time as a response to the Securities and Exchange Commission's order-handling rules.[31] The creation of new nonexchange trading systems across the EU was facilitated with the implementation of MiFID on November 1, 2007. The regulatory basis for sanctioning new trading systems has also begun to occur in some other jurisdictions, including Australia, Canada, and Japan.[32]

Most new trading systems that have sought to compete with incumbent exchanges have failed. In the EU, for example, the UK Competition Commission examined the history of entry and expansion by regulated exchanges for new trading ventures in Europe over the period 1995–2005.[33] Of the seven initiatives listed, one was never implemented, three stopped operating during the period, and the remaining three only obtained minimal trading volumes.

There have, however, been some new trading systems, some classified as exchanges and others not, that have successfully competed against incumbent exchanges in capturing significant order flow, and in some

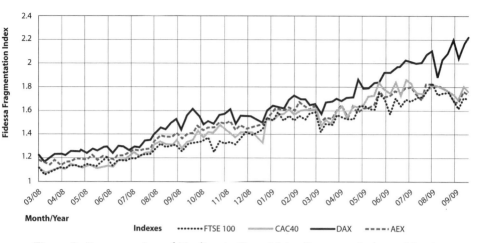

Figure 3: Fragmentation of Trading in Four Major European Indexes, March 2008–September 2009
Source: http://fragmentation.fidessa.com

instances, the whole market. Three prominent examples include when Deutsche Terminbörse (DTB) captured all the trading in German government bond futures (the Bund contract) from the London International Financial Futures and Options Exchange (LIFFE) in 1998;[34] when the National Stock Exchange in India began competing against the Bombay Stock Exchange (BSE), and exceeded the volume of the BSE within one year from November 1994;[35] and when the International Securities Exchange (ISE), an automated trading market for options, was launched in May 2000 in the United States to compete against the dominant incumbent floor-based markets, the most important of which was the Chicago Board Options Exchange (CBOE).[36]

It is in the EU and the United States that competition between trading systems in the equities markets has been most intense. In Europe, following the introduction of MiFID, a series of MTFs were established—including BATS, Burgundy, Chi-X, NEURO, and Turquoise—to compete with the primary national exchanges, and some of these exchanges themselves also sought to compete with each other. Following the introduction of MiFID in November 2007, the market share of most major European exchanges in trading their primary national stocks dropped.[37] This is illustrated in figure 3, which shows how a particular measure of fragmentation, the Fidessa Fragmentation Index (FFI), varied over the period March 2008–September 2009 for the trading in four major European indices. The four indices are the FTSE 100 for the UK, the CAC 40 for France, the DAX for Germany, and the AEX for the Netherlands. The

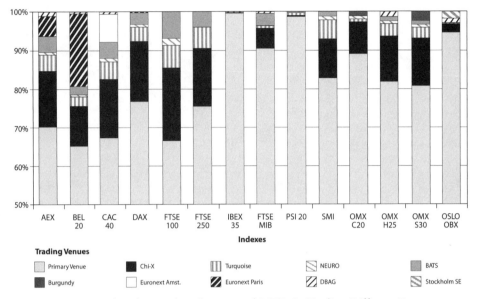

Figure 4: Market Shares of Exchanges and MTFs in Trading Different European Indexes, Week Ending September 18, 2009
Source: http://fragmentation.fidessa.com

FFI takes the value 1 when all trading is concentrated on a single system, and higher values when trading is split between trading systems. If trading were divided equally between *n* trading systems, the FFI would take the value *n*.[38] As figure 3 illustrates, order flow in trading equities in the four specified indices became progressively more fragmented over the relevant period.

An illustration of the market shares of different trading systems in the EU as of the week ending September 18, 2009, is presented in figure 4, based on the data presented in table 4. Each column represents the trading in the constituent shares of a particular index, as identified below the column. The bottom section of each column shows the percentage of trading that took place in the relevant week at the primary trading venue for the relevant index, which was typically the national exchange. So, for example, the primary trading venue for the FTSE 100 index was the London Stock Exchange. It is important to note that there were different primary trading venues for the different stock. The other sections of the column show the percentages of trading in the relevant shares obtained by trading systems other than the primary trading venue.

The percentage of trading in the shares in a particular index that remained on the relevant index's dominant national exchange varied from

TABLE 4

Market Shares of Different Trading Systems in Shares of Major European Indices, Week Ending September 18, 2009

| Index | Primary venue | | Alternative venues | | | | | | | | |
	Venue	Share	Chi-X	Turquoise	NEURO	BATS	Burgundy	Amst.	Paris	Xetra	Stockholm
AEX	Amsterdam	70.34%	14.82%	4.25%	0.61%	4.11%			5.60%	0.17%	
BEL 20	Brussels	65.78%	10.82%	2.62%	0.33%	2.41%			17.76%	0.05%	
CAC 40	Paris	68.73%	14.52%	4.52%	0.91%	3.98%		6.16%		0.22%	
DAX	Xetra	77.60%	14.36%	3.72%	0.40%	3.09%		†	0.02%		
FTSE 100	London	67.66%	18.22%	5.94%	1.27%	6.90%					
FTSE 250	London	75.50%	15.85%	4.50%	0.24%	3.91%					
IBEX 35	Madrid	99.58%	0.29%	0.04%	†			†		0.03%	
FTSE MIB	Milan	91.78%	4.71%	0.80%	0.05%	2.61%		†	†	0.03%	
PSI 20	Lisbon	98.31%	0.61%	1.02%	0.03%	0.03%					
SMI	SIX	83.19%	9.58%	5.15%	0.77%	1.30%					
OMX C20	Copenhagen	88.76%	9.84%	0.89%	0.16%	0.23%	0.02%				
OMX H25	Helsinki	82.00%	11.59%	3.82%	0.43%	0.69%	†	0.03%			1.25%
OMX S30	Stockholm	81.07%	12.00%	3.21%	0.41%	0.79%	2.40%				
OSLO OBX	Oslo	94.63%	2.98%	0.38%	0.02%	0.11%	†				1.88%

Source: Fidessa Fragmentation Index (http://fragmentation.fidessa.com).

Notes: Data are compiled from order book trades only. Totals only include stocks contained within the major indices. † Market share < 0.01%. The name of the primary trading venue represents the major national exchange that has historically operated in the relevant country. So Amsterdam, Brussels. Lisbon, and Paris are Euronext, Xetra is Deutsche Börse, London is the LSE, Madrid is BME, Italy is Borsa Italiana, Copenhagen, Helsinki, and Stockholm are Nasdaq OMX, and Oslo is Oslo Børs.

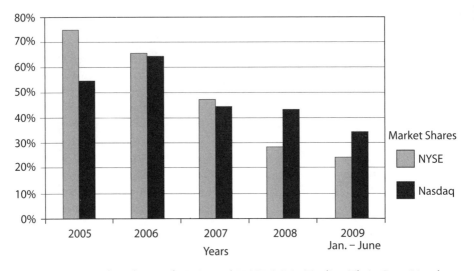

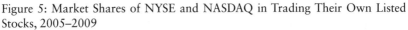

Figure 5: Market Shares of NYSE and NASDAQ in Trading Their Own Listed Stocks, 2005–2009
Source: www.arcavision.com

99.57% for the Spanish index traded on the Bolsas y Mercados Españoles (BME), to 65.78% and 67.66% for the major Belgian and British indices traded respectively on Euronext Brussels and the London Stock Exchange.

Competition between trading systems in the United States has had a complicated history, even over the last 10 years. Following the implementation of the SEC's order-handling rules in 1997, a series of ECNs were established to compete with the two primary markets, the New York Stock Exchange (NYSE) and NASDAQ. These ECNs included Archipelago, Attain, Brut, B-Trade, GlobeNet, Instinet, Island, MarketXT, NexTrade, Redi-Book, and Track. Subsequently, both the NYSE and NASDAQ purchased several of their major competitor ECNs—with the NYSE purchasing Archipelago in December 2005, and NASDAQ purchasing Brut in July 2004 and Instinet in December 2005. Since 2005, two new trading systems, namely BATS and Direct Edge, have provided the primary competition to NYSE and NASDAQ, now themselves both restructured as part of the larger corporate groups NYSE Euronext and NASDAQ OMX. The market shares of the NYSE and NASDAQ in stocks listed on their respective exchanges over the period 2005 to the first half of 2009 are illustrated in figure 5.

The market share of the NYSE in trading NYSE-listed shares fell from 76.1% to 24.9% over this period. However, the proportion of NYSE-listed shares traded on the NYSE Group as a whole, which included both the NYSE and NYSE Arca, fell less sharply, from 78.9% to 40%. The market share of NASDAQ in trading NASDAQ-listed shares fell from 55.5% to 35.1% over the same period.[39]

Even in markets where new trading systems and exchanges have been authorized, there is disagreement about the extent of competition that obtains in such markets. Most national securities still trade on their home national stock exchange. In Europe there used to be a widespread view that, in the words of the LSE chairman in 2002, there was "no effective competition between exchanges. Dominant providers in domestic markets are the order of the day."[40] Deutsche Börse similarly stated in 2006 that "no competition exists between cash equity exchanges on a European level," but also argued that exchanges did face a major competitive constraint in the form of off-exchange trading.[41] Deutsche Börse provided an unofficial estimate that such trading accounted for 50% of volumes traded in equities in Germany at the time.

The extent to which alternative venues for trading compete with exchanges has, however, been challenged. LIBA maintained in 2005, for example, that "off-exchange trading and internalization constituted at best partial substitutes for electronic on-exchange trading."[42] Similarly, when examining what competitive factors constrained the LSE at the same time, the UK Competition Commission concluded that the relevant product market was the provision of on-book, namely on-exchange, trading services, as off-book trading was not considered an important economic substitute.[43]

There is also disagreement about the extent of contestability in the provision of trading services. Domowitz and Steil (1999, 46–47) claimed that the industry is "showing clear signs of increasing contestability," putting forward two central pieces of evidence to justify their position: the existence of price undercutting by new entrants, and the erosion of cross-subsidies previously employed by incumbent national exchanges. Such cross-subsidies included the cross-subsidization of large trades by small trades, of "on-exchange" by "off-exchange" trades, and of retail by institutional trades. Pirrong (2007a, 3) has taken the opposite viewpoint, maintaining that trade execution, and indeed also clearing and settlement, are all "subject to pervasive economies of scale, and have strong natural monopoly tendencies. Moreover, specific assets and coordination problems impair the contestability of these natural monopolies."

Competition between exchanges and trading systems in the derivatives markets appears to be somewhat different from that in securities markets. As noted by Russo, Hart, and Schönenberger (2002, 11), "Derivatives exchanges rarely offer duplicate contracts on their respective markets and the trading of particular contracts (and the liquidity associated with that trading) tends to concentrate on a single market (or at least on one market per time zone)." There are different views regarding both the extent of market power that derivatives exchanges have, and the nature of the competition that exists between, and to, them. Some view derivatives exchanges essentially as monopolies for the trading of the contracts listed on them. Such monopolies may arise because of the intellectual property rights that derivatives exchanges hold in their contracts, the order flow externality present in all markets, or the lack of access granted to potential competitors to the CCPs that clear such exchanges' contracts.[44]

A second, and opposing, view accepts that different exchanges may not trade contracts that are the same or similar, but argues that the OTC market offers significant competition to derivatives exchanges. A range of exchanges, such as the Chicago Mercantile Exchange (CME), have taken this position based on several key arguments: comparable OTC products are available for all futures contracts, the two market places are converging in terms of products and processes, and OTC markets are much larger, and growing faster than exchange-traded derivatives.[45] Competition from OTC products to on-exchange traded contracts may occur in the absence of fungibility between the two.[46]

A third view about the level of competition in the derivatives markets, which has for example been espoused by LIFFE, has been to reject that "competition in derivatives trading is between exchanges and the OTC markets," given that "there is a clear difference between the customized contracts traded OTC and standardized contracts traded on-exchange."[47] While accepting that derivatives exchanges do not compete with each other for order flow, it is argued instead that they may compete with each other in other ways, specifically in products, pricing, services, and technology.

Generic Propositions about Industry Structure

Seven generic propositions characterizing the exchange industry's structure, focusing on the delivery of trading services, are articulated here.

   Proposition 1: Competition to exchanges for the provision of trading services may come from various sources: other exchanges, ATSs, OTC trading, internalization, investor-to-investor trading, or related cash and derivatives markets.

   Proposition 2: Competition for trading services varies both over time and geographically.

   Proposition 3: A range of factors make it likely that a single trading system will both obtain and keep market power in the provision of trading services in any one market.

Proposition 4: All the factors consolidating market power in a single trading system can in principle be overcome, and in a small, but growing, number of jurisdictions have been.

Proposition 5: In many countries, a single national stock exchange either operates a monopoly or has a dominant position.

Proposition 6: Most new trading systems have failed, but a few have been very successful.

Proposition 7: Although there has been little international competition between exchanges to provide trading services to date, such competition is growing.

CCPs

The extent to which CCPs have market power is explored in this section. It is composed of four parts. The key factors that lead towards consolidation of market power, and some mitigating factors that may enhance competition, are identified first. The types of competition that CCPs may face are discussed next, together with an analysis of some difficulties with such competition. Brief comments on the industry structure in practice are then presented. Finally, some generic propositions about the industry's structure are articulated.

Factors Amplifying Market Power, and Others Enhancing Competition

Network Externalities: A CCP typically benefits from two positive network externalities. The first arises because the benefits of netting trades in a single asset are dependent on the number of traders using the CCP. The more traders that use a CCP, the more that netting is likely to reduce the number and volume of trades that need to be settled. Once a CCP has been established in a market to deliver netting, all market participants therefore have an incentive to use this CCP to net their trades over any potential competitor.

A second network externality normally arising from the operation of a CCP provides an incentive for many assets or contracts to be cleared on the same CCP. It concerns the collateral that market participants are required to put up to support their trading activity via a CCP. The more assets that are cleared through a single CCP, and the more this CCP is able to offset margin requirements in one type of asset against positions in other types of assets that are economically correlated, the lower the total amount of collateral that is likely to be required of each individual participant. The total margin required for a diversified portfolio in more than one market operating under a single CCP is less than it would be in an environment where positions in each market are margined in separate CCPs. This is because the risk of a combined portfolio is less than the sum of the risks of the individual components of the portfolio. Even if there were no risk offsets that served to reduce the total amount of collateral required, a single CCP could make collateral movements between different markets more operationally efficient for members, minimizing the amount of collateral trapped in one market that could not be deployed in another. As putting up capital is expensive, this means that once a CCP starts to dominate clearing in one or more assets, it will be difficult for new competitors to offer market participants similar reductions in collateral for this range of assets, or potentially for other assets, without compromising their risk-management procedures. This factor tends to provide an incentive for different assets to be cleared by the same CCP.

Economies of Scale: It is widely accepted that CCPs exhibit economies of scale, due to the relatively large fixed costs of operating them, and the low variable costs for clearing additional trades.[48]

Monitoring Costs: Without the existence of a CCP, market participants need to monitor the creditworthiness of all their counterparties individually, in order to minimize the possibility that one of them may default. As individual traders will only have information about the trades they execute with their individual counterparties, and not information about all the trades executed by all their counterparties, the effectiveness of each individual market participant's monitoring will necessarily be based on a restricted information set.

The presence of a CCP obviates the need for bilateral monitoring, as the CCP undertakes centralized monitoring of all its members in order to minimize the possibility of a default.[49] This means that the overall monitoring costs incurred by the market are substantially lower, as only one institution needs to undertake such monitoring.[50] The quality of monitoring by a CCP is also likely to be higher than that possible by each individual market participant, given that the CCP would have information about all trades in a market undertaken by all market participants—or at least information about all trades cleared through the CCP. Consolidating such monitoring in a single CCP also reduces the costs, and enhances the quality, of monitoring compared to what would be undertaken with competing CCPs. If there were more than one CCP, each CCP would only have information about those trades it cleared, and would have to incur the costs of monitoring all its members.[51]

Switching Costs: In order to access a CCP, both an exchange and its trading members need to have an IT connection to the CCP. These connections are not standardized and have to be tailored to each CCP's specific IT systems. Switching to another CCP is therefore costly, both for an exchange and for its users.[52] There have been differences of opinion about the importance of such costs. When the UK Competition Commission (2005, 61) assessed whether the LSE could feasibly consider employing a new CCP, it noted that

> LCH.Clearnet and Euroclear told [it] that the costs that would be incurred by trading firms ... were not high, with the bulk of any cost arising from a change in the hardware or software. LIBA, however, said that rearranging clearing arrangements for UK equities would carry considerable one-off costs due to the need to change systems.

The Competition Commission considered that the estimated switching costs could represent "quite a large proportion of the trading firms' annual trading fees," and concluded that "any switching between clearing providers would be likely to be constrained to some degree by the switching costs that would be faced by trading firms."[53]

Rules/Regulations/Market Practices: Different types of market practices, regulations, and laws constrain entry into the provision of clearing services.[54] Some are explicitly restrictive in nature, as for example occurs when an exchange chooses to employ only one CCP.[55] Russo, Hart, and Schönenberger (2002, 34) note that an exchange "may perceive its clearing operations to be an adjunct of its trade execution services and may perceive that its clearing arrangements give it a competitive advantage over other competing exchanges." A vertically integrated exchange may thus seek to restrict access by CCPs other than the one it operates, both to the exchange itself and to its CCP.

All regulators of CCPs are concerned that such institutions operate in a safe and sound manner, and that the various risks inherent in clearing are appropriately managed. In order to ensure this, a range of regulatory requirements are typically imposed on CCPs, in a manner similar to exchanges. By their nature such requirements restrict entry into the clearing business only to those institutions able to satisfy them. Given the concentration of risk in a CCP, regulators have been particularly concerned about how systemic risk is monitored and managed.

Various regulations and market practices may, however, also make the consolidation of clearing different markets in a single CCP unappealing.[56] Some CCPs require clearing members to be jointly and severally liable for any obligations arising from defaults at the CCP. If there is little overlap in the membership of different CCPs, the members of each individual CCP may prefer to keep them separate, in order not to face potential losses from defaults at other CCPs. If different CCPs employ different risk management practices, the members of a particular CCP may also prefer their CCP's risk management practices, to the possibility that other processes might be imposed if they merged with another CCP. There may also be regulatory concern about consolidation among CCPs, as such consolidation would concentrate systemic risk in a smaller number of institutions.

The possibility of competition between CCPs in an international context gives rise to many additional complications. The issue has received most attention in the EU. The Giovannini Group (2001 and 2003) identified and discussed 15 barriers that prevented the development of an efficient clearing and settlement industry in the EU. The barriers were classified into three groups, relating to national differences in technical requirements and market practice, national differences in tax procedures, and issues relating to legal certainty. In tandem with seeking to resolve these issues, the European Commission considered whether a legislative approach to facilitate the recognition of CCPs on a cross-border was appropriate.[57] After a variety of official consultation processes, a private sector approach was adopted, initiated at the instigation of the EU Commission, as being most effective in enhancing competition in the EU for clearing and settlement services. A Code of Conduct for the clearing and settlement industry was formulated in 2006, and implemented in a staged manner by February 2, 2008.[58] The code focused on three broad issues— price transparency, access and interoperability, and service unbundling and account separation.

Reduction of Barriers to Competition: Many of the barriers to competition noted above may be removed or lowered in principle, although in practice it is often difficult to do so. In particular, the *netting externality* may be reduced if there is a mutual offset system between competing CCPs, so that positions taken on one CCP may be set off against positions taken on another CCP. Automation may reduce *economies of scale.* The cost advantage of *centralized monitoring* of counterparties creditworthiness over bilateral monitoring may be reduced with better disclosure of credit information and better information sharing processes. Harmonization of market rules and practices, and agreement between different CCPs on standardized connection protocols, will reduce the *switching costs* that exchanges and financial intermediaries may need to incur in moving to a new CCP.

Nature of Potential Competition

Competition for the Market: Competition for the market refers to a situation where at any one time an exchange chooses to employ only one CCP to clear trades conducted on the exchange, but the selection of the CCP is open to competition on a periodic basis.[59] Even if there is competition *for* the market, the provision of clearing services will not necessarily be contestable if there are switching costs, either for the exchange or for all clearing members, to move to a new CCP.[60]

Competition in the Market: Competition in the market means that exchanges, and individual market participants, have a choice over which CCP they can use at any one time. For competition in the market to be feasible, CCPs need to be interoperable in a range of ways.[61]

If there is more than one CCP in a market, and market participants choose to use more than one of them, then there will be net exposures between the CCPs. This may be seen by considering an example where a seller of securities clears a trade via CCP A, and its counterparty buyer clears with CCP B. Then CCP A will have a long position, while CCP B will be short. Some form of agreed-on procedure between the competing CCPs will then be required to manage their net exposures to each other.[62] In particular, CCP A needs to effect a sale to CCP B, the result of which will be that both CCPs then will have net zero securities positions: CCP A will have a long position from its purchase from its customer, and a countervailing short position from its sale to CCP B; CCP B will have a short position from its sale to its customer, and a countervailing long position from its purchase from CCP A. One way of structuring such an arrangement between two CCPs is for each CCP to maintain an account with, and become a member of, the other. Sometimes each CCP has a special clearing status with each other. Sometimes one CCP functions as an "umbrella" CCP, and the other becomes a general clearing member with the umbrella CCP. Interoperable CCPs also need to agree a range of other issues with each other, including in some contexts how to share losses between their different sets of members.

There are a range of potential difficulties with interoperability between CCPs:[63]

1. The costs may not exceed the benefits.[64] Multiple CCP arrangements are commercially, operationally, legally, and financially complex to establish and maintain.[65]
2. An incumbent CCP may not grant unconditional access to new CCPs.[66] A dominant CCP has little incentive to make interoperability with other CCPs work effectively, as to do so would allow other CCPs to compete for its business.
3. If one CCP becomes a member of another CCP, this may jeopardize both CCPs' risk management processes, as each will be exposed to the other's risk management methodology.[67]
4. If one CCP becomes a general clearing member of another CCP, it may obtain an unfair advantage in competing with other general clearing members.

5. An exchange may not grant unconditional access to new CCPs.[68] This may be more likely if the exchange operates a vertical silo, and thus owns a dominant incumbent CCP, as it may not wish to sanction competition to its CCP.

6. A CSD may not offer access to a new CCP on the same terms available to an incumbent CCP. This may again be more likely if an exchange operates a vertical silo, owning both a CCP and a CSD. If the exchange-owned CSD does not grant access to competing CCPs, it will restrict competition to its own CCP.

7. In some contexts, CCPs may need access to central bank money. If new CCPs are not granted such access on the same terms as an incumbent CCP, this may once again restrict competition. The use of a payment bank to obtain access is possible, but involves additional costs.

Competition from Sources Other Than CCPs: Sources and institutions other than CCPs can offer competition to some of the services provided by CCPs, either by offering services that are close substitutes, or by allowing market participants the possibility of avoiding the services offered by a CCP.[69] For example, rather than using a CCP to net trades, market participants could net trades with their counterparties on a bilateral basis though legal novation, and seek to minimize counterparty risk by requiring margins or appropriate collateral, or by purchasing appropriate insurance or equivalent risk-shifting protection. Such bilateral netting will not, however, provide the same magnitude of benefits as multilateral netting, in terms of the reduction in the number and sizes of trades to be settled. Some exchanges and CCPs allow market participants to opt out of the CCP for specific transactions. The existence of a CCP is also not necessary for trades to be netted multilaterally, as long as contracts are enforceable under applicable law. Multilateral netting without novation to a CCP is, however, likely to provide only operational benefits. If one counterparty is unable to settle for any reason, the whole settlement process will need to be unwound.[70]

Industry Structure in Practice

CCP services are now widely, though not universally, used in equities trading. In almost all countries where CCP clearing of securities trades does take place, there is only one provider, and if there is more than one CCP, each one is normally for a different asset class.[71] While it is difficult to be definitive given the rapidly changing circumstances in financial and derivatives markets, all derivatives exchanges now have a CCP, and no derivative exchange has more than one.[72]

There is a widespread belief that clearing organizations operate monopolies with market power, that such monopolies face little competition, and that the contestability of providing clearing services is low.[73] Not everybody agrees with this view, however. Deutsche Börse, for example, maintains that "every post-trade function [including clearing] is offered by a number of different post-trade services providers and is open to competition."[74]

There have historically been only a few instances of competition *for* the market to provide clearing services. One such situation arose in 2003 when Eurex Clearing made a bid to supply CCP services to the LSE. At the time the LSE employed LCH.Clearnet as its only CCP. After due consideration, the LSE chose to stay solely with LCH.Clearnet. Although LCH.Clearnet did reduce its charges in response to Eurex Clearing's threat of entry, a factor that was reportedly more important in the LSE's decision to remain with LCH.Clearnet was that its members believed that the switch to a new CCP would involve excessive costs—arising both from new IT investments, and from the loss of efficiency in the joint netting and margining of exposures on the LSE.

Historically, there have been very few instances of competition *in* the market to provide clearing services, and as of June 2009 there had been no instances where a new entrant CCP had successfully challenged an incumbent to become the dominant CCP in clearing the same securities. Historically, there have also been a very limited number of links between CCPs, and of these only some sought to facilitate competition between CCPs.

The first example of interoperability between CCPs was the Mutual Offset System (MOS) established in 1984 to provide joint clearing arrangements between two derivatives exchanges, the CME and SIMEX (now SGX), the Singaporean exchange.[75] Each exchange owned its own CCP. The MOS allowed certain futures contracts to be traded in one jurisdiction and closed out in another, and market participants to choose whether to clear trades at CME or SGX. Each CCP became a special clearing member of the other. The arrangement required agreeing on common margining, emergency management, information sharing, and taxation issues. The rationale for the MOS was not to facilitate competition, either between the CCPs or the exchanges, but rather to widen the use of the contracts that were available for clearing via the MOS. Users of the different integrated exchanges/CCPs appeared to be partitioned, with those working through Singapore tied to SGX, and those working through Chicago tied to CME. New customers who wished to trade remotely could in principle choose between each exchange.

In Europe, virt-x, a London-based stock exchange, facilitated two CCPs, LCH (now LCH.Clearnet) and SIS x-clear, to provide competing clearing services in May 2003.[76] Each CCP offered clearing services for all eligible virt-x traded securities, and operated an account with each other. The choice of CCP was determined by each member. Each member only cleared trades with the CCP of which it was a member. Each CCP retained the responsibility for any defaults of its members, so as to avoid any duplication of risk management exposures.

virt-x identified three features of its dual clearing model that it believed were key to the perceived success of the model.[77] First, it was established when CCP clearing was first introduced in the market. Neither CCP thus had to capture a significant share of business from an established CCP in order to enter the market. Second, as virt-x had no economic interest in either CCP, it was able to offer active and neutral leadership in ensuring that the commercial and technical issues arising between the competing CCPs were resolved adequately. Third, the model reflected market demand, with users tending to select the provider with which they already had an existing relationship, or which was located within their domicile. As with the CME/SGX linkage, the model appeared to effect a partitioning of the market, with Swiss users clearing via SIS x-clear, and the major UK market participants clearing through LCH.Clearnet.

In the bond markets, MTS Italy, the bond trading platform, facilitated competition in 2005 between the Italian CCP, Cassa di Compensazione e Garanzia (CC&G), and LCH.Clearnet, to clear government and corporate bond trades executed on MTS.[78] MTS Italy also allowed its participants to decide whether or not to have their transactions cleared through a CCP at all. The division of the CCPs appeared again to reflect a dual structure of the market: almost all domestic Italian investor trades cleared through CC&G, while most foreign investor trades cleared through LCH.Clearnet.

The jurisdiction in which competition both *for*, and *in*, the market for clearing has been most intense over the past few years has been the EU, following the development of the Code of Conduct. A few new CCPs have been founded to service both existing and new exchanges and trading systems, even though other CCPs were already operating in the same jurisdictions, and in some instances, clearing trades in the same securities. Fortis Bank's European Multilateral Clearing Facility (EMCF) began clearing trades for Chi-X, a trading system owned by Instinet, on March 30, 2007.[79] EuroCCP, which the Depository Trust & Clearing Corporation (DTCC) had previously operated in 2001, then closed down, was revived and started providing clearing services on August 15, 2008, for Turquoise, a trading system owned by a consortium of investment banks.[80] EMCF and Euro CCP began competing with the major incumbent CCPs in the market—Eurex Clearing, LCH.Clearnet, and SIS x-clear. In order to do so, various bilateral interoperability agreements between the potentially competing and the incumbent CCPs, facilitated by the exchanges and MTFs whose business they were looking to clear, were agreed.[81]

The effect of this competition appears to have been strong downwards pressure on the prices CCPs charged. EuroCCP (2008a) made some estimates about the prices that the various CCPs operating in Europe were charging in July 2008. Subsequently, many of the competing CCPs lowered their fees.[82]

Two aspects of the competition between CCPs in the EU are noteworthy. First, while it was the users, and typically the financial intermediaries, who paid the fees charged by CCPs, the choice of which CCPs exchanges employed were made by the exchanges themselves and not the users. There appeared to be various reasons why an exchange may have chosen a particular CCP to clear its trades, even if the exchange's users might have preferred another CCP that offered better services at lower prices. Most importantly, if a potential CCP supplier already cleared trades for another trading system that competed with the exchange, then the exchange might have been unwilling to sanction use of the particular CCP, as to do so might have increased the competition in trading that it faced. There was also concern about whether competition between CCPs in the EU was compromising risk practices at CCPs, in their attempt to lower prices. EuroCCP (2009a) believed that this was an important enough issue to warrant a European convention on interoperability between competing CCPs in order to achieve appropriate levels of transparency in risk management processes. Subsequently LCH. Clearnet noted that some of its regulators had raised concerns about the clearing link agreements it had signed with other CCPs, in particular about inter-CCP margin requirements.[83]

The use of CCPs for OTC markets is still relatively rare, although following the credit crisis beginning in 2007, there has been a growing belief that CCPs should be employed to clear OTC derivatives contracts, as the failure of such contracts, and particularly credit default swaps (CDSs), was thought to have led to, or exacerbated, the crisis.[84] In 2009 the US Treasury proposed a law requiring that standardized OTC derivatives be centrally cleared by a regulated derivatives clearing organization, and be traded on a regulated exchange or "alternative swap execution facility."[85] The proposed law also aimed to encourage substantially greater use of standardized derivatives versus OTC customized products. Similar proposals were developed in the EU to shift derivative markets from predominantly OTC bilateral trading to more centralized clearing and trading via CCPs.[86]

Several CCPs sought to respond to this policy trend for increased use of clearing. Over the period 2008–9, Deutsche Börse and the CME separately established in Europe and the United States facilities to clear CDSs and other OTC derivatives, and LCH.Clearnet indicated it planned to do so by December 2009.[87] The DTCC and NYSE also set up a joint venture in 2009 to clear fixed-income cash and derivative instruments.[88]

Consolidation: A prominent example where competing CCPs existed was in the US securities markets in the 1970s, but this situation did not last, as all the CCPs were subsequently merged into a single institution.[89] Prior to the consolidation, clearing and settlement was a paper-intensive activity conducted by seven vertically integrated exchange subsidiaries. The revenue from each CCP accounted for a significant component of the revenue of most of its affiliated exchanges.

Growth in trading volumes led to a paperwork crisis on Wall Street, and to problems in the operations of the CCPs and also the settlement institutions. These problems became so severe that the exchanges had to shut down entirely one day a week just to keep up with processing trades. In order to resolve this issue, the NYSE, AMEX, and NASDAQ created a single depository to immobilize securities certificates (the Depository Trust Corporation [DTC]), and a single equities clearing corporation to automate and standardize the clearing process (the National Securities Clearing Corporation [NSCC]). In the rest of the United States, the five regional exchanges, in Boston, Chicago, Cincinnati, Pacific, and Philadelphia, initially maintained their own clearing and depository businesses.

The development of the NMS in the mid-1970s focused attention on clearing and settlement. There was, however, no regulatory mandate for the securities industry to consolidate clearing and settlement, or to direct its post-trade business to the newly created DTC and NSCC. Fair access to the various clearing and settlement providers was required by the regulator, but the decision about where trades should be cleared and settled was left to trading firms. Over time all clearing business tipped towards the NSCC, which gradually also took over the other systems. The key reasons for this were that brokerage firms and banks were concerned about redundant systems and rising costs, and believed that standardization, the risk reductions available via consolidation, the existence of a central collateral facility, and market-wide netting could lower costs substantially and bring a range of other benefits. The last of the regional depositories and clearing businesses, in Philadelphia, was integrated into DTC and NSCC in 1997. The monopoly positions of DTC and NSCC (subsequently merged into DTCC) were only potentially challenged in 2008, when NASDAQ OMX indicated its intent to provide CCP services in the United States via its NASDAQ Clearing Corporation,[90] although subsequently these plans were abandoned.[91]

Generic Propositions about Industry Structure

Seven generic propositions characterizing the CCP industry's structure are articulated here:

Proposition 8: A range of factors make it likely that a single CCP will both obtain and keep market power in the provision of clearing services in any one market.

Proposition 9: All the factors consolidating market power in a single CCP could in principle be overcome, but this is hard to achieve.

Proposition 10: Competition to CCPs could come from other CCPs, both for and in the market, and from other sources, including OTC trading without clearing.

Proposition 11: Almost all CCPs operate monopolies in their respective markets.

Proposition 12: A few instances of competition for the market in clearing have occurred, but no new CCP has yet replaced an incumbent CCP.

Proposition 13: Although few instances of competition in the market in clearing have occurred historically, such competition has become more common recently in some jurisdictions.

Proposition 14: Where competition in the market in clearing has occurred, no new CCP has yet gained significant market share from an incumbent.

CSDs

The extent to which CSDs have market power is explored in this section. It is composed of four parts. Some key factors that lead towards consolidation of market power are identified. The nature of the types of competition that CSDs may face, and some difficulties with such competition, are discussed next. Brief comments on the industry structure in practice are then presented. Last, some generic propositions about the industry's structure are articulated. The two key functions that CSDs typically undertake, namely operating a central register and providing a central settlement system via book-entry transfer of securities, are examined at different points in the discussion.

Factors Amplifying Market Power

Network Effects: A settlement system accepts transfer requests from its members to exchange cash for securities and visa versa, and then determines an efficient arrangement and scheduling of transfers, subject to the constraints given by the securities and cash account balances of its different members. The algorithm adopted by a settlement system, namely the set of rules that determine which transfers get effected and according to what criteria, typically seeks to minimize three sources of risks and costs in a market: credit risk exposure by market participants to other market participants, liquidity consumption by market participants, and settlement delays.[92] There are normally trade-offs between achieving these three goals. Although no simple characterization is possible for how settlement systems operate, pooling the settlement of a large number of securities in the same system is likely to reduce the need for costly liquidity usage on the part of market participants.[93] This will give an incumbent CSD a competitive advantage against any potential new entrants.

Economies of Scale: It is widely believed that a large fixed investment is required to build a sound and efficient settlement system, but that once built, the marginal cost of adding a new user, a new security, or settling an additional transaction is low.[94] Schmiedel, Malkamäki, and Tarkka (2006) investigated data from 16 depository and settlement systems across different regions for the years 1993–2000. They found the existence of significant economies of scale, with the degree of such economies differing both by the size of settlement institution and by region. Smaller institutions could realize significant scale economies, and larger CSDs could also reduce costs by increasing their size, although to a lesser extent. Over the period, clearing and settlement systems in Europe and Asia exhibited substantially larger economies of scale than those in the United States. Van Cayseele and Wuyts (2005) examined data for eight European CSDs over the period 1997–2003, and drew similar conclusions. Their results also pointed towards the existence of economies of scope in providing settlement and safekeeping services together.

Switching Costs: There are fixed costs associated with holding accounts at CSDs.[95] It is thus cheaper for users of CSDs to hold all their shares in the same CSD, and not to transfer their shares to CSDs of which they are not already members.

Rules/Regulation/Market Practices: A range of different types of rules may constrain entry into the provision of central register and settlement services.[96] Some are explicitly restrictive in nature. These include national rules that require security issuers to deposit their securities in the national CSD,[97] and requirements imposed by exchanges for settlement to be routed through a particular CSD.

As with exchanges and CCPs, all regulators of CSDs are concerned that such institutions operate in a safe and sound manner, and that the risks inherent in providing central register and settlement services are appropriately managed. In order to ensure this, a range of regulatory requirements are typically imposed on CSDs, which by their nature restrict entry only to those institutions able to satisfy the requirements.

International competition between CSDs is complicated. A CSD from one country could in principle compete with an incumbent in another country to be the primary CSD for issuersfrom that country. In order for a CSD to compete for issuer customers across borders, it needs to be granted the right to operate in a foreign country. The conditions necessary for cross-border recognition currently do not, however, yet exist. There are also many differences across countries in fiscal, regulatory, and institutional arrangements that have meant that in practice only domestic CSDs have provided depository and settlement services for national issuers, apart from the two ICSDs that provide such services for the international Eurobond market.[98]

Nature of Potential Competition

Competition for the Market for Central Register Services: Competition for the market in central registers would allow an issuer to choose to use the services of a single central register at any one time, but tender for such services should it wish to change providers. Where a CSD is also the central register (an "issuer CSD"), the presence of switching costs for market participants to move to a new register would reduce the contestability of the market. However, where registrars or stock transfer agents do compete in major markets, an issuer switching from one registrar to another is usually invisible to shareholders, implying switching costs are low.

Competition in the Market for Central Register and Settlement Services: Issuers could choose to have more than one central register for their securities operating simultaneously. If there were more than one register for the same issue of securities, however, some form of mechanism for reconciling the holdings of all the competing registers, and for ensuring that the total number of securities in circulation did not exceed the number issued, would be required. If a market participant held securities in one register and sold to a buyer who wished to hold its shares in another register, a "supra-central register" would normally need to reconcile the differences in holdings, and transfer the shares from the first to the second register.[99]

Competition in the market between issuer CSDs to provide settlement services in the same securities requires interoperability between CSDs.[100] If two counterparties to a transaction held their securities in different issuer CSDs, securities would need to be transferred between the two CSDs. This is normally accomplished by each CSD holding an account in the other, each effectively acting as a custodian in the competing CSD until a point when the positions are transferred in the books of the supra-central register.[101] Each CSD would thus provide its customers with a single point of entry to any other CSDs with which it was linked. This would allow its customers to hold and transfer securities into any other linked CSD, but still maintain a membership, and connectivity, solely with their existing CSD. CSDs offering this service would compete with each other and also with custodians. While this model of competition is valid for both domestic and international competition between CSDs, cross-border linkages are more difficult to establish and have other complexities.

There are a range of difficulties with interoperability and linkages between CSDs, some of which are similar to those with CCPs:

1. Links between CSDs are expensive to build and maintain, and result in higher costs for transactions that settle across two CSDs, as compared to within the same one.[102] Linking all the CSDs in a region, such as the EU, would also require a large number of separate bilateral connections.

2. In order to achieve interoperability, agreement on standards, communication protocols, and common operation methods is required. This is difficult, as the Giovannini Reports demonstrate. The European Central Securities Depositories Association (ECSDA) did, however, seek to provide a common model for such links in 1997, and initiated a program in 2002 to harmonize message standards for linkages between EU CSDs.[103]

3. Market participants may prefer links that provide settlement against payment, since such links reduce risks. Delivering interoperable links that offer delivery versus payment (DVP), however, may require those CSDs that are not banks to have direct access to the intra-day liquidity provided by national central banks, or to use a payment bank, and this can be difficult and expensive to achieve. Other obstacles to achieving DVP across CSDs are operational inefficiencies and risk exposure that could result from timing differences in the CSDs' settlement processing.

4. Interoperability creates custody exposure of CSDs to one another. In the case of the ICSDs, this includes financial exposure as both institutions settle in commercial bank money and hold cash with each other.

5. Competition may mean competing CSDs have to implement costly rebalancing and risk-monitoring procedures. It may also reduce settlement efficiency by generating settlement failures and encouraging the recourse to automatic securities borrowing offered by CSDs, due to restrictions in the timing and frequency of information exchanges between the CSDs.

6. Incumbent CSDs may be reluctant to implement interoperability with other CSDs, as doing so will reduce the costs of switching between suppliers and also the costs of entry by new com-

petitors.[104] Furthermore, even if perfect interoperability between CSDs is effected, the interconnections that are created between CSDs may not be efficiently priced.[105] A dominant CSD may have an incentive not to reduce the price of a link to a competitive level, again because by doing so the CSD would expose itself to competition from other CSDs via the link.[106]

Internalization: Internalization of settlement occurs when a transfer of ownership between a seller and a buyer in a securities transaction is reflected on the accounts of a financial intermediary used by both parties, typically a custodian, rather than a CSD.[107] Two conditions are necessary for internalization. First, at some point in the chain of settlement providers, a financial intermediary must be able to keep the securities of different customers in a single omnibus account. If omnibus accounts are not allowed in a market, then all end-investors must have an account in the relevant CSD, and all settlement movements will be reflected there. Second, the intermediary must have as customers both the buyer and the seller for any given transaction, or at least their agents, and the positions of both buyer and seller must be held in the same omnibus account. A transfer of their positions can then take place on the books of the intermediary, without any change in ownership reflected on the accounts of the CSD.

Several factors may increase the probability of internalization on an intermediary's books. In particular, the more customers an intermediary has, and the more they trade with one another, the more likely it is that internalization will occur.[108] Similarly, the more concentrated is the market in which an intermediary operates, the more likely it is that the intermediary will be able to internalize trades, given that the proportion of market users that are customers of the intermediary is likely to be higher. Internalization tends to be more prevalent when clients are international firms, because local brokers typically do not use an intermediary in their local markets as they have direct access to their local CSD. The settlement of on-exchange trades is, however, less likely to be internalized than the settlement of OTC trades, as stock exchanges often send transactions automatically to CSDs or ICSDs for settlement, or to CCPs for clearing that in turn send the netted transactions directly to a CSD or ICSD.

Four aspects of internalization are important to note. First, in a number of jurisdictions, it is not possible, as all end-investors have an account directly with the CSD. Second, it not normally an elective option for either a custodian or a client. This is because custodians cannot control whether trades are internalized on their books, nor can clients choose to have their trades internalized.[109] In order to offer such a service with a reasonable likelihood of success, a custodian would need to know in advance of settlement that all potential counterparties to a trade already had an account with it. Although a custodian may offer a different price for a transaction settled on its books, it cannot guarantee its occurrence. A third important aspect of internalization is that any transactions that cannot be settled on an intermediary's books must be settled on the books of the relevant CSD.

Finally, any holdings on a custodian's books, even if they are in an omnibus account, will need to be listed in the accounts of the central register. In markets where the CSD is also the central register, a custodian must therefore be a customer of the CSD in order to be in the custody business. A CSD may thus have market power over central register services, even if it faces competition in settlement. If a CSD is able to discriminate in pricing between central register and settlement services, it may be able to raise its rivals' costs to their disadvantage.[110] In particular, since custodians cannot operate without keeping securities at a CSD, a CSD threatened by internalization could replace lost revenues by increasing safekeeping fees.

There are a significant number of transfers effected on the books of an intermediary without any need for corresponding transfers on the book-entry accounts of a CSD, which are not, however, transfers of ownership between a seller and a buyer in a securities transaction. These transfers are undertaken in order to move securities between the accounts of brokers and those of their clients. They are typically pre- or post-trade security movements undertaken as part of brokers' services to clients. If both use the same custodian, such movements may not be reflected on the books of the CSD.

The issue of whether holding a security in an account with an intermediary or a custodian is a close substitute for holding it in a CSD central register, assuming both possibilities are allowed, can only be determined by assessing market participants' preferences. Nevertheless, the two options are not identical, specifically with regards to the rights and risks associated with each of the two types of ownership.[111] Three examples illustrate this point:

1. An investor whose ownership interests in securities is recorded in its account at a CSD central register has a direct property right to the securities. In contrast, if an investor uses a custodian, which in turn has an account at the CSD, the investor must enforce its rights through the custodian. The investor's rights will then be derivative of those of the custodian.

2. If an investor's securities are held in an omnibus account at a custodian, the investor's securities will be commingled with, and thus indistinguishable from, other customers' securities. The investor's direct property rights in its commingled items may be

eroded by other entities' interests in the same pool of securities. Such a possibility is dependent on the specific legal circumstances in question. In France, for example, an investor's securities are considered to be deposited with the custodian it opens an individual account with in the first place. The investor's property rights remain unaffected even if the custodian opens an account with a global custodian that has an omnibus account for customers' securities at a CSD.

3. In the EU, settlement on a custodian's books does not benefit from the protection provided by the Settlement Finality Directive.[112] In contrast, a CSD that is defined as a "system" in the Settlement Finality Directive is eligible to be protected under the directive, including when it acts as an intermediary.[113]

Industry Structure in Practice

Many of the institutional arrangements for post-trade processing now regarded as standard in developed financial markets are of fairly recent origin. In the 1960s, while there were some arrangements for centralized holdings of securities, almost all security ownership and transfer was paper-based, resting on the issue and holding of physical certificates. Malkamäki reports that the number of CSDs across the globe grew from 2 in 1950, to 7 in 1970, 28 in 1990, and 102 in 1999.[114] The 1989 seminal G30 report established the provision of DVP settlement on a time scale of T + 3 or better as a minimum standard for safe and efficient securities processing, and recommended the centralization of securities issues in a CSD as the way to achieve this standard.[115] Only after the G30 report did present CSD arrangements become universal in developed securities markets.

In most countries now, there is only one national CSD.[116] Where there is more than one CSD, typically each CSD specializes in a specific securities segment, such as equities or government bonds. Europe is unique in that, in addition to the national domestic CSDs, there exist the two ICSDs.

Competition both for, and in, the market for central registers has occurred, but only rarely. There is competition for the market in the UK, where issuers choose a single central register, but may change their supplier if they wish. There are two central registers in the Eurobond market, where issuers issue securities into the two ICSDs: Euroclear and Clearstream International. There is, however, no competition for the central registry function because issuers do not choose one ICSD over the other. A number of so-called common depositaries have been appointed jointly by the two ICSDs to serve as supra-central registers. As the ICSDs' policy is to appoint the paying agent of an issue as the common depositary for that issue, competition for the supra-central register function exists, but is determined by winning the paying agency appointment from issuers.

There have been a very limited number of occurrences where a significant number of market participants have switched settlement provider at the same time, so that a new CSD has competed successfully against an incumbent.[117] Such competition has occurred as a result of coordinated action by the major participants in a market, typically in response to a specific problem in the market.

The foundation of Cedel (now Clearstream International) to challenge Euroclear as an ICSD for Eurobonds is one such instance. Its creation was possible because the financial institutions that founded it, together with some other institutions, collectively moved their Eurobond holdings to Cedel in order to limit the dominance of Euroclear. The continued duopolistic existence of two such settlement institutions has occurred very rarely.[118]

Another switch occurred in the 1970s when the majority of settlements in German government securities moved from the German CSD to Euroclear. This occurred again as a result of a coordinated decision by the large market participants. In this instance, they wished to avoid paying a German income tax on repo transactions, which was due if transactions settled in the national German CSD. Since these firms were already active in the Eurobond market, they were already customers of Euroclear, and switching costs were thus low.

The main, if not the only, location where internalization has been widely discussed as providing a potential competitive threat to CSDs has been in the EU. There are few publicly available data about the level of internalization in the various European markets, however, so, as noted by Directorate General Competition Services (2006, 9 n. 17), its actual extent and importance "remains unknown, with banks claiming it is marginal and CSDs claiming it is widespread." Euroclear quotes some evidence from two nonpublic reports as follows:[119]

> A study in France organised by the Banque de France [in 1998] revealed that significant internalisation of settlement is happening for transactions involving non-residents active in the French listed shares.
>
> In Italy, a study carried out in 2002 by Monte Titoli found similar characteristics, but recent evidence suggests that as new providers have come into the market, internalisation in Italy has substantially declined, because buyers and sellers now find themselves on the books of different providers.

Two reasons were identified for the stated level of settlement internalization in France. A relatively small proportion of it was due to OTC transactions that bypassed Euroclear France. More importantly, many settlement movements were undertaken to "realign securities from broker/dealers used by non-residents to their custodians." It is unclear whether such movements should be considered competition to the incumbent CSD.

In February 2009 the Committee of European Banking Supervisors (CEBS) sought to examine the extent of settlement internalization in the EU by calling for evidence from interested parties. It received 33 responses—17 from its member supervisors, and 16 from market participants representing most of the major European custodian banks. In addition, CEBS organized a public hearing on March 24, 2009, to discuss its preliminary views based on the responses it had received. CEBS noted that the lack of a harmonized definition of internalization might mean that the responses it received were not based on a common understanding of the term. CEBS itself defined settlement internalization as settlement activities that would otherwise have been carried out by a CSD. After examining the evidence it had received, CEBS concluded that

> the practice of internalisation is not currently widespread across the custodian bank community. However, the answers provided by market participants show great variety on the materiality of internalisation of settlement from the point of view of the institution. It can also be said that internalisation appears more widespread for certain markets/products. Even in these areas though, large differences remain across Member States. These results are in line with those of previous studies where this practice was found to be concentrated in some markets/products.[120]

There is a widespread belief that CSDs operate monopolies with market power, that such monopolies face little competition, and that the contestability of providing settlement services is low. CPSS and IOSCO (2001b, 20), for example, maintain that the economies of scale that characterize the activities of CSDs (and CCPs) "impair the forces of competition that might otherwise be relied upon to ensure that they operate safely and efficiently." The Directorate General (DG) Competition of the European Commission (2006–9) concludes that the limited degree of competition in EU securities posttrading markets (as well as in the trading markets) is "striking." The Directorate General Internal Market and Services of the European Commission (2006b, 20 and next quote) argues that "the markets in which CSDs/CCPs operate are not perfectly contestable" given the presence of sunk costs and switching costs. DG Market and Services also states that "there appears to be no evidence that internationalisation of settlement represents a net competitive constraint on the pricing of a CSD."[121]

These views are not, however, universally held. The European Central Securities Depositories Association (2006, 7), for example, contends that "there is competition in the market for clearing and settlement services but ... the degree of competition varies according to the service provided." Euroclear (2004, 10), a member of ECSDA, argues that "practically all the services offered by (I)CSDs are in fact, in one market or another, contestable and in practice are contested by third parties such as agent banks."[122] Euroclear also maintains (2006b, 5) that "because intermediaries compete with (I)CSDs, they are able to exercise pressure on prices. This will vary by market according to the level of internalisation."

Many links between CSDs, including ICSDs, have been established, with more than 60 in Europe alone.[123] Although data about their use are for the most part unavailable publicly, these links appear to attract minimal business, except those established by the ICSDs. The ICSDs' links are used for fixed-income securities traded by the same population of market participants that trade Eurobonds, and settle transfers between two ICSDs or between an ICSD and a CSD.

Generic Propositions about Industry Structure

Seven generic propositions characterizing the CSD industry's structure are articulated here:

Proposition 15: A range of factors make it likely that a single CSD will both obtain and keep market power in the provision of central settlement services in any one market.

Proposition 16: All the factors consolidating market power in a single CSD could in principle be overcome, but this is very hard to achieve.

Proposition 17: Almost all CSDs operate national monopolies.

Proposition 18: Competition for the market for central register services has occurred in a very few instances.

Proposition 19: Competition in the market for central register services has occurred in a very few instances.

Proposition 20: Competition between CSDs in the market for central settlement services has occurred in a very few instances.

Proposition 21: Settlement internalization could in principle provide a competitive threat to a CSD, but there is no evidence as to whether it has yet done so in practice.

CONCLUSIONS

A critical determinant of whether exchanges, CCPs, or CSDs should be considered infrastructure institutions is whether they have market power. This chapter explores whether they do, specifically in the provision of trading, clearing, central register, and settlement services. No assessment is made about whether any particular institutions have market power. Instead four general issues are examined. Some broad comments are provided on the nature of market power. The key factors that lead towards consolidation of market power in each industry sector, and those that tend to promote competition and reduce market power, are discussed. Brief comments on the industry structure in practice in each of the three sectors are presented. Finally, a range of generic propositions about the industry structure in each of the three sectors are articulated. The propositions seek to capture and summarize the relevant accumulated knowledge and experience in a simple manner. It is accepted, however, that by their nature they cannot be comprehensive and may oversimplify a complex reality.

A range of factors may impede competition, and accordingly amplify market power, in each industry sector. These include network externalities (the order-flow externality for exchanges, the netting externality for CCPs, and a liquidity externality for CSDs), economies of scale, switching costs, and restrictive laws, regulations, and market practices. In principle all these and other types of factors limiting competition may be overcome to facilitate competition in each industry sector. So access to a network and appropriate interoperability can allow a new competitor not to be at a disadvantage compared to an incumbent provider, without market participants losing the benefits of an existing network externality; automation can reduce economies of scale; harmonization of market rules and practices, and agreement on standardized connection protocols, can reduce switching costs; and restrictive laws, regulations, and market practices can be liberalized. These factors impeding competition are, however, hard, though not impossible, to overcome in practice.

Unsurprisingly, the answer to the question of whether a particular exchange, CCP, or CSD does have market power is that it depends on the specific circumstances in which it operates. The analysis presented here nevertheless indicates that in many contexts each type of institution may have market power. To date, competition, the associated lack of market power, and potentially also contestability appear more prevalent in the market for trading services than in the markets for clearing and settlement. In a few jurisdictions, however, competition in the provision of clearing services also appears to be increasing.

PART TWO

Survey Evidence

CHAPTER THREE

The Allocation of Regulatory Powers over Securities Markets

THERE IS GREAT DIVERSITY in the way in which jurisdictions allocate regulatory powers over their securities markets. Typically such authority is divided between central governments, independent regulatory agencies, market infrastructure institutions, and SROs. This chapter seeks to compare how different jurisdictions allocate regulatory powers over their securities markets. It is difficult to do this for various reasons: the manner in which regulatory powers are allocated to different institutions in any single jurisdiction is complicated; the nature of market infrastructure institutions and SROs varies widely across countries, with, for example, some jurisdictions requiring market infrastructure institutions to be SROs, and others not doing so; different countries have different models for allocating regulatory responsibilities; and many jurisdictions have been changing the way in which they allocate regulatory responsibilities for their securities markets. Rather than seek to present detailed descriptions of how any specific jurisdictions allocate such regulatory responsibilities, three surveys on the topic, covering various jurisdictions and institutions, are described and evaluated.

The chapter is composed of four sections. The first two summarize in turn key results from two surveys that examine the regulation of securities markets, and how regulatory powers over such markets are allocated—one prepared by the World Federation of Exchanges (WFE) in 2004, and the other by the International Council of Securities Associations (ICSA) in 2006. The third section presents the results of a survey undertaken in 2006 for this book on how regulatory authority is allocated in eight jurisdictions with large securities markets. Conclusions are presented in the last section.

WORLD FEDERATION OF EXCHANGES

The WFE is the global trade organization for regulated securities and derivative markets, settlement institutions, and related clearinghouses.[1] In 2004 the WFE conducted a survey of its member exchanges regarding the changing role of stock exchanges in regulation.[2] Thirty-nine exchanges responded to the survey, although not all respondents answered all questions.[3] Responses to the survey were rendered anonymous.

The survey obtained information about the manner in which the respondent exchanges undertook 10 areas of regulation as follows.

1. *Market Regulation:* Virtually all of the respondent exchanges established market trading rules, and conducted real-time and post-trade surveillance. Virtually all exchanges enforced these trading rules either with fines, bars, or suspensions of trading members. Enforcement of trading rules was frequently shared with government regulators.

2. *Licensing:* 88% of the respondent exchanges licensed trading members, and over half of these exchanges shared this responsibility with government regulators. A little over half of the respondents were responsible for licensing clearing members.

3. *Capital Adequacy and Position Risks:* Approximately half of the respondent exchanges established or monitored capital adequacy rules. A greater number established or monitored position risk rules, and an even larger number enforced such rules. Government regulators in a number of jurisdictions established or enforced such rules, and often responsibility for such rules was shared between exchanges and government regulators.

4. *Clearing and Settlement:* Over half the respondent exchanges undertook clearing and settlement functions, but only about one-third had a depository; 49% managed guaranty funds. Such functions were generally not shared, but undertaken either by exchanges or by government regulators.

5. *Conduct of Business Rules:* Approximately 80% of the exchanges established, monitored, and enforced conduct of business or fair dealing rules by their trading members. Responsibility for these rules was sometimes handled solely by government regulators, and frequently shared with government regulators.

6. *IPO and Advertising Rules:* About a quarter of respondent exchanges reviewed underwriting agreements and IPO allocations, and about one-third reviewed advertising by members. Some of this work was conducted by government or other agencies.

7. *Arbitration:* Over half the respondent exchanges provided arbitration facilities. Four exchanges noted that arbitration facilities were provided by government regulators.

8. *Listing Standards:* Among the respondent exchanges, 79% established quantitative listing standards, and 69% established corporate governance standards. Such standards were monitored by and enforced by a large number of exchanges. Government regulators also shared these responsibilities.

9. *Issuer Disclosures:* About 75% of respondent exchanges established and monitored disclosure standards by listed companies, including annual and periodic disclosures, but only 49% vetted prospectuses. Many exchanges shared these responsibilities with government regulators.

10. *Other Regulatory Activities:* Of 33 respondent exchanges, 88% designed new products, while 44% of 34 respondent exchanges monitored money laundering regulations, 42% of 26 respondent exchanges established cross-border trading rules, and 42% of 26 respondent exchanges monitored cross-border trading rules.

The WFE survey also sought to obtain some qualitative information about "the direction of regulatory activities and current problems in the performance of regulatory functions by exchanges." Three relevant sets of questions posed by the survey, together with summaries of the responses to the questions, are noted here as follows.

a. What regulatory areas does your exchange wish to retain? What areas would it be willing to dispose of? How would you like to see market regulation evolve?

Virtually all exchanges wished to retain regulation of their trading markets, and most exchanges also wished to continue regulating some aspects of listed companies' corporate governance. Only three exchanges responded that there were regulatory tasks they no longer wished to undertake. Such activities included "upstairs activity and surveillance for insider-trading," and "multi-market investigations into potential market manipulation and abuse."

Many exchanges expressed the view that there should be a reduction of duplicative government and exchange regulation, some complaining that there was not a clear-cut delineation of responsibilities between the relevant government authority and the exchange. More coordination and transparency between different agencies was requested. Some exchanges asked for an increased separation of functions between the government and independent regulatory bodies. Some exchanges, particularly from Europe, expressed the view that there should be more uniform regulation by exchanges in different jurisdictions.

b. Is regulation a significant part of your brand or your commercial strategy? What corporate purposes are served by engaging in regulatory activities?

Almost all the respondent exchanges replied that regulation was a significant part of their brand or commercial strategy. Only two exchanges answered this question negatively.

c. If your exchange has demutualized/and or become a public company within the past three years, did this impact market regulation? How?

Five out of the 14 exchanges that answered that they had demutualized did not notice any significant changes in their regulatory responsibilities. There were, however, some changes in the way they carried out such duties. For those exchanges that said that there had been some changes in their responsibilities, some mentioned the introduction of mechanisms to respond to new conflicts of interest in being a commercial market place and remaining a regulator at the same time. Such mechanisms included the creation of information barriers or Chinese walls, spinning off regulation into a separate subsidiary, and ceding some functions to a regulatory service provider.

INTERNATIONAL COUNCIL OF SECURITIES ASSOCIATIONS

ICSA is an association of 14 trade associations and self-regulatory associations for participants operating in 11 national capital markets, and also the global capital markets.[4] In 2006, ICSA carried out a survey of 10 SROs the aim of which was to describe the core responsibilities and activities that characterized SROs.[5] The survey examined four key topics: (1) the sources of SROs' regulatory authority, (2) their regulatory and other activities, (3) mechanisms for controlling conflicts of interest, and (4) governance arrangements and the role of SROs' members. Key results in each of these areas are noted here. Responses to the survey were rendered anonymous.

1. *Mandates and Sources of Regulatory Authority:* The mandates of all the respondent SROs emphasized public interest objectives, including the enhancement of market integrity, investor protection, and market efficiency. Some also included improving the competitiveness of national capital markets and market infrastructures, providing education for market professionals and the general public, and increasing or maintaining investor confidence.

Government regulators actively supervised all the respondent SROs. This supervision was carried out primarily through periodic examinations or inspections, although more than half of the SROs in the survey reported that government regulators exercised continuous oversight of their operations. In most cases government regulators were required to approve SROs' bylaws, rules, and regulations. Government regulators were also allowed to initiate rulemaking for more than half of the respondent SROs.

All of the respondent SROs had statutory authority for their regulatory activities, and half also had authority that was delegated by their government regulators. None of the SROs in the survey relied exclusively on contractual authority with their members.

2. *Regulatory and Related Activities of SROs:* All the SROs surveyed had the authority to regulate member firms. This was done primarily by establishing sales practice and business conduct rules, and monitoring firms' compliance with these rules. The SROs in the survey also established and monitored compliance with capital adequacy standards, licensed or registered member firms, and monitored compliance with rules on other areas such as anti-money-laundering and customer identification requirements. Almost all of the respondent SROs also regulated markets, principally by establishing and monitoring compliance with trading rules and conducting surveillance of trading activities.

Most of the SROs in the survey regulated employees of member firms and, in some jurisdictions, also independent contractors that were active in the markets they regulated. SROs regulated individuals primarily through setting accreditation or proficiency standards, and licensing or registering the individuals that met those standards. Most of the SROs that regulated individuals also set educational standards for the individuals that they regulated, and licensed or registered the individuals who met these standards.

A relatively small number of SROs in the survey regulated issuers. All of the SROs that did so established, and monitored compliance with, disclosure, listing, and corporate governance standards.

All of the SROs in the survey had the authority to investigate complaints against the firms and individuals that were subject to their authority, and to take disciplinary action against firms and individuals that were found to have violated their rules and regulations. Such disciplinary actions most commonly took the form of monetary fines, suspensions, and sanctions. Most of the SROs in the survey were allowed to expel members, and to force the disgorgement of profits.

4. *Dealing with Potential Conflicts of Interest:* Slightly more than half of the SROs in the survey owned or operated an exchange or market that they also regulated. Two of the SROs also functioned as third-party suppliers of regulatory services, as they regulated exchanges that they did not own or operate. Two of the SROs did not regulate exchanges or markets at all.

The majority of SROs in the survey that regulated an exchange or market that they also owned or operated, maintained a formal separation between their regulatory and commercial activities. In all cases, these separations included separate reporting lines and completely separate staff for the SRO's regulatory and commercial activities. In addition, three of the five SROs that had a formal separation between their commercial and regulatory activities had established completely separate corporate entities for their regulatory activities.

Three of the SROs in the survey that regulated an exchange or market that they owned or operated did not have a formal separation between their regulatory and commercial activities. However, two of these SROs had formal policies and procedures in place for managing potential conflicts of interest that the relevant government regulators had reviewed.

4. *Governance Arrangements and the Role of Members:* Half of the SROs in the survey reported that industry participants accounted for less than half of their board members, while the other half of the SROs reported that industry participants accounted for the majority of their board members.

All of the SROs surveyed reported that members played an important role in the development of their regulatory policies, primarily through committees organized by the SRO, comment letters, and regular contact with the SRO. However, in a previous survey carried out by ICSA, all SROs reported that they also relied extensively on analysis by their own staffs and on developments in other jurisdictions when formulating new regulatory policies.

Members played an important role in the enforcement process at most SROs surveyed. Most SROs reported that their members were not involved in an initial decision to investigate a complaint against another member. However, once the SRO had made a decision to investigate a member firm or individual, almost all the SROs reported that their members played a role in the adjudication process. In general, members participated in the adjudication process through public or private discipline panels and on arbitration panels. Slightly more than half of the SROs in the survey also reported that members played a role in the decision to take disciplinary action against member firms or individuals that had been found to have violated the SRO's rules and regulations.

INFRASTRUCTURE INSTITUTIONS IN MAJOR MARKETS

This section contains the results of a survey undertaken in 2006 for this book of how regulatory responsibilities were allocated in eight jurisdictions with large securities markets: Australia, Canada, France, Germany, Hong Kong, Japan, the UK, and the United States.[6] Although there was enormous diversity between all eight jurisdictions, there was sufficient similarity at the broadest level for three generic models of allocating regulatory responsibility to be identified. The models are referred to, respectively, as the Government-Led Model, the Flexibility Model, and the Cooperation Model. The models capture key elements of the regulatory approaches employed at the time in all but one of the jurisdictions under scrutiny, namely the UK.

Three points about these generic models are noteworthy. First, they are intended only to provide a very broad characterization of how regulatory responsibilities are allocated in a jurisdiction. By construction, therefore, they are bound to oversimplify the nature of how regulatory responsibilities are allocated in practice in any single jurisdiction. Second, the models are simply descriptive in nature. No implications should therefore be drawn about the merits of any particular country's way of allocating regulatory responsibilities from the fact that it is classified under any one of the models. Finally, given the changes that are constantly occurring in the way in which countries allocate regulatory responsibilities, the models should not necessarily be taken to represent up-to-date characterizations of the approaches currently adopted by the countries in question, and indeed in some of these countries significant changes in how regulatory duties are allocated were made subsequent to the survey.

The methodology employed in the survey is briefly described first in this section. Each model is then described in turn, with comments provided on three key questions: How are regulatory responsibilities divided between regulatory agencies, market infrastructure institutions, and SROs? What types of rules define the interaction between market infrastructure institutions and administrative agencies? What is the role of central government in the securities markets regulatory framework? The regulatory approach employed in the UK is then summarized. It is viewed as having elements of both the Flexibility and Government-Led models, but as belonging to neither category. Finally, some brief comments on the effects of various EU directives on the regulatory approaches adopted in EU jurisdictions are presented, and in particular on how their implementation has meant that the approaches adopted in EU member states for allocating regulatory responsibilities are converging.

Methodology

In order to investigate the allocation of regulatory powers in countries with major securities markets, a questionnaire was sent to stock exchanges and lawyers in the eight jurisdictions examined.[7] Answers to the questionnaire were supplemented with research into relevant legal and regulatory provisions. The questionnaire sought to ascertain how the regulation of 45 functions in the securities markets was divided. For each of these functions, respondents were asked to indicate the regulatory body responsible for rulemaking, for monitoring, and for enforcing relevant laws and regulations. Responses to the questionnaire yielded a breakdown of 135 different regulatory powers for each jurisdiction. A detailed map of the allocation of regulatory powers in each jurisdiction was thus obtained. Areas that were unregulated, or that fell within the sphere of competence of more than one regulatory body, were also identified.

A functional approach was employed to avoid confusion caused by open-ended jurisdictional assignments, as well as ambiguities resulting from legal provisions that had not been fully implemented. It also facilitated comparisons across jurisdictions and between regulatory entities.

The survey sought to capture the interplay between market infrastructure institutions, SROs, and state authorities in three main ways. First, the different types of public authorities that may be involved in the regulatory process, including central government bodies (such as ministries), regulators (such as agencies or specialized authorities), and courts, were distinguished. Second, varying degrees of interaction among these regulatory authorities were identified, by separating instances where an institution acts alone, from others where approval by another institution was required. This was deemed crucial given that the role of an institution in a regulatory framework is defined not only by its own powers, but also by the powers of other entities to set out, limit the scope of, or overturn the institution's actions. Third, the roles of different levels of government authorities (for example at the federal or state level) were noted, where relevant.

The results of the survey are summarized in tables 5–12.[8] Each table outlines the results for one jurisdiction, in the following order: France, Japan, Germany, Australia, Hong Kong, the United States, Canada, and the UK. In order to present the results in a concise manner, the 45 functions examined in the survey are grouped together in the tables into nine general categories: (1) prospectus disclosure, (2) securities distribution, (3) listing and ongoing disclosure, (4) issuer corporate governance, (5) market abuse, (6) trading rules, (7) marketplace oversight,[9] (8) brokers and investment firms, and (9) clearing and settlement.

For each jurisdiction, the types of institution that regulated each of these categories of functions are identified. The names in each table in bold face illustrate government or administrative agency authority, while the areas in white indicate market infrastructure institution or SRO authority. This manner of constructing the tables captures key elements of the regulatory approaches in each jurisdiction, but necessarily simplifies what in each case are highly complex regulatory arrangements.

TABLE 5
Overview of the Regulatory Framework in France, 2006

	Rulemaking		Monitoring		Enforcement	
Prospectus disclosure	AMF	E	AMF	E	AMF/C	E
Securities distribution		AMF	AMF		AMF	
Listing—ongoing disclosure	AMF	E	AMF	E	AMF	E
Issuer corporate governance	AMF		AMF		AMF	
Market abuse	Ministry/AMF		Ministry/AMF		AMF/C	
Trading rules	AMF	E	AMF	E	AMF	E
Marketplace oversight	Ministry/AMF		Ministry/AMF		AMF	
Brokers— investment firms	CECEI/CB	E	CECEI/CB	E	CECEI/CB	E
Clearing & settlement	AMF	LCH	AMF	LCH	AMF	LCH

KEY

AMF: Autorité des Marchés Financiers   E: Euronext Paris   LCH: LCH.Clearnet

CB: Commission Bancaire   CECEI: Comité des Établissements de Crédit et des Entreprises d'Investissement   C: Courts

TABLE 6
Overview of the Regulatory Framework in Japan, 2006

	Rulemaking		Monitoring		Enforcement	
Prospectus disclosure	FSA	TSE	FSA	TSE	FSA/C	TSE
Securities distribution	FSA		FSA		FSA	
Listing—ongoing disclosure	FSA	TSE	FSA	TSE	FSA	TSE
Issuer corporate governance	FSA		FSA		FSA	
Market abuse	FSA		FSA		FSA	
Trading rules	FSA	TSE	FSA	TSE	FSA	TSE
Marketplace oversight	FSA		FSA		FSA	
Brokers—investment firms	FSA/JSDA		FSA/JSDA		FSA/JSDA	
Clearing & settlement	Ministry	JSCC	Ministry JSCC		JSCC	

KEY

FSA: Financial Services Agency   TSE: Tokyo Stock Exchange   JSCC: Japan Securities Clearing Corp.

JSDA: Japan Securities Dealers Association   Ministry: Ministry of Finance   C: Courts

TABLE 7
Overview of the Regulatory Framework in Germany. 2006

	Rulemaking		Monitoring		Enforcement	
Prospectus disclosure	Ministry/Parliament		BaFin		BaFin	C
Securities distribution	Ministry/Parliament		BaFin		BaFin/C	
Listing—ongoing disclosure	Ministry/Parliament	DB	BaFin	DB	BaFin	DB
Issuer corporate governance	Ministry of Justice		BaFin		BaFin/C	
Market abuse	Ministry/Parliament		BaFin/HÜSt		BaFin/C	
Trading rules	Ministry/Parliament	DB	HÜSt	DB	BaFin	DB
Marketplace oversight	Länder/BaFin		Länder/BaFin		Länder/BaFin	
Brokers—investment firms	BaFin/Bundesbank		BaFin		BaFin	
Clearing & settlement	BaFin/Bundesbank	DB	BaFin	DB	BaFin	DB

KEY

BaFin: Bundesanstalt für
Finanzdienstleistungsaufsicht
Länder: State Ministries
  of Economics

DB: Deutsche Börse
Ministry: Ministry of Finance

C: Courts
HÜSt: Market Surveillance
  Office

TABLE 8
Overview of the Regulatory Framework in Australia, 2006

	Rulemaking		Monitoring		Enforcement	
Prospectus disclosure	Treasury	ASX	ASIC	ASX	ASIC/C	ASX
Securities distribution	Treasury		ASIC		ASIC	
Listing—ongoing disclosure	ASX		ASX		ASX	
Issuer corporate governance	Government		ASIC		ASIC	
Market abuse	Government		ASIC		ASIC	
Trading rules	ASX		ASX		ASX	
Marketplace oversight	Treasury	ASX	ASIC	ASX	ASIC	ASX
Brokers—investment firms	Treasury	ASX	ASIC	ASX	ASIC	ASX
Clearing & settlement	Treasury	ASX	ASIC/RBA	ASX	ASIC/RBA	ASX

KEY

ASX: Australian Stock Exchange
ASIC: Australian Securities
  and Investment Commission

RBA: Reserve Bank of Australia

C: Courts

TABLE 9
Overview of the Regulatory Framework in Hong Kong, 2006

	Rulemaking		Monitoring		Enforcement	
Prospectus disclosure	**SFC**	HKEx	**SFC**	HKEx	**SFC**	HKEx
Securities distribution		HKEx		HKEx		HKEx
Listing—ongoing disclosure		HKEx		HKEx		HKEx
Listing—corporate government		HKEx		HKEx		HKEx
Market abuse	**SFC**	HKEx	**SFC**	HKEx	**SFC**	HKEx
Trading rules		HKEx		HKEx		HKEx
Marketplace oversight	**SFC**	HKEx	**SFC**	HKEx	**SFC**	HKEx
Brokers—investment firms	**SFC**	HKEx	**SFC**	HKEx	**SFC**	HKEx
Clearing & settlement	**SFC**	HKEx	**SFC**	HKEx	**SFC**	HKEx

KEY

SFC: Securities and Futures Commission   HKEx: Hong Kong Exchanges and Clearing Limited

TABLE 10
Overview of the Regulatory Framework in the United States, 2006

	Rulemaking		Monitoring		Enforcement	
Prospectus disclosure	**SEC**		**SEC**		**SEC/C**	
Securities distribution	**SEC**	SROs	**SEC**	SROs	**SEC**	SROs
Listing—ongoing disclosure	**SEC**	SROs	**SEC**	SROs	**SEC**	SROs
Issuer corporate governance	**SEC**	SROs	**SEC**	SROs	**SEC**	SROs
Market abuse	**SEC**	SROs	**SEC**	SROs	**SEC**	SROs
Trading rules	**SEC**	SROs	**SEC**	SROs	**SEC**	SROs
Marketplace oversight	**SEC**	SROs	**SEC**	SROs	**SEC**	SROs
Brokers—investment firms	**SEC**	SROs	**SEC**	SROs	**SEC**	SROs
Clearing & settlement	**SEC**	SROs	**SEC**	SROs	**SEC**	SROs

KEY

SEC: Securities and Exchange Commission   SROs: Self-Regulatory Organizations   C: Courts

Table 11
Overview of the Regulatory Framework in Canada, 2006

	Rulemaking		Monitoring		Enforcement	
Prospectus disclosure	OSC	TSX	OSC	TSX	OSC/C	TSX
Securities distribution	OSC		OSC		OSC	
Listing—ongoing disclosure	OSC	TSX	OSC	TSX	OSC	TSX
Issuer corporate governance	OSC	TSX	OSC	TSX	OSC	TSX
Market abuse	OSC	TSX	OSC	TSX	OSC	TSX
Trading rules	OSC	TSX	OSC	TSX	OSC	TSX
Marketplace oversight	OSC	TSX	OSC	TSX	OSC	TSX
Brokers—investment firms	OSC	TSX	OSC	TSX	OSC	TSX
Clearing & settlement	OSC	TSX	OSC	TSX	OSC	TSX

KEY

OSC: Ontario Securities Commission   TSX: Toronto Stock Exchange   C: Courts

TABLE 12
Overview of the Regulatory Framework in the UK, 2006

	Rulemaking	Monitoring	Enforcement
Prospectus disclosure	Treasury	FSA	FSA/C
Securities distribution	Treasury	FSA	FSA
Listing—ongoing disclosure	Treasury	FSA	FSA
Issuer corporate governance	FSA/Panel	FSA	FSA
Market abuse	Treasury/FSA	FSA	FSA
Trading rules	LSE	LSE	LSE
Marketplace oversight	Treasury/FSA	FSA	FSA
Brokers—investment firms	Treasury/FSA	FSA	FSA
Clearing & settlement	Treasury/FSA	FSA	FSA

KEY

FSA: Financial Services Authority   LSE: London Stock Exchange   C: Courts

Panel: Panel for Takeovers and Mergers

Government-Led Model

In three of the jurisdictions surveyed—namely France, Japan, and Germany—the allocation of regulatory powers favored administrative agencies and central government officials over market infrastructure institutions. The approach adopted in these jurisdictions is referred to here as the Government-Led Model. Laws in these jurisdictions tended to require greater involvement of central governments in certain key actions and regulatory measures than existed under other models. The regulatory powers of market infrastructure institutions were specific, carefully defined, and related to areas where their involvement was most beneficial, such as the regulation of the trading process. Even in these limited areas, the exercise of regulatory powers by market infrastructure institutions was often subject to approval by an administrative agency. The similarities in the pattern of allocation of regulatory responsibilities among the countries in the Government-Led Model is demonstrated in tables 5, 6, and 7, for France, Japan, and Germany respectively.

DIVISION OF REGULATORY RESPONSIBILITIES

In the Government-Led Model, the allocation of regulatory responsibilities between administrative agencies and market infrastructure institutions was issue-specific: statutes directed market institutions' regulatory efforts to precisely delineated areas of activity and regulatory responsibility, assigning specific tasks and granting them specialized powers. Market institutions derived their regulatory powers from a complex set of different provisions, each one aiming to provide regulatory solutions to a particular concern. The regulatory role of market infrastructure institutions thus came together in a piecemeal fashion, rather than through a general authorization to uphold securities laws and formulate rules for their implementation. A consequence of the issue-specific approach to the allocation of regulatory powers is that in these jurisdictions the government agency was the default regulator for the securities markets, in the sense that when a power had not been expressly assigned to a market infrastructure institution, it rested with the government agency.

Jurisdictions employing the Government-Led Model were also distinctive with regards to the specific areas in which they allocated regulatory powers to market institutions. Market infrastructure institutions typically had powers in the following areas: setting out prospectus disclosure requirements, establishing listing requirements and ongoing disclosure obligations, setting the trading rules according to which transactions were effected on a stock exchange, and setting out clearing and settlement procedures. Stock exchanges thus had a key role in controlling whether issuers could obtain access to their markets and how trading could take place. Clearing and settlement institutions were responsible for designing the clearing and settlement process.

This allocation of powers is consistent with the view that stock exchanges may be more effective than government agencies in regulating certain aspects of the securities markets. It also implements the regulatory approach of limiting market infrastructure institutions' regulatory role to the minimum, and specifically to areas where their involvement is highly beneficial for the smooth operation of the market.

The limited rulemaking and review authority granted to exchanges with regards to initial and ongoing issuer disclosure constitutes a channel through which they familiarize themselves with their issuers. Similarly, an exchange's trading system is one of the core aspects of its activity and one over which it has a high level of expertise. It is thus not surprising that regulation of the exchange trading process was one of the few areas where all the jurisdictions in the survey, including those with the Government-Led Model, coincided in granting significant regulatory powers to exchanges. Given the complicated technical issues associated with market microstructure, most jurisdictions left wide discretion to exchanges in this field, and limited themselves to setting high-level principles that a trading system must satisfy. An analogous argument held for clearing and settlement regulation, where government agencies focused on financial stability and infrastructure adequacy issues, leaving the design of the technical clearing and settlement systems to the institutions operating them.

The degree of discretion market institutions had in these areas in Government-Led jurisdictions varied. For example, government intervention in rules that determined which issuers would have access to public financing was relatively strong, as statutes and agency rulemaking usually prescribed the conditions that triggered the requirement for a prospectus and outlined a prospectus' required contents. On the other hand, governments were usually less interested in specifying rules that determined market microstructure issues, leaving trading technicalities for exchanges to determine.[10]

In the areas where market infrastructure institutions enjoyed regulatory responsibilities, their powers were almost always not exclusive: regulators also often bore some authority over the same areas. Frequently, the law would subject a market infrastructure institution's discretion in the exercise of its powers to government agency oversight. Regulators thus typically had an all-encompassing scope of authority.

The administrative agencies operating in the Government-Led Model jurisdictions as of 2006 sprung out of regulatory reforms in these countries at the turn of the millennium. In France, the Autorité des Marchés Financiers (AMF) succeeded a number of smaller agencies specializing in securities markets oversight.[11] In Japan, the Financial Services Agency (JFSA) came into being as a high-level supervisory body for agencies regulating the banking and securities markets. In Germany, the federal regulator, Bundesanstalt für Finanzdienstleistungsaufsicht, was an amalgamation of the administrative agencies previously responsible for the insurance, banking, and securities industries.[12] These extensive reorganizations were justified as necessary to respond to the increasing complexity of, and constant innovations and changes in, modern financial markets, including in some instances stock exchange demutualizations.

INTERACTION BETWEEN STOCK EXCHANGES AND ADMINISTRATIVE AGENCIES

In Government-Led Model jurisdictions, the regulatory powers of market infrastructure institutions generally coexisted with powers afforded to the administrative agencies active in securities markets regulation. Given this overlap, the risk of clash between these bodies' actions was almost inevitable. A number of solutions were employed to counter this problem, most of which resulted in giving precedence to agency powers over those held by market infrastructure institutions. Three are noted here.

First, stock exchange rules often required agency approval to enter into force. Although a similar requirement existed in other models, the implications in the Government-Led Model were different, because market infrastructure institutions' powers were more narrowly prescribed given their issue-specific character. As a result, the regulatory space over which market infrastructure institutions had rulemaking power was much narrower in comparison to what occurred under the Cooperation Model, for example. The law often also granted regulatory agencies the ability to direct market infrastructure institutions to adopt certain measures in areas where agencies enjoyed the power of prior approval of market institution rulemaking.

A second frequent way of resolving clashes between agency and market infrastructure institution power was that agencies were granted the power to reverse decisions by market infrastructure institutions.

Finally, the character of SROs' rulemaking and enforcement actions in the Government-Led Model was secondary to agency initiatives. On the rulemaking side, SRO rules often sought to implement agency directives in a concrete way, rather than define new regulatory objectives. On the enforcement side, SROs' powers often came in support of agency initiatives, such as by expelling issuers from an exchange whose fraudulent activities had already been the target of agency investigations.[13]

In sum, the regulatory mission of market institutions in the Government-Led Model consisted largely in supplementing agency regulatory actions, rather than bringing concrete regulatory initiatives to the fore.

In Government-Led Model jurisdictions, central government shaped the securities regulatory framework so as to maintain important channels of influence over the operation of market infrastructure institutions. Sometimes these channels of influence were direct, such as via powers to approve the establishment of a stock exchange or a clearinghouse that rested with a central government official, typically a Minister.[14] These channels might often also be indirect, and expressed through a tight relationship between central government and the administrative agency responsible for the regulatory oversight of the securities markets. In Japan, for example, the JFSA was positioned under the Prime Minister's Cabinet in the Japanese regulatory hierarchy, and some of its rules required the Prime Minister's approval before entering into force. In France, the AMF was seen as an independent public authority,[15] but all AMF rules required the approval of the Ministry of Finance before entering into force. Moreover, the Ministry could influence the AMF's deliberation process through its directly appointed representative on the AMF board.[16]

Flexibility Model

The regulatory approach adopted in Australia and Hong Kong was to grant as much leeway as possible to market infrastructure institutions in structuring their activities, while still ensuring that they fulfilled their regulatory obligations. This approach is referred to here as the Flexibility Model. It did not necessarily entail a lack of clarity or rigor in setting out firm objectives for securities markets regulation, nor did it signal laxity in enforcement. On the contrary, regulatory objectives remained clear, and enforcement efforts in these jurisdictions were often strong. However, in considering how to implement these objectives, regulated entities normally had the ability to shape their own solutions, sometimes through reaching an understanding with the regulator directly. These jurisdictions might also achieve flexibility by having regulatory agencies issue nonbinding guidance rather than, or in addition to, prescriptive rules, and by limiting central government involvement in the monitoring and enforcement stages.

The allocation of regulatory powers in the Flexibility Model was issue-specific in a similar manner to the Government-Led Model: government entities, public agencies, market infrastructure institutions, and SROs had distinct responsibilities for regulatory oversight. There were, however, differences between the two approaches. First, the core powers each entity had in Flexibility Model jurisdictions were designed to be distinct, although in some cases they were complementary, unlike the Government-Led approach. Second, the Flexibility Model might facilitate market- or industry-led initiatives to shape regulatory policy and enforcement, unlike in the Government-Led Model.

Tables 8 and 9, for Australia and Hong Kong respectively, illustrate that market infrastructure institutions in Flexibility Model jurisdictions enjoyed a wide range of regulatory powers, covering primary markets' disclosure rules, regulation of stock exchange member firms, and regulatory oversight of the marketplaces themselves. A comparison between these tables and those of the Government-Led jurisdictions reveals three important differences between the two models.

First, the areas over which market infrastructure institutions had regulatory powers in Government-Led Model jurisdictions were also areas over which market infrastructure institutions had regulatory powers in Flexibility Model jurisdictions. These included prospectus disclosure rules, listing and ongoing disclosure rules, trading rules, and clearing and settlement rules. These powers constituted "the bare minimum" regulatory role assigned to market institutions. Second, Flexibility Model jurisdictions entrusted market infrastructure institutions with substantially more powers than Government-Led jurisdictions. Third, there were many areas in the Flexibility Model where market infrastructure institutions were the exclusive regulators, without significant powers residing with government entities or administrative agencies. This characteristic of the Flexibility Model sets it apart both from the Government-Led Model and the Cooperation Model, neither of which allowed such leeway to market infrastructure institutions.

As the traditional role of market infrastructure institutions in the regulatory structure of Flexibility Model jurisdictions was more important than in the other models, demutualization of stock exchanges had a profound impact on these regimes. They responded to stock exchange demutualization by strengthening the position of regulators towards stock exchanges, and by implementing additional governance measures where necessary. Such jurisdictions nevertheless also preserved significant powers in the hands of market infrastructure institutions.

In Hong Kong, the government, although fully supportive of the demutualization process, resolved to strengthen the powers of the regulator following the demutualization of the exchange.[17] The 2003 Securities and Futures Ordinance increased the regulator's powers in some respects, and also led to further discussions about transferring other powers of the stock exchange to the regulator.

Following the demutualization of the Australian Stock Exchange (ASX), Australia maintained an important regulatory role for ASX, but established an enhanced governance regime over the stock exchange. ASX entered into an MOU with the Australian Securities and Investments Commission (ASIC), its regulator, regarding its supervision as a listed entity that enhanced ASIC's supervisory role.[18] In November 2000 ASX established ASX Supervisory Review, a wholly owned subsidiary of ASX, to monitor and oversee ASX's supervisory functions, and to report on the general policy direction, funding, and administrative arrangements of ASX's market supervision operations.[19] Following the merger of the ASX and the Sydney Futures Exchange on July 7, 2006, subsequently rebranded the Australian Securities Exchange, ASX Supervisory Review ceased operations on October 31, 2006, and ASX's supervisory activities were transferred to a new subsidiary of ASX called ASX Markets Supervision. In 2009, the Government decided to give ASIC responsibility for supervising real-time trading on all of Australia's domestic licensed markets.[20]

INTERACTION BETWEEN STOCK EXCHANGES AND ADMINISTRATIVE AGENCIES

In the Flexibility Model, regulatory agencies imposed limited administrative process constraints on market infrastructure institutions. In Australia, ASIC's approval was generally not required for a stock exchange rule to enter into force.[21] Given that the allocation of regulatory responsibilities was issue-specific, the absence of a prior approval requirement effectively granted market infrastructure institutions wide flexibility in the exercise of their rulemaking authority over the areas they regulated. In Hong Kong, Hong Kong Exchanges and Clearing Limited (HKEx) was required to obtain prior approval from the Securities and Futures Commission (SFC) before HKEx's rules could enter into force. However, there were many areas over which HKEx enjoyed the exclusive power to initiate regulation, even if SFC approval was ultimately necessary. In other areas, HKEx and SFC might both establish their own rules. This structure strengthened the presence of HKEx as a market regulator in Hong Kong.

A central characteristic of the regulatory process in the Flexibility Model lies in the nonintrusive approach these jurisdictions employed with regards to capital markets regulation in general, and rulemaking in particular. As in all jurisdictions in this study, the laws passed by the legislature required implementation by second-tier legislative measures specifying the practical details of enforcement. Unlike other types of jurisdictions, however, the task of implementation often fell to a central government entity, like a Ministry of Finance, which was required to issue the necessary legislative instruments with which government agencies and market infrastructure institutions had to comply and ensure compliance.

Often, these second-tier measures contained general principles that did not lend themselves to direct implementation in practice in the same way that rules of a day-to-day regulator did. These measures might thus require further elaboration by the agency or market infrastructure institutions under whose sphere of competence they fell. Moreover, the issuing government entities were often reluctant to revisit these second-tier measures. In many cases, administrative agencies were further authorized to issue regulations implementing such measures. Regulatory power was thus devolved from central government.

Administrative agencies in the Flexibility Model jurisdictions also developed the practice of issuing "guidance" to regulated entities, to illustrate their approach in the implementation of specific legal requirements. Such guidance resembles rulemaking in that it is phrased in terms of general applicability and is not addressed to a specific entity.[22] However, the language in guidance is normally not prescriptive, and often phrased in "best practice" terms, rather than imposing firm regulatory obligations. In cases of noncompliance with guidance, agencies might not threaten sanctions against regulated entities, but instead ask them to disclose noncompliance to the public, and explain the reasons for such noncompliance. Overall, Flexibility Model jurisdictions were more ready than other types of jurisdictions to recognize that adherence to general principles might require different actions from different entities.

ROLE OF GOVERNMENT IN REGULATORY FRAMEWORK

The relatively nonintrusive character of capital markets regulation in Flexibility Model jurisdictions stemmed also from the relationship between central government, the administrative agencies, and market infrastructure institutions, that underpinned the regulatory framework in such jurisdictions. Agencies in the Flexibility Model enjoyed greater independence from central government, and greater flexibility in monitoring and enforcing securities laws than in other models. A comparison of the institutional arrangements in the Government-Led Model with those of the Flexibility Model illustrates this.

In the Government-Led Model, central governments sought to influence securities markets regulation through their sway over administrative agencies, which dominated the full spectrum of regulatory responsibilities, namely rulemaking, monitoring, and enforcement. In the Flexibility Model, central governments provided more independence to administrative agencies and market infrastructure institutions, maintaining only limited ways to affect their day-to-day operation and decision-making processes. In most such jurisdictions, the main direct power central governments maintained over the operation of securities markets consisted in their power to approve the agency decision for the establishment of a new stock exchange or clearinghouse. Although central government might influence the operation of the agencies indirectly, through the appointment of agency officials, governments did not typically have other means of influencing a particular agency decision.

In return, central governments in the Flexibility Model retained significant rulemaking powers, often having a central government entity issuing implementing legislation that in Government-Led jurisdictions would have been issued by an administrative agency.[23] Tables 8 and 9, for the two Flexibility Model jurisdictions model in the survey, illustrate that the presence of central government entities in the rulemaking column was strong. However, as noted above, the legal instruments that government entities produced often required further elaboration by agencies before they could be implemented. The fact that agencies were exclusively responsible for monitoring and enforcing implementing legislation meant that their interpretations of these rules, sometimes in the form of guidance, dominated the oversight process. Given the nonprescriptive character of guidance, there was also room for market participants to negotiate with the agency, and for arguing in favor of a regulatory approach different from one put forward by a regulatory agency before a court in the final analysis. As a result, although central governments were the promulgators of an initial rule, agencies still possessed significant tools to frame the implementation of rules in practice.

Cooperation Model

The main characteristic of the regulatory approach adopted in Canada and the United States—referred to here as the Cooperation Model—was the pervasiveness of self-regulation. Market infrastructure institutions and SROs historically were granted wide powers and extensive responsibilities for ensuring the fair and efficient operation of securities markets in these jurisdictions. They also had a role in almost all aspects of securities markets regulation, devoted significant resources to assist and support regulatory agencies' efforts, and undertook their own independent regulatory initiatives. In addition, SROs and market institutions devoted significant efforts and resources to enforcement. The importance of self-regulation in the United States and Canada is illustrated in tables 10 and 11, which summarize their respective regulatory frameworks.

There were several reallocations of self-regulatory duties among different entities in the private sector in both Canada and the United States over the period 2007 to 2008, as discussed below. Although the allocation of regulatory duties among the newly created SROs and the market infrastructure institutions in these Cooperation Model jurisdictions changed, both the SROs and the market infrastructure institutions retained their private, namely nongovernmental, status. The key attribute of the Cooperation Model was thus unaffected by these reallocations of regulatory duties among different private sector organizations.

While central governments in jurisdictions following the Cooperation Model had a very limited role in regulatory oversight, specialized agencies were actively involved in market oversight responsibilities, often sharing jurisdiction with SROs, and also pursuing independent enforcement actions. Rather than delegating specific and limited powers to market institutions or SROs, as was the case under the Government-Led Model, or granting broad latitude to these entities, as occurred in the Flexibility Model, administrative agencies operating under the Cooperation Model tended to engage in continuous dialogue with market infrastructure institutions and SROs. The boundaries of regulatory responsibility, and even the content of regulatory requirements, thus tended to remain in a constant state of flux.

DIVISION OF REGULATORY RESPONSIBILITIES

The Cooperation Model tended to avoid the issue-specificity of the Government-Led and Flexibility Models in favor of a structure where the regulatory powers of market institutions and SROs were pervasive, extending across most areas of the regulatory spectrum. Statutes in the Cooperation Model jurisdictions did not attempt to draw clear lines between the authority of the government agencies and the authority of market infrastructure institutions or SROs, nor did they seek to avoid jurisdictional overlaps and create separate spheres of competence. Instead, they called on administrative agencies, SROs, and market institutions to cooperate in almost all aspects of securities markets regulation, so as to achieve better the high-level objectives the law identified, such as investor protection and the fair and efficient operation of markets. While the law set out certain obligations for administrative agencies, SROs, and market infrastructure institutions, and sketched out the basic framework of securities markets operation, agencies, SROs, and market institutions maintained significant leeway as to the functions they could choose to regulate, the manner in which they chose to regulate, and the sanctions they might apply to violators of regulation.

This regulatory philosophy differed markedly from the approaches of jurisdictions employing the other models. Although Flexibility and Government-Led Model jurisdictions reached a similar allocation of regulatory powers to agencies, SROs, and market infrastructure institutions in certain isolated areas, only in the Cooperation jurisdictions did this approach become the dominant regulatory technique. Inspired by the self-regulatory tradition of common-law jurisdictions, this regulatory approach was a political choice that sprung out of a New Deal compromise in the United States, and sought to maintain market infrastructure institutions as the frontline regulators under the scrutiny of a public interest-minded agency.[24] The benefits that self-regulation brought, which included the enhanced expertise and the de facto supervision of market operation by market institutions, justified the attempt to channel input from market participants to regulation through the market infrastructure institutions of which they were members. The pervasive character of the Cooperation Model in the exercise of rulemaking authority also extended to monitoring and enforcement authority. Under the Cooperation Model, market institutions and SROs were responsible for monitoring and enforcing compliance both with their own rules and with securities laws in general.

Although it is clear how this approach differed from the Government-Led Model, where agencies dominated the pattern of allocation of regulatory powers, it is perhaps less clear how it differed from the Flexibility Model, which also sought to combine market initiatives with government power to achieve regulatory efficiency. The main difference lay in the way agencies, market infrastructure institutions, and SROs exercised their regulatory powers. Flexibility Model regulatory agencies were predisposed to issue guidance to regulated entities, as opposed to exercising direct rulemaking, in order to assist the implementation of central government rules, although Flexibility Model regulatory agencies did also undertake much direct rulemaking. In contrast, regulatory agencies in Cooperation Model jurisdictions were active rule-makers, often dominating the regulation of securities markets, and used guidance infrequently, if at all. Moreover, in Cooperation Model jurisdictions, agencies, SROs, and market infrastructure institutions often shared enforcement responsibilities, with parallel enforcement proceedings taking place by both to investigate the same alleged violations.

For market professionals in Cooperation Model jurisdictions, participation in SROs was typically mandatory. Such mandatory membership illustrates both the central role these organizations played in the regulatory structure, and the pervasive sharing of responsibilities between SROs and government agencies.

A defining characteristic of the Cooperation Model was the delegation of significant regulatory functions and enforcement powers to SROs. When scandals revealed weaknesses in SRO oversight of market practices, or when other regulatory challenges arose such as those posed by stock market demutualizations, dramatic reductions in SRO oversight responsibilities—conceivable in Government-Led Model jurisdictions— were difficult to accomplish in Cooperation Model jurisdictions. Instead, such jurisdictions were the countries most apt to experiment with different self-regulatory structures.

Several recent developments highlight this possibility. The first was the segregation of the provision of regulatory functions from the operation of the market. In the United States, this occurred both at the National Association of Securities Dealers (NASD), with the incorporation of NASD Regulation separate from the NASDAQ Stock Market, and at the NYSE, with the development of a separate NYSE Regulation division.

The second such development was the creation of institutions focused solely on the provision of regulation, but which no longer had any ties with market operators. These new institutions remained SROs, however, in the sense that they were privately operated, financed, and managed. The merger of the NASD with the member regulation, enforcement, and arbitration functions of the NYSE, to form the Financial Industry Regulatory Authority (FINRA) in July 2007 is one key example of this.[25] In Canada, the formation of Market Regulation Services Inc. (RS) on March 1, 2002, and the subsequent formation of the Investment Industry Regulatory Organization of Canada (IIROC) in 2008, were similar, although they led to different allocations of self-regulatory duties than in the United States.[26] Prior to the formation of RS, each exchange in Canada, and the Investment Dealers Association (IDA), had their own market regulation staff and set of rules. RS was created as a joint initiative of TSX Group and the IDA. It amalgamated the in-house surveillance, trade desk compliance, investigation, and enforcement functions of the TSX and TSX Venture Exchanges to produce a single entity to monitor and enforce trading rules without preference to one marketplace over another.[27] IIROC was created through the consolidation of the IDA and RS to oversee all investment dealers and trading activity on debt and equity marketplaces in Canada.

INTERACTION BETWEEN STOCK EXCHANGES, SROS,
AND ADMINISTRATIVE AGENCIES

The essence of the Cooperation Model lies in the manner in which government agencies, exchanges, and SROs work together to regulate securities markets. The approach arises as a result of certain key features of both the regulatory regime and the securities markets in the relevant jurisdictions. In the Cooperation Model regulatory regime, SROs are typically required to obtain the approval of the government agency for any rule changes they wish to make. Although the requirement for agency approval in SRO rulemaking in the Cooperation Model appears similar to a similar requirement in the Government-Led Model, a number of features differentiate the two models.

First, Cooperation Model jurisdictions have historically been home to multiple and diverse SROs that are often in competition with each other. For the SROs, rulemaking has been a method of attracting members and gaining business from their competitors. As the SROs in the Cooperation Model jurisdictions have been merging, however, the importance of this factor has diminished.

A second difference between the Cooperation Model and the Government-Led Model turns on the way regulatory agencies intervene in SRO rulemaking. In the Cooperation Model, the law grants government agencies the power to intervene by rulemaking when they deem it necessary. As a result, SROs in Cooperation Model jurisdictions are constantly seeking to convince agencies that their rules successfully achieve the objectives set out in the law, so as to avoid a loss of powers to the regulatory agency, and more intrusive regulation for their members. SROs thus compete not only among themselves, but also against the regulatory agency. As a result, SRO rulemaking under the Cooperation Model is different than rulemaking by the same type of organization under the Government-Led Model, where the requirement for prior approval of SRO rules by agencies prevails. In the Cooperation Model, SROs are not limited to the role of a second-tier regulator whose mission consists of implementing agency rulemaking. On the contrary, SROs take their own initiatives and develop their own regulatory programs.

ROLE OF GOVERNMENT IN REGULATORY FRAMEWORK

Central governments in the Cooperation Model maintain high-level oversight of the securities markets, expressed mainly through their law-making powers and their influence over government agencies. As the Cooperation Model assigns SROs with the power to undertake regulatory initiatives, lawmakers must consider the successes and failures of the combined SRO- and agency-promulgated regulatory framework before they decide to act. Moreover, while SRO rules require prior agency approval, agency rules do not require prior government approval in the Cooperation Model. Thus, the entities that constitute the main actors in the Cooperation Model—market infrastructure institutions, SROs, and regulatory agencies—perform their day-to-day rulemaking tasks without direct interference from the central government. However, once lawmakers establish the need to intervene in securities markets regulation, often in response to a crisis, they may establish rules that hold agencies and SROs to higher standards than in the past. In effect governments thus constitute the final institutional layer that guarantees protection to investors, intervening when there is a perceived agency failure, often in addition to an SRO failure.

While the Cooperation Model does not provide for direct channels of government intervention in securities markets regulation, some indirect channels of intervention still persist. Most importantly, governments maintain the power to appoint regulatory agency officials. However, local law often limits the level of influence central governments are able to exercise through indirect channels in comparison with other jurisdictions, allowing agency officials to set their own political goals independent of central government.[28] In the United States and Canada, the federal structure of the government also limits the combined influence central government entities exercise over securities markets. In addition, the presence of SROs with strong regulatory powers and agencies that possess highly regarded market expertise ensure that any high-level changes in securities markets regulation will be the subject of much debate and criticism, thus increasing the political cost a central government must pay in case it decides to intervene. Consequently, in the Cooperation Model central governments normally exercise only limited and indirect influence over securities markets regulation.

The United Kingdom: A Mixture of Flexibility and Government-Led

The UK regulatory approach is not easily categorized into any one of the three models described above. Instead, it is best viewed as having elements of both the Flexibility and the Government-Led Models. Over recent years, the British approach has moved closer to the Government-Led Model for various reasons, including government determination to sever links with an era of self-regulation that was perceived to have failed as a result of various crises associated with it, and EU harmonization measures.

The regulator in the UK, the Financial Services Authority (FSA), had an extremely wide scope of powers as of the time of the survey, as illustrated in table 12. This scope was broader than typically presented in any of the three generic models identified above, but closest to that of the Government-Led jurisdictions. The regulatory role of the LSE was very restricted, being limited essentially to setting its own trading rules and providing the FSA with information on trading activity. Other powers retained by the exchange were only secondary and complementary to the FSA's rules. As well as all the specific areas over which the FSA had regulatory powers, the FSA was granted in December 2006 a general power to prevent UK Recognized Investment Exchanges (RIEs) and Recognized Clearing Houses (RCHs) from making changes to their regulatory provisions that were disproportionate to the end they were intended to achieve, or that did not pursue a reasonable regulatory objective.[29] The reason for the government granting such authority to the FSA was that at the time it was thought possible that NASDAQ might buy the LSE, and the government was concerned that were this to happen, US regulation might be imported into the UK via ownership of the LSE. It was believed this could adversely affect the competitiveness of the UK financial markets. The legislation effectively thus gave the FSA a veto over any attempt to impose US regulatory jurisdiction over UK exchanges and financial markets via ownership of an RIE or RCH.

The status of the FSA was unlike that typical in the Government-Led Model. It was not a government agency, but instead an independent nongovernmental body organized in the form of a company limited by guarantee. The financial industry paid for the operation of the FSA. The government could, however, exert some influence over the FSA. In particular, HM Treasury (HMT) appointed the FSA Board, and the FSA was accountable to government in a variety of ways.[30] These included the following: it was required to deliver four statutory objectives,[31] it had to consult extensively, its rules were subject to competition review by the Director General of Fair Trading, its rulings in respect of individual cases could be reviewed in a variety of ways, it had to report annually to HMT on the extent to which its regulatory objectives had been met, and its nonexecutive directors had to report on the discharge of their functions, including on whether the FSA was using its resources in the most efficient and economic way. These elements of accountability did not, however, imply that the UK government had the same level of influence over the FSA, or indeed over market infrastructure institutions, as was the case in Government-Led jurisdictions. On the contrary, the government granted the FSA much independence, maintaining only limited mechanisms to influence its day-to-day operations and decision-making process.

The exercise of rulemaking power by the FSA was also different in character from that employed by agencies in the Government-Led Model, resonating more with the approaches followed in the Flexibility jurisdictions. The FSA did promulgate many specific rules binding market infrastructure institutions, and other types of market participants, as well as itself. However, in respect of some important aspects of securities regulation, covering, for example, issues regarding exchanges and clearinghouses, the FSA followed a policy of issuing either nonbinding guidance on the implementation of the provisions it was charged with overseeing, or of operating through principles-based regulation. Both approaches allowed a degree of flexibility to exchanges and other market infrastructure institutions in deciding how to comply with FSA regulation.

Given the preeminence of London as an international financial center and the competition it provides to US markets, comparisons between the US and the UK regulatory frameworks have often been made.[32] Two differences frequently identified between the SEC and the FSA are the wide range of powers afforded to the FSA, and the variety of objectives of the FSA's mandate, as compared with the SEC's focus on investor protection. However, two other differences are more significant in differentiating the UK regulatory approach from that employed in the Cooperation Model, as evidenced in the United States. First, the SEC is primarily an enforcement agency, pursuing a large number of individual cases each year.[33] In contrast, the FSA only initiates a limited amount of enforcement actions against the entities it oversees, relying instead on other tools to ensure compliance with its rules.[34] Second, SEC rulemaking is more detailed and prescriptive than the relatively flexible approach of the FSA.

In the past the LSE carried out its own extensive investigations and disciplinary process, before handing cases to the UK Government's Department for Trade and Industry (DTI). However, with the Financial Services and Markets Act 2000, the DTI's responsibilities passed to the FSA. Subsequently the LSE carried out extensive monitoring of its markets and reported any suspicious trading to the FSA, but it was the FSA's responsibility to take such investigations forward and determine further enforcement action. The LSE did, however, continue to operate a disciplinary process in respect of breaches of its own rules.

The difficulty in categorizing the nature of the UK regulatory regime may be illustrated by considering two views presented by different officials on the topic. In 2006, Ed Balls, Economic Secretary to the Treasury, and the Minister in charge of the UK financial markets at the time, stressed the government's "determination to engage effectively with our European partners to entrench principles-based, light touch regulation in Europe that are key to Britain continuing to attract foreign direct investment in the future."[35] He also noted that it "is important that the FSA continues to deliver a light-touch and risk-based regulatory approach."[36] In contrast, Sir Callum McCarthy, chairman of the FSA, when describing the nature of the UK's regulatory regime, stated in 2007:

> I have questioned the description of the FSA as both "principles based" and "light touch." The former is half true; the latter even less true. Both are misleading. I have set out the reality, which is more complex: a mixture of both principles and rules, with a determined effort ... to move towards greater use of principles and to rely less on detailed rules; and an approach which is risk based, and which recognises that we cannot achieve and should not seek to avoid all financial failure.[37]

Impact of EU Directives

EU directives have increasingly limited the discretion over how regulatory powers may be allocated between governments, regulators, market infrastructure institutions, and SROs in the EU. This has meant that the regulatory models adopted in all EU member states are converging, although the manner in which EU directives have affected the governance of EU exchanges has depended on the applicable national arrangements in place. The key directives concerning financial markets in the EU, under the Financial Services Action Plan (FSAP), require that a single "competent authority"—typically a national regulator—be designated in each member state to assume final responsibility for supervising compliance with the provisions of the directives, as well as for international cooperation. The individual directives specify particular powers and functions be given to these competent authorities. For many jurisdictions, some of these functions have historically resided with the national stock exchange. As a result, the FSAP is leading to a shift of regulatory powers away from exchanges. The effects of the FSAP on three issues are briefly noted here: the regulatory role of exchanges in the primary market for new issuance of shares, the regulatory role of exchanges in the secondary market for trading shares, and exchange governance.

1. *Regulation of Issuers:* Exchanges in the EU were historically responsible for the listing of securities in their local markets. However, the FSAP focuses on the concept of market operators running "regulated markets," as defined in various FSAP directives, onto which they admit securities. The Prospectus Directive (PD) aims to harmonize the contents of issuers' prospectuses, thereby creating a passport for an issuer so that it can have its securities admitted to any EU Regulated Market.[38] The PD sets out the required contents of a company's prospectus when undertaking a public offer or being admitted to a regulated market, and how such prospectuses should be approved by the competent authority. The PD has already had a significant impact upon the role of EU exchanges, and a sunset clause will mean that by 2011 all exchanges will need to transfer the function of approving prospectuses to an independent competent authority.

The implementation of the Transparency Directive (TD) on January 20, 2007, resulted in a similar transfer of authority with respect to ongoing issuer disclosure.[39] Historically, the national stock exchange in a number of European jurisdictions was closely involved in the provision and dissemination of corporate information to market users, including in some cases a level of vetting of corporate announcements. However, under the TD, competent authorities have a responsibility to monitor that issuers disclose timely information in a manner ensuring fast access on a nondiscriminatory basis.[40] It is also the responsibility of the competent authority to ensure that there is an officially appointed mechanism for the central storage of regulated information.

The Markets in Financial Instruments Directive (MiFID) requires that regulated markets have clear and transparent rules regarding the admission of financial instruments to trading.[41] It also requires a regulated market to establish and maintain effective arrangements to verify that issuers comply with their admission requirements (as per the PD), and their obligations in respect of initial, ongoing, or ad hoc disclosure obligations (as per the TD).[42] In effect, this permits a regulated market to have admission and ongoing disclosure rules that exceed those set out in the respective directives, in which case the regulated market will be responsible for ensuring compliance. While the PD and TD transfer many of exchanges' traditional responsibilities to national competent authorities, and MiFID confirms compliance with these directives as EU-wide minimum standards, MiFID does still envision a role for exchanges in designing listing standards that go above and beyond EU minimum standards. This leaves some limited flexibility for exchanges to retain some independent listing function—should they wish to do so.

2. *Regulation of Trading:* The first FSAP directive to have a significant impact on the regulation of secondary market trading was the Market Abuse Directive (MAD).[43] It requires that the competent authority in a member state be given final responsibility for the supervision of markets,[44] but also recognizes that market operators, namely exchanges, should contribute to the prevention of market abuse and adopt structural provisions aimed at preventing and detecting market manipulation practices. Various provisions in MiFID also affect the regulation of regulated markets. In particular, it requires regulated markets to

> have transparent and non-discretionary rules and procedures that provide for fair and orderly trading and establish objective criteria for the efficient execution of orders;[45]
>
> establish and maintain effective arrangements and procedures for the regular monitoring of the compliance by their members or participants with their rules;[46] [and]
>
> monitor the transactions in order to identify breaches of those rules, disorderly trading conditions or conduct that may involve market abuse.

Operators of regulated markets must report significant breaches of their rules, or disorderly trading conditions, or conduct that may involve market abuse to the competent authority, and supply relevant information and provide full assistance to the competent authority in investigating and prosecuting market abuse occurring on or through the systems of the regulated market.[47]

MiFID is important in defining the relationship between competent authorities and exchanges. It states that member states shall require the operator of a regulated market to perform tasks relating to the organization and operation of the regulated market under the supervision of the competent authority.[48] Supervision of the markets is therefore the dual responsibility of both market operators and competent authorities. However, it is clear that final responsibility for supervising compliance with the provisions of MiFID rests with the competent authority.

3. *Governance of Exchanges:* MiFID includes provisions relating to the control of exchanges, the powers of competent authorities in relation to the organization of exchanges, and also the suitability and good repute of those managing, or exerting significant influence over those managing, an exchange.[49] A competent authority is required to refuse to approve proposed changes to the controlling interests of a regulated market, or market operator, where there are objective and demonstrable grounds for believing that they would pose a threat to the sound and prudent management of the regulated market.[50] As a result, competent authorities have to be kept informed whenever certain criteria are met that affect a person's shares or voting power in an exchange. A competent authority also has the power to suspend or remove a financial instrument from trading on an exchange.[51]

CONCLUSIONS

This chapter compares how regulatory powers over securities markets are allocated across a range of jurisdictions. Three surveys on the topic are evaluated, prepared respectively for the WFE in 2004, for the ICSA in 2006, and for this book in 2006. The evidence presented in the surveys supports a range of broad conclusions.

1. There is great diversity and complexity in the way in which jurisdictions allocate regulatory powers over their securities markets.

This is evident in several ways: (1) in the types of institutions to which regulatory powers are allocated—including central governments, independent regulatory agencies, market infrastructure institutions, and SROs; (2) in the different areas of securities market regulation allocated to different institutions—including authority over the public offer and listing process, issuer regulation following a public offer or listing, trading, financial intermediation, and clearing and settlement, and, (3) in the types of regulatory authority allocated to different institutions—including rulemaking, licensing, monitoring, and enforcement powers.

2. There are common trends in the way in which jurisdictions allocate regulatory powers over their securities markets.

Almost all stock exchanges regulate their markets, in the sense of establishing trading rules, and conducting real-time and post-trade surveillance. Most exchanges license trading members, regulate conduct of business by trading members, and establish and monitor listing standards and issuer disclosures. Similarly, most SROs regulate their markets and members. The distinction between exchanges and SROs is not explored in detail here.

3. All jurisdictions maintain a multifaceted and fragmented regulatory structure for their markets, despite the trend to concentrate supervisory powers in a single regulator.

The regulatory structure within each jurisdiction utilizes a wide variety of regulatory bodies, both public and private, and also a wide variety of regulatory approaches, more or less interventionist, to address different concerns.

4. All the regulatory regimes of jurisdictions with major securities markets are relatively complete.

Specifically, the major securities markets all have a regulatory framework that covers rulemaking, monitoring, and enforcement for all the key functions of securities regulation. These functions may be broadly grouped into nine general categories: prospectus disclosure, securities distribution, listing and ongoing disclosure, issuer corporate governance, market abuse, trading rules, marketplace oversight, brokers and investment firms, and clearing and settlement.

5. The traditional approach of classifying regulatory regimes in jurisdictions with major markets as relying either on self-regulation or on statutory-based regulation implemented by a government agency is not insightful any longer.

In some jurisdictions, central governments shape the regulatory framework to ensure that they maintain a relatively tight grip over securities markets regulation, despite the existence of a specialized administrative agency. Other countries have sought to grant much greater leeway to market infrastructure institutions in structuring their activities, while still ensuring that they fulfill their regulatory obligations. Yet other countries grant a much wider regulatory role to market infrastructure institutions and SROs, while at the same time having government agencies exercise strong oversight of these institutions in respect of their regulatory tasks.

6. None of the jurisdictions with major securities markets removed all regulatory powers from stock exchanges or other market infrastructure institutions in response to demutualization.

CHAPTER FOUR

Regulation and Governance of Market Infrastructure: Global Perspective

THE DEVELOPMENT AND STABILITY of national financial markets have become two paramount goals in most countries' strategies for sustainable economic growth, and the regulation and governance of market infrastructure institutions are now thought essential components of such strategies. This chapter examines a unique set of assessments of securities markets and their regulation, from countries around the world, in order to provide a global perspective on policymakers' viewpoints about the regulation and governance of market infrastructure institutions.[1] The assessments were undertaken as part of an initiative called the Financial Sector Assessment Program (FSAP), implemented jointly by the International Monetary Fund (IMF) and the World Bank.[2] Each assessment evaluates the extent to which a country's securities markets regulatory regime reflects internationally recognized standards. The assessments prepared for the FSAP since its inception in 1999 up until 2006 are analyzed. Together they provide insights on three topics of key relevance here: how exchanges, CCPs, and CSDs are regulated and governed globally; official perceptions on the optimal way of regulating markets and market infrastructure institutions; and the assumptions that are often made when examining the governance and regulation of market infrastructure institutions.

The chapter is composed of three sections. In the first, the nature of the FSAP and of the assessments undertaken as part of it are examined, and some limitations with both in the context of evaluating the regulation and governance of market infrastructure institutions are noted. The next section contains some observations, drawn from the set of assessments, on the regulation and governance of market infrastructure institutions around the world. Brief conclusions are presented in the last section.

THE FINANCIAL SECTOR ASSESSMENT PROGRAM AND SECURITIES MARKETS ASSESSMENTS

Following the Asian Crisis in 1997, the G7 Finance Ministers identified "a gap in the current international system with respect to surveillance of countries' financial supervisory and regulatory systems," and concluded that "enhanced surveillance in this area would help encourage national authorities to meet international standards and help reduce financial risk."[3] The IMF and the World Bank responded by creating the FSAP in May 1999. At the broadest level, the aims of the program were "to increase the effectiveness of efforts to promote the soundness of financial systems in member countries,"[4] "to reduc[e] the likelihood of crisis and improve[] global financial stability, and to foster[] financial sector development and its contribution to economic growth."[5]

A joint mission by the IMF and the World Bank visits each country participating in the FSAP to assess its financial sector, except for developed countries where assessments are undertaken exclusively by the IMF. The assessments have the following main objectives:[6]

1. To identify the strengths, vulnerabilities and risks of the country's financial system.
2. To determine how key sources of risk and vulnerabilities are managed.
3. To evaluate the observance and implementation of international financial sector standards, codes, and good practices.
4. To ascertain the financial sector's development and technical assistance needs.
5. To help prioritize policy responses.

The mission team produces a range of different outputs for different purposes. Typical outputs include[7]

1. A report to the country's authorities with the mission's findings. This type of report was initially called an FSAP report, and subsequently an aide-mémoire.
2. A volume of detailed assessments of the country's compliance with relevant financial sector standards and codes.
3. One or more additional volumes on selected issues.
4. A summary report of the FSAP, or aide-mémoire, for the Board of the IMF, called a Financial System Stability Assessment (FSSA). FSSAs focus on the strengths, risks, and vulnerabilities in a financial system in a broad macroeconomic and macroprudential context. They examine the likely consequences of alternative macroeconomic policy mixes and exogenous shocks, and the implications of financial sector reforms for financial sector profitability, solvency, and liquidity.
5. A summary report of the FSAP, or aide-mémoire, for the Board of the World Bank, called a Financial Sector Assessment (FSA). FSAs emphasize the main points identified in the FSAP related to developing and strengthening institution-building in a country's financial system.

6. Summaries of the detailed assessments of the country's compliance with relevant financial sector standards and codes, which are referred to as Reports on Observance of Standards and Codes (ROSCs).[8]

Participation in the FSAP by a country is voluntary. It is seen as delivering a range of potential benefits to different types of countries as follows:

The main perceived benefit of the FSAP in high-income countries with global financial systems is that it offers an independent check-up of the health of the financial system, its infrastructure and regulatory framework from an international perspective. In low- and medium-income countries, the FSAP is also seen as a tool that helps identify gaps and issues that need to be addressed to develop a more diversified, competitive and inclusive financial sector.[9]

As of April 2006, assessments had been undertaken of 108 countries. Table 13 presents a list of the countries that had participated, or planned to participate, in the FSAP as of October 2005. An assessment program was also established in 2001 for offshore centers. It is much the same as the FSAP, but tailored to offshore jurisdictions. Twenty-seven reports on offshore centers had been completed as of April 2006.

The focus of the FSAP has evolved over time. One gradual change has been that the perceived importance of nonbank financial institutions in a country's financial sector compared with that of the banking sector has grown. The reason for this, as explained by the IMF in examining development issues with regards to the FSAP, was that although nonbank financial institutions and markets had typically played a small role in the economies of developing countries, "in the medium- to long-term, ... nonbank financial institutions have been characterized as a spare wheel which can prevent excessive reliance on banking from making a financial system vulnerable. ... Thus, development motives call for a strong nonbank financial sector."[10] Two sets of internationally recognized standards and codes relevant for the regulation and supervision of market infrastructure institutions have been used: the "Objectives and Principles of Securities Regulation" prepared by IOSCO, and the "Recommendations for Securities Settlement Systems" jointly prepared by the CPSS and the Technical Committee of IOSCO.[11]

As of 2006, IOSCO identified three overarching objectives of securities regulation: (1) the protection of investors; (2) ensuring that markets are fair, efficient, and transparent; and (3) the reduction of systemic risk.[12] (These objectives were in the process of being revised as of mid-2010). IOSCO also specified 30 principles that needed to be implemented in order to deliver these objectives. The principles are grouped into eight

TABLE 13

FSAP: Completed and Ongoing/Planned (in italics) per Fiscal Year (as of October 2005)[1]

2000	2001	2002	2003	2004	2005	2006
			Initial FSAPs			
Cameroon	Armenia	Barbados	Algeria	Austria	Albania	Australia
Canada	Croatia	Brazil	Bangladesh	Azerbaijan	Bahrain	Bosnia and Herzegovina
Colombia	Czech Republic	Bulgaria	Bolivia	Chile	Belarus	Brunei Darussalam
El Salvador	Dominican Republic	Costa Rica	Germany	ECCU	Belgium	Denmark
Estonia	Finland	Egypt	Honduras	Ecuador	Greece	Fiji
Hungary	Georgia	Gabon	Hong Kong	France	Italy	Guyana
India	Ghana	Korea	Japan	Jordan	Madagascar	Jamaica
Iran	Guatemala	Lithuania	Kyrgyz Republic	Kenya	Mauritania	Montenegro
Ireland	Iceland	Luxembourg	Malta	Kuwait	Norway	Namibia
Kazakhstan	Israel	Morocco	Mauritius	Macedonia	Paraguay	Portugal
Lebanon	Latvia	Nigeria	Mozambique	Moldova	Rwanda	San Marino
South Africa	Mexico	Philippines	Oman	Netherlands	Serbia	Spain
	Peru	Russia	Romania	New Zealand	Sudan	Turkey
	Poland	Slovak Republic	Singapore	Nicaragua	Trinidad and Tobago	Uruguay
	Senegal	Sri Lanka	Tanzania	Pakistan		
	Slovenia	Sweden		Saudi Arabia		
	Tunisia	Switzerland				
	Uganda	Ukraine				
	United Arab Emirates	United Kingdom				
	Yemen	Zambia				
Total: 12 (pilot countries)	Total: 20	Total: 20	Total: 15	Total: 16	Total: 14	Total: 14 (prelim.)

Grand Total: 111

2000	2001	2002	2003	2004	2005	2006
			FSAP updates			
	Lebanon	Hungary	Iceland	El Salvador	Armenia	Georgia
	South Africa			Ghana	Colombia	Guatemala
				Kazakhstan	Hungary	Iran
				Slovenia	Peru	Ireland
					Senegal	Mexico
					Uganda	Poland
						Tunisia
Total: 0	Total: 2	Total: 1	Total: 1	Total: 4	Total: 6	Total: 7 (prelim.)

Grand Total: 21

Source: This table reproduces a table from IMF, Independent Evaluation Office (2006: 124). Countries have been arranged in alphabetical order. The country names and totals in the table are not exactly the same as those presented on World Bank, Independent Evaluation Group (2006: 43).

categories concerning, respectively, the regulator, self-regulation, enforcement of securities regulation, cooperation in regulation, issuers of securities, collective investment schemes, market intermediaries, and secondary markets.

The specific IOSCO principles relevant for the governance and supervision of market infrastructure institutions and SROs are the following:

Principle 6: The regulatory regime should make appropriate use of self-regulatory organizations (SROs) that exercise some direct oversight responsibility for their respective areas of competence, to the extent appropriate to the size and complexity of the markets.

Principle 7: SROs should be subject to the oversight of the regulator and should observe standards of fairness and confidentiality when exercising powers and delegated responsibilities.

Principle 25: The establishment of trading systems including securities exchanges should be subject to regulatory authorization and oversight.

Principle 26: There should be ongoing regulatory supervision of exchanges and trading systems which should aim to ensure that the integrity of trading is maintained through fair and equitable rules that strike an appropriate balance between the demands of different market participants.

Principle 30: Systems for clearing and settlement of securities transactions should be subject to regulatory oversight, and designed to ensure that they are fair, effective and efficient and that they reduce systemic risk.

The CPSS/IOSCO recommendations "are intended to promote implementation of measures that enhance the safety and efficiency of SSSs and reduce systemic risk."[13] An SSS was defined "broadly to include the full set of institutional arrangements for confirmation, clearance and settlement of securities trades and safekeeping of securities."[14] The CPSS/IOSCO recommendations relevant for the governance and supervision of market infrastructure institutions are the following:

Recommendation 13 *Governance*: Governance arrangements for CSDs and CCPs should be designed to fulfil public interest requirements and to promote the objectives of owners and users.

Recommendation 14 *Access*: CSDs and CCPs should have objective and publicly disclosed criteria for participation that permit fair and open access.

Recommendation 18 *Regulation and Oversight*: Securities settlement systems should be subject to transparent and effective regulation and oversight. Central banks and securities regulators should cooperate with each other and with other relevant authorities.

The people who undertook the securities markets assessments for the FSAP, the assessors, are drawn from IMF and World Bank staff, a pool of consultants, and from IOSCO members. IOSCO's selection process consists of requesting volunteers from member organizations, and selecting the one with the most suitable background, for example, with the right language skills. Assessors have been, for the most part, regulators or ex-regulators. In 2003, IOSCO developed a methodology for assessing the implementation of the principles that prescribed criteria for evaluating compliance with each principle and provided assessors with a grade key.[15] Each recommendation was to be judged according to whether it was "fully implemented," "broadly implemented," "partly implemented," "not implemented," or "not applicable."

Limitations

The IOSCO and CPSS/IOSCO assessments undertaken for the FSAP contain a valuable body of information regarding how countries structure their markets and regulatory regimes, policymakers' recommendations for enhancing market regulation and development, and the assumptions that underpin policymakers' approaches in evaluating markets and regulatory regimes. There are, however, various limitations with the information presented and conclusions reached in the assessments, some of which are general in nature, and others of which are important specifically in the context of an examination of the governance and regulation of market infrastructure institutions. Eight relevant limitations are noted here, as follows:

1. *Limited Time Available for Each Assessment:* Assessors spend only a limited time in any country they are assessing, usually two weeks. They are therefore constrained as to how deep an analysis they can prepare.

2. *Inconsistent Quality:* The quality of assessments has varied considerably.[16] A review of all assessments concluded that the quality was directly related to the experience and skill of the assessor. One-half to two-thirds of assessments were conducted by first-time assessors, and most assessors did not undertake more than one assessment. In order to enhance the quality of assessments, IOSCO introduced a methodology for assessing implementation of the standards in 2003.[17] This appears, however, not to have had a significant impact on the quality or consistency of assessments, further underscoring the conclusion that the individual assessor is the most important variable in influencing an assessment's quality.

3. *Concerns about Candor:* Although the candor of assessments has been thought to be generally satisfactory, there have been instances where it has been thought to be compromised.[18] This may occur for various reasons. The preparation of an FSAP report necessarily requires a dialogue between a country's national authorities and the IMF/World Bank mission team undertaking the assessment.[19] A World Bank evaluation unit noted that both governments and management had sometimes "pressured staff to soften the written messages." There were also concerns about the potentially adverse consequences that could arise if an FSAP document that contained sensitive information about a country's financial sector strategy, or criticism of such a strategy by the IMF or World Bank, was published or leaked.[20] An IMF evaluation unit noted that the language used in FSSAs

> was often very cautious and a franker presentation of key messages would have been useful. Officials of the various standard-setting organizations made a similar point, stressing that they found the overall messages of FSSAs highly informative but often couched in overly technical and oblique language (which some commentators referred to as "Fundese").[21]

4. *Pro-Statutory Regulator Bias:* A common theme running through the IOSCO assessments is a general bias in favor of regulation by a statutory regulator over self-regulation. Two factors may contribute to this. First, the purpose of the assessments is to focus on regulation from the statutory regulator's point of view. Second, assessors are almost always regulators or ex-regulators—and not industry participants, or current or former exchange officials. This bias manifests itself in several ways. There is a strong belief that regulators do not act in a self-interested way, and this seems to block any analysis of whether an exchange or other institution is overregulated, or whether a regulator has the skill and knowledge to make the decisions that it sometimes makes for market infrastructure institutions. There is also a pervasive lack of reflection among assessors about the conflicts of interest that may be present in a statutory regulator, with an assumption that self-regulatory organizations are alone in struggling with such problems. In some cases, an assessor questioned the "cozy" relationship between government, industry, and the regulator, from the point of view of strong regulation, but generally assessors did not question whether a statutory regulator had the skill or ability to make relevant market decisions.

5. *Greater Focus on Stability Than Development:* There has been a tendency for assessors to place a greater focus on stability, to be achieved by regulation, than on development. Two factors, in addition to the fact

that most assessors have a regulatory background, may contribute to this bias. First, as an evaluation unit of the IMF noted,

> In contrast to the more comprehensive use of various indicators and assessment tools for financial sector stability, most FSAPs still present a more limited analysis of financial development issues including access to financial services. Tools for the analysis of such issues remain less well developed.[22]

Second, it is much harder to develop a market than to ensure that the regulation of a market satisfies international standards, at least in appearance. The IOSCO assessments have sometimes been criticized as box-ticking exercises, where countries and assessors seek to ensure that the relevant IOSCO criteria are satisfied on paper, at the potential expense of ensuring that regulation is applied by a country that is appropriate and proportionate for its stage of development.

The difficulties of making recommendations for market development are illustrated in a weakness identified with various FSAP assessments:

> Many FSAPs have significant shortcomings as a platform for organizing follow-up TA [i.e., technical assistance], reflecting insufficient prioritization of recommendations and sense of sequencing as well as limited judgments on implementation capacity.[23]

The bias in favor of regulation over development is evident in the "more regulation is better" recommendations that are often made in assessments. There is rarely a discussion as to whether the development of the market or exchange is affected by regulatory burdens, while there is much analysis regarding the need to "tighten up" regulation. In one very small market, the assessor suggested that bringing in "best practice" listing standards from developed markets was burdensome to local companies, and would have a detrimental effect on market development, but this was an unusual report.

6. No Direct Focus on Governance: The template used for the IOSCO assessments does not focus directly on the governance of market infrastructure institutions. Governance arrangements are therefore often not explicitly mentioned in an assessment, or if they are, the assessor may not express an opinion about whether they are adequate or not. Assessors tend to look at the regulator's or government's role in the governance of market infrastructure institutions, rather than at governance more generally. If the government or regulator does have a role in the governance of a market infrastructure institution, the assessments often analyze whether or not such a role is effective. If the government or regulator has no such role, the governance of market infrastructure institutions is typically ignored. Assessors do not often comment on the performance of market infrastructure institutions other than as regulators. Where market infrastructure institutions are regarded as underperforming, recommendations are often made for improving supervision, or for bringing in more comprehensive legislation or better enforcement, but few assessments contain recommendations on improved governance generally.

7. *Out of Date:* The FSAP assessments can become dated, especially in a rapidly changing environment. The FSAP started in 1999, and an average of about 16 FSAP assessments per year have been undertaken since then. With 185 member countries of the IMF and World Bank, and assuming that each country chooses to participate in the program, it will take over 10 years to undertake assessments of all countries. The FSAP reports on the Eastern Europe accession countries appear particularly dated, as they were among the first countries to be assessed, over the period 1999 to 2002, and have changed a great deal in the interim.

8. *Confidentiality:* Most of the outputs of the FSAP reports are confidential. As participation by a country in the FSAP is voluntary, national authorities are free to decide whether or not to publish any of the written outputs of an FSAP. The full FSAP report or aide-mémoire is published only very rarely.[24] More frequently, countries may decide to publish the associated FSSA, FSA, or ROSCs. These, however, do not contain the detailed assessments of countries' compliance with relevant financial sector standards and codes.

OBSERVATIONS

This section contains some observations about the regulation and governance of market infrastructure institutions around the world, based on an analysis of 78 full IOSCO assessments undertaken for the FSAP.[25] Information has also been obtained from some CPSS/IOSCO assessments, and from some relatively limited experience at the IMF with technical assistance projects in the financial sector. The countries assessed come from all regions and income levels in the world.[26] Given the confidential nature of the full IOSCO assessments, the analysis presented here either discusses information that is in the public domain, or draws generic lessons without referring to specific countries, or, if an example from a specific country is employed that is not in the public domain, presents the information without revealing the identity of the country.

Observations are presented on five interrelated issues: (1) the role of market infrastructure institutions; (2) the use, definition, and merits of self-regulation; (3) the governance of market infrastructure institutions; (4) demutualization; and (5) regulation and governance. The observations seek to reflect the factual information presented in the assessments, assessors' views on relevant issues, and also key assumptions underlying assessors' approaches.

Role of Market Infrastructure Institutions

There was almost universal consensus among jurisdictions that some form of exchange was needed in their country, no matter how small the economy. Only a tiny minority of the countries assessed—such as the offshore centers of Liechtenstein and Monaco—did not utilize market infrastructure institutions. The functions and structure of these organizations did, however, differ widely across jurisdictions. In Bhutan, for example, where they were only 65 trades annually and 16 listed companies, the exchange played an important role as the center of the nonbank financial system, the depository of ownership and price information, and the only source of market information. Bhutan had no natural locus for a capital market: there were no brokerage firms, and market activity was carried out through two banks. There were no law firms and no accountants. There were, however, interested investors and companies seeking capital. Without the exchange, no secondary market would be possible. In this low-capacity environment, the only skills for guiding companies through an issuance, for handling investor inquiries and complaints, and for educating government on the functioning of a secondary market, existed among the exchange staff. The exchange also possessed the only platform for communication between issuers and investors, or among investors.

It was common for countries to overinvest in systems, and to build exchanges with a broad functionality and large capacity, even though there was little trading. Although it was clear in some countries that the exchange would never recover its costs of operation because the market was so small, maintaining the operation of the exchange was seen as a reasonable expense given its broader public role. In other jurisdictions, however, where very costly systems had been established in small markets, such nonrecoverable expenses were not seen as justified by the wider role the exchange might play in the economy.

In many small economies, the exchange and clearing and settlement systems were created by government in order to further the development of the market. Their creation often preexisted any trading volume or listings. In Poland, for example, the Warsaw Stock Exchange was originally 90% owned by the government, with 10% owned by industry. In Lithuania and Estonia, similar structures were put in place until the exchanges became fully private exchanges, and subsequently part of a larger regional business grouping. In Jordan, the exchange and central depository were created and delegated responsibilities by statute. No business case was prepared for building the exchange, there was no "organic" growth of the exchange from off-exchange trading, and the industry did not band together to create the exchange. In some countries with even newer exchanges, the regulator, rather than the government, created the exchange and remained closely connected with it, such as in Kuwait and Oman. Even in larger economies, some exchanges and other market infrastructure institutions had their origins as publicly established institutions.

Some regional differences were apparent in the way market infrastructure institutions had been established and developed. In the Middle East, where most markets were very new, market infrastructure institutions were, almost without exception, creations of government, and most remained almost an arm of government. In emerging market countries in Asia, there were close connections between government, the regulator, and the exchange, even in countries with a long history of functioning markets, such as India. In Indonesia and the Philippines, regulators and the executives of the exchanges and clearing and settlement systems generally worked very closely together in discussing and formulating policy decisions concerning market development, even if they did not always agree. In the larger Latin American countries, market infrastructure institutions preceded government policy and regulation, and tended to operate quite independently from government policy. In Argentina and Brazil, for example, exchanges existed long before regulation and had not been nurtured into being by a close relationship with the regulator. The result was that exchanges had active but sometimes difficult relationships with their regulators.

Participation by a government or regulator in an exchange was sometimes seen by assessors as impeding both effective regulation and the development of the market as a business. A governmental entity was regarded as lacking the ability to operate a market, which might be better undertaken by the private sector or industry, and also as more likely to avoid setting a high standard of regulation, if it perceived strong regulation could be a hindrance to market development. Two core difficulties often faced by exchanges with close government or regulatory involvement were that they were micromanaged by the government or regulator, and that, if the exchange was an SRO, the distinction between the regulator and the SRO, or the Ministry of Finance and the SRO, was often blurred.

In many countries the exchange was granted a monopoly as a deliberate public policy choice. In some such countries, the assessor noted that given the size of the market, a monopoly was appropriate, but in others the assessor concluded that a rule allowing for another exchange or trading system to establish itself in the jurisdiction would improve markets by introducing competition. Countries with very small markets were often loathe to admit more than one exchange into the market for fear of market fragmentation.

There were a number of developing and emerging market countries with more than one exchange. This was the case for some smaller markets, including Bangladesh, Chile, Croatia, Indonesia, Pakistan, and the Ukraine, as well as some larger emerging markets like Argentina, Brazil, China, and Russia. While the presence of more than one exchange might suggest healthy competition, which could keep trading fees low and promote innovation, in small markets more than one exchange was often thought to impose too big an overhead cost on the industry—both in terms of infrastructure and regulatory costs, and in terms of fragmented liquidity. In one country with a very small market, the assessor concluded that the cost of regulating a number of exchanges was too great, and was causing regulatory resources to be spread too thin. In another country with a weak regulatory system, the assessor concluded that the lack of regulatory capacity at one exchange undermined the credibility of the other exchange, so that competition led to a "race to the bottom" in terms of regulatory standards.

In stronger markets, some exchanges that had begun as government-created and sponsored institutions had grown into more independent institutions that were able to generate sufficient funding internally and even make a profit. This was the case, for example, in Korea, where the exchange was created by government statute, but grew into a profitable ongoing business. In other, smaller, jurisdictions, such as Labuan or Bhutan, the government-created exchange remained small and underused.

Many market infrastructure institutions in developing and emerging markets struggled for funding. The volume of trading and listing on exchanges did not generate sufficient fees to keep them going financially, and they thus relied on direct or indirect public funding or government subsidy to survive. The search for new sources of revenue was a constant preoccupation. One concern that arose from the involvement of governments in exchange development was that in many small markets governments attempted to construct policy in a way that generated revenue for the exchanges, or at least were under pressure to do so. For example, it was not uncommon in developing and emerging market countries for there to be proposals to list treasury bills or other money market instruments on the exchange, as a means of channeling business toward the exchange, whether or not this was in the interest of market development or monetary operations. It appears from the assessments that these strategies were not generally successful: "forced" development of exchanges through listing of debt or money market instruments did not appear to work. Three factors that did appear to give exchanges a successful boost were the removal of taxation impediments to trading or raising capital in the secondary market, allowing foreign investment into the market, that simply improved general economic conditions. Clearing and settlement systems did not tend to have the same concerns about funding, since their services were necessary in the primary market, and this generally provided sufficient revenues to support their continued operation.

The assessments appeared to show that market infrastructure institutions functioned better in wealthier countries than they did in poorer countries. For example, there were fewer settlement failures and market disruptions in wealthier markets. There did not, however, appear to be any significant regional differences in market infrastructure institution performance.

In most countries market infrastructure institutions, and particularly exchanges, acted as the voice of the industry vis-à-vis new policy and rules. This was seen as a vital role. There were often no other active industry groups, and exchanges were seen as having an interest in market development, as well as sound regulation, even if they were not always in step with the regulator's views.

A major issue for exchanges and other market infrastructure institutions in emerging market countries was a lack of capacity. There was often a lack of understanding and skill in staff and management of the exchange. and this, depending on its severity, led to a lack of effective operation and a lack of credibility as an operator of a fair market or as a regulator, or both.

The assessments make clear that the operation of market infrastructure institutions could not be separated entirely from public policy, even in the most robust and developed markets, although the connection sometimes proved difficult both for regulators and for the institutions themselves. This tension, namely whether an exchange was simply a commercial enterprise operating a market, or whether it also served the public good, was evident in many jurisdictions' approaches to regulation and to governance, and also ran through many assessments.

In developing and emerging market countries there was less reluctance to view privately owned market infrastructure institutions as being public utilities—in the sense of having an obligation to serve the public good. Public policy development frequently directly addressed their role and activity. A key reason for this was that exchanges were seen as having critical importance in developing markets. This was particularly evident in markets where the exchange or clearing and settlement system had been created by the government or regulator, as compared to countries where such institutions began as businesses or as creations of the financial community. The legal framework for market infrastructure institutions in some countries supported this approach. Often the legal framework for the exchange or clearing and settlement system was established in a dedicated piece of legislation dealing only with the exchange or clearing and settlement system, which was separate from the general securities law. The exchange or clearing and settlement system was thus seen as clearly having a defined public role, as opposed to being simply a regulated entity.

Self-Regulation: Its Use, Definition, and Merits

The use of self-regulation varied considerably from country to country. Correlations between where it was employed and particular types of legal systems or cultures were hard to identify; there were no discernable regional trends, and each regulatory system usually had strong historical and domestic roots. It was evident from the assessments, however, that most market infrastructure institutions had some regulatory responsibilities, though of different kinds. Many countries relied on exchanges or SROs to carry out detailed regulation of intermediaries, including business, sales, and market conduct regulation. Where an exchange or another SRO did not regulate intermediaries, such regulation was often incomplete or nonexistent. Regulators might impose basic capital requirements, but often did not conduct detailed intermediary regulation.

Regulatory responsibilities were delegated to market infrastructure institutions either directly in legislation, as in Kenya, where the statute gave the exchange direct responsibility, or indirectly through delegation by the regulator. In Turkey, the Istanbul Stock Exchange was created by statute, and its chairman was appointed by the government, in the same way as the head of the statutory regulator. The exchange was heavily relied on to regulate intermediaries and the market, and was given this responsibility in its constituting statute, rather than as a delegation by the regulator.

There were relatively few SROs that were not also exchanges or clearing and settlement organizations. Such "stand-alone" SROs were found in Canada, Jordan, the Philippines, and the United States. In Jordan, the SRO was created by statute at the same time as the securities commission. The statute set out its powers, governance structure, and responsibilities. The SRO board was composed of market participants, but the SRO operated under the strictures of the statute. In many jurisdictions there were also informal SROs, which were organizations such as trade associations that effectively carried out some regulatory functions, but were not formally recognized or regulated as SROs.

In some countries, such as Argentina, Brazil, Canada, India, Indonesia, Jordan, the Philippines, and Russia, SRO membership was mandatory for all market intermediaries trading on an exchange, and in a subset of these countries, including Canada and Russia, this requirement extended to market intermediaries that did not trade on exchanges. In a few cases this structure gave rise to abuse, as governance of these institutions was controlled by a few interests that used SRO membership as a means of eliminating competition. Such a situation was sometimes compounded by the regulator's lack of authority or practical ability to enforce its rules.

The FSAP was reviewed in 2002 and again in 2006.[27] In these reviews, it is clear that there was stronger regulation, as measured by compliance with the IOSCO principles, in wealthier countries. This was a consistent trend across all areas of regulation, and across all regions. The strength of regulation appeared to be directly related to the resources available to the regulator and the capacity of its staff. High-income countries had, for example, better licensing and oversight programs for exchanges and clearing and settlements systems, and more complete legislation; lower-income countries tended to have less complete legislation, and a lack of proper oversight, usually related to a lack of resources and a lack of authority.

At a general level, there was broad implicit agreement in the assessments that an SRO was an organization that took on some regulatory responsibilities, but was neither a statutory regulator, such as a securities commission, nor a branch or department of government. Beyond this general agreement, however, widely different and inconsistent views were presented about what constituted an SRO. Some assessors believed that any regulatory function carried out by a market infrastructure institution should be viewed as self-regulation. The definition of what constituted a regulatory function was itself also open to controversy, however, as all market infrastructure institutions had to set some kind of operating rules for their users, but the question of which of these should be considered self-regulatory in nature was debatable. Some countries, generally those in Europe, were adamant that their exchanges not be considered SROs, even though the exchanges carried out some regulatory functions, such as listing or surveillance. Some assessors agreed with this analysis, but others did not. Some assessors did not consider an exchange that regulated its member brokers or users, but was not formally delegated such power by the statutory regulator, to be an SRO. Many traditional and mutually owned exchanges and clearing and settlement systems were considered SROs, but there appeared to be some reluctance to consider demutualized, privately funded, and privately operated institutions as SROs. Some assessors also acknowledged the existence of "informal" SROs that were not formally delegated responsibility as an SRO, but were relied on in practice as part of the regulatory system.

Two fundamental and contradictory themes concerning self-regulation were evident across the assessments. On the one hand, the use of market infrastructure institutions as regulators was generally welcomed by assessors, and in fact normally taken for granted. The regulatory capacity of market infrastructure institutions was often taken to be crucial to a regulatory system. On the other hand, many assessors believed that market infrastructure institutions, whether mutually or privately owned, were hopelessly self-interested, and therefore unable to carry out serious regulation.

In some countries, an assessor was critical of the lack of delegation to the exchange of regulatory responsibilities, where the regulator did not have sufficient capacity to carry out regulation but would not delegate, which then resulted in gaps in regulation. Where market infrastructure institutions failed to carry out adequate regulation, the assessor often saw this as a failure of the supervising regulator. An extreme example of this was in the Philippines, where corruption at the regulator was, in part, blamed for the failure of the exchange to enforce its rules. The failure of a supervising regulator was usually attributed in assessments to a lack of capacity in the quality and skill set of its staff. This raised a difficult problem where on the one hand a regulator did not have the capacity to oversee appropriately a delegation of regulation to an exchange or SRO, but on the other hand did not have the capacity to undertake the regulation itself.

Assessors generally favored the inclusion of informal SROs in a country's regulatory framework. A range of reasons were presented for this approach, including the expertise available in such institutions, their relatively close ties with market participants, the belief that industry input into the policymaking process would result in better outcomes, and the view that such trade associations were better placed to police particular aspects of industry activity than other institutions.

Assessors were not critical of the use of stand-alone SROs per se, but did believe that they were suitable primarily for sophisticated and developed markets. The stand-alone model appeared to be expensive and difficult to fund in emerging market countries, in part because of the low profitability of market intermediaries. An inability to manage conflicts of interest also appeared to be a large factor in the lack of success of stand-alone SROs and their limited use. In addition, some regulators were reportedly uncomfortable overseeing a complex environment with both an exchange and a separate SRO, preferring the exchange to carry out relevant regulation.

An important problem in regulatory frameworks often identified was a lack of clarity in the roles and responsibilities of market infrastructure institutions, in both their regulatory and market functions. This appeared particularly relevant in countries where a market infrastructure institution was stronger than the regulator, or was founded before the regulator. Assessors frequently noted that such institutions were "left to their own devices," and this was seen as damaging the public good.

Where there were multiple SROs, an assessor often identified as problems a lack of coordination between the SROs, especially in enforcement, and overlapping regulatory requirements that could burden the industry. Such issues were particularly evident where the SROs had similar mandates, such as when they were all exchanges.

The assessments suggested that there were some governance arrangements that completely ruled out effective regulation. This was thought in particular to be the case when one part of a government, such as the Treasury, Ministry of Finance, or Central Bank, either owned or championed an exchange or central depository, and would not allow the regulator to carry out effective supervision of the institution.

Governance of Market Infrastructure Institutions

The assessments show that the governance structures of exchanges, and other market infrastructure institutions, varied widely across institutions and countries. The same country could have one exchange that was mutually owned and governed by market intermediary members, and another that was privately owned. Most governance structures appeared to be products of historical and current circumstances, and were designed to suit the particular needs of the relevant institution and market in which the institution functioned. There were no evident regional trends. There was, however, one clear difference between developing and emerging markets on the one hand, and developed countries on the other: in developing and emerging market countries there was more direct involvement by the government or the regulator in the governance structures of market infrastructure institutions.

A representative of either the ministry of finance or the regulator often sat on the board of a market infrastructure institution. Typically this was a nonvoting position. The key reason why governance structures often involved government officials or regulators was that the developmental role of the exchange was seen as being complemented by the involvement of the regulator or the government, and public policy was coordinated among these bodies. While such an approach was more commonly a feature of developing and emerging market countries, it was also found in some developed markets. In Austria, for example, the Ministry of Finance participated in all material decisions of the board of the Vienna exchange. In some countries, such as Bhutan, Egypt, and Israel, the central bank was also represented on the board of the exchange. This was even more frequent for clearing and settlement systems, given their close ties to the payment systems overseen by the central bank.

Assessors treated official representation on the boards of market infrastructure institutions in two opposing ways. A minority viewed it as something that unduly interfered in the exchange; more commonly it was seen as something that was desirable for effective oversight. Exchange officials in most countries did not appear critical of such arrangements. In some cases, the exchange relied on the regulator or ministry for funding, or for support in obtaining public funding, and believed the presence of a regulator or ministry official on its board gave the exchange the profile that it needed to ensure such funding. In developing and emerging markets, it may also have been helpful to have such close ties because the exchanges were more dependent on government policy than in more developed markets. Exchange officials complained more frequently about a lack of adequate skill at the regulator, a lack of understanding of their business, and slowness of decision-making at the regulator than about representation of a ministry or regulator on their governing boards.

Requirements that mandated issuer or investor representation on the board of a market infrastructure institution were rare, although they were present in a few countries, including Senegal. Sometimes seats on the board of an exchange were allocated to representatives of other market infrastructure institutions, such as the national clearing and settlement system.

There was rarely a requirement for independent directors on the board of market infrastructure institutions. A certain number of independent directors were, however, required for some of the largest exchanges, with Slovenia being an unusual example where all board members were independent. A requirement for independent board members was also not always mentioned in the assessments. In developing and emerging market countries, there appeared to be little attention paid to the role of independent directors, or any discussion of what independence might mean in the relevant context. The definition or understanding of independence across jurisdictions was also quite inconsistent. Some jurisdictions considered a member of government, or an ex officio board member who represented the central bank or another public agency, to be independent. In others, independence was more narrowly defined to mean someone not from government or industry or related to the exchange operator.

Assessors did not necessarily view the presence of independent directors on the board of a market infrastructure institution as solving particular governance problems. In one country, the exchange was seen as performing very badly, and not able to overcome its inherent conflicts of interest, even though the board had a majority of independent directors. The independent directors were viewed as lacking the necessary skill and authority to govern the exchange well. The mere fact they were independent did not mean that they were able to overcome the exchange's inability to enforce compliance with regulation against member brokers. The assessor also concluded that the exchange's inability to regulate properly was the result of a lack of effective oversight by the regulator. The presence of independent directors was thus not seen as a substitute for a strong statutory regulator. In another report, however, the assessor did find that the poor performance of the exchange in executing its regulatory responsibilities was directly linked to its not having any independent directors on its board. In this country, a small number of intermediaries controlled the exchange, and effectively acted to block new memberships. The market itself was small and underdeveloped, and there was little incentive to carry out credible self-regulation. The assessor believed that only if governance of the exchange was opened up to include "outsiders" would the culture of the exchange and the market change. A similar viewpoint was also presented for a few countries with larger emerging markets.

While board composition and the relationship between an exchange and its regulator or government was sometimes discussed, it was very rare for an assessment to consider other aspects of governance. Only one assessment looked at how the board of an exchange handled conflicts of interest, and how its code of conduct functioned. Where the effectiveness of the market infrastructure institution was related to its governance structure in reports, there was always a mention of the clash of interests between big, bank-owned brokers and smaller independent brokers. This was a common theme across countries. No one solution, however, was recommended to address this governance problem.

One underlying concern about governance in most assessments was its relationship to fair access to the exchange or clearing and settlement system. Even when governance was not mentioned directly, there was often a discussion about fair access. In some countries, concerns were expressed that powerful participants in the market that dominated the exchange, or clearing and settlement system, effectively shut out new or smaller participants. In other countries, the requirement that users own shares of the market, and the lack of available shares, acted as a barrier to entry for new market participants. Participants were able to set standards for entry into membership, and therefore access to the market, that were advantageous to the existing membership and precluded competition. Requirements for membership were thus used as an anticompetitive tool and were not necessarily related to regulatory or market operation standards. Self-interest on broker-controlled boards was blamed in a few assessments for fragmentation and a lack of efficiency among markets and clearing and settlement systems. An assessor in one country with such a problem described the broker-owners of the country's market infrastructure institutions as a "cartel" that needed to be broken up before the market could flourish.

There appeared to be a link between the poor functioning of a governance structure and the poor functioning of the market infrastructure institution. In assessments, poor governance was linked to poor performance, and often poor performance was what prompted a discussion of the governance structure in the first place. However, the assessments provided no clear answer to the question of what was an optimal governance structure.

Demutualization

The trend of demutualization among stock exchanges was evident across all types of countries—developing, emerging, and developed. It was seen in many places as a means of breaking the hold that some broker interests had on policy—whether over regulation or over market development.

In the Philippines, a lack of credibility of the exchange, which was perceived to have been caused by the concentration of its ownership among brokers, rose to scandal level in 1999, and resulted in a forced demutualization. A market manipulation scandal gave rise to sharp criticism of the Philippines Stock Exchange (PSE) and also of the statutory regulator, the Securities and Exchange Commission, and prompted a number of changes. The assessment found that

> the PSE has been criticized for being a cozy club of member brokers at the expense of their client investors ... the PSE's SRO license was once suspended by the SEC [following the scandal and] ... the demutualization was made a requirement and a majority of directors of its board had to be non-brokers. The PSE implemented the demutualization and associated reform of its board ... [and] by doing so successfully persuaded the SEC to restore its SRO status.[28]

Demutualization was in fact made a requirement in the securities legislation.[29] The assessment also noted that the "concentration of the ownership [of the PSE] appears to be making it difficult for the SCCP [the Securities Clearing Corporation of the Philippines—a subsidiary of the exchange] to act against the business interest of the participating brokers."[30] A number of brokers were "habitually" failing to settle trades, and efforts by the PSE and SCCP to impose discipline were mixed. The assessment concluded that "diversification of the PSE's ownership by going public needs to be carried out as soon as possible" so that the market could regain lost credibility.

In India, a connection was drawn between the governance structure of a mutually owned exchange, the Bombay Stock Exchange (BSE), with a board consisting solely of brokers, and a lack of credibility in regulating the market. The BSE did not have regulatory responsibility beyond market surveillance and listings. Two serious market scandals resulted in a change of governance structure, with regulators forcing the BSE to demutualize in order to improve its ability to regulate the market. The National Stock Exchange (NSE) in India was created partially in response to this lack of credibility at the BSE. Although the NSE's board was also dominated by member-owners, these members were large state-owned financial institutions rather than just brokers.

In other countries, authorities regarded removing regulatory responsibilities from the exchange as "breaking a monopoly," or chose not to move regulatory duties to an SRO if it was an exchange, because of its concentration of ownership. Where market infrastructure institutions with self-regulatory functions were totally member-run, there were sometimes problems with brokers violating rules and also with the credibility of the SRO as a regulator. This was usually linked to the exchange's monopoly in the market. The combination of member-ownership and monopoly was seen as detrimental to appropriate regulation.

There was a fairly strong thread of opinion that demutualization or "privatization" of an exchange would make the exchange more difficult to regulate, or would render the exchange unable properly to undertake regulation itself. Without fully exploring the conflicts of interest that existed prior to demutualization, many assessors tended quickly to reach the conclusion that regulation must be moved from the demutualized exchange.

Regulation and Governance

While governance per se was not often discussed directly by assessors, a large amount of attention was devoted to understanding the regulation and oversight of market infrastructure institutions. Indeed, the topics of appropriate regulation and governance were often fused together, so that assessors only considered governance insofar as it effected how exchanges were regulated. Hence the emphasis in assessments on direct regulatory involvement in market infrastructure institutions' boards, with no information given, or sought, as to how governance structures worked otherwise.

Most countries had explicit licensing regimes for market infrastructure institutions. The licensing was often not undertaken by the relevant regulator, but by the ministry of finance or a similar government department. It was usually also not up to the regulator to decide whether competition for an exchange should be allowed. This was typically considered a political decision regarding market development and financial sector policy generally.

Governance requirements normally only formed a minimal part of an exchange's licensing criteria. Many countries required board members and officers to undergo fit and proper tests. In most cases there was no provision for independent directors or representation of particular stakeholders. A requirement for some independent directors did appear, however, to be becoming more common, possibly drawn from the OECD corporate governance principles. Issues of ownership, namely who was allowed to own shares in a market infrastructure institution, and how much they were allowed to own, were also often a concern of licensing requirements. Most regulatory regimes required the owners of an exchange seeking a license to be explicitly approved. Changes of ownership above a de minimis amount also often required notice and approval. There were, however, no mentions in the assessments of restrictions on foreign ownership, although such restrictions did exist in many countries. A number of assessments did mention restrictions on the number of shares any single institution could hold. For example, the Philippines required that the brokerage industry be restricted to no more than 20% ownership in aggregate of the exchange.

There was a consensus, at least in developed countries, that appropriate oversight of market infrastructure institutions by regulators included the right to approve rules, to approve material changes and ownership of the institutions, and to receive in-depth annual reporting. In most jurisdictions, exchanges and other market infrastructure institutions had to comply with ongoing oversight rules, which included submitting new rules for approval to the regulator and submitting daily, monthly, and annual reports. Daily reports were usually operational reports, including volumes, prices, errors, and defaults. Monthly reports summarized daily reports and sometimes included broader management information. Annual reports included financial statements and business planning information.

In some countries an exchange's prudential condition was also monitored. This appeared to be a growing trend among emerging market countries, where capital requirements were applied to exchanges. Capital requirements were designed to give the regulator a tool to monitor the exchange's financial fitness and to prevent a sudden and significant loss. In Morocco and Malta, the public auditor also undertook a prudential audit of the exchange annually, as a check against financial problems at the exchange.

Inspections emerged as a relatively new component of regulatory oversight, but there was no consensus among assessors about whether inspections of exchanges were necessary, or what they should entail. The IOSCO principles suggested that adequate oversight should require regulators to carry out on-site inspections. However, the assessments found that it was a common failing among regulators that inspections were not carried out, and if they were, that they were inadequate. This often appeared to arise as a result of a lack of capacity in both resources and skilled personnel at the regulator. In many cases, assessors found that staff at the regulator had a weak understanding of exchange, clearing, and settlement system operations, and in particular risk management and internal controls.

This failing was not confined to emerging market countries, but was also common in developed countries. For example, an assessment of Sweden in 2002 found that inadequate attention was paid to oversight of risk management in the clearing and settlement system. In particular, it was determined that "the clearing and settlement system [did] not adequately prevent an unwinding in the event of the failure of a participant to meet its obligations," and that the "inadequacy of this system is well-known but [the regulator] has been unable to exercise its supervisory authority to solve the problem."[31] The assessment concluded by pointing to shortcomings in the skill and organization of the regulator, saying that "it is not clear that [the regulator] has developed sufficient supervisory skills to enable it to fully understand and address ... the clearing and settlement system."[32]

One clear trend in emerging market countries was the presence of real-time monitoring of markets at the regulator: many regulators were directly linked into their exchanges' computer system, and could watch market activity in the same way that exchange staff could. This often existed despite a lack of capacity in the regulator, and many other regulatory weaknesses that needed to be addressed, but for which there were no resources. A significant number of assessors agreed with this approach to oversight, and were critical if real-time surveillance was not in place. Another set of assessors, however, believed that such an arrangement was a waste of regulatory resources, and resulted in micromanagement of the exchange. There appeared thus to be some confusion as to whether the proper role of oversight should be to watch over an infrastructure institution's activity continuously, or to apply an audit function.

It was common for regulators to have the right to give an exchange "direction." In some jurisdictions this authority was very broad, while in others it was restricted to circumstances where the exchange had violated the law. Usually there was a "public interest" element to the power, so that the regulator was allowed to order the exchange to carry out a particular action if the public interest required it. There was little discussion in the assessments of the actual use of this power, or of the effects of not having sufficient authority. The focus was on whether the regulator had sufficient power. It appears from the reports that regulators were more likely to use their rule approval powers to resolve outstanding concerns than to initiate rule changes.

In some jurisdictions, however, regulators sometimes did not have the authority to give direction to market infrastructure institutions. This was a common problem in countries in which the exchange was created by statute with a mandate directly from parliament, or operated under a license granted by government, rather than the regulator. Assessors noted that such a situation could create various difficulties for the regulator, and could also be confusing for the market if the regulator had a responsibility to regulate the market, but did not have sufficient power to do so. It could also cause a problem in practice, if not in law, when the regulator had sufficient legal authority, but was undermined by an exchange's relationship with government, or by a relationship between the exchange's members with government, and was thus unable to enforce its authority as a result.

A very few countries, such as New Zealand, employed a light regulatory approach with regards to regulatory oversight of exchanges' rules, using a "non-objection" system. The exchange was allowed to develop rules as it wished, and these were then provided to the Ministry of Finance, which did not have to approve them, but could object to them if necessary. The nature of the New Zealand regulatory system was, however, complicated by the fact that the Australian regulatory system also had a de facto role in the New Zealand regulatory system, as most companies listed in New Zealand were also listed in Australia and subject to Australian regulation, as were most brokerage firms.

In many countries, direct involvement in the governance structure of an exchange was a replacement for, or a complement to, regulation of the exchange. Sometimes the regulator or relevant government ministry was involved at the decision-making level, by being present on the board, as well as at the rule-approval level. In Indonesia, the regulator was represented on the board of both exchanges. In Austria, Croatia, and Egypt, among other countries, the ministry of finance had a direct role in the consideration of all material decisions made by the exchange, including the listing and delisting of securities. In the Czech Republic, the regulator was directly involved in the governance of the Prague Stock Exchange via the presence of a "commissioner" at the exchange, who was appointed by the regulator to attend listing, member, and trading committee meetings. The commissioner had the power to suspend the exchange's powers if it violated the law or relevant regulations, but did not vote at the committees the commissioner attended. The assessor found this to be an effective system of oversight, as the regulator instituted little other oversight, and the exchange was regarded as better resourced and more skilled at regulation than the regulator.

Cross-border exchanges provided a challenge for their regulators, and also presented difficulties for assessors. One weakness of the assessments is that they were undertaken on a national basis, and little attention was paid to regional or cross-border functions. The assessments showed that exchanges that operated on a cross-border basis could be difficult to fit within an existing regulatory framework. In some cases where exchanges were regulated by more than one regulatory body, an MOU between the market infrastructure institution and the relevant regulators had been put in place. This was the case in the Nordic countries supervising OMX, in the European countries (Belgium, France, Netherlands, Portugal, and the UK) supervising Euronext, and in Canada, where exchanges were subject to regulation by a number of provincial regulators. These MOUs set out how regulation would be coordinated, and how the regulators would communicate among themselves and with the exchange. Typically the MOUs also designated a lead regulator. In the case of Euronext, for example, the lead regulator designation was done by function, with the French regulator being primarily responsible for market surveillance. In the case of Canada, the lead regulator was designated by institution, so the Toronto Stock Exchange was regulated primarily by the Ontario Securities Commission, and the Montreal Exchange by the Quebec regulator. Under both agreements, working parties of staff were set up to deal with both operational issues, such as inspections, and policy issues. All regulators had the right to participate in decisions through the lead regulator.

Formal coordination by regulators was seen in assessments as a positive step in reducing regulatory burdens for exchanges, but it was also sometimes deemed too early to conclude how effective such agreements were in practice. The smaller regulators in such regulatory coordination groups often felt that they had little influence in practice over the exchange, and were at the mercy of the larger country regulators. There was a great deal of interest in emerging markets in exploring cross-border relationships as a means of bolstering market interest, and assessors and technical assistance advisors were often asked how these agreements worked in practice.

Conclusions

This chapter examines a unique set of assessments of securities markets and their regulation from countries around the world in order to provide a global perspective on policymaker's viewpoints about the regulation and governance of market infrastructure institutions. The assessments were undertaken as part of the FSAP, implemented jointly by the IMF and the World Bank. The assessments prepared for the FSAP since its inception in 1999 up until 2006 are analyzed. Each assessment evaluates the extent to which a country's securities markets' regulatory regime reflects the internationally recognized standards for the regulation of securities markets and exchanges prepared by IOSCO. Some assessments also examine the extent to which a country's SSS satisfies the recommendations jointly prepared by CPSS/IOSCO.

While recognizing the limitations of the assessments, observations are nevertheless drawn from them on five interrelated issues:

1. *Role of Market Infrastructure Institutions:* There was almost universal consensus among jurisdictions that some form of exchange was needed in their country, no matter how small the economy. In many small economies, the exchange and clearing and settlement systems were created by government in order to further the development of the market. Participation by a government or regulator in an exchange was sometimes seen by assessors as impeding both the development of the market as a business and effective regulation. Two core difficulties often faced by exchanges with close government or regulatory involvement were that they were micromanaged by the government or regulator, and that, if the exchange was an SRO, the distinction between the regulator and the SRO or the ministry of finance and the SRO, was often blurred.

In most countries, exchanges acted as the voice of the industry vis-à-vis new policy and rules. A major issue for exchanges and other market infrastructure institutions in emerging market countries was a lack of capacity. Many exchanges in developing and emerging markets also struggled for funding, and relied on public subsidy to survive.

The assessments make clear that the operation of market infrastructure institutions could not be separated entirely from public policy, even in developed markets. There was a tension over whether an exchange was simply a commercial enterprise operating a market, or whether it also served the public good. There was less reluctance in developing and emerging market countries than in developed market countries to view privately owned market infrastructure institutions as being public utilities—in the sense of have an obligation to serve the public good.

2. *Self-Regulation:* The use of self-regulation varied considerably from country to country. Correlations between where it was employed and particular types of legal systems or cultures were hard to identify, there were no discernable regional trends, and each regulatory system usually had strong historical and domestic roots. Most market infrastructure institutions, however, had some regulatory responsibilities, though of different kinds. There were relatively few SROs that were not also exchanges

or clearing and settlement organizations. In many jurisdictions there were also informal SROs that effectively carried out some regulatory functions, but were not formally recognized as SROs. In some countries, SRO membership was mandatory for all market intermediaries trading on the exchange.

At a general level, there was broad implicit agreement in the assessments that an SRO was an organization that took on some regulatory responsibilities, but was neither a statutory regulator nor a branch of government. Beyond this general agreement, however, widely different and inconsistent views were presented about what constituted an SRO.

Two fundamental and contradictory themes concerning self-regulation were evident across the assessments. On the one hand, the use of market infrastructure institutions as regulators was generally welcomed and normally taken for granted. The regulatory capacity of market infrastructure institutions was often taken to be crucial to a regulatory system. On the other hand, many assessments argued that market infrastructure institutions, whether mutually or privately owned, were hopelessly self-interested, and therefore unable to carry out serious regulation.

An important problem in regulatory frameworks often identified was a lack of clarity in the roles and responsibilities of market infrastructure institutions, in both their regulatory and market functions. Where there were multiple SROs, two problems were often identified: a lack of co-ordination between the SROs, and overlapping regulatory requirements that could burden the industry. The assessments suggested that there were some governance arrangements that completely ruled out effective regulation: in particular when one part of government championed an exchange or central depository and did not allow the regulator to supervise it effectively.

3. *Governance of Market Infrastructure Institutions:* Governance models of market infrastructure institutions varied widely across institutions and countries. There were no evident regional trends. One clear difference between developing and emerging markets on the one hand, and developed countries on the other, was that in developing and emerging market countries there was more direct involvement by the government or the regulator in the governance structures of market infrastructure institutions. Assessors treated official representation on the boards of market infrastructure institutions in two opposing ways. A minority viewed it as something that unduly interfered in the exchange. More commonly it was seen as desirable for effective oversight. Exchange officials in most countries did not appear critical of such arrangements, although they did complain about a lack of adequate skill and understanding and a slowness of decision-making at the regulator.

Requirements that mandated issuer or investor representation, or independent directors, on the board of a market infrastructure institution were rare. The definition of independence across jurisdictions was quite inconsistent. For the most part, assessors did not view the presence of independent directors as solving particular governance problems, although in some jurisdictions, it was seen as important, as it opened up the governance of an exchange to "outsiders."

Where the effectiveness of the market infrastructure institution was related to its governance structure in assessments, there was always a mention of the clash of interests between big, bank-owned brokers and smaller independent brokers. Another underlying concern about governance in most assessments was its relationship to fair access to the exchange or clearing and settlement system. A common worry was that some powerful participants in a market dominated an exchange or a clearing and settlement system and could thus restrict competition in a variety of ways.

4. *Demutualization:* The demutualization of stock exchanges was evident across all types of countries—developing, emerging, and developed. It was seen in many places as a means of breaking the hold that some broker interests had on policy—whether over regulation or market development. The combination of member-ownership and monopoly was seen as detrimental to appropriate regulation. There was, however, a fairly strong thread of opinion that demutualization of an exchange would make the exchange more difficult to regulate, or would render the exchange unable properly to undertake regulation itself, as a result of conflicts of interest.

5. *Regulation and Governance:* Most countries had licensing regimes for market infrastructure institutions. Governance requirements, however, normally only formed a minimal part of such licensing criteria. Many countries required board members and officers to undergo "fit and proper" tests. Issues of ownership, namely who was allowed to own shares in a market infrastructure institution, and how much they were allowed to own, were also often a concern of licensing requirements. In many countries, direct involvement by the government or regulator in the governance structure of an exchange was a replacement for, or a complement to, regulation of the exchange. This was sometimes viewed by assessors as an effective system of oversight, if the regulator instituted little other oversight, and the exchange was regarded as better resourced and more skilled at regulation than the statutory regulator.

Governance of Market Infrastructure Institutions: A Snapshot

THE AIM OF THIS CHAPTER is to survey how infrastructure institutions in the equity markets around the world—namely exchanges, CCPs, and CSDs—were governed in 2006. As has been widely recognized, the governance of stock exchanges has been radically transformed over recent years.[1] Exchange demutualization began in 1993 when the Stockholm Stock Exchange demutualized.[2] Prior to this time, most stock exchanges had been nonprofit mutual organizations run by their members since their inception, or in some instances organizations controlled by the state. By December 2007, however, 76% of the WFE's member exchanges that responded to a survey it conducted (namely 39 out of 51 respondent exchanges), operated on a for-profit basis.[3] Over the same period a range of new exchanges were created in both emerging and developed markets, many of which were established as private companies, but some of which were founded, controlled, and owned by various governments.

The governance of clearing and settlement entities has also changed over the recent period. Many automated clearing and settlement institutions were developed and owned largely by exchanges, often in response to a crisis when volumes rose that the existing structures could not handle. Some markets, however, opted to create CSDs that were controlled by collectives of users, typically the commercial banks who were the major participants in the relevant settlement and custody businesses. Some central banks have also been involved in the governance and operation of their national CSDs, primarily because of the links between their countries' settlement systems and payment systems.

This chapter examines and surveys a database of global exchanges and their governance as of 2006 prepared for this book. Although there were some changes in both the list of exchanges and the manner in which they were governed over the period 2006–9, they are not substantive to the results of the survey and are noted in the text where appropriate. The chapter is composed of three major sections. In the first, the data employed in the survey are described. The analysis is presented in the second section. Conclusions are presented in the last section.

DATA

In order to undertake a survey of how infrastructure institutions in the equity markets around the world were governed, a database was constructed identifying the stock exchanges in the world, and their associated clearing and settlement institutions, and values for five key parameters relevant to assess the governance of these institutions were determined: (1) how they are controlled, (2) whether they operate for profit or not, (3) their size, (4) their region, and (5) their level of development.[4]

Scope

The stock exchanges examined for the analysis were the members of the WFE as of 2006. The WFE has three levels of membership: Full Members, Affiliate Members, and Corresponding Members. Full members have been through an acceptance process that includes an objective assessment of their regulatory and operational capacities.[5] Corresponding and affiliate stock exchanges are exchanges that either do not seek full WFE membership or do not comply with the WFE's standards and have therefore not achieved full membership.[6] At the time of the analysis, the WFE had 51 Full Members, 6 Affiliate Members, and 33 Corresponding Members, for a total of 90 exchanges.[7]

The Full Members represented the vast bulk of the world's stock exchanges by business—some 97% of global equity turnover in 2005. Corresponding exchanges represented a total of 2.8% of 2005 global equity turnover (of which Saudi Arabia comprised three-quarters), and Affiliate exchanges represented 0.37%. There were a large number of other stock exchanges in the world in addition to the WFE members; however the difficulty of obtaining relevant information about these smaller exchanges made it difficult to include them in this survey.[8]

The clearing and settlement entities analyzed here are those institutions used by participants to clear and settle trades executed on the WFE member stock exchanges. There was a wide variety among such institutions, but these differences were ignored, and they were simply categorized into two broad catchall groupings: "clearing institutions" or "CCPs," and "settlement institutions" or "CSDs." In some instances, more than one stock exchange was associated with the same clearing or settlement institution.

Control Model

In order to provide an overview of the control models adopted by the market infrastructure institutions in the sample, a limited number of generic control models were specified, and each institution's actual control model was classified as one of these generic models. Given the wide variation among the models adopted globally, this approach necessarily led to the loss of some granularity.

Four generic control models for exchanges were identified:

1. *Mutual Control:* A mutual exchange is controlled by its members, and its shares are typically not transferable. Control and trading rights are combined and inseparable. The governing body of such an exchange—its council or board—is normally elected by the membership. Often mutual exchanges also have some sort of independent or public interest representation on their governing body. Their mandate is normally not-for-profit, so there is no distribution of surpluses, which are either retained or refunded to members through reduced fees.

2. *Government Control:* Government-controlled exchanges are controlled by government. Typically they are not-for-profit institutions, have government representation on their boards, and have a large stake owned by government.

3. *Private Company Status:* In a private exchange, the control of the exchange and the right to trade on the exchange are normally separate, private institutions dominate the exchange's ownership, and trading in the exchange's shares is normally limited or restricted in some manner. Many private exchanges have demutualized, but some were originally constituted as private companies and were never mutuals. Although it is possible for control and ownership to be separate in private exchanges, members often remain the dominant owners. Sometimes transfers of shares to nonmember shareholders may be restricted, the size of holding by any single shareholder may be limited, or existing shareholders may have a preemption right on any shares offered for sale by other shareholders. Board membership tends to have a high proportion of representation from broking firms and also usually some representation from customer groups and public interest members. Private exchanges may be for profit or not-for-profit.

4. *Listed Status:* A listed exchange is one that has been offered for sale through an IPO to a wide range of investors. Sometimes listed exchanges have formal control restrictions to prevent foreign control. Even if no such formal restrictions exist, there may be de facto restrictions on foreign control of a listed exchange. Listed exchanges attract a wider range of investors than do private exchanges including speculative investors such as hedge funds. Board membership may have representatives from the broking community as well as from other stakeholder groups, but they typically form a minority in the decision-making process.

Four generic control models were also identified for CCPs and CSDs:

1. *Government Control*: A government-controlled CCP or CSD is controlled by government, including potentially the relevant central bank. Board members are appointed by government and may include the finance minister or central bank governor. Typically such institutions are not-for-profit, and have a large stake owned by government.

2. *User Control*: A user-controlled CCP or CSD is one in which a consortium of a wide range of users controls the institution. It thus has no obviously dominant shareholder. These institutions usually operate on a not-for-profit basis.

3. *Exchange Control*: An exchange-controlled CCP or CSD is one in which an exchange is the dominant stakeholder of the institution. This arrangement would arise if an exchange has outright control, but may also be applicable in cases where the control structure and other features suggests that an exchange has a dominant position regarding the control of the clearing or settlement institution. In cases where two exchanges each have a 50% stake, such as in China, it is concluded that neither exchange is dominant, and the institution is classified as being user-controlled. Although exchange-controlled clearing or settlement entities may or may not operate on a for-profit basis, in many cases they are associated with for-profit exchanges.

4. *Independent Control*: An independently controlled clearing or settlement institution is one in which control lies with a nonexchange company (or companies). In some cases the owner or owners are clearly commercial, independent entities. This category also includes, however, some examples where the shareholder list included some users. These users did not, however, appear representative of the bulk of users. Although such entities could be characterized as being user-controlled, the instances examined suggested that they were not run as user-controlled cooperatives but more as private companies with shareholders. Typically these institutions operate on a for-profit basis.

A range of sources were examined in order to assess the control model of each market infrastructure institution in the survey. These included the relevant institution's articles of association or incorporation, any statements it made concerning its structure and purpose, its board membership, its financial statements, relevant shareholder meeting resolutions, and other pertinent information.[9] The assignment of who controlled a market infrastructure institution was taken to be a function of the following variables:

- *Ownership.* Who owns the institution's shares? Are there any shareholders that have a dominant shareholding? Is the distribution of shareholdings within a group, such as users, representative of the whole group or a subset of that group? Are there barriers to certain types of shareholder or to changes in shareholding, and who controls those barriers?
- *Voting Power.* Who actually has the controlling power? Do the shareholders have equal power?
- *Board Membership.* Who is represented on the board? Do external board members have significant extra powers? Are the board members professionals in the corporate sense or do they represent interest groups? Does some special stakeholder, such as the government, have the right to appoint board members?
- *Profit Mandate.* Is the entity clearly in business to make a profit and serve its investors by generating dividends? Or do the shareholders have other reasons for holding shares?

It was often not easy to determine the precise control model of an institution. Relevant information was frequently unavailable, and the information that was available was also commonly either insufficient or ambiguous. Furthermore, there were many nuances of control beyond the generic models identified here. There were many hybrid structures, for example, where a government was a significant shareholder in a market infrastructure institution, but the articles of association stressed the private nature of the entity. Government ownership was frequently combined with a large measure of private autonomy. It was also difficult to identify at what point a shareholder had a stake so large in an infrastructure institution that it was able effectively to control the entity. The allocation of the control model to the institutions under analysis was thus a matter of judgment.

In order to address uncertainties in determining an institution's control model, the following guidelines were used:

- Entities where most of the board members were government appointees were classified as being government-controlled.
- Entities where the articles or other documentation referred to *associations* or the like were classified as mutual associations.
- Clearing or settlement entities where a wide range of market users were strongly represented as shareholders were classified as user controlled—even where one or more exchanges, or the government, were shareholders.
- However, if the owners of a clearing or settlement institution were a subset of users, for example a few major banks, then the entity was taken to be independently controlled. In practice this was a rare occurrence.
- Entities where government owned over 30% and there were no other similarly large shareholders were classified as government-controlled.

- Clearing or settlement entities where an exchange owned over 30% and there were no other similarly large shareholders were classified as exchange-controlled.
- Clearing or settlement entities where an exchange was one of several significant shareholders were defined as user-controlled.

For-Profit Status

The determination of whether an institution operated on a for-profit basis or a not-for-profit basis was also difficult. The following guidelines were used to make such a determination:

- Specific statements in the institution's articles of association or incorporation, or in relevant securities law that an entity was a not-for-profit institution, were accepted at face value.
- In the absence of specific documentation:
  - Entities where the shareholders included entities that were likely to be seeking investment returns (for example foreign investors) were classified as being for-profit.
  - Listed entities were classified as being for-profit.
  - Government-controlled entities were classified as being not-for-profit.
  - Mutually controlled or user-controlled entities were classified as being not-for-profit.
  - Entities that appeared to be private companies, but where all profit was routinely retained, were classified as being not-for-profit.
  - Private entities where the list of shareholders or the historic distribution of profits suggested that profits were at least an important element in the business were classified as for-profit.
  - If a clearing or settlement institution was controlled by a for-profit exchange, it was classified as being for-profit.

Size, Region, and Development Level

Each of the market infrastructure institutions examined was categorized according to its size, region, and level of development. Equity turnover was taken as the measure of size. The data used were the 2005 total equity turnover as reported by the WFE. Exchanges were categorized into five size bands as shown in table 14, from "very small," with an annual turnover in 2005 of under $US5 billion to "very large," with a turnover of US$1 trillion. Table 15 shows the number of exchanges in each size category and the share of total turnover covered by the exchanges in that category. The WFE classifies exchanges geographically in line with their time zone, as shown in table 16. In order to identify variations specific to

Table 14
Size Bands of Exchanges in Database

Category	WFE equity turnover, 2005 (US$)
Very large	Over 1 trillion
Large	200 billion–1 trillion
Medium	50 billion to 200 billion
Small	5 billion to 50 billion
Very small	Under 5 billion

TABLE 15
Numbers and Percentage Turnover of Exchanges in Database by Size Bands

Size category	Number of exchanges	Percentage of global equity turnover
Very large	10	84
Large	12	12
Medium	15	3
Small	19	1
Very small	34	0
Total	90	100

the Middle East, Africa and South America, the WFE regions were further subdivided as shown in table 17.

Institutions were categorized by their level of development according to a set of criteria developed by FTSE International that defines the following categories for use in its indices: developed (D), advanced emerging (E1) and secondary emerging (E2).[10] The FTSE International categories covered 56 of the 90 exchanges examined in this survey. The remaining 34 exchanges were not covered, as they did not meet the FTSE requirements in terms of freedom of capital movement, investor interest, or liquidity. For this survey, these 34 were classified as tertiary emerging (E3). Table 18 shows the number of stock exchanges by region in each category of development.[11]

ANALYSIS

This section analyzes in turn the governance of stock exchanges, clearing entities, settlement entities, and also integrated institutions. For each

TABLE 16
Time Zones of Exchanges in Database

WFE zone	Number of exchanges
Americas	15
Europe, Middle East, and Africa	52
Pacific and Asia (including South Asia)	23
Total	90

Table 17
Expanded Regional Categories of Exchanges in Database

WFE Categories	Expanded categories	Number of Exchanges
Americas	North America (including offshore)	6
	South and Central America	9
Europe, Middle East, and Africa	Western Europe	18
	Eastern Europe	12
	Middle East	12
	Africa	10
Asia Pacific	Pacific Rim Asia	15
	Australasia	3
	South Asia	5
Total		90

TABLE 18
Development Level of Exchanges in Database by Region

	Developed	Advanced emerging	Secondary emerging	Tertiary emerging	Total
North America	6				6
S. and C. America		2	5	2	9
Western Europe	15		1	2	18
Eastern Europe			2	10	12
Middle East		1	2	9	12
Africa		1	1	8	10
Pacific Rim Asia	5	3	7		15
Australasia	2			1	3
South Asia			3	2	5
Total	28	7	21	34	90

type of entity the analysis discusses (1) the number of institutions in each control model, (2) the number of institutions by profit mandate, (3) the share of global turnover for each control model, (4) the distribution of control models by size of exchange, (5) the distribution of control models by region of exchange, and (6) the distribution of control models by development level of exchange.

Exchanges

The most common control model for exchanges was that of a private company at 40.0% (36/90) of the sample, as shown in figure 6. These included both demutualized exchanges and recently created exchanges that had never been mutually controlled. Of the other exchanges, 27.8% (25/90) were under mutual control, 16.7% (15/90) were listed (including several smaller ones), and 15.6% (14/90) were government controlled.

The government-controlled and mutually controlled exchanges operated on a not-for-profit basis, and the listed exchanges were all for-profit (figure 7). The exchanges that operated as private companies were split, with 16 not-for-profit and 20 for-profit.

The listed exchanges included the bulk of the largest exchanges (five of the top 10 by equity turnover), and constituted 72% of the total equity turnover in 2005 (figure 8); private exchanges represented 22%, and government-controlled and mutual associations each represented 3% of the global total (with Saudi Arabia alone being over one-third of this percentage). The other large mutuals were Amex, Shanghai, Shenzhen, Istanbul, São Paulo, and Karachi.

None of the very largest exchanges had a mutual control model (figure 9). The majority had moved to listed status, and the four private exchanges in the very large group—Tokyo, Korea, Spain, and Italy— were actively considering or planning a listing at the time the database was prepared. Subsequently the Tokyo Stock Exchange decided to postpone its listing in 2009,[12] the Korea Exchange was designated a "quasigovernmental institution" in early 2009,[13] the Spanish exchange, BME, became a listed company in 2006, and the Italian Exchange, Borsa Italiana, became part of the listed London Stock Exchange Group in 2007. The Saudi exchange, which recorded record equity turnover in 2005 (equivalent to approximately 8% of NYSE turnover) was government controlled.

The listed exchanges were almost all in the most developed markets and concentrated in Europe and North America, with eight of the 15 listed exchanges (figures 10 and 11). In other regions, it was the exchanges in the most developed markets (Australia, New Zealand, Singapore,

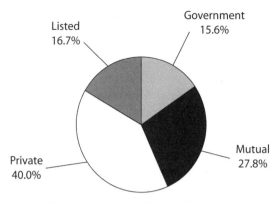

Figure 6: Exchange Control Models

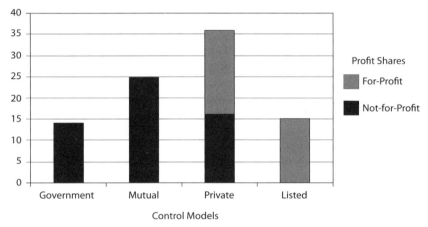

Figure 7: Exchange Control by Profit Mandate

Hong Kong) that had listed—with Bursa Malaysia and the Philippines (where there was very strong regulatory pressure to list) and Panama among the emerging markets. This changed subsequently with the listing of the JSE (the South African exchange) in 2006, Bovespa (the Brazilian stock exchange) in 2007, and the Bolsa Mexicana de Valores (the Mexican stock exchange) in 2008.

Government control of exchanges was common in Europe but was declining. The newer exchanges in Eastern Europe (though not Russia or Ukraine, which favored mutual associations) generally followed the private company model, though often with significant government interest. However, the newer Middle Eastern exchanges, which were all in

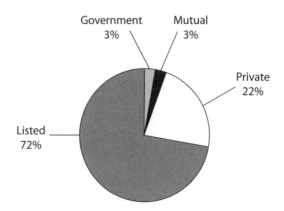

Figure 8: Share of Global Turnover by Exchange Control Model

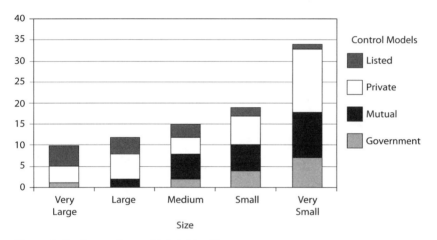

Figure 9: Exchange Control Model by Size

the tertiary emerging development category, were all set up with government control.

Mutual control remained the dominant control model among the long-established exchanges in South America and was also a widely adopted model in Africa—although this was in the process of changing as evidenced by the changes in governance at the JSE, Bovespa, and the Bolsa Mexicana de Valores. Only Amex among the developed markets retained a mutual structure. The mainland Chinese exchanges—which ranked as "large" by volume—were classed as mutual exchanges, as were Istanbul and São Paulo, which were of similar size.

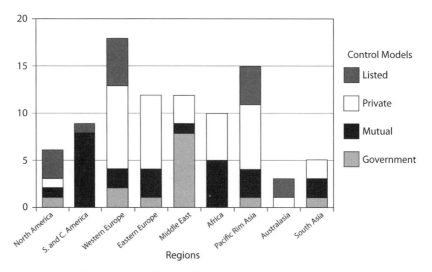

Figure 10: Exchange Control Model by Region

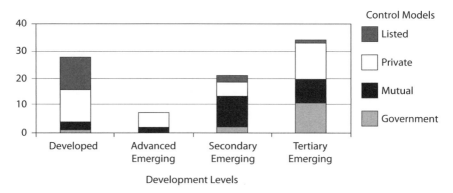

Figure 11: Exchange Control Model by Development Level

Clearing Institutions

Of the 90 exchanges analyzed, all but three had a defined entity performing clearing. Control of clearing entities was dominated by exchange control at 37.9% (33/90) and user control at 40.2% (35/87), as illustrated in figure 12. Government control was low at 13.8% (12/87), as was control by Independent entities at 8.1% (7/8).

Profit mandates for clearers and CCPs (figure 13) generally followed control type, with government-controlled institutions being not-for-profit, and independent institutions being for-profit. Exchange-controlled entities were roughly evenly split between not-for-profit and for-profit.

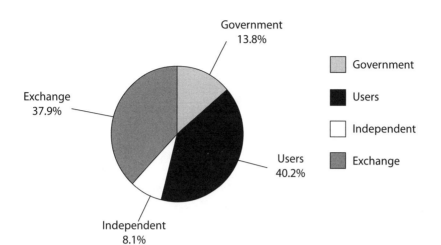

Figure 12: Clearing/CCP Control Models

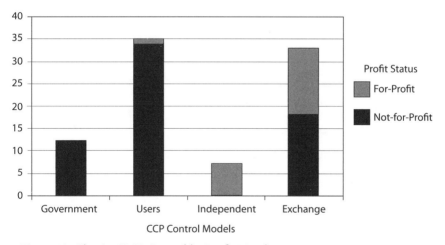

Figure 13: Clearing/CCP Control by Profit Mandate

User-controlled for-profit institutions were rare—with only one example in Austria, where the CCP was controlled by commercial banks but distributed significant dividends.

In terms of share of total equity turnover, CCPs that were user-controlled represented 64% of total turnover (figure 14). This largely reflected the size of the three largest exchanges with user-controlled clearers—NYSE and NASDAQ (which used the same clearinghouse), and Tokyo—which jointly represented 54% of equity trading. Independent clearers also showed a

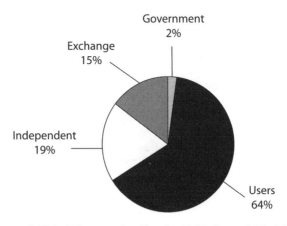

Figure 14: Share of Global Turnover by Clearing/CCP Control Model

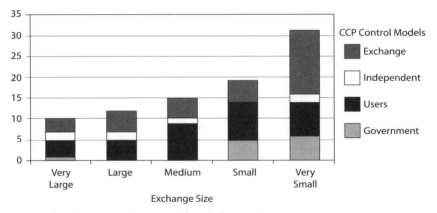

Figure 15: Clearing/CCP Control by Exchange Size

high share of global trading, reflecting the situations at the two largest exchanges with independent clearers—the LSE and Euronext (LCH.Clearnet was categorized as being independent of the LSE and Euronext)—which represented 16% of 2005 trading. The three largest exchanges that owned their clearing systems were Deutsche Börse, Borsa Italiana, and BME, which represented 9% of global equity turnover.

The clearing entities associated with the larger exchanges tended to be roughly evenly split between exchange and user control (figure 15). Exchange control was most significant among the group of "very small" exchanges, reflecting the tendency of new exchanges to install integrated trading and clearing systems, with the exchange retaining control of

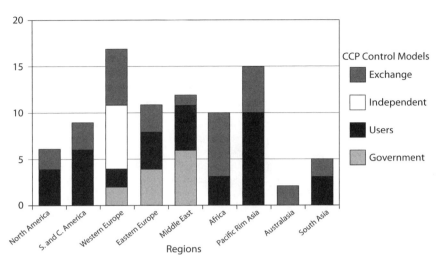

Figure 16: Clearing/CCP Control Model by Region

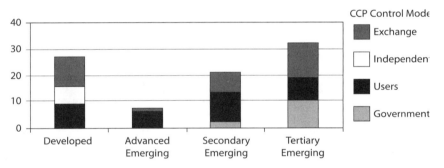

Figure 17: CCP/Clearing Control Model by Development Level

both. Government control (except for Saudi Arabia) was only present among the smallest exchanges.

Figure 16 indicates that independent control of clearing entities was exclusively a western European phenomenon. Government control of clearers, as of exchanges, was important in the Middle East, though no more so than user control. Government control was also significant in Eastern Europe, in contrast to the pattern of exchange control there.

Figure 17 shows that exchange control of CCPs was fairly common throughout the development spectrum—though the reasons tended to differ, with more developed exchanges seeing integration as a business opportunity. Government control of clearing was a feature of the developing Middle East and East European exchanges.

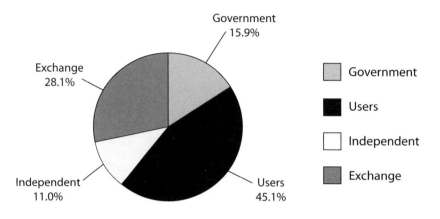

Figure 18: CSD Control Models

Settlement Institutions

Of the 90 exchanges covered in the analysis, 82 had a depository. Of the other eight, three had no apparent formal mechanism for clearing or settlement (i.e., no CCP or CSD). The remaining five had a clearing function but no depository. User control of CSDs was the dominant model at 45.1% (37/82)—even more so than among clearing entities (figure 18). Exchange control of CSDs was far less common than exchange control of clearing institutions, though it still stood at 28.1% (23/82). The number of Independent CSDs at 11.0% (9/82) and Government-controlled CSDs at 15.9% (13/82); were at low levels similar to those of similarly controlled clearing institutions.

The profit mandate split (figure 19) of CSDs was almost identical to that of clearing institutions, with 23 for-profit and 59 not-for-profit (with five exchanges having some form of clearing organization but no CSD, and three having no apparent clearing or settlement entity). As their ownership suggests, almost all government- and user-controlled CSDs were not for profit, independent CSDs were for profit, and exchange-controlled CSDs split roughly equally between for profit and not-for-profit.

As with clearing institutions, exchanges with user-controlled CSDs represented 64% of global equity turnover in 2005 (figure 20), again reflecting the importance of the two largest US exchanges and Tokyo.

The distribution of CSDs by control and exchange size (figure 21) shows a pattern very similar to that for clearing institutions, except that among the very small exchanges, user control of CSDs was more common and exchange control was less common.

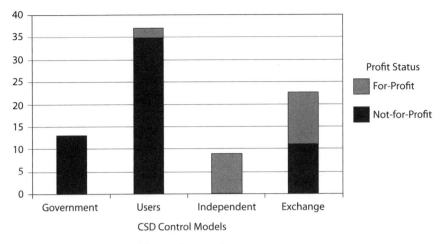

Figure 19: CSD Control by Profit Mandate

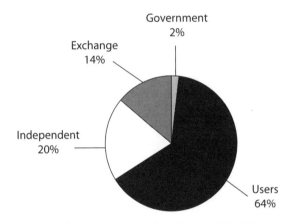

Figure 20: Share of Global Turnover by CSD Control Model

Overall the patterns of control for Clearer/CCPs and for CSDs were almost exactly the same, as illustrated in Table 19. There were 82 exchanges with both clearing and settlement institutions. Of these, in only five exchanges were the control models of their clearing and settlement institutions different. In these five jurisdictions, although all the exchanges controlled the clearing/CCP function, there were differences for the CSDs—in particular, at the two major Indian exchanges the independent CSDs were controlled by subsets of major banks and market users, at Chittagong the CSD was controlled by market users, and in Ghana and the Philippines the CSD was controlled by a group including the exchange and the bankers association.

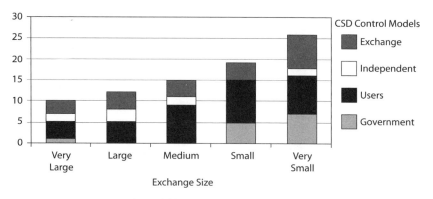

Figure 21: CSD Control Model by Size

Table 19
CCP/Clearer versus CSD Control Model

Clearer control	CSD control				
	Government	Users	Independent	Exchange	Total
Government	12				12
Users		35			35
Independent			7		7
Exchange	1	2	2	23	28
Totals	13	37	9	23	82

Figure 22 shows the control models for settlement institutions organized by region. The results are very similar to those for clearing entities. Independent control of CSDs was exclusively a western European phenomenon, government control of CSDs was important in the Middle East, though no more so than user control, and government control was also significant in Eastern Europe, in contrast to the pattern of exchange control there.

Figure 23 shows the control models for settlement institutions organized by level of development. Once again the results are similar to those for clearing institutions. Exchange control of CSDs was fairly common throughout the development spectrum, though the reasons tended to differ, with more developed exchanges seeing integration as a business opportunity. Government control of CSDs was a feature of the developing Arab and East European exchanges.

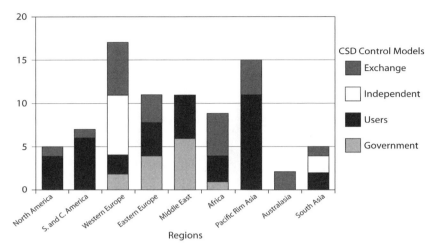

Figure 22: CSD Control Model by Region

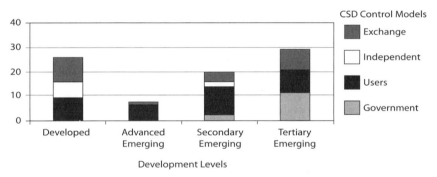

Figure 23: CSD Control Model by Development Level

Integrated Trading, Clearing, and Settlement Institutions

Figure 24 illustrates the extent to which exchanges and CCPs were integrated in the same organization. The four control models for exchanges are shown on the x-axis. For each of these models, the number of CCPs with the different control models are shown. The first column, for example, shows all the 14 exchanges under government control, and lists the control models of their associated CCPs. Of these 14 CCPs, seven were under government control, three were under user control, and four were under exchange control. These last four CCPs were thus integrated with their associated exchanges. The figure shows that the majority of listed exchanges were integrated, and that there were also integrated exchanges with each of the other control models.

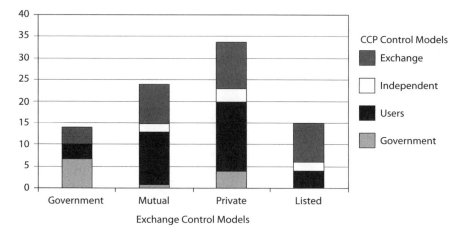

Figure 24: Clearing/CCP Control by Exchange Ownership

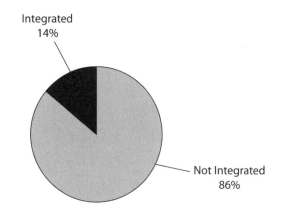

Figure 25: Global Equity Turnover by Vertical Integration

In terms of share of global equity turnover (figure 25), integrated exchanges were a small part of the total—only 14%—reflecting the importance of the nonintegrated US, London, and Tokyo exchanges.

Conclusions

The chapter provides an overview of how market infrastructure institutions in the cash equity markets around the world were governed as of September 2006. The 90 member exchanges of the World Federation of Exchanges, and their associated clearing and settlement entities, were examined.

Exchanges: The dominant control model for exchanges, at 40% of the population, was that of a private company. 27.8% of the population were under mutual control, 16.7% were listed, and 15.6% were government controlled. All the government controlled and mutually controlled exchanges operated on a not-for-profit basis. All the listed exchanges were for-profit, as were just under half of the private exchanges. Listed exchanges constituted 72% of global equity turnover, private exchanges represented 22%, and government-controlled and mutual associations each represented 3% of the global total. Exchanges in developed markets were mostly either private companies or listed. Mutual control was more common among the secondary emerging markets, and remained the dominant control model among the long-established exchanges in South America. The newer exchanges tended to be constituted as private companies, except in the Middle East, where government control was the norm.

Clearing Entities: Of the 90 exchanges analyzed, all but three had a defined entity performing clearing. The dominant control models for clearing institutions were exchange control at 37.9% of the population and user control at 40.2%. Government control was low at 13.8%, as was control by independent entities at 7.8%. Government-controlled and user-controlled clearing institutions were mostly not-for-profit, independent institutions were mostly for-profit, and exchange-controlled clearing entities were roughly evenly split between not-for-profit and for-profit. User-controlled clearing entities represented 64% of global equity turnover—reflecting the size of the U.S. and Tokyo exchanges, which had user-controlled clearers. Government control of clearing entities was most common among secondary and tertiary developing markets, predominantly in the Middle East and Eastern Europe. Independent control was restricted to developed markets. Markets at all levels of development exhibited a mix of user control and exchange control of their clearing entities.

Settlement Entities: Of the 90 exchanges examined, 82 had a CSD to effect transfers of ownership. User control was the dominant model at 45.1% of the population, with exchange control still common at 28.1%, although less important than for clearing entities. The proportions of independent CSDs at 11.0% and government-controlled CSDs at 15.9%, were at similarly low levels to those of similarly controlled clearing institutions. Almost all government- and user-controlled CSDs were not-for-profit, independent CSDs were for-profit, and exchange-controlled CSDs split roughly equally between for-profit and not-for-profit. The control models for settlement institutions organized both by region and by development level were very similar to those for clearing entities.

Integrated Control of Trading, Clearing and Settlement: Overall the patterns of control for clearing institutions and for settlement institutions were almost exactly the same. There were 82 exchanges with both clearing and settlement institutions, and of these, for only five exchanges did the control models of their associated clearing and settlement institutions differ. The majority of listed exchanges were integrated. There were also integrated exchanges with each of the other control models. Exchanges with ownership of clearing and settlement entities represented only 14% of global equity turnover. The 86% share held by nonintegrated exchanges reflected the importance of the U.S., Tokyo, and London exchanges, none of which owned their clearing or settlement entities.

PART III

Case Studies

CHAPTER SIX

Exchanges

A SERIES OF CASE STUDIES illustrating how specific exchanges have actually been governed in particular contexts are presented in this chapter. The following institutions and contexts are described in turn: the proposed iX merger between Deutsche Börse and the LSE, and its subsequent collapse, in 2000; the "Penny Stocks Incident" at HKEx in 2002; the attempted takeover of the LSE by NASDAQ over the period 2006–8; Euronext's purchase of LIFFE in 2001; the resignation of the chairman/ CEO of the NYSE in 2003; and the purchase by the "Murakami Fund" of a major block of shares in the Osaka Securities Exchange in 2005. A few brief general lessons from each case study are also identified.

The case studies are presented for several reasons. The detail contained in them complements the conceptual and abstract analyses provided elsewhere in the book, both by highlighting issues the conceptual analyses need to address and by illustrating the strengths and weaknesses of particular conceptual approaches in different circumstances. The case studies also show that the way market infrastructure institutions are governed may be highly complex, that there is enormous diversity in the manner in which market infrastructure institutions are governed in practice, and that different elements of governance are important in different contexts. In addition, they demonstrate that there sometimes exists a difference between the formal and publicly stated governance structure of a market infrastructure institution, and how it is actually governed in practice.

Two main sources of information were used in preparing the case studies. First, pertinent primary and secondary documentation was examined. Second, interviews were held with a range of parties interested in the governance of the relevant institutions, including, wherever possible, board directors, management, owners, users (both direct and indirect), other types of commercial stakeholders, regulators, government, independent commentators, and other interested parties.

Each institution examined was advised that a case study on key aspects of its governance was being prepared, and was also provided with details about the aims and anticipated contents of the case study. Draft versions of each case study were also sent to each institution and other key interested parties for their comments. Widely differing responses were received from the various institutions being studied. Some were fully interested and happy to share documents and make introductions to relevant people; some were indifferent, ignored letters, or procrastinated; and some did not respond, or decided not to share information or participate in the process. These reactions did not stop relevant and useful information for all the case study institutions from being obtained.

The descriptions presented in the case studies should be considered as being illustrative, rather than authoritative, for four main reasons. First, they are based only on nonconfidential information—full access to relevant board papers and other pertinent strategic documentation was not available. Second, on average 20 people were interviewed for each institution, and thus interviewee participation in the development of each case study was limited. Any opinions described in the text therefore do not necessarily represent the majority view about any particular context, and indeed where there are conflicting views, are in some contexts bound to represent a minority view. Third, the diversity of perspectives among interviewees, and in some cases the direct opposition of interviewees' interests, both commercial and otherwise, meant that contradictory information about specific institutions was sometimes obtained. Finally, while the descriptions are believed truthful and accurate, they may contain omissions or mistakes. They should thus only be viewed as presenting a considered judgment about how governance may have operated at the relevant institutions in particular contexts.

At the end of each case study a few brief lessons are identified. Given the illustrative nature of the case studies, these morals are not intended to be definitive conclusions either about the specific exchanges being examined, or more generally about how market infrastructure institutions are governed in practice. Many interpretations of each case study are possible, and as a result many possible conclusions may be drawn from them. The aim here is simply to highlight a few morals that may be generally relevant for how market infrastructure institutions are governed in practice.

DEUTSCHE BÖRSE/LONDON STOCK EXCHANGE: PROPOSED iX MERGER 2000

On May 3, 2000, Deutsche Börse and the LSE proposed a merger of equals to create Europe's biggest stock exchange.[1] The intention was to create two new markets. The first, called "iX," was intended to target Europe's blue-chip companies for listing and trading, and would be owned 50% by the LSE's members and 50% by Deutsche Börse. It would consist of all of the LSE's and Deutsche Börse's businesses, including Eurex, but excluding Deutsche Börse's 50% stake in Clearstream International, its settlement arm, which Deutsche Börse would continue to hold. The chairman of iX would be Don Cruickshank, the chairman of the LSE, and its chief executive would be Werner Seifert, the CEO of Deutsche Börse. It would be based in, and managed from, London with major operations in Frankfurt, and would use a single trading platform, Deutsche Börse's Xetra, for all its cash markets. The stock exchanges in Italy and Madrid also signed an MOU to join iX at a later date.

The second market the two exchanges intended to launch was to be a joint venture between iX and NASDAQ to create a pan-European, high-growth market. This would have replaced the existing growth markets of London and Germany, techMARK and the Neuer Markt respectively, as well as the vehicle that NASDAQ had previously indicated would be its launching pad into Europe, namely NASDAQ Europe. iX and NASDAQ would be equal shareholders in the joint venture, which would be incorporated in, and managed from, London, and operated in Frankfurt.

Deutsche Börse and the LSE also indicated that they would support initiatives to set up a central counterparty and establish straight-through processing (STP). In the meantime, however, settlement would continue to be delivered by the current providers, Clearstream International and CrestCo Limited.

The key objectives of iX were to

become the premier global exchange organisation and provider of exchange-related services; be the lowest cost provider of exchange trading and related services; and create significant benefits for all customers and value for shareholders.[2]

It was anticipated that the merger would benefit both customers and shareholders, principally as a result of

the critical mass that will be created by combining the markets of the Merger Partners and bringing together their respective intermediaries, investors and issuers on a global platform; and the economic effects of creating a single electronic trading platform and rationalized infrastructure.

The merger was expected to result in significant benefits for all customer groups:

Private client brokers and other intermediaries: *reduced technical complexity*: the use of a single electronic trading platform for all Group cash markets should reduce the complexity and cost of information technology operations and increase the potential for integrating cash and derivatives markets in the medium term; *lower charges*: by generating economies of scale and adopting a competitive pricing model, iX-international exchanges should be able to reduce its own costs, with a positive impact on dealing charges for intermediaries; *easier access to markets*: the single electronic trading platform will offer access to a wider range of securities, investors and intermediaries and allow Retail Service Providers to expand their service range; *central counterparty*: iX-international exchanges will support initiatives to link the single electronic trading platform to one central counterparty, offering benefits to intermediaries through cross-product netting and margining and reduced counterparty risk, as well as establishing straight-through processing at lowest cost; and *information and news services*: the creation of pan-European markets will increase the range and depth of market information and company news available for dissemination to market users and customers.

Investors retail and wholesale: *lower transaction and dealing costs*: the operating cost synergies expected to arise as a result of the Merger, primarily in technology and systems, should have a positive impact on dealing charges; *improved pricing of securities*: combining the volume and liquidity of the London and Frankfurt markets and facilitating access through the single electronic trading platform should result in increased visibility in the price formation process, leading to narrower spreads and more competitive pricing; and *pan-European market visibility*: the combined markets of iX-international exchanges will facilitate cross-border sectoral, rather than national, comparison and investment.

Issuers: *concentration of investor focus*: the proposed pan-European markets of iX-international exchanges will concentrate investor focus and deepen the pool of capital available to companies of all sizes; and *higher trading volumes*: the single electronic trading platform and combined intermediary membership should attract trading volumes from other markets and concentrate liquidity in European equities, improving the profile and liquidity of companies whose shares are traded.

In addition, it was expected that shareholders would also benefit from the merger, as a result of a range of synergies, including

higher revenue growth: the single electronic trading platform will concentrate trading volumes, which should produce higher revenue growth than either Deutsche Börse or London Stock Exchange could achieve alone; *higher operating margins*: a large proportion of the cost base of the Merger Partners is in respect of information technology systems which is not volume related. Increases in revenues can be achieved without a commensurate change in costs and, accordingly, operating margins should benefit from any increase in revenues; and *cost savings*: the Merger will create opportunities for operating cost synergies. Such synergies will be realised through specific projects, which have been identified as part of the integration plan following the Merger, and should result from: operating all of the Group's markets and winning new business on a single system rather than operating two high-tolerance, high-capacity operating centres; reduced systems development expenditure as a result of eliminating the need for regularly upgrading two separate systems; and eliminating overlapping support, administration, marketing and management information functions.

The project was aimed at meeting demand from the big traders of equities for a simpler and cheaper way to trade major shares from different European countries, without having to be a member of many national exchanges and their corresponding clearing and settlement operations, which duplicated costs.

Within three months of its proposal, the iX project collapsed. Many reasons were put forward for its failure.[3]

There appeared to be a central flaw in the economic logic for the merger. A key stated goal of the merger was to reduce costs. However, the core strategy of the merger was to replace two old exchanges—the LSE and Deutsche Börse—with two new exchanges, iX for Europe's top companies, and the iX-NASDAQ joint venture for pan-European high-growth companies. To save expenses, it was clear that operations should have been based in a single city. Rather than being a rational way to save costs, this element of the proposal thus appeared to be a political compromise.[4]

It was argued that the distinction between iX and the iX-NASDAQ joint venture would inevitably have led to conflict. NASDAQ would never have supported the possibility of companies choosing to graduate from its high-tech growth market to iX. This would have meant creating a market that had the seeds of its own destruction contained within it.

Management's valuation of the LSE implied in the iX proposal was believed to have been too low. The LSE and Deutsche Börse were effectively estimated as having the same value, a decision that was purely political, as no other terms would have been acceptable on an agreed basis to either the Germans or the British. The valuations were, however, not accepted by many market participants. Their logic was simple—if the market capitalization of the London Stock Exchange was twice that of Deutsche Börse, why concede to a merger of equals?

The project was criticized for lacking the detail that brokers and banks said they needed in order to respond to it properly. There was a belief that the merger was being rushed through, partly as a riposte to news of a planned merger between the stock exchanges in Paris, Brussels, and Amsterdam to form Euronext. Poor communication between the two companies and users also seemed to have played a part. A survey in August 2000 estimated that only 23.2% of LSE shareholder members were in favor of the merger just two weeks before they were due to vote on it in September 2000 of that year, and 14.2% were against, with the rest undecided or not prepared to comment.[5] Shareholders controlling 15% of the votes were anxious about a lack of information on clearing and settlement, with 12.5% concerned about management's track record. A smaller-companies' markets committee, chaired by Brian Winterflood of market-maker Winterflood Securities, asked the LSE to clarify 28 points about the merger three months after it was unveiled.[6]

Regulation also became an issue. The proposal envisaged two separately regulated exchanges: iX to operate under FSA rules, and the iX-NASDAQ joint venture to be regulated by the German authorities. On August 21, 2000, the German and British supervisory authorities issued a joint statement on regulatory issues concerning iX.[7] Six working groups were created to develop joint arrangements in order to deliver efficient and effective supervision of iX. These groups' main goal was to work towards further harmonization of the supervisory standards where a common approach was appropriate. The working groups were to examine issues concerning market structure, listing and ad hoc requirements, transaction reporting and market surveillance, legal issues in connection with insider dealing and market abuse, corporate takeovers, and clearing and settlement of securities transactions.

The FSA, however, gave mixed signals about the project. One speech by its chairman, Howard Davies, was widely interpreted as a veiled attack on the concept of iX through its play on the word "No" in German:

> Just two weeks ago the London and Frankfurt stock exchanges announced their intention to merge. In future they will be run by a Scottish chairman and a Swiss chief executive, and will be called iX which, if I remember my schoolboy Latin, is pronounced "nein." The Exchange will be based in Finanzplatz London, but its newtech brother, NASDAQ Europe, will be based in what we must now know as Mainhattan.[8]

A couple of weeks later he stated:

> We are now working with the exchanges, and with our German regulatory counterparts, to clarify the way in which the regulation of these two exchanges would work in practice. We see no insuperable obstacles, but we will need a high degree of co-operation and collaboration between regulators.[9]

However, Davies also quoted an observation from a recently published book on European capital markets, coauthored by Seifert, which implied that the FSA could be the sole regulator for both exchanges:

> "[I]t would be entirely in keeping with the spirit of the EU's directives if European exchanges, operating in more than one country, could opt for being regulated by, say, the FSA." Why? Because, [the authors] say, "Most professionals in the securities industry have been impressed by London's FSA. Despite its sweeping powers, market participants have noted its flexible and informal approach as well as the competence of its staff."

The two merger partners underestimated the power that the smaller brokers and market-makers had when they combined their votes. Winning over Winterflood and the retail brokers in their trade association, the Association of Private Client Investment Managers and Stockbrokers (APCIMS), was essential, as together they controlled about a third of the 290 votes in the then mutual LSE. For any merger to go ahead, a 75% majority would be needed, making it easy for the smaller brokers to act together and block the deal.[10] The smaller brokers felt particularly aggrieved because iX was seen as a project promoted by a handful of London-based US investment banks, without prior discussion with the rest of the market before being announced. There had been strong support for iX from an alliance of executives at Merrill Lynch, Goldman Sachs, and Morgan Stanley Dean Witter, who were together known colloquially as MGM.[11] George Cox, director-general of Britain's Institute of Directors, said the deal was being pursued by a small group of American banks whose interests did not necessarily match those of the LSE.[12]

There was also some concern about iX's proposed governance structure. Under the terms of the deal, Deutsche Börse's half of the merged company would be controlled by Deutsche Börse's supervisory board and not its shareholders.[13] This was because German capital gains tax laws would impose a heavy bill on every shareholder in Deutsche Börse if iX shares were distributed to them. Governance issues generally were not believed to have been adequately addressed in the merger proposal, as they only focused on the shareholders of the stock exchange and not on the requirements of the users.

Corporate governance specialist Manifest said different corporate governance rules in Germany and Britain raised fundamental questions for shareholders, with the UK code seen as robust and effectively mandatory, while the German code was voluntary. There was too little leadership from the iX partners on how corporate governance would be handled, and it was left to the investment community to determine what was required to protect fundamental shareholder rights.[14]

Nationalistic sentiment in the UK may also have played a role, and some anti-German feeling was evident—for example, there was a picture in the *Telegraph* newspaper of the LSE building with the phrase "Bosch Exchange" daubed on the wall. When the CEO of the LSE, Gavin Casey, said it would "make sense for all companies on the merged bourse to list in euros in the future," British anti-European and euro-skeptic sentiments were further inflamed.[15]

Deutsche Börse received criticism in Germany as well. German corporate leaders "predicted a bureaucratic nightmare as companies grappled with conflicting securities regulations in Britain and Germany."[16] There was also concern that Deutsche Börse's DAX index could be scrapped, which in turn could lead investors to cut their holdings in German blue chips.[17] Deutsche Börse dismissed this concern, noting that the DAX index would remain as long as needed. German car manufacturer Porsche also said it would not agree to its shares being listed in London.[18] The German media noted that Britain was taking over the Neuer Markt, Germany's prized growth stock market, which at the time was feted by the business press and small investors, but which subsequently collapsed.

Support for the merger among shareholders of Deutsche Börse also appeared not to be sufficient for the merger. Backing from 75% of them was needed to secure German approval for the merger, but in a poll conducted by Boersen-Zeitung, a key German financial newspaper, there was stated support for the merger among only 28.4% of Deutsche Börse's shareholders.[19] A deputy chairman of Deutsche Börse's supervisory board, Manfred Zass, also was equivocal in his support of the merger, stating: "The total of what is in the small print must not result in London taking over Frankfurt."[20]

There were various worries about technology issues concerning the merger. Some people questioned the reliability of the German trading platform, Xetra.[21] There was concern about necessary future investments in technology. If the merger went ahead, the plan was for the LSE to scrap the existing electronic trading system, Sets, and to migrate to the German electronic trading system, Xetra. The LSE offered £30,000 to each existing customer of the trading service to cover their migration costs over two years.[22] However, industry consultants suggested that the total conversion costs for the larger member firms of the LSE would come to at least £500,000 each. This was also against a background where London stockbrokers had spent an estimated £1 billion in 1996 to implement the Sets system. APCIMS questioned whether the offer of £30,000 would be enough to cover the charges of employing IT consultants and demanded more guidance on the mechanics of migrating to Xetra.

Other factors may have also contributed to the failure of iX. There was a concern that the merger would lead to a complex post-trading environment, as the two exchanges used different clearing and settlement service providers that it was believed could not easily be integrated. Sir Ron Brierley, a corporate raider who headed the Guinness Peat fund management group, also demanded that shareholders be compensated for exchange property included in the deal.[23]

Together, all these factors undermined the iX plan. When the Swedish bourse operator OM Gruppen came forward with a hostile bid for the LSE in August 2000, the LSE withdrew its support for the iX proposal. The board gave two key reasons for doing so: to focus attention wholly on the hostile bid from OM Gruppen; and because it would not be possible to resolve a number of shareholder, customer, and regulatory issues raised by the proposed merger, in parallel with preparing a bid defense under the UK's Takeover Code timetable.[24]

On September 14, 2000, the LSE held its annual general meeting. There was a vote by show of hands on whether to reelect chief executive Gavin Casey.[25] Shareholders were furious over the attempt by the board to push through the "deeply unpopular plans" to merge with Deutsche Börse.[26] Although Casey survived a ballot with a narrow 56.3% majority, he still chose to resign. Cruickshank—who had led the iX project and been its public face—survived a shareholder ballot, as did Michael Marks, chairman of Merrill Lynch Europe, a board member of the LSE, and one of the chief proponents of iX.

Morals

- The views of constituencies other than those that have formal legal power over a particular market infrastructure institution may influence decisions taken at the institution.
- There may be many constituencies that seek to influence market infrastructure institutions' decisions.
- Foreign ownership of a national market infrastructure institution may be viewed as against the national interest.

EURONEXT: PURCHASE OF LIFFE 2001

In 2001 Euronext, now a subsidiary of NYSE Euronext Inc., bought LIFFE, the second largest derivatives exchange in Europe. Several years prior to the purchase, LIFFE had been in serious difficulty, having lost trading in its biggest contract, the bund, to its German rival Eurex (then called DTB) in 1998, in part because it had been too slow to adopt electronic trading. In 2000, two venture capital firms, Blackstone Group and

Battery Ventures, invested £44 million in the still-struggling exchange, together with an additional injection of £16 million from existing share-holders, in return for a 30% stake.[27] The cash inflow, together with the leadership of Brian Williamson (chairman) and Hugh Freedberg (CEO), triggered a turnaround in the exchange's fortunes, helped by an emphasis on sales of the company's LIFFE CONNECT™ trading system. The ex-change even began preparing for a listing.[28]

The turnaround triggered talk of a possible merger with the LSE. As both exchanges used the same clearinghouse (LCH), such a link would potentially have given users the possibility of significant savings by being able to cross-margin cash and derivatives trades, and by requiring a single and smaller pool of collateral than would be required if they continued to operate separately.[29] Ms. Clara Furse, the LSE's then new CEO, was a LIFFE board member for nine years and held the position of deputy chairman until 1999. Furse first met Freedberg to explore possible areas of cooperation on March 19, 2001.[30] There was some media speculation about a potential combination of the LSE and LIFFE from May 2001.[31] Garban Intercapital, a broking firm, was also trying to buy a 29% stake in LIFFE.[32] Two months later, in July 2001, the LSE board backed a potential £400 million bid for LIFFE.[33] Reports of this led to interest from other exchanges, including Deutsche Börse,[34] but cash-rich Euro-next emerged as the main potential competitor to the LSE.[35]

On receiving these various indications of interest in purchasing LIFFE, its board decided to assess whether any of the proposals would achieve greater value for shareholders than the alternative of continuing to pur-sue LIFFE's strategy as an independent exchange. As explained by the chairman of LIFFE and the CEO of Euronext subsequently:[36]

> The primary focus of the Board in assessing the merits of each offer proposal was the maximisation of shareholder value, in accordance with its fiduciary duties and the requirements of the UK Takeover Code. In addition, however, the Board focused on a number of other key ele-ments of each offer proposal, being the extent to which it would
>
> - give a commitment to LIFFE's existing customers and relationships;
> - give LIFFE the ability to increase its business momentum beyond that which it could achieve on its own;
> - reflect a strategic awareness of the role of electronic exchanges in fast-changing markets;
> - demonstrate an acceptance of the importance of globally accessible and functionally rich technology.

The Board was mindful that many shareholders were also customers whose approval of an offer would depend not simply on price, but on the effect that the offer would have on the consequent quality and potential of the market. Accordingly, these additional criteria were important in the Board's assessment of the various offer proposals and each potential bidder was asked to address them specifically in their presentation.

The process for assessing which proposal, if any, was most attractive to the LIFFE board was not simply an auction to obtain the highest price—it included requiring presentations to the board by the prospective bidders. After due consideration, the board unanimously endorsed Euronext's offer on October 29, 2001, of £555 million even though the notional value of LSE's final offer was higher. Euronext offered £18.25 per share in cash, while the LSE provided a £19 cash-and-stock bid, of which £12.00 was cash and the balance was LSE shares.[37] The CEOs of LIFFE and Euronext identified five main reasons for the exchanges combining:[38]

(i) The combination of LIFFE and Euronext will treble the volume of business that is transacted through LIFFE's world-beating electronic trading system, LIFFE CONNECT™.

(ii) Euronext and LIFFE have highly complementary customer and product bases. LIFFE is particularly strong in interest rate futures and options, whereas Euronext's deepest and most mature derivatives markets are in equity-related products.

(iii) The consolidated business meets customer needs. It gives customers access to a wider range of products in a larger and more liquid market through a single trading platform. This offers the potential for greater efficiency for the combined customer base.

(iv) We believe the combination of LIFFE and Euronext will be a catalyst for consolidation of European clearing and settlement, which has been long-awaited by international users of derivative markets.

(v) The management teams of Euronext and LIFFE have a common vision based on delivering excellent customer service through the provision of technology-rich trading platforms and innovative and liquid products.

Several factors were put forward for Euronext's success. First, and probably most important, the venture capital shareholders, Blackstone and Battery, preferred Euronext's all-cash bid to the LSE's part-paper offer, as they were keen to cash in on their investment at a time when a weak stock market had hit their investments elsewhere. Second, Euronext offered to leave the LIFFE CONNECT™ technology platform in place, which had been at the core of Williamson's recovery strategy for the exchange. In contrast, it was perceived that the LSE wanted to abandon this technology program in favor of creating an integrated trading platform based on the LIFFE CONNECT™ system.

Third, the LSE initially only offered Williamson the vice chairmanship of the combined LSE and LIFFE group, rather than the chairman's position,[39] even though he was credited, along with Freedberg, with having turned around an exchange that had lost its way. In contrast, Euronext's offer gave Williamson and Freedberg the autonomy to carry on running not only LIFFE's business, but also all of Euronext's derivatives business from London. The deal was also seen as being worth more to Euronext, as it needed LIFFE to gain both critical mass and credibility in derivatives trading, and a foothold in London, which it might employ later as a springboard for buying the LSE.

Morals

- Foreign ownership of a major exchange can occur.
- Price may not be the sole factor affecting the purchase of a market infrastructure institution.

HONG KONG EXCHANGES AND CLEARING:
THE PENNY STOCKS INCIDENT 2002

In 2002 a "three-tiered" regulatory structure was in operation in Hong Kong, comprising the Government, the Securities and Futures Commission (SFC), and HKEx—each with its own anticipated role.[40] The Government's role was to set overall policy direction and initiate legislation. The SFC was viewed as a market watchdog, an independent statutory body responsible for administering the laws governing and regulating the securities and futures markets in the HKSAR (Hong Kong Special Administrative Region), including HKEx, as well as for facilitating and encouraging the development of these markets. HKEx was seen as having frontline responsibility for market regulation, including the operational administration of the Listing Rules.

On July 25, 2002, the SFC held a press conference to release the principal findings of a research paper it had prepared on the quality of markets and the case for a more effective delisting mechanism. The paper had been written principally by staff from the SFC's Corporate Finance Division and Research Department, and represented the views only of its authors and not necessarily of the SFC. Key findings from the paper were as follows:[41]

- Although the SEHK [Stock Exchange of Hong Kong] is the tenth largest in the world, as measured in terms of market capitalization at the end of 2001, it nonetheless does not enjoy the same status when assessed by valuation, weighting in world portfolio investments and liquidity.

- At the end of 2001, the weighted average price/earning ratio for the thirty-three constituent companies on the Hang Seng Index was fifteen; this lags significantly behind its blue chip counterparts in London (thirty-four), New York (thirty) and Australia (twenty-four).
- The SEHK has a high incidence of stocks with low nominal values. Twelve percent of its companies on the Main Board were capitalized at less than HK$100 million, or US$13 million, which would not have qualified them for an initial listing. In addition, about eight in every ten of such companies incurred losses.
- There were 107 "penny stocks" as of May 31, 2002, defined in the research paper as shares which trade at or below HK10 cents or about US1.3 cents.

The paper viewed the prevalence of penny stocks as being inconsistent with international standards, and argued that this gave rise to three main policy implications. First, the pricing mechanism of the trading system worked less efficiently for penny stocks than for those with higher prices. This provided opportunities for market manipulation, as a few transactions would usually suffice to cause substantial fluctuations in the price of these securities. Second, the absence of an effective delisting mechanism deprived the holders of such stocks of an orderly exit option that they could use to cash in their investments.[42] Third, an accumulation of a large number of underperforming penny stocks was perceived to reflect poorly upon the standing of the exchange. It was thought this might lead otherwise suitable listing candidate companies to avoid the exchange, and in the long term adversely affect the liquidity of the market. The paper concluded:

> It is important for us [i.e. Hong Kong] to have an effective delisting mechanism to facilitate an orderly exit of companies that are no longer suitable for listing. The accumulation of a large number of these companies runs counter to the interest of the investing public and could seriously affect the reputation of the Hong Kong market.[43]

Later on the same day that the SFC issued its research paper, the HKEx published a consultation paper on proposed amendments to its Listing Rules, with particular reference to continuing listing eligibility and the cancellation of listing procedures.[44] On its publication, the media focused immediately and almost exclusively on Part C, which sought to cancel the listing of securities that were traded on the main board of the SEHK if they failed to meet specified criteria. Although 11 broad quantitative and qualitative criteria were specified, the minimum share price criterion was highlighted. This proposal would have deemed an issuer in default if its share price traded below HK$0.50 for more than 30 trading days. A determination that an issuer was in default could then lead to the delisting of the issuer's shares, unless specified remedial actions, including the consolidation of shares or reverse stock-splits, were undertaken.

The proximity of the release of the SFC research paper and the HKEx consultation paper gave rise to a widespread presumption of an official agenda to remove penny stocks from the Hong Kong markets.[45] The key reasons for the SFC's support for such an agenda were that it sought to make the regulation of capital markets in the HKSAR on par with international standards, and viewed the existence of the penny stocks as lowering the status of Hong Kong's capital markets. With the introduction of the more politically inclined ministerial system of governance in Hong Kong from July 1, 2002,[46] it is likely that the release of the research report by the SFC may also have been expedited at the instigation of the Financial Secretary or the Secretary for Financial Services and the Treasury.[47]

The HKEx put forward similar reasons for making its proposals. In particular, it noted that they sought to raise the standards of corporate governance among issuers listed on the exchange, to enhance the quality of the issuers listed on the exchange, and to bring its requirements on a par with international standards.[48] Some commentators suggested, however, that the HKEx was influenced by its status as a for-profit company.[49] Its role as a frontline market regulator was, at least in the short term, seen as a cost center with minimal, if any, immediate financial returns. This was argued as being especially relevant regarding the regulation of penny stocks since the corporate transactions that they undertook were usually large relative to their size, which in turn necessitated various levels of approvals to ensure that the interests of shareholders were protected. The fact that it was also not uncommon for these companies to run into financial difficulty, requiring corporate restructurings, was also thought to increase the cost of regulation because such restructurings involved large amounts of documentation. It was therefore argued that it may have been cost effective for the HKEx to delist penny stocks given the direct positive implication this would have had for its profitability as a listed entity.

The immediate market reaction to the release of the SFC research paper and the HKEx consultation paper was rather muted, as evidenced by the lack of abnormal activity on the SEHK during the afternoon trading session on July 25, 2002. The next day, however, share prices of the penny stocks started to collapse after the first hour of trading. The fall in the share prices was relatively widespread, with more than 220 companies, representing about a third of the total number of companies that were listed on the main board of the SEHK at that time, seeing their share price drop by at least 5% on July 26, 2002.

Eventually, following a barrage of heavy selling, some HK$10.9 billion (approximately US$1.39 billion) was wiped off this sector at the close of trading on the SEHK, representing some 10% of the market capitalization of penny stocks. The prices of individual shares dropped by as much as 88% from their previous close as investors rushed to sell their penny stock holdings. No fewer than 62 penny stocks suffered price declines of at least 20%, and concerns were raised about the financial health of brokerage firms that had been exposed to significant margin financing of their clients' trading activities. The possibility of market confidence being shaken by the closure of some of these adversely affected brokerage firms prompted a series of actions by key individuals commencing on Saturday, July 27, 2002.[50] Meetings were seemingly hastily organized over the weekend resulting in announcements that appeared to be made to placate a highly vocal group of investors and their stockbrokers. These are summarized as follows:[51]

Saturday July 27, 2002	Following a clarification a day earlier, the HKEx announced an extension of the proposed consultation period for the HKEx consultation paper from August 31 to October 31.
Sunday July 28, 2002	The chairman of the HKEx announced the withdrawal of the delisting proposals following meetings with the Secretary for Financial Services and the Treasury, the chairman of the SFC, and market participants. A new set of proposals was planned to be published in its place at the end of October.
Monday July 29, 2002	In the wake of persistent public outcry, the Secretary for Financial Services and the Treasury, the SFC chairman, and the HKEx chairman were summoned by the Financial Affairs Panel of the Legislative Council to a meeting on July 31 to explain their respective roles in the "penny stocks crash." The prices of penny stocks improved but generally failed to recover fully to their levels prior to the release of the HKEx consultation paper.
Tuesday July 30, 2002	The SFC launched an investigation into the penny stocks crash to determine whether market manipulation was the cause. Particular emphasis was directed at allegations that some brokers had colluded to engineer the plunge in the prices of penny stocks to exploit the uncertainties surrounding the issue and create panic selling among investors.

Wednesday July 31, 2002	Preempting the call for the establishment of an official commission of inquiry, the Financial Secretary exercized his administrative prerogative to establish a two-person Panel of Inquiry into the Penny Stocks Incident. Although definitive answers proved elusive at times, the Financial Services Panel of the Legislative Council subjected the Secretary for Financial Services and the Treasury, the chairman of the SFC, and the chairman and the chief executive of the HKEx to intense questioning. These officials extended their apologies for "underestimating" the market reaction to the delisting proposals.
Thursday August 1, 2002	As the chief executive of HKSAR expressed his support for the panel of inquiry, public pressure grew for the chairman of the SFC and the chief executive of the HKEx to resign from their respective roles in the handling of the penny stock issue. Victims of the penny stock crash announced their intention to initiate legal action against regulatory bodies for compensation for their losses.

Soon thereafter, K. C. Kwong, the inaugural CEO of HKEx, announced that he would retire from office when his term expired in April 2003.[52]

Initially, public attention focused on the release of the HKEx consultation paper as the root cause of the penny stock sell-off. The view that the market crash was the result of hasty and ill-conceived proposals did not, however, appear to tally with the reality that the proposals were the result of detailed and lengthy discussions between the HKEx and the SFC, the last of which was an endorsement by the SEHK Listing Committee that was comprised of market practitioners. Discussions between the SFC and HKEx are illustrated by the following chronology of events:[53]

July 30, 2001	The HKEx submitted a preliminary draft proposal to the SFC seeking to require the consolidation of stocks that traded at HK$0.01, for more than 20 trading days within a three-month period. It further proposed that the minimum consolidated price be no less than HK$0.10, and that issuers be barred from undertaking any corporate transaction that would result in the stocks' theoretical value falling below this threshold.
August 8, 2001	The SFC responded by stating that the criterion should either be HK$1 or HK$5.

December 12, 2001	The HKEx revised its proposals to mandate that issuers seek consolidation of stocks when their shares traded at below HK$0.20 for the period in question.
January 25, 2002	The SFC insisted that the threshold be set at no less than HK$1.
April 30, 2002	The HKEx further revised its proposal by increasing the threshold to HK$0.30, and for a minimum initial public offering (IPO) price of HK$1 for all new issues that followed the amendment of the Listing Rules.
May 13, 2002	The SFC reiterated its position that the minimum price threshold should be set at HK$1 while the minimum IPO price should be HK$5.
May 15, 2002	The HKEx responded by stating that the proposed HK$1 minimum price threshold was "too hasty" and agreed to discuss a range between HK$0.30 and HK$0.50 as an interim measure.
June 8, 2002	The HKEx submitted its second draft proposals, which included revised thresholds set at HK$0.50 as the minimum share price at which consolidation would be required and HK$2 as the minimum price of IPOs.
June 17, 2002	The SFC replied that it had "no definite views" on the proposed revised thresholds.
July 10, 2002	The HKEx sent the fifth draft of its consultation paper to the Listing Committee of the SEHK for comments and approval after the SFC replied that it had no further significant opinion on HKEx's fifth draft of the consultation paper, which included the $0.50 threshold proposal.

Following the fall in prices in the penny stocks, the Financial Secretary of HKSAR appointed a panel of inquiry to look into the circumstances relating to the preparation and release of the HKEx consultation paper, as noted above. Its main terms of reference were

(a) To examine the existing procedures for the preparation and making of new or amended HKEx rules and regulations, including the process of consultation with the trade and the public;
(b) Having regard to the findings in (a), to review the arrangements for the preparation and release of the Consultation Paper; [and]

(c) To make recommendations as to the measures to be adopted to improve, where necessary, the co-ordination in and procedures for the preparation and making of similar rules and regulations in the future, including the process of consultation with the trade and the public.[54]

The report of the panel (*Report of the Panel of Inquiry on the Penny Stocks Incident* or "PIPSI Report") was published in September 2002. When discussing the causes of the incident, the report's authors stated that it

seemed to have been the outcome of a combination of factors which fed on and magnified each other. There was the prevailing unfavourable market sentiment, the generally weak investor confidence, and the inherent volatility of these stocks. We have noted criticisms of the contents of and the arrangements surrounding the release of the Consultation Paper. Clearly its release triggered the reaction on the 26 July, but it would be simplistic and inaccurate to identify the consultation Paper as the single cause of what happened. Unfounded rumours about margin calls, panic reaction to the dumping, an element of when fortune smiles, take advantage as well as unreflecting herd instincts also played a part.[55]

For example, other reasons for the incident were also put forward. For example, David Webb, a prominent corporate governance activist, argued:

The result of the proposals was a panic sell-off of micro-cap stocks on Friday, as investors quite rationally believed they were about to lose both the market place for their shares and also the protection of the listing rules, which require a certain level of financial reporting, corporate disclosure and approvals of connected transactions. The Listing Rules may be inadequate in many areas, but they are a lot better than no rules at all, which is what you get with a delisted stock.[56]

Others believed that the sell-off could be attributed primarily to an overreaction by investors to proposals for market consultation that were misunderstood by some to be policy changes that were to be implemented. This perception led to a domino effect the ultimate consequence of which was a "herd mentality" market reaction to the fear that all penny stocks would soon be delisted or untradable on the SEHK. It was noted that investors in penny stocks had not in fact lost all their money overnight on July 26, 2006. Most of the declining stocks had in fact experienced sustained price declines over a period of six months prior to the release of the HKEx consultation paper, making some of the losses of July 26, 2006, look relatively small by comparison.[57]

While the PIPSI Report was supportive of the spirit of the HKEx consultation paper, which was premised on fostering good corporate governance, increasing transparency, and enhancing the quality of the market in Hong Kong, its authors identified what they believed to be a crucial weak link that contributed to the Penny Stocks Incident that they expressed in the following manner:

> The crux of what went wrong is that the public associated the [proposed HK$0.50] threshold with delisting rather than consolidation. Consolidation, initially the focus, was no longer at the forefront in the paper. Media discussion in the two or three months preceding the release also concentrated on delisting. In addition, the two issues were intertwined in a lengthy, complex and technical Consultation Paper. The $0.5 threshold thus played a more important role in the Consultation Paper than originally envisaged in the previous stand-alone proposal on share consolidation. Neither the SFC nor the HKEx apparently focused enough on this subtle change. The SFC, in particular, assumed, not unreasonably, that the distinction between delisting and consolidation would be clear and therefore readily understood. This turned out not to have been the case.

The PIPSI Report also examined the process leading to the publication of the HKEx consultation paper, which in its authors' opinion suffered from the lack of an appropriate consultative network. While acknowledging the diligence of both the SFC and the HKEx in preparing the paper, the authors opined that the gestation process for such complex proposals would have been smoother had there been more preconsultation with a wider base of constituents. In particular, "Due process was, in a sense, followed, perhaps too rigidly" and "The lack of engagement of its [i.e., the HKEx] extended family, the somewhat unclear role of the Listing Committee, the slightly tense relationship with the SFC all perhaps contributed to not making full and complete use of the available knowledge, experience and expertise."

In addition, different statements and actions by different parties may have compounded the state of confusion following the collapse of the share prices of penny stocks. While the authors of the PIPSI Report acknowledged the overwhelming support for the continuation of the "three-tiered" regulatory structure, they nonetheless stated that there was an urgent need for clearer delineation of responsibilities as well as for better coordination between the three parties. In particular, they expressed the view that "the handling of regulatory issues by both the HKEx and the

SFC and the splitting of roles and functions between them not only lead [*sic*] to inefficiencies but also to confusion." Recognizing the tension between the SFC and the HKEx pertaining to listing matters, the authors considered it "timely for the present arrangement to be reviewed," recommending that

> the Government in conjunction with the SFC and the HKEx review how best to redefine the roles and functions over listing matters with a view to increasing effectiveness, efficiency, clarity, fairness and credibility of the regulatory system. We would only add that the perceived conflicts within the HKEx and the inefficiency and confusion caused by the dual regulatory functions have been commented on not only by market practitioners and financial analysts, but also by many who were and still are members of the extended family of the HKEx. In particular, most have suggested that if a Listing Committee is to be retained, as most believe it ought to be, it cannot be housed under the HKEx. Within the current structure, the only entity under which it can be accommodated is the SFC.

As regards the government, it "should clearly reposition itself as a facilitator and a co-ordinator and not as a regulator, leaving market forces to work within the broad policy framework and without political interference." The structure of the government also gave rise to some confusion given the perceived overlap in some functions that were exercised by the Financial Secretary and the Secretary for Financial Services and the Treasury, prompting the authors to call upon the government to review the exercise of their statutory powers and functions, as well as to clarify the division of responsibilities and lines of command between these two important offices.

The PIPSI Report identified the HKEx as being a regulator only in a limited sense of the term. Its wholly-owned subsidiary, the SEHK, possessed no statutory powers of investigation and derived its powers through an interpretation of the contractual terms of the Listing Agreement that it entered into with the issuers. Subsequent attempts to enforce the terms of this agreement gave rise to some legal uncertainty, as evidenced by the increasing number of judicial reviews that were launched against the SEHK.

Morals

- Politics may matter in the governance of market infrastructure institutions.
- With multiple regulators, it is not always easy to determine precisely which institution has what regulatory powers and responsibilities.

NASDAQ: ATTEMPTED TAKEOVER OF
LONDON STOCK EXCHANGE 2006–8

Over the period 2004 to early 2006 the LSE was subject to several bids and approaches from various institutions interested in purchasing it. In December 2004, Deutsche Börse bid 530 pence per share for a total of £1.35 billion.[58] Euronext subsequently approached the LSE about a possible merger, although it did not place a formal offer.[59] In March 2005, Deutsche Börse dropped its takeover plans.[60] In December 2005, Macquarie Bank bid 580 pence per share for the LSE for a total of £1.5 billion, an offer the LSE rejected as "derisory."[61] In February 2006 Macquarie retracted its offer.[62]

On March 10, 2006, NASDAQ then made an unsolicited and indicative offer to acquire the LSE for 950 pence per share in cash, for a total of £2.4 billion.[63] NASDAQ identified a range of benefits of its proposed offer. The indicative cash offer was said to represent

- 72% premium over the closing price of 552 pence on 12 August 2005, the business day immediately prior to Macquarie's announcement of its potential interest in a possible formal approach to LSE;
- 64% premium to the cash offer share price of 580 pence per share offered by Macquarie;
- 12% premium to the closing price of 845.5 pence on 8 March 2006; and
- multiple of 29.8 times adjusted earnings for the 12 months to 31 December 2005.[64]

The proposal was also thought to offer a range of potential benefits to issuers and market participants by creating

- the only global, cross-border equity market platform giving issuers the ability to dual-list simultaneously in London and New York;
- the leading global exchange for listing companies of all sizes and the natural choice for international issuers;
- a powerful equity market place by number of listings with over 6,266 listed companies with a total market capitalization of approximately £4.2 trillion (US$7.3 trillion); and
- significant efficiencies which would benefit the users of both platforms, and fully execute on the efficiencies that both companies offer their market participants.

There appeared to be several other factors motivating the bid. Taking over the LSE would have been the biggest acquisition for NASDAQ since the NASD founded it in 1971. The bid would preempt the possibility of the NYSE purchasing the LSE—although subsequently the

NYSE purchased Euronext. NASDAQ may have also been trying to take advantage of its stock multiple that was much higher than that of the LSE at the time.

The LSE rejected NASDAQ's indicative bid, however, and NASDAQ withdrew it on March 30, 2006.[65] Under the UK Takeover Code, NASDAQ was then barred from making another bid for six months until October 2, 2006, unless it could arrange an agreed deal, or a rival bidder made another bid. NASDAQ was, however, allowed to buy another 10% stake in the LSE after a week's time, and a further 5% the following week, taking its stake up to the maximum 29.9% allowed, before it would be obliged to make a full bid. Over the next few months NASDAQ progressively increased its stake in the LSE. On April 11, 2006, NASDAQ bought a 14.99% stake in the LSE (35.4 million shares) at £11.75 per share from the LSE's largest shareholder at the time, Threadneedle Asset Management, and on April 12, 2006, it purchased a further 2.69 million shares from Scottish Widows Investment Partnership.[66] By May 10, 2006, NASDAQ had raised its stake to 24.1% of the LSE.[67]

Under the UK Takeover Code, these acquisitions created a "floor" for the price NASDAQ would be required to pay, until March 2007, should it wish to bid again for the LSE. The floor was the highest price NASDAQ had paid in acquiring its stake, and was £12.43 a share. After March 2007 NASDAQ was allowed to rebid at a lower price. On November 20, 2006, NASDAQ increased its holding in the LSE to 28.75% and tabled a "final offer" at a price of £12.43, the minimum permitted bid, for a total of £2.7 billion. The LSE immediately rejected this bid, stating that it "substantially undervalues" the company.[68]

On December 12, 2006, NASDAQ revised its offer, but this time it indicated that it sought to purchase just over 50% of LSE's shares, rather than the 90% it had initially been seeking. While the approach of seeking to buy over 50% of the LSE's shares would not allow NASDAQ to force a mandatory buyout of all other shareholders,[69] if successful, it would still allow NASDAQ to control the board of the LSE and its dividend policy.[70] In this second offer, NASDAQ did not raise its bid, however, and many hedge funds that had accumulated large holdings of the LSE's shares, as well as the LSE's CEO, indicated that the bid was still inadequate.[71] NASDAQ's bid was made more difficult because it had described its offer as "final," which, under the UK Takeover Panel's bidding rules, restricted its ability to raise its offer except under certain circumstances. Unlike Deutsche Börse's previous bid, however, there were no objections to NASDAQ's bid on competition or regulatory grounds.[72]

A week prior to the closing deadline for receiving acceptances of the NASDAQ bid, the NASDAQ CEO confirmed that he was considering working with a group of banks that were seeking to create a new trading system called Turquoise to compete with the LSE, if he was not successful in purchasing the LSE.[73] This approach was widely questioned, however, since it did not appear logical that NASDAQ should both seek to buy the LSE, and at the same time look to undermine the success and share price of the LSE by supporting a potential competitor.[74] NASDAQ's offer was rejected by LSE shareholders—it received acceptances of only 0.41% of the rest of the register by the closing deadline of February 10, 2007.[75] The offer then lapsed on February 12, 2007.[76]

In order to pay for its acquisition of LSE shares, NASDAQ utilized US$287.6 million in cash, with the balance financed through credit facilities. In an SEC filing in April 2006, NASDAQ revealed that it was replacing a US$748.1 million credit facility arranged by J.P. Morgan Chase and Merrill Lynch in 2005 with money from a Bank of America loan. Moody's Investors Service cut the rating on NASDAQ's debt to Ba3, and Standard & Poor's put the company's triple-B-minus rating on a watchlist. Both organizations said they were concerned that NASDAQ was taking on too much debt to complete the purchase of its stake in LSE.

The proposed merger led to a regulatory reaction in the UK. Both HM Treasury and the FSA were concerned about the merger, not because they were worried that the ownership of the LSE might not be based in the UK, but because they did not want the US regulatory environment to be imposed on the LSE were it to be bought by NASDAQ.[77] In response, the government decided to legislate to protect the UK's regulatory environment.

On September 13, 2006, Ed Balls, the economic secretary to the Treasury, stated:

> We have resisted pressure for heavy-handed responses to US corporate scandals. Four years ago, the WorldCom accounting scandal broke in the US. The calls from Parliament and commentators were for a regulatory crackdown. And we could have sought easy headlines. Instead, we responded with a measured, proportionate response. We were initially criticised for that, but the alternative approach, as the Americans have found with Sarbanes-Oxley, would have been wrong for Britain. I believe that we were right not to go down that road. I am very well aware that regulatory mistakes can be very costly. And we are determined that our regulatory regime continues to be the best in the world.

Balls emphasized two points with respect to NASDAQ's interest in the LSE.[78] First, the government was neutral with respect to the nationality of the ownership of the LSE. Second, the government's interest in the ownership of the LSE was that it should not affect the existing light-touch, risk-based regulatory regime under which the exchange and its members and issuers then operated.

The government's key aim was to enhance the FSA's powers in relation to recognized exchanges by giving it the power to veto rule changes that would be disproportionate. Balls justified and outlined the elements of the legislation the government proposed to enact as follows:

> It has been put to me that the right approach is Government intervention to protect the LSE from foreign ownership. I reject this argument. This would fly in the face of the traditions that have underpinned the City's success. A policy of protecting "national champions" would damage, not bolster the interests of London and the UK.
>
> The Government's interest in this area is specific and clear: to safeguard the light touch and proportionate regulatory regime that has made London a magnet for international business. That has made London an economic asset for the UK, for Europe, and for countries throughout the world. I can therefore announce today that the UK Government will now legislate to protect our regulatory approach.
>
> This legislation will confer a new and specific power on the FSA to veto rule changes proposed by exchanges that would be disproportionate in their impact on the pivotal economic role that exchanges play in the UK and EU economies.
>
> It will outlaw the imposition of any rules that might endanger the light touch, risk based regulatory regime that underpins London's success.
>
> Nothing in this legislation has any consequence for the nationality of the ownership of UK exchanges. It will neither make overseas ownership easier or more difficult. We remain open to overseas investment that will continue to be able to benefit from our regulatory regime.

The legislation was enacted on December 19, 2006.[79]

Given the difficulties NASDAQ faced in purchasing the LSE, it decided to pursue a different target, and this had significant implications for the ownership of the LSE. On May 25, 2007, NASDAQ agreed to buy OMX for US$3.7 billion.[80] On August 9, 2007, however, Borse Dubai offered US$4 billion for OMX, prompting speculation of a bidding war.[81] Borse Dubai's bid was potentially put into jeopardy, however, as it did not correctly follow the takeover rules in Sweden. The Swedish regulator, Finansinspektionen, ruled that the press release that Borse Dubai made public on August 9, 2007, was a public takeover bid, and that Borse Dubai had not undertaken to follow the rules and accept the sanctions that OMX Nordic Exchange Stockholm AB stipulated for such offers. Finansinspektionen decided, however, that as Borse Dubai had subsequently complied with the relevant legislation on takeovers, it would take no further action against Borse Dubai.[82]

On August 20, 2007, NASDAQ announced that it was abandoning its plan to take over the LSE, and subsequently began looking for options to divest its 31% shareholding in the company, in order to obtain more money to increase its offer for OMX.[83] The Qatari Investment Authority (QIA) appeared to be the favorite to buy this block of shares.[84] On September 20, 2007, however, NASDAQ and Borse Dubai agreed on a complex deal that determined both the control of OMX and that of NASDAQ's shareholding in the LSE.[85]

The key elements of the deal were the following:

1. Borse Dubai would continue its previously announced offer for OMX, at 230 kronor per share valuing OMX at $3.97 billion.
2. NASDAQ would acquire all OMX shares purchased by Borse Dubai after its offer for OMX completed.
3. Borse Dubai would become a 19.99% shareholder in NASDAQ, with its voting rights capped at 5%, which was the maximum allowed by NASDAQ's certificate of incorporation and bylaws. NASDAQ would issue to Borse Dubai approximately 60.6 million NASDAQ shares, and also pay 11.4 billion kronor in cash to Borse Dubai, assuming that Borse Dubai acquired all outstanding OMX shares. Borse Dubai would then retain approximately 42.6 million of the NASDAQ shares (approximately 19.99% of the total) with the balance of approximately 18.0 million shares being held in trust. The shares in trust would eventually be sold.
4. NASDAQ would become a strategic shareholder and the principal commercial partner of Dubai International Financial Exchange (DIFX), the holding company for Borse Dubai, by purchasing 33.3% of its shares for US$50 million.[86]
5. Borse Dubai would acquire 28.0% of the LSE's shares that NASDAQ owned at a price of UK£14.14 per share for approximately $1.6 billion.
6. The DIFX would be rebranded with the NASDAQ brand and licensed with technology from the NASDAQ/OMX combination.

This deal enraged the Qatar Investment Authority,[87] and on the same day it bought a 20% stake in the LSE and a 10% stake in OMX.[88] The QIA initially asked OMX shareholders to hold off on a decision about the NASDAQ–Borse Dubai offer pending its evaluation of the situation—but subsequently decided not to pursue its purchase of OMX. On September 26, 2007, NASDAQ sold the balance of shares it still held in the LSE through the market for $193.5 million in cash, following Borse Dubai's purchase of most of its block shareholding in the LSE. Part of the proceeds NASDAQ received from its sale of LSE shares was used to repay its credit facilities. In December 2007, NASDAQ obtained clearance from the Committee on Foreign Investment in the United States concerning Borse Dubai's investment in NASDAQ.[89] Borse Dubai's offer to buy all the outstanding shares of OMX expired on February 12, 2008, at which time it announced that it had successful purchased 97.6% of the outstanding shares of OMX via the tender. The full deal between NASDAQ and Borse Dubai was finally concluded on February 27, 2008.[90]

Moral

- A national regulator is unlikely to be allowed to give up regulatory sovereignty over its national markets and its market infrastructure institutions, whoever owns such infrastructure institutions.

NEW YORK STOCK EXCHANGE:
RESIGNATION OF CHAIRMAN-CEO 2003

In May 2003 it was revealed that the NYSE chairman and CEO Richard "Dick" Grasso[91] had received a 2002 pay package valued at more than US$10 million, and had a retirement package valued at between US$80 million and US$100 million.[92] At this time, the NYSE operated on a not-for-profit basis under New York corporation law. Grasso's compensation significantly exceeded the annual pay received by other regulators and exchange officials.

Some corporate governance experts questioned Grasso's pay level. "I think you would have to equate his salary to something like a public oversight board," asserted Charles Elson, director of the John L. Weinberg Center for Corporate Governance at the University of Delaware. His pay, Elson argued, should have been "in line with someone occupying a quasi-public job: head of a major foundation, head of a major university."[93] In May 2003, Elliot Spitzer, the New York Attorney General, stated, "There are many problems with the NYSE governance structure. They need to be addressed."[94]

By June 2003, there was a growing consensus among NYSE governance committee members that Grasso's full compensation package should be disclosed. On June 6, 2003, the NYSE announced a 10-step plan to overhaul its corporate governance.[95] One of the reforms was the disclosure of executives' compensation, including that of Grasso, in its annual report. Other changes included a bar on directors of Wall Street firms being members of NYSE's compensation committee, and the prohibition of exchange executives from serving on other public company boards. Public criticism of the governance of the NYSE continued to grow (as evidenced in Council of Institutional Investors [2003]). In August 2003, Grasso was awarded a two-year contract extension and US$140 million in accumulated savings, retirement benefits, and incentives.[96] Under the new contract, Grasso would maintain his US$1.4 million annual base salary and could continue to collect a yearly bonus of at least US$1 million. The contract running to May 2007 replaced one that was signed in 1999 and was set to expire in 2005.

In response to this, the SEC began contemplating a probe of salaries of senior executives at the major exchanges, including the NYSE. On September 2, 2003, SEC chairman William Donaldson requested that the NYSE provide a detailed accounting of its decision to pay out nearly US$140 million in accumulated retirement benefits to Grasso, as well as extending his contract to 2007.[97] Donaldson said that Grasso's pay package "raises serious questions regarding the effectiveness of the NYSE's current governance structure." He ordered the NYSE to submit minutes from several board meetings on Grasso's compensation, a description of how every NYSE compensation committee member was chosen, and detailed terms of the chairman's pay.

On September 9, 2003, traders at the NYSE started a petition to oust Grasso as chairman, in anger at his salary. James Rutledge, an NYSE member and former director of the Alliance of Floor Brokers, issued a memo to exchange firms to "initiate the changes we desperately need to begin to move forward."[98] He also released a copy of a letter he had sent to SEC chairman Donaldson that asked the agency to examine Grasso's compensation and NYSE's corporate governance structure.

On September 10, 2003, Grasso defended receiving US$140 million for his work at the exchange and said he would forgo a previously undisclosed additional US$48 million he was due to receive over the next four years.[99] Some corporate governance advocates, however, said that Grasso obtained his lucrative remuneration package partly because NYSE had avoided governance practices adopted by many major public companies, including the establishment of a collegial process for choosing its compensation committee. Since taking over the chairmanship of NYSE in 1995, Grasso had recommended all committee-membership assignments to the full board for approval, including the compensation committee that set his pay, and had done so without formal input from anyone else on the board.[100] Grasso's case represented "the most egregious example of excessive pay and the lack of corporate governance," asserted Alan Johnson, managing director of New York pay consultants Johnson & Associates.[101] There was also concern about the governance of the NYSE, given its wide regulatory responsibilities.[102] Grasso's description of his job as two-thirds businessman, one-third regulator suggested that he placed greater emphasis on the first than on the second role.[103]

On September 16, 2003, the California State Treasurer and the heads of California's two giant pension funds, California Public Employees' Retirement System (CalPERS), and California State Teachers' Retirement System (CalSTRS), called for Grasso's resignation, saying that the size of Grasso's pay package endangered attempts to reform corporate governance.[104] They indicated that they had deep concern about Grasso's compensation and wanted the pay revised, together with Grasso's resignation.[105] On September 17, 2003, Grasso resigned as chairman and CEO of the NYSE, and John Reed was appointed as interim chairman and CEO on September 21, 2003.

Reed subsequently commissioned a report from the law firm Winston & Strawn to investigate and review issues relating to Grasso's compensation, and the process by which the compensation was determined.[106] The NYSE provided this report to the SEC and the New York Attorney General, who then commenced his own investigations into these issues in January 2004. The fact that the NYSE was a not-for-profit corporation gave the Attorney General broad authority to enforce New York law regarding not-for-profit corporations, a key element of which in this context was that such firms were only entitled to pay reasonable compensation.

On about February 12, 2004, Reed wrote to Grasso stating that the NYSE had determined that the compensation and benefits that he had received "were excessive and at unreasonable levels."[107] The NYSE also demanded that Grasso repay the NYSE $120 million and reserved its rights to seek additional amounts beyond that. Grasso refused to return any part of the US$188 million compensation package. In fact, Grasso argued that he was still owed US$50 million by his former employer. Grasso's legal counsel stated in a letter dated February 26, 2004, that Grasso "has no intention of returning any portion of his compensation to the exchange."[108]

On May 24, 2004, the New York Attorney General filed a lawsuit in New York Supreme Court against Grasso, seeking the return of at least US$100 million from Grasso's US$188.5 million pay package. At a press conference, Spitzer said the process that determined Grasso's compensation was "rigged" and "wholly inappropriate and illegal." He said that Grasso, who was also the NYSE chairman, at turns misled and intimidated some of the exchange's board members. The lawsuit also named as defendants Kenneth Langone, the NYSE compensation committee's former chairman, who played a role in the approval of the pay package, and the exchange itself.[109] "When this case comes to trial, we will seek well over US$100 million back from Mr. Grasso," Spitzer said. "The amount that was paid was simply not reasonable." Frank Ashen, a former NYSE executive vice president who had participated in fashioning Grasso's compensation package, reached a settlement with Spitzer's office, under which he would return US$1.3 million to the NYSE, Spitzer also said.

Spitzer asserted eight causes of action—six against Grasso, one against Kenneth Langone (chairman of the NYSE Compensation Committee from 1999 to June 2003), and one for declaratory and injunctive relief against the NYSE. Of the six causes of action against Grasso, four were nonstatutory common-law claims and two were statutory claims brought under New York's nonprofit corporation law. In response, Grasso denied the New York Attorney General's allegations of wrongdoing, and also asserted claims against the NYSE and NYSE chairman John Reed, including claims that the NYSE terminated Grasso without cause in September 2003 and breached his 1999 and 2003 employment agreements, and that the NYSE and Reed defamed him. Grasso also asserted third-party claims against former director Carl McCall for negligence, negligent misrepresentation, and contribution. In May 2004 Grasso said that although he would not give up any of the US$139.5 million he had already received— he would cede an additional US$48 million he believed he was owed, in exchange for an NYSE apology "for destroying my reputation." Grasso stated: "If they say I am an honorable man and I did nothing wrong, it's the end of the issue. If not, let's go to war."[110]

A complicated series of court decisions and appeals reviewing the Attorney General's claims against Grasso, and Grasso's counterclaims, ensued.[111] The final result came in two judgments on June 25, 2008, and July 1, 2008.[112] The first dismissed the four nonstatutory causes of action against Grasso—three for lack of standing on the part of the Attorney General, and the fourth for lack of proper pleading. The second judgment dismissed the remaining two legal claims against Grasso. The court ruled that following the merger in 2006 of NYSE Inc, a nonprofit entity, with Archipelago Holdings Inc. to form NYSE Inc., a for-profit entity, the Attorney General no longer had standing to sue Grasso under not-for-profit corporation law. As the Attorney General had only been seeking the return of money from Grasso to NYSE Inc., and as any money received from a successful claim would benefit solely the private interest of the for-profit NYSE Inc. and not the public interest, it was deemed that any ruling against Grasso would thus no longer serve the public interest.[113]

As a result of these two judgments, the Attorney General's spokesman, representing a new Attorney General following the earlier resignation of Spitzer, stated: "We have reviewed the court's opinion and determined that an appeal would not be warranted. Thus, for all intents and purposes, the Grasso case is over."[114]

Moral

- Public outcry can lead to political and regulatory intervention in executive compensation levels at a market infrastructure institution.

Osaka Securities Exchange: "Murakami Fund" Purchase of Shares 2005

The manner in which a stock exchange operating as a for-profit joint-stock company should be governed became a controversial issue in Japan when MAC Asset Management Inc. ("Murakami Fund") announced that it had acquired a large stake in the Osaka Securities Exchange (OSE) at the end of March 2005.[115] The OSE had listed its shares on its own "Hercules" market in April 2004.[116]

The Murakami Fund was an activist fund managed by Yoshiaki Murakami, a former official at the Ministry of International Trade and Industry, and president of M&A Consulting Inc. He was a well-known shareholder activist, who announced his vociferous and direct attempts to persuade companies to increase their shareholder value on his company's website. After acquiring an initial stake in the OSE, Mr. Murakami called on the exchange to return a larger share of its earned surplus of some ¥20 billion to shareholders in the form of a significantly higher dividend, or possibly through share buybacks. He stepped up these calls from March 2005, when he acquired 10% of the exchange's shares.

The response of the OSE was to argue that it needed to keep a certain amount of cash and deposits in order to ensure that it would always be able to settle derivative trades. The exchange had had experience of the potential need for such funds in 1995. At that time, the Nikkei 225 stock index futures contract, the OSE's main trading product, was used in the illicit trades that brought about the downfall of the British merchant bank Barings. The huge positions in the Nikkei 225 and TOPIX futures that Barings' head futures trader in Singapore, Nick Leeson, had built up were left unsettled when the bank collapsed. It was then decided that other members of the exchange would settle on behalf of Barings in order to liquidate Leeson's positions, and that Barings' margin deposits would be used to cover the resulting losses. When Barings collapsed, it was estimated that the losses on its Nikkei 225 futures positions on the OSE amounted to some ¥30 billion. Although this was roughly the same amount as Barings' margin deposit, it was agreed that if this were not enough to cover the loss, the exchange's "default compensation reserve," namely the clearing reserve to which members contributed and which the exchange held, would be used to cover the rest of the loss. In the event, the exchange was in fact able to liquidate Leeson's positions, which had a nominal value of not less than ¥300 billion, quite easily, and the losses were less than had at first been feared. At the time, however, it was an anxious and exhausting experience for both the officials of the OSE and the supervisory authorities.

As of September 2004 the OSE's holdings of cash and deposits amounted to ¥25.8 billion, or 16.8% of its total assets. Although this was a sizeable amount both in absolute terms and as a percentage of total assets, it was not out of line with the practice of futures exchanges outside Japan. The CME, for example, held $357.56 million, or 12% of its total assets, in the form of cash or cash equivalents as of December 2004. As a public company the OSE was, however, obliged to record the funds in its default compensation reserve as a capital surplus on its balance sheet. Similarly, it had to post a corresponding amount under "assets" for all the cash, deposits, and securities in the form of which it held these funds. At least some of the cash and deposits that Murakami called on the OSE to return to its shareholders were thus settlement funds that it might have to draw on in the event of a default by one of its members.

Following the OSE's rejection of Murakami's demand, he sought to become a nonexecutive director of the company. He continued to voice his opinions about how the OSE should be run and to call on the company to return its considerable retained earnings to shareholders in the form of an increased dividend. He also criticized the exchange for suspending listings on its Hercules market because of a computer system failure. In July 2005 OSE set up a panel to advise it on how a listed stock exchange that was also a clearinghouse could best manage its cash.[117]

On June 13, 2005, Murakami filed an application with the Japan Financial Services Agency (JFSA) to increase his stake of the OSE to 20%, as required under the Securities and Exchange Law. The reason he decided to apply to increase his stake in the company was apparently that he wanted to reduce the large proportion of the company's shares held by securities companies, to call for the appointment of some nonexecutive directors, and to strengthen the company's corporate governance. On August 13, 2005, a hearing was held to give both Murakami and the JFSA an opportunity to voice their views. The agency indicated that it was going to reject the application and later announced this officially.

The JFSA explained that it rejected Murakami's application because he did not meet the requirement that there be no risk that an applicant might use its voting rights to interfere with the proper functioning of a demutualized stock exchange.[118] The agency justified its position by arguing that because Murakami had a large stake in the investment fund he managed, and because this fund invested in companies that were, or might be, listed on OSE, this might lead to a conflict of interest between the fund's investment activities and the OSE's self-regulatory responsibilities. This argument implied, however, that all listed companies, securities companies, or companies that might list at some point in the future would also have an application to become a major shareholder of a stock exchange rejected. It also appeared that if an applicant had to prove that there was no risk that it might interfere with the proper functioning of a stock exchange, its application would have little chance of being approved unless it already operated a properly functioning stock exchange. As Japanese stock exchanges and securities dealers associations were exempt from meeting the three requirements specified in the Securities and Exchange Law in order to obtain approval to become major shareholders of stock exchanges, the requirements thus appeared to be relevant only to potential non-Japanese stock exchanges, stock exchange holding companies, or securities dealers associations, which might wish to purchase a substantial stake in a Japanese stock exchange.

Murakami is reported to have said at the hearing that if the JFSA's case was upheld, nobody's application would ever be approved, showing that the law as it stood was a bad law. Although Murakami accused the agency of an "abuse of its discretionary powers," he did not seek to have the decision overturned in the courts.

On December 29, 2005, Murakami announced that his fund had sold its entire stake in OSE to the systems development company CSK Holdings Corp. CSK, which had close ties with the OSE through its stock price information service, said it would strive to forge a "friendly relationship" with the stock exchange.[119] The panel set up to advise OSE on how to manage its cash reserves also published a report in December 2005 proposing new rules for setting up a reserve fund and new procedures for its use. The exchange then established a permanent committee for its settlement business in February 2006 to implement the proposals made by the panel.

Moral

- A for-profit integrated exchange/CCP may seek to sacrifice appropriate risk management procedures in order to enhance profits.

CHAPTER SEVEN

CCPs and CSDs

A SERIES OF CASE STUDIES illustrating how some specific CCPs and CSDs have been governed in particular contexts are presented in this chapter. The following institutions and contexts are described in turn: the relationship between The Canadian Depository for Securities' owners, its users, and board directors from the company's inception to 2008; the establishment of EuroCCP by DTCC over the period 2000–2002; the creation of Clearstream International by Deutsche Börse over the period 1999–2002; some aspects of how Euroclear was governed regarding its creation, ownership, and board structure up until 2006; and the creation of LCH.Clearnet and some difficulties it faced over the period 2003–6. A few brief general lessons from each case study are also identified, in a manner similar to that undertaken in the previous chapter.

CANADIAN DEPOSITORY FOR SECURITIES: OWNERSHIP, USAGE, AND BOARD REPRESENTATION TO 2008

The Canadian Depository for Securities Ltd. is the parent holding company for the CDS group that includes CDS Clearing and Depository Services Inc., the operator of Canada's national securities depository for nonderivative securities, and the provider of clearing and settlement services for Canada's equities, debt, fixed-income, and money markets. The relationship between the company's owners, users, and board directors from its inception until 2008 is examined here.

A brief note on the use of the term "CDS" is important. It has been, and still is, widely used to refer both to the group's holding company, The Canadian Depository for Securities Ltd. (CDS Limited), and to the group's current main operating subsidiary, CDS Clearing and Depository Services Inc. (CDS Clearing). This double use is due in part to the fact that in 2006 CDS Ltd. restructured its business units, and in fact created the subsidiary CDS Clearing to provide the core clearing and settlement services, which previously had been delivered by CDS Limited itself. At this time the management and supervision of CDS Clearing was assigned to the board of directors of the parent holding company. Prior to 2006, CDS Limited was often referred to as CDS, and there was no CDS

Clearing. Subsequent to the reorganization, The Canadian Depository for Securities Ltd. has normally been referred to as CDS Limited, and CDS Clearing and Depository Services Inc. has been referred to as CDS (or CDS Clearing). Given that the description presented here examines the company both before and after 2006, the term CDS is used here to refer to both institutions. Where necessary, a more specific identification of which institution is being referred to in the text is included in order to avoid ambiguity.

The evolution of the relationship between CDS's owners, users, and board directors has been complicated. The creation of CDS was relatively informal. In order to raise the necessary finance to start the company, "the hat was simply passed round" among industry participants. Following the establishment of a study group, an Agreement of Trust was entered into on June 9, 1969, among 13 trustees who sponsored the depository concept and together provided C$1 million funding. This, together with the results of four subsequent fund-raising tranches, raised a total of C$6.1 million for the company. It is unclear how this money was accounted for by the sponsors at the time. A range of different types of organizations participated in these fund-raisings, including mutual funds and their associations, life insurance companies, the Canadian Investor Protection Fund, the Trust Companies Association of Canada, the Investment Funds Institute of Canada, the Vancouver Stock Exchange (VSE) and the Alberta Stock Exchange (ASE).

The last and most recent funding for CDS took place in the early 1980s, raised C$2.6 million, and resulted in the issuance of the 2.6 million common shares. At the same time, 6.1 million preferred shares in the company were issued to recognize the earlier funding tranches. At that time, the Canadian financial sector was divided up into different industry groups or "pillars"—including banks, brokerage firms, and trust companies—which were prohibited by regulation from operating in each others' activities, either directly or through subsidiaries.[1] Each of these three industry groups contributed one-third of the funding for CDS's final tranche of funding, and as a whole, representatives of each group were each allocated one-third of the common shares issued. The reason for this structure, as described by a "blue ribbon" review committee established in 1974, was that

> if any one element of the financial community were in full ownership and control of the Depository the other groups would have concern about its financial integrity and responsibility, fear about losing control over the manner and methods of achieving objectives and misgivings that important parts of their business may be taken over on a rate-cutting competitive basis by the Depository.[2]

The brokerage industry contributed funds via the three SROs of which they were members at the time: the IIROC (then named the Investment Dealers Association of Canada), the Toronto Stock Exchange (the TSE as it then was, and now the TSX), and the Montreal Stock Exchange (the MSE as it then was, and subsequently the Montreal Exchange [ME]). The amount each individual member of the brokerage industry contributed was that proportion of the total raised by the brokerage industry, specified by the individual member firm's capitalization divided by the total capitalization of the brokerage industry at the time. Each individual member did not, however, receive shares in CDS. Instead, each SRO identified which members were based within its audit jurisdiction, and shares were allocated to each of the three SROs, in proportion to the total capitalization of the brokerage industry represented by the aggregate of these members' contributions. Based on their members' contributions, the TSE was allocated 12.7% of the common shares of CDS, the ME was allocated 5.4%, and the IIROC was allocated 15.2%.

The precise shareholdings originally allocated to the individual banks and trust companies is not public information. The one-third of the company's shares issued to the banks was registered in the name of a bank nominee (Lake and Co.), and held for the six banks. The one-third of the company's shares issued to the trust companies was registered in the name of a trust company (Montreal Trust Co.) and held as nominee for the various trust companies.

At the time of issuing the common shares, preferred shares were also issued to the institutions that had participated in the five previous funding-raising tranches.[3] It is unclear why the earlier funders were allocated preferred shares rather than common shares. Some of the institutions that had participated in the five first fund-raising tranches did not continue their support. For example, the VSE and ASE instead created their own clearing and settlement companies, the Vancouver Stock Exchange Service Corporation, which later became the West Canada Depository Trust Company (WCDTC) and the West Canada Clearing Corporation (WCCC). The preferred shares have few rights. They are noncumulative preferred shares, so that if no dividends are declared in any particular year, then the rights to the dividends not paid are not rolled over, and due in the next year. In the event of a winding up of CDS, the preferred shareholders' original investment must be repaid prior to any distributions to the common shareholders. They have no voting rights over most issues facing CDS, except in extraordinary circumstances mandated by the Canada Business Corporations Act.

Three broad industry developments led to a range of changes in the ownership of CDS. The first was the breakdown of the three-pillar model in the financial industry. In 1987 Canada had its "Little Bang," in which the regulatory barriers between the three sectors of the financial industry were dismantled. Both the regulatory process to achieve this, and the subsequent industrial restructuring, were complicated in nature, but the end result was that banks were permitted by new regulations to enter the trust business through the acquisition of trust companies as subsidiaries. Within a few years after the enactment of these regulations, all of the trust companies that were shareholders in CDS were acquired by a number of banks that were shareholders in CDS. Of the 33.33% initially allocated to the trust companies, 16.6% is now registered to a nominee on behalf of the Toronto-Dominion Bank, 5.5% is now registered to a nominee on behalf of Royal Bank of Canada, and 11.1% is now registered to a nominee on behalf of Bank of Nova Scotia.

The second industry development that led to changes in the ownership of CDS was the restructuring of the Canadian exchanges. Under a memorandum of agreement dated March 15, 1999, between the ASE, the MSE (as it then was), the TSE (as it then was), and the VSE, the TSE became Canada's sole exchange for the trading of large-capitalized (senior) equities.[4] The ME assumed responsibility for the trading of options and derivatives, and the VSE and ASE merged to form the Canadian Venture Exchange, handling trading in small-cap (junior) equities. The latter subsequently merged with the Canadian Dealing Network, Winnipeg Stock Exchange, and the equities portion of the ME. On March 31, 2000, in the last phase of the restructuring, the ME became the sole owner of the Canadian Derivatives Clearing Corporation, when TSE transferred its 50% shareholding in the corporation to the ME, while the ME transferred its 5.4% shareholding in CDS to the TSE.

The third industry development that led to changes in the ownership of CDS was the demutualization of the Toronto Stock Exchange. Prior to its demutualization, the TSX had been holding its shares in CDS on behalf of the brokerage industry. In the demutualization process, completed on April 3, 2000, the TSX issued its own shares in exchange for its members' seats, then completed an initial public offering to become a public for-profit company. Some members sold these shares to the public, while others kept them. The TSX demutualization led to no formal change regarding the TSX's holdings in CDS. In particular, the share registration did not change, the number of shares registered to the TSX did not change, and the TSX had no agreement or trust instrument with its members that it needed to amend or terminate. The TSX did, however, become a public company with a for-profit mandate. The change in incentives facing the TSX following demutualization may have changed the attitude of the TSX regarding its shareholding in CDS. Where prior to the demutualization, the TSX may have sought to exercise the rights associated with its holding in CDS shares on behalf of the brokerage industry, post-demutualization the TSX may have sought to exercise those same rights to further its own profit objectives.

The power to nominate directors to the CDS board has also evolved over time. Since 1981, a Pooling Agreement between CDS's shareholders has specified how they nominate directors to its board. Initially, the Pooling Agreement specified that each of the three industry groups would nominate three directors, there would be five independent directors, and one officer from CDS. A quorum rule at board meetings was implemented to safeguard the interests of each of the pillars of the Canadian financial sector operating at the time of CDS's creation.[5] The CDS by-laws, together with relevant board resolutions, classified the board into three industry quorum groups, consisting of a "bank," a "brokerage," and a "trust company" quorum group.[6] In addition to requiring a quorum for the transaction of business at any board meeting of at least six directors, at least one member from each industry quorum group had to be present as part of a quorum for the transaction of business at board and board committee meetings.[7] This gave each industry group an effective veto over board decision-making. If any one industry group decided not to send any of its directors to a particular meeting where a decision with which it might disagree was being discussed, the board would not have a quorum, and would thus not be able to come to a decision.

The Pooling Agreement was amended in October 1996 when CDS merged operations with the WCDTC and the WCCC. At that time a concession was provided such that two of the independent director seats were allocated to the VSE and to the ASE, and one each to the owners of the WCDTC and WCCC. When the VSE and the ASE merged to form the Canadian Venture Exchange in 1999, one of these Western director seats was dropped and the remaining director position was assumed by the merged Canadian Venture Exchange. When the TSX bought the Canadian Venture Exchange in 2002, it assumed the directorship allocated to the Canadian Venture Exchange. Formally this nominee was an industry (namely a "nonindependent"), but also a nonquorum, position. This directorship, however, was in fact never filled.

Under the Pooling Agreement at that time, out of a total of 15 board directors, the bank shareholders nominated six directors, TSX nominated two directors, TSX Venture Exchange nominated one director, the IIROC nominated one director, and the CDS board nominated four independent directors from outside the securities industry, and one officer from CDS, namely its president-CEO.[8] By custom, one of the independent directors was an ex-deputy governor of the Bank of Canada, there was at least one director from Québec and also one from the west of the country.

The Pooling Agreement was revised again on August 10, 2007, following which the board was to consist of nine members appointed by the shareholders, the CEO of CDS, and five independent members. The industry quorum rules were also abolished, and replaced with the rule that a quorum at a board meeting obtained if 60% of the directors were present.

The nature of the individuals nominated to the board has also varied. When the industry quorum groups rules were present, the banks had to nominate some directors to be part of the "banking" quorum group, and others to be part of the "trust company" quorum group. However, there were no requirements that any particular nominee work in any particular part of a banking group. So, for example, somebody working for the brokerage arm of one of the banking groups could be nominated to be part of the trust company quorum group.

Traditionally, the IIROC nominated as a director somebody from an "independent" firm, where in this context "independent" referred to a broker-dealer that was not owned by one of the big six Canadian banks. The IIROC saw its role in holding the CDS shares as being to hold them in trust for its members. However, this role was complicated by various factors. First, the identities of its members changed significantly since the time when the IIROC was first allocated its shares. If the IIROC were ever to be wound up, attempting to locate its original beneficiary owners would likely be impossible. Second, key members of the IIROC became owned by the banks.

When the ME owned its shares, it used to appoint a senior officer of the exchange to sit on the CDS board. Historically, the TSX nominated a senior person from the financial industry who also sat on its board. When the TSX obtained the shares from the ME, it followed the custom of the ME, and appointed one of its senior officers to the CDS board.

Since its inception, a key goal has been to ensure that CDS's ownership structure, board representation, and usage are closely linked. Although information about what revenues CDS receives from which institutions is not publicly available, there appear, however, to be five reasons why the shareholding structure and board composition may not reflect the usage: (1) collectively the six banks' usage of CDS may not be the same as their collective ownership share; (2) individually, each bank's share of usage may not equal its share of ownership; (3) the TSX owns 18.1% of CDS but is not a direct user of it, in that it does not pay any fees to CDS; (4) the usage by the non-bank-owned brokerage firms may not be the same as the IIROC's 15.2% shareholding on their behalf, even disregarding the fact that key members of the IIROC are the bank-owned brokerage firms; and (5) there are many users of CDS that are not owners or represented by one of the eight owners, including smaller banks, trust companies, and credit unions.

Morals

- The ownership and usage of a market infrastructure institution may change in different ways.
- If the governance framework of a mutual market infrastructure institution cannot easily respond to changes in its ownership and usage, disparities between the two may arise.

DEPOSITORY TRUST & CLEARING CORPORATION: EUROCCP 2000–2002

The DTCC is a holding company for a group of operating companies providing securities clearing, settlement, custody, and information services in the United States and other jurisdictions. This section examines the establishment of EuroCCP by DTCC. The creation of EuroCCP went through three phases: first, a generic industry blueprint for clearing in Europe was prepared by the European Securities Forum over the period 2000–2001; second, DTCC developed EuroCCP for NASDAQ Europe over the period 2001–2, after which it was closed down; and third EuroCCP was revived in 2008 by DTCC to provide clearing services to a number of trading venues in the EU. The first two phases are described here.

ESF Industry Blueprint, 2000–2001

In 2000, six large European investment banks had concerns about the emergence of multiple CCPs in Europe, each tied to a particular national market, in spite of an increasing trend towards issuers cross-listing on multiple markets, especially in the pan-European single capital market environment. These investment banks began pressing for a Europe-wide CCP to avoid the duplication of up-front investment, operating costs, and collateral management expenses associated with multiple clearing infrastructures. This core group of investment banks brought their proposal to the European Securities Forum (ESF), which had been established in 1999 as the European Securities Industry User Group, to represent the views of primarily global, institutional users of clearing and settlement services in Europe. Originally created by 14 of the largest global custodian banks and brokerage firms, led by UBS and Morgan Stanley Dean Witter, the group grew to 26 members and in April 2000 changed its name to the European Securities Forum.

In June 2000 the ESF called for the creation of a single European central counterparty that it said should satisfy the following criteria:[9]

- It should be a single legal entity delivering central counterparty and netting services on a European basis.
- It should deliver a reduction in risk at a member and systemic level, savings in investment and running costs and reliability, scalability and integrity of service.
- The central counterparty should be able to handle all products and be open to all providers of trading systems. Netting for equities should be a key priority.
- Ownership and governance of the central counterparty should be separate from that of trading platforms and, in the foreseeable future, from settlement providers.
- The central counterparty should be a not-for-profit institution with a majority user ownership.
- A single legal jurisdiction should govern the central counterparty.
- Regulation of a European central counterparty should be located ideally within a single regime, or effective co-operation between regulators should minimize the duplication of compliance required by members.

The ESF set a six-month deadline for the region's central counterparty and netting organizations to commit themselves to a timetable for a merger that, it said, would eventually save users nearly a billion euros annually. Pen Kent, executive chairman of the ESF, said:

> I have been concentrating on seeking to create a single central counterparty, and I am hoping for action by the end of the year, by which I mean getting commitment from the providers. I have not got that commitment yet, but I am cautiously optimistic.[10]

There was much industry talk about efforts to collaborate among Europe's clearinghouses, and even at a global level. Clearnet and the London Clearing House (LCH) announced their intention to extend their planned European netting platform to create a "pipeline" interlinking the United States, Europe, and Asia. This global pipeline would, it was hoped, improve users' profitability by creating the opportunity for further margin offsetting. A global netting platform would be achieved through alliances with similarly structured entities in other time zones, such as the DTCC's Government Securities Clearing Corp.

LCH and Clearnet also planned to merge their operations and extend the use of Clearing 21, a CCP netting system that had been adapted for equities by Paris Bourse (Clearnet's parent company) and licensed from a futures clearing platform co-owned by the Chicago Mercantile Exchange and the New York Mercantile Exchange. The merged LCH-Clearnet entity, in announcing its merger, said that it would also welcome approaches from other clearinghouses within the euro zone, especially Eurex Clearing.

The world's CCP providers convened at a conference in London on February 1, 2000, including 12 clearinghouses from Europe, Asia, and the Americas who joined together to create an association called CCP 12 to improve global clearing, netting, and central counterparty services. The first meeting of representatives from the 12 clearinghouses took place in May 2001. The group planned to meet about every six months, and agreed on some objectives, including sharing information, improving collateralization, and analyzing other linkage models. Real integration, however, was far less advanced. With little indication that the protagonists were serious about cooperation, market participants became increasingly concerned.

In October 2000, the ESF decided to press ahead with a proposal to create a single CCP for Europe. The ESF's aim was to provide an inclusive facility for netting all securities, including equities, bonds, and derivatives, to reduce risk, and to bring savings in investment and running costs as well as greater reliability. The ESF wanted the CCP to handle all products and be open to all providers of trading systems, and for its ownership and governance to be separate from that of trading platforms and settlement providers. The ESF proposed a conceptual model for a European CCP, reportedly with assistance from DTCC,[11] that would adhere, as far as possible, to the following set of fundamental principles:[12]

Principles	The model must
Credible and quickly implementable	Not develop a "de novo" clearinghouse.
	Offer a realistic and achievable solution that satisfies participants' functional requirements while quickly achieving greater efficiency, cost and risk reduction on a pan-European scale.
Scalable	Enable maximum connectivity with members' back office systems at lowest cost.
	Offer the most practical implementation solution, consistent with prudent financial management of counterparty risk.
	Be the "best of breed" CCP solution for participants, regulators, trading spaces, and settlement houses.
Compliant	Operate in a single location for regulatory purposes.
	Comply with international standards for clearing systems including the Lamfalussy standards.

Extendable	Provide a single CCP entity across product lines and pan-European markets. Facilitate cross-border settlement.
Flexible	Accommodate, complement, and be accessible to all providers of trading services. Interface with local CSDs and ICSDs. Provide multicurrency capability.
Efficient	Have an ability to connect to multiple points to enable optimum settlement processes for post-transaction processing across European markets. Support and enhance straight-through processing. Be a catalyst for significantly reducing participants' investment spending with utilities.
Legally robust	Use a netting mechanism that can withstand the insolvency of a participant in all relevant jurisdictions.
Capital optimizing	Benefit from optimal counterparty status for regulatory capital purposes.
Voluntary	As far as possible, provide users freedom to choose all or part of the service. Users should in principle only pay for functionality that they do use.

The ESF also issued a request for proposals to build the European CCP, but received no responses. By July 2001, the ESF had effectively given up on trying to create a pan-European CCP, with its chairman, Pen Kent, saying that to go forward "would require resources that our membership [is] not prepared to pay for."[13]

The ESF's efforts to build a European CCP were undermined by a range of factors, including politics, disconnects between different constituencies' strategies, vested interests, and lack of commercial drive and funding. As Maguire (2001b) noted,

Although many market participants recognised the validity for Europe of a single market in financial services—and indeed in most cases saw a central role within it for themselves—there are also many profound obstacles of law, regulation, technology, national and commercial interest, and frankly cost, which make immediate progress towards a single EuroCCP unlikely.

More bluntly, Kent stated that "the institutions involved in the discussions did not feel that they had, at this time, the required volume of resources to commit to such a project."[14]

The ESF was also stymied by the demutualization of the major EU exchanges whose shareholders stood to gain more from owning their own clearing and settlement facilities than from subcontracting out clearing to an independent provider. In response to the flotations by Deutsche Börse and Euronext, the ESF noted that "the move by some trading platforms to public flotation, dependent in part on income streams from clearing and/or settlement services, has raised the stakes, and at the same time the barriers to a single EuroCCP."[15] In a later statement the ESF said that it "continues to believe strongly in a horizontal structure that separates governance of clearing and settlement from trading platforms."[16]

Whilst the ESF's efforts were coming to nothing, two exchanges—virt-x and Deutsche Börse—also abandoned or put on hold CCP projects.[17] In response, some ESF members held unofficial discussions with DTCC regarding the possibility of creating a pan-European CCP. At the same time NASDAQ was looking for a provider of clearing and settlement services to support its NASDAQ Europe venture.

Central Counterparty Clearing for NASDAQ Europe, 2001–2

NASDAQ Europe was the new name for Easdaq, which NASDAQ had acquired in March 2001. At the time of acquisition, Easdaq had attracted just 62 companies for listing in five years, compared with the nearly 5,000 listed on NASDAQ. NASDAQ persuaded eight big investment banks to take stakes in Easdaq and to promise to contribute order flow. At the heart of NASDAQ Europe would be a European CCP based on the one NASDAQ employed in the United States. This use of a central counterparty was key to cutting clearing and settlement costs in half.

NASDAQ tried to interest various European CCPs in providing CCP services to NASDAQ Europe and spent some time during 2000–2001 discussing possibilities with them. However, for various reasons, none was able to provide a service, certainly within the aggressive timescale set to support the launch of NASDAQ Europe's new hybrid market structure. In response to this situation, DTCC established its own pan-European CCP in 2001, to which it gave the name EuroCCP. Headquartered in London, EuroCCP was created to deliver seamless, low-cost, safe, and efficient cross-border clearing and settlement. Initially, its aim was to provide clearing for transactions executed on NASDAQ Europe in both European and US securities. EuroCCP was, however, also free to bid for the clearing business of other exchanges, and NASDAQ Europe had no influence or control over EuroCCP's direction or strategy. A key aim of DTCC was to expand market opportunities and revenues to markets outside the United States. Although this may not have been stated publicly, the user-owners of DTCC may also have hoped that such an innovation by DTCC, even if only moderately successful, might provide an incentive for the European providers of similar services to become more efficient, and also to consider merging or consolidating.

EuroCCP, a company registered in England and regulated by the UK's FSA, was 100% owned by DTCC, but had its own governance structure. A board with a majority of representatives from the user community governed the company, with a separate European user committee comprising 12 members. An agreement between NASDAQ and DTCC to build EuroCCP was reached in spring 2001, after NASDAQ had received and reviewed proposals from other clearing and settlement houses. EuroCCP was declared operational in December 2001.

Listing and trading on NASDAQ Europe never took off, however, due both to a severe downturn in technology stocks, and to the fact that company failures significantly reduced the number of stocks listed on NASDAQ Europe. The events of 9/11 in New York probably also contributed to its closure, as there was less appetite to undertake new and innovative projects, and more focus on ensuring safety and soundness of existing systems. NASDAQ Europe was thus closed in November 2002. Two months earlier, in September, EuroCCP withdrew as CCP for NASDAQ Europe, without processing any trades. As Jeff Smith, then CEO of EuroCCP noted, "The number of trades that Nasdaq Europe was able to execute was not at the level that Nasdaq Europe, EuroCCP and the participants felt was essential to bring in a central counterparty."[18]

Subsequently DTCC undertook a postmortem of its decision to create EuroCCP. Although the results of this review are not public, several aspects of the project were heralded by DTCC. Technically the system worked well. It was built and implemented in a short period of seven months. The technology behind EuroCCP was also reused on DTCC's other entities and products. The approval of EuroCCP by UK regulators in a short five-month period reflected a new sense of urgency at DTCC and the FSA.

The decision to build EuroCCP was approved by DTCC's board, which included representatives from users, such as banks and broker dealers, and European-based as well as US-based organizations. The decision to proceed with EuroCCP would thus have been made with the full knowledge and recognition of the potential risks of doing so. The potential benefits to DTCC had NASDAQ Europe been successful were set off against the costs and other risks of implementing the project in the first place. In retrospect, the creation of EuroCCP also enabled DTCC to gain experience of the UK-recognized clearinghouse requirements, and to establish a legal entity that increased the speed to market and reestablishment of EuroCCP, which was reactivated in 2007.

Moral

- A mutual market infrastructure institution may be innovative.

DEUTSCHE BÖRSE: CREATION OF CLEARSTREAM INTERNATIONAL 1999–2002

Clearstream International was formed initially as a joint venture owned 50% by Cedel International and 50% by Deutsche Börse AG. Clearstream International was the parent company of Clearstream Banking SA, the ICSD based in Luxembourg, and Clearstream Banking Frankfurt AG, the CSD for Germany.[19] Deutsche Börse subsequently bought out the remaining 50% of Cedel International's shares, held by over 90 banks and brokers. The simplicity of these two transactions masks a complicated corporate history that was affected by a multitude of different market participants' agendas.

Cedel was created in 1971 by over 60 of the world's major financial institutions in response to the development of Euroclear, which was set up and dominated initially by Morgan Guaranty Trust of New York (subsequently J.P. Morgan Chase).[20] The intention was that Cedel should not be dominated by any single bank, unlike Euroclear, so the company's constitution was established in such a way that no single shareholder was permitted to own more than 5% of Cedel's share capital.[21] The main clients of Cedel were the European universal banks. In contrast, the London-based and primarily American broker-dealer firms, who were the main participants in the European securities markets, tended to concentrate the majority of their business with Euroclear, although they usually maintained accounts with both institutions. Since its creation, there was both a rivalry between Euroclear and Cedel, and also strong support, among a range of market constituencies, in favor of a merger of both institutions—but no agreement on how such a merger should be effected.

The possibility of such a merger came to a head in 1999. In May that year, Euroclear issued a paper, entitled *The Hub and Spokes Clearance and Settlement Model*, putting forward its views as to the appropriate clearing and settlement solution for efficient and competitive capital markets in Europe.[22] Euroclear proposed that it become the main point of entry (the "hub") to every European CSD (the "spokes") for international fund managers, custodian banks, and broker-dealers. A key implication of the hub and spokes proposal was that it left no room for Cedel—at least in theory.

Euroclear issued a formal merger proposal to Cedel on May 4, 1999. This was, however, immediately rejected by André Lussi, the CEO of

Cedel. He had seen such a proposal coming, and to preempt it, had already agreed on a joint venture with Deutsche Börse. This venture was called the European Clearing House (ECH). When ECH was announced 10 days later, Lussi had also secured an MOU with the Société des Bourses Françaises (SBF), the holding company of the Paris Bourse, and Sicovam, the French depository, to join the new venture by January 2000.[23]

The deal between Cedel and Deutsche Börse offered several benefits to Cedel. Of most importance, Lussi was against a merger with Euroclear at that time, as Cedel would have ended up being taken over by the larger Euroclear. Lussi saw the joint venture as a merger of equals with Deutsche Börse's settlement unit, and viewed it as a way of building size so that Cedel could compete with Euroclear. In addition, Cedel's strategies to attract the American broker-dealer community by providing a range of new products—including Liberty (an order-routing business), and Global Credit Support Service (an electronic book-entry collateral management service for the derivatives markets)—were not successful at that time.

The prime benefit of the deal for Deutsche Börse was that it allowed the exchange to reinforce its entry into the pan-European arena, and support its strategy of vertical integration between trading, clearing, and settlement. The German CSD also needed a new technical platform for its settlement business, and Cedel had been developing such a real-time system, called CREATION.

Some investment banks, led by UBS of Switzerland, one of the banks owning Cedel, tried to prevent the merger with Deutsche Börse because they wanted to continue controlling Cedel as a useful counterforce to Euroclear. The banks also suspected that a deal with Deutsche Börse would end up being of more strategic value to Deutsche Börse than to Cedel. Many banks were, however, willing to accept a merger between Cedel and the user-owned Euroclear in the hope of creating a more efficient and cheaper pan-European settlement system that would avoid duplicating technology costs. They were represented at the time in the European Securities Industry Users' Group (ESIUG), a group of 14 leading investment and custodian banks, some of which were board members and shareholders of Cedel, and indeed also of Euroclear. Cedel dismissed calls by the ESIUG, however, to postpone a shareholder vote on the merger, as it considered the user group to be biased towards Euroclear.[24]

Cedel's deal with Deutsche Börse was a major setback for Euroclear, as it had sought to merge with Cedel for years. In addition, the proposal that Sicovam join the ECH was a shock to Euroclear, as in December 1998 Sicovam had been set to announce an alliance with Euroclear. At that stage, however, Euroclear rejected the proposal, believing that such an alliance would foreclose its preferred option of merging with Cedel.

The key reason SBF and Sicovam agreed to join the ECH appeared to be political. Lussi had portrayed the ECH as a "European" alternative to an "American" domination of securities clearing and settlement by Euroclear. SBF and Sicovam came under pressure from the Banque de France, the owner of a 40% stake in Sicovam, to participate in what was perceived as the "European" solution.

On November 22, 1999, however, Sicovam withdrew its support for the ECH, choosing subsequently to merge with Euroclear in 2000. A range of reasons were suggested for this change of mind. The proposed terms of the merger were of major importance. The percentage of ECH that was to be owned by the French was to be determined by a mutually agreed valuation of the assets Sicovam brought to the venture, including their own settlement platform (Relit à Grande Vitesse [RGV]), their transaction volumes and potentially also Clearnet, the netting platform owned by the Paris Bourse. There was, however, disagreement on an appropriate valuation. The French wanted a one-third share of the new, joint company, despite being willing to contribute only around 22% of the total valuation of the company. It might also have been politically sensitive in such a European merger if Sicovam had been given a share of less than one-third of the venture. Neither Cedel nor Deutsche Börse, however, was willing to sanction such an expense of shareholder money to offer this level of shareholding to Sicovam. In addition, French customers wanted to continue using RGV, rather than pay for a new single platform.

During the first two years of the Deutsche Börse-Cedel venture, there was tension between Frankfurt and Luxembourg, although at the same time, the two companies were able to integrate their technical platforms and enhance their financial returns. The company renamed itself Clearstream over this period. In response to the Euroclear-Sicovam merger, Clearstream sought rival takeover bids for the Cedel-owned half of Clearstream from both Deutsche Börse and Euroclear. At this stage, Lussi changed his mind to argue in favor of a deal with Euroclear, rather than selling the other 50% to Deutsche Börse.[25] Various reasons were suggested for his change. He may have wanted to balance the German power in Clearstream with a corresponding French influence. He may have felt more comfortable with the ESIUG than previously. Lussi, himself, argued that the most compelling reason was that large cost savings could be achieved by integrating the sales, corporate functions, network management, and collateral management systems of Clearstream and Euroclear.

Two events that were immaterial to the economic merits of the merger were perceived as contributing to Clearstream's vulnerability to a takeover. First, Lussi was forced to stand down as CEO of Clearstream in May 2001 amid an investigation by Luxembourg regulators into allegations of money laundering made by a French journalist—which were later completely dismissed. Second, Clearstream admitted overstating its assets under custody by 2.5 trillion euros. The overstatement was due to an operational statistical error and not a book-keeping mistake, and was also rectified as soon as Clearstream Banking AG became aware of it.[26] Nevertheless, the two incidents made it look as though Clearstream was not being managed properly. Lussi was replaced, initially on a temporary basis, by André Roelants of Benelux Bank Dexia. Clearstream was by then increasingly being run from Deutsche Börse's head office in Frankfurt rather than Luxembourg.

In January 2002, the board of Cedel International agreed to sell the group's 50% stake to Deutsche Börse for the equivalent of 1.6 billion euros, based on a valuation of 3.2 billion for the whole company. A range of factors contributed to this decision. Deutsche Börse CEO Werner Seifert voted against Euroclear's bid using Deutsche Börse's 50% stake in the company. Euroclear only offered 1.0–1.2 billion euros, a significantly lower figure than that offered by Deutsche Börse. It also appeared that Euroclear would fire the whole management, while Deutsche Börse was more equivocal on this issue.

The sale price was well below what Cedel management had first suggested, with Clearstream CEO André Roelants indicating it was worth more than 3.4 billion dollars or 3 billion euros.[27] This valuation was, however, open to debate for at least two important reasons. First, the valuation was based on a "four-year plan," using financial assumptions based on the previous five years (1995–2000). There was a widespread view, however, that in 2001 this valuation was overstated. There was also a question about the sustainability and volatility of the customer base. Euroclear had sarcastically said that it had no need to buy Clearstream International, since the Clearstream International customers would progressively migrate their business to their Euroclear accounts. Some major participants threatened to do just this. J.P. Morgan Chase said it would move all of its estimated $150 billion of assets out of Clearstream and into Euroclear. Swiss bank UBS, also one of Clearstream's biggest clients, said it would switch some assets to Euroclear as it also opposed Deutsche Börse creating a vertical silo.[28] It was never confirmed whether any of these switches were fully or partially executed.

The sale went ahead despite users, now under the banner of the European Securities Forum (ESF) (which was formerly the ESIUG), campaigning for a merger between the Cedel part of Clearstream and Euroclear, in order to speed up industry consolidation and create a dominant settlement house to help cut costs.[29] Euroclear had predicted that a merger would save 300 million euros a year in costs.[30] Of the 93 shareholders in Cedel International, 44 of them also had stakes in Euroclear.[31]

The Cedel users, who were also shareholders, initially wanted to stop the creation of a vertical silo, whereby Deutsche Börse would have full ownership of trading, clearing, and settlement operations, giving it strong pricing power. As no shareholder in Cedel could own more than 5%, however, individual shareholders had little controlling influence because Cedel's ownership was too widely dispersed, and it proved difficult for the shareholders to act with a single purpose. In addition, not all the users were broker-dealers, and they may have preferred Deutsche Börse as an owner to Euroclear. It also proved hard for the shareholder banks to resist a tempting take-it-or-leave-it cash offer from Seifert. The short-term cash gain from selling to Deutsche Börse proved more attractive than sticking to their avowed principles of fostering wider industry consolidation. The top 10 shareholders of the non-Deutsche Börse half of Clearstream gained a total of 722.7 million euros by selling out to the German exchange operator, even though seven of them were members of the ESF, which had campaigned against vertical silos.[32] In some cases the profits they made by selling their stakes were more than their entire investment banking income for the previous year when the stock market fell sharply.

Moral

- Financial institutions' stated and actual goals regarding the governance of a market infrastructure institution may differ.

EUROCLEAR: CREATION, OWNERSHIP, AND BOARD STRUCTURE UP TO 2006

Euroclear plc (Euroclear) is the holding company for a group of companies that provide settlement services in more than 80 countries for domestic and international transactions in bonds, equities, and investment funds. Five issues and contexts regarding how Euroclear was governed in practice from its creation to 2006 are examined here in turn: (1) the history of Euroclear's corporate structure up until 2006; (2) the nature of some competition faced by Euroclear in 2006, and the implications this had for the existence of competing interests among some of its users and shareholders; (3) Euroclear's ownership rebalancing in 2002; (4) the role and independence of directors in 2005; and (5) the transparency of Euroclear Bank's revenues in 2005.

One introductory point concerning the descriptions presented here is noteworthy. As of 2006 Euroclear was the largest settlement institution in Europe, and its governance structure had underpinned its attaining this position. Governance was a critical issue for the Euroclear group, and the core principle behind its governance model was that of user governance. It stated that

> a fundamental Euroclear value [is] that the users of the Euroclear services should both own and govern the Euroclear group. The fact that almost all of Euroclear's shareholders are direct or indirect users of Euroclear services results in alignment of the interests of the shareholders and users to a far greater degree than would be possible in a listed company, and generally means that decisions taken in the longterm interest of the company and its shareholders are also in the interest of its clients.[33]

Given Euroclear's importance in the Europe settlement industry, however, and given also the regulatory and industry concern about the costs of clearing and settlement generally in Europe, the vigorous debate about the optimal way of structuring the clearing and settlement industry in Europe at the time, and the potential and actual conflicting interests among and between Euroclear's shareholders, its various types of users, and other stakeholders, it is unsurprising that differences of opinion about Euroclear's governance sometimes arose.

Euroclear believed user governance had a wide range of benefits, it had a stated commitment to respond to the markets it served, and it found it difficult to imagine how users could be more directly involved in its business than they were at the time. Consequently, it believed that some of the differences of opinion about its governance structure noted here were generic criticisms of user governance.

Brief History of Corporate Structure

The Euroclear system was founded by Morgan Guaranty Trust Company of New York ("Morgan Guaranty," now J.P. Morgan Chase), Brussels branch, to process Eurobonds settlement in 1968.[34] In 1971, a group of European banks established an alternative and competing system when they created Cedel, a user-owned cooperative, domiciled and regulated in Luxembourg.[35] In response, Morgan Guaranty created a company called Euroclear Clearance System plc (ECS plc). The term "clearance" was used at the time for the service that is currently called "settlement."

ECS plc acquired the license of the Euroclear system from Morgan Guaranty and offered the main users and founding members of the Euroclear system, approximately 120 institutions, the opportunity to purchase its shares, up to a capped maximum of about 4% per institution. ECS plc appointed Morgan Guaranty as the operator of the Euroclear system, and paid it a management fee for supplying premises, equipment, and employees. Revenues and costs associated with settlement and safe-keeping services were for the account of ECS plc, while Morgan Guaranty retained its role as sole banker to the system. ECS plc historically maintained and publicized a policy of low costs to users, while Morgan Guaranty's profits from the exclusive arrangement for banking services were not disclosed.

In the mid-1980s, Euroclear Clearance System Société Coopérative was created to spread the ownership of the system among all its users—each was offered a share in the cooperative. It operated the Euroclear system on the basis of a yearly license paid to ECS plc.[36] And it was a company domiciled and regulated in Belgium, and majority owned by ECS plc. In July 2000, ECS Société Coopérative was granted a banking license in Belgium and became Euroclear Bank. Euroclear Bank acquired Morgan Guaranty's rights as banker to the Euroclear system, with a maximum payment of US$295 million per year from 2000 to 2002, for a total of just under a billion dollars.

In January 10, 2001, ECS plc acquired 100% of the capital of Sicovam, the French CSD. Sicovam was acquired in a two-stage process. Initially a group of French banks that together owned 60% of Sicovam bought the 40% of Sicovam owned by the Banque de France, partly through an immediate cash payment, and partly through a progressive yearly payment based on Euroclear's financial results. More specifically, there was a 200 million euro up-front cash payment and an additional payment of a minimum 20 million euros and a maximum 47.1 million euros' dependent on Euroclear's future profits. The two French stakes were then combined into Sicovam Holding, which exchanged its Sicovam SA shares for a 16.7% shareholding in ECS plc shares. Sicovam Holding's voting rights were limited to 5%, according to the general restriction on voting rights. It was given four seats on the ECS plc board (out of 26), a number proportional to its shareholding percentage, but no seat on the board of Euroclear Bank. Euroclear Bank became the CSD parent company.[37] Sicovam was subsequently renamed Euroclear France. ECS plc was renamed Euroclear plc on June 1, 2001.

In 2002, Euroclear acquired 100% of the capital of Nederlands Centraal Instituut voor Giraal Effectenverkeer, the Dutch CSD, from Euronext, over a phased period. On this occasion, Euroclear also gained an option to acquire 20% of Clearnet, plus the right to appoint directors onto the Clearnet board, and Clearnet's commitment to develop a direct link into Euroclear Bank. In 2004, Euroclear acquired most of the settlement and custody business of Caisse Interprofessionnelle de Dépôts et de Virement de Titres/Interprofessionele Effectendeposito-en Girokas, the Belgian CSD. In December 2000 Euroclear Bank also assumed responsibility for the settlement of Irish government bonds, following the decision of the Irish government and the Central Bank of Ireland to delegate this activity to Euroclear.

In September 2002, Euroclear Bank acquired 100% of the capital of CRESTCo, the British CSD. The acquisition of CRESTCo was negotiated directly by CRESTCo and its owners. CRESTCo's shareholders decided not to follow the route followed by Sicovam when the British settlement house was taken over by Euroclear. Instead of creating a holding company, they exchanged CRESTCo shares directly for Euroclear shares. This meant that they did not have a voting cap on their shares, as no single holder held more than 5% of the shares. CRESTCo also negotiated the right to nominate seven directors to the Euroclear plc board. In addition, CRESTCo obtained the right to nominate four of the 12 nonexecutive directors to the Euroclear Bank board, until the migration of the CREST securities to the Single Settlement Engine had been completed, which occurred in August 2006.

In 2004/5, Euroclear's corporate structure was changed.[38] Euroclear Bank, the ICSD and former parent company of the individual CSDs, was transformed into a sister company of those companies, and Euroclear SA/NV was created as the new nonbank holding company to house Euroclear Bank and the other CSDs. Euroclear SA/NV, in turn, became wholly-owned through Euroclear Investments SA/NV by Euroclear plc, the ultimate holding company. Euroclear SA/NV thus owned and operated the group platforms and ran all major functions: strategy and development, regulatory affairs, sales, audit, and technology (functions that were formerly within Euroclear Bank).

The new corporate structure sought to provide the following benefits: (1) to address potential systemic risk concerns for the CSDs, in case of a bankruptcy of Euroclear Bank; (2) to confirm that Euroclear Bank did not have a preferential status within the group compared to the CSDs; (3) to confirm that Euroclear Bank did not divert resources from the CSDs, for example, in terms of dividend flow; (4) to address concerns that Euroclear Bank would use its position as owner of the CSDs to compete unfairly with third parties; (5) to increase transparency in how services were delivered within the group of companies and in cost allocation; and (6) to increase the flexibility of the corporate structure for potential alliances and mergers.[39]

Competition and Competing Interests in 2006

The nature of the various services that the Euroclear group provided, together with its ownership structure, meant that it became the focus for different and sometimes competing interests, both between differing types of users and between users and shareholders. Each set of interests, or constituency, typically supported a governance structure for Euroclear that maximized the realization of its own goals. The nature of how these different interests operated in 2006 are briefly outlined in this section.

Euroclear Bank competed with some custodian or agent banks, particularly those that had a significant presence in the markets where the CSDs were part of the Euroclear group. The plans of the Euroclear group to combine its national CSDs and Euroclear Bank on the same IT platform—namely the Single Settlement Engine and the Single Application Platform—raised particular concern. Some agent banks believed that Euroclear Bank could use this platform to gain unfair competitive advantage through privileged access to the national CSDs under the common ownership of the Euroclear group, which they could not match if they did not have equivalent conditions of access. Such privileged access could be in the form of service quality, such as preferential processing of transactions, availability of data, and timing of instructions and reporting.

In order to combat the competitive threat from Euroclear Bank, some of the agent banks set up a lobbying group called Fair & Clear to campaign for internal changes at Euroclear.[40] Fair & Clear sought to highlight the necessity for Euroclear to separate its so-called infrastructure CSD operations from its banking services, in order, it argued, to avoid possible cross-subsidies or privileged conditions extended by the Euroclear group CSDs to Euroclear Bank. Fair & Clear also said that a technical link established between LCH.Clearnet and Euroclear Bank illustrated the Euroclear group strategy of diverting transactions from the CSDs to Euroclear Bank, where more revenues and profits could be generated, via the bundling of banking and settlement services.

From the start of Fair & Clear's campaign, Euroclear argued against its claims, saying that nothing Euroclear did was anticompetitive. It saw its role as eliminating inefficiencies in the European financial market, and argued that competing with other more traditional suppliers, and in particular the agent banks, was necessary to deliver such efficiencies. Furthermore, Euroclear provided assurances that there was no cross-subsidy between the group ICSD and CSDs, and supported this assurance with an annual attestation on this issue provided by an independent auditor.

The competition to provide commercial banking services between Euroclear Bank and agent banks led to a conflict of interest between the users of the Euroclear CSDs and the users of Euroclear Bank—although there were overlaps among their interests as well. The large users of Euroclear Bank were the major international and U.S. firms, mainly broker-dealers, investment banks and global custodians. The interests of Euroclear Bank's users were to enhance Euroclear Bank as an efficient and low-cost single gateway to the Euroclear group CSDs, and to further the development of Euroclear Bank's securities finance services. They also sought the reduction of Euroclear Bank prices, either directly, or through year-end rebates.

Many of the large users of Euroclear Bank also used services provided by agent banks competing with Euroclear Bank. The long-term goal of some of these users, however, was to disintermediate the agent banks, by having direct access to a single European settlement institution, thus obviating the need to have agent bank intermediation to the many settlement institutions in operation in Europe.

The large users of the Euroclear group CSDs were generally European firms, primarily custodians and some brokers, and some regional firms. They often also had an account with Euroclear Bank for Eurobonds. These users had three key interests: first, the reduction of the costs the CSDs charged them for settlement and custody, in order to be able to reduce their own and their clients' costs; second, efficient settlement systems spanning the Euroclear group CSDs, in order to be able to expand their market coverage; and third, access to the CSD platforms on the same basis as Euroclear Bank, so they could compete on an equal footing to serve as the single gateway to the Euroclear group CSDs. They were wary that Euroclear group rebates might be diverted from CSD users to Euroclear Bank users.

Euroclear's reform of its corporate structure sought, in part, to answer Fair & Clear's concerns. However, even after its implementation, Fair & Clear continued to argue that the restructuring did not resolve the central problem as they saw it, namely that the single application IT platform gave Euroclear Bank a structural advantage of privileged access conditions not available to its agent bank competitors.

In addition to the tension between the different types of users of Euroclear group's services, a conflict also arose between users and shareholders. Shareholders were driven by a range of objectives, including, self-evidently, the maximization of dividends and return on capital. A return on equity was particularly important to many shareholders, given the illiquidity of Euroclear's shares, which meant that it was difficult for shareholders to realize capital gains. For Sicovam Holding, the Euroclear group's largest shareholder, dividends had an added importance as the French banks counted on these revenues to pay the Banque de France for their purchase of its shares in Sicovam. The French banks were the only Euroclear shareholders who paid for their shares in cash, rather than by an exchange of paper. Shareholders, and particularly those whose usage patterns benefited less from rebates, preferred the distribution of dividends, and did not in general support rebates.[41]

The appropriate balance between rebates and dividends was much debated at the Euroclear group, and was considered by the board each year. In June 2001, Euroclear announced that the board would determine how financial surpluses available for distribution would be allocated between fee reductions and rebates for customers and dividends to shareholders, after providing for the future investment needs of the business. Euroclear said it would distribute dividends at least equal to 60% of the first 15% return on equity. In practice, Euroclear had paid out rebates to Euroclear Bank users for years before this, a practice that reflected the historical ECS plc policy. In 2004, certain Euroclear group shareholders started pressing for what they believed to be a more effective implementation of the dividend policy, and the Euroclear board decided to increase dividends. In 2006, the Euroclear group board noted that it "tries always to balance the need to retain a loyal client base to ensure the company's long-term viability with the requirement of an appropriate return to shareholders on their invested capital."[42] In addition, Euroclear affirmed that "as a user-owned/user-governed organization there is no conflict between providing shareholder value and value to our users."[43]

Some shareholders were also concerned that the value of Euroclear group's shares was not written down, as any decrease in value, for example via impairments, would impact their own financial results. Past acquisitions, in particular the Sicovam SA and CRESTCo deals, had led to significant impairments.

Preservation of the value of Euroclear Bank was seen as essential by shareholders. Euroclear Bank represented a major percentage of the value of the Euroclear group, and was also the main generator of profits, and thus of potential dividends. This created an incentive for Euroclear group to make sure that transaction flows went through Euroclear Bank rather than the CSD side.

Ownership Rebalancing in 2002

User governance has been central to the Euroclear group's approach to governance. Euroclear does not, however, have a method of rebalancing its shares according to usage of its systems. Following the purchase of CRESTCo in 2002, Euroclear plc agreed to consider implementing a share-rebalancing process, similar to that which had been in use by CRESTCo. Given the valuation put on Euroclear, however, the amount of money needed for such an ownership restructuring was deemed inappropriate at a time of significant investment in Euroclear's new single settlement platform, and given also the need to increase the capital of Euroclear Bank.

In addition, none of the users targeted by the rebalancing, primarily the US banks who were large users of Euroclear bank but had relatively small shareholdings, were ready to make such an investment, especially in a context where Euroclear group shares were illiquid. Although these users were the main recipients of Euroclear Bank rebates, they preferred to continue receiving these rebates, rather than have the money allocated towards purchasing Euroclear group shares in order to effect the rebalancing process.

Roles and Independence of Directors in 2005

A crucial element of Euroclear's governance approach has been that its users' views should not only be represented on its board, but indeed be central to the board's deliberations in order to ensure that "decisions taken in the long-term interest of the company and its shareholders are also in the interest of its clients."[44] To effect this goal, most nonexecutive directors on the board work for users of Euroclear services.

There have been different views about the manner in which nonexecutive directors both do, and are allowed to, represent users' interests on the Euroclear board. As directors, the nonexecutive directors have a fiduciary duty to promote the interests of Euroclear. This means that they are legally not allowed to promote solely the interests of either their firm, or any "constituency" of stakeholders of which their firm might be a part, on the Euroclear board. As long as directors are never put in a position where they need to choose between supporting their firm or supporting Euroclear, however, then they will not be breaking their fiduciary duty if they do represent their firm's interests. But if a director is faced with such a choice, then a tension arises for the director as to whether he or she represents the interests of his or her firm, or similarly his or her firm's constituency, as a user of Euroclear, or the interests of Euroclear. Given that there are conflicts between different types of users, and that some users compete with Euroclear, conflicts have arisen between user representation and the interests of Euroclear. When directors are reminded that they need to fulfill their fiduciary duty to act in Euroclear's interests, this has been interpreted in different ways: either that the director in question is promoting the interests of his or her own firm at the expense of Euroclear, or that Euroclear is promoting its own interests at the expense of at least one user's, and possibly a group of users', interests.

Other factors also affect the extent to which Euroclear board directors can represent users' interests. Euroclear notes that "The user-governance structure of Euroclear means that, in practice, the majority of directors of Euroclear are regularly accessible to the stakeholders of the group (shareholders and clients alike), because they are actively working in the same industry."[45] The extent to which directors are accessible to stakeholders may be limited by various factors, however. Directors' obligations to maintain confidentiality about Euroclear business matters means that they may not be allowed to discuss issues of importance with stakeholders in general, or even internally in their own firms, and this restricts the utility of such interaction for stakeholders. In addition, the directors are senior industry figures who are therefore likely to be regularly accessible only to a limited circle of stakeholders.

Another issue affecting the manner in which directors can represent users' interests concerns the independence of directors from management. Euroclear seeks to comply with established best practice in the field of corporate governance. In order to do so, it voluntarily adopted the UK Combined Code on Corporate Governance as its governance model, recognizing, however, that the code was designed primarily for publicly listed companies, and thus might not be fully appropriate for itself. A key element of the code is to allow companies to describe the extent of their compliance with the code, or explain any departures from its provisions. The code states that at least half of a company's board (except for small companies) should consist of nonexecutive, independent directors,[46] where independence may be compromised by the existence of material relationships between a director, or the firm for which the director works, and the company on whose board the director sits.

As of year-end 2005, the boards of Euroclear plc/Euroclear SA/NV confirmed that both companies were compliant with the code, with the primary exception arising from the group's commitment to ownership and governance by its users. At that time, 23 of the 26 nonexecutive directors on the Euroclear board were affiliated with users. This necessarily meant that most directors' companies did have a material relationship with Euroclear, given that they used its services. In order to explain this departure from the code, the boards undertook an assessment of the independence of their nonexecutive directors. They noted:

> The concept of director independence has been applied in light of the user-governance philosophy which necessarily means that the majority of Euroclear directors will have a business relationship with Euroclear. Each Board evaluate[d] whether any such relationship could influence a director to the detriment of the company in carrying out director duties, in line with the spirit of the Code provisions on independence. The Boards ... adopted objective guidelines in order to support such assessment. In addition to this objective test regarding material business relationships, each Board also examine[d] whether any other relationships or circumstances exist[d] that could affect, or appear to affect any director's judgment, using as a guide the factors mentioned in the Code (for example, employment with the group in the previous five years, receipt of non-director related remuneration from the group).

Following the application of these objective tests and additional reviews, each board determined that the 23 members of its Board that [were] affiliated with users of the group's services [were] sufficiently independent in character and judgment to be considered independent from management and from influences that would affect their performance as a director to the detriment of the company within the spirit of the Code.[47]

Euroclear noted the importance both of the independence of its directors, and also of the appearance of such independence. There were, however, a range of relationships between the firms for which nonexecutive directors worked and Euroclear that could affect, or appear to affect, their judgment, in addition to whether any director's firm was a user of Euroclear's services. In particular, many directors' firms were also suppliers of services to Euroclear, and in some instances they were also actual or potential competitors with Euroclear. An examination of the roles of the Euroclear directors at year-end 2005 provides an illustration. A list of the board directors of Euroclear SA/NV and the relationships their firms had with Euroclear, as of April 2006, is provided in table 20.

There were at least six types of relationships that directors' firms had with Euroclear that went beyond being simply users of Euroclear group's services:

1. Some banks provided a "common depository" service for Eurobonds. A common depository is appointed by the two ICSDs jointly to hold the entirety of a Eurobond issue. It essentially provides a settlement function between the two ICSDs. Common depositories are typically custodian banks with secure vaults to hold Eurobond certificates.
2. Some banks acted as "cash correspondent banks" for Euroclear Bank. A cash correspondent bank makes payments in the local currency on behalf of Euroclear Bank, and if necessary will fund Euroclear Bank through extension of intraday liquidity or overnight credit.
3. Some banks acted as underwriters for Euroclear Bank when it issued bonds.
4. Some banks may have acted as corporate advisers to Euroclear group on its mergers and acquisitions strategy. Details of such relationships are typically not public information.
5. Euroclear Group was the preferred settlement partner of Euronext, which had a seat on the board.
6. Some banks were competitors of Euroclear Bank as custodians of non-Eurobond securities, and as providers of banking services.

These relationships between directors' firms and Euroclear raised questions about the appearance of independence of directors from management. If a director is appointed from a firm acting as a supplier to the company, this could allow management to exert pressure over the director's decisions, given the fees paid to the director's firm as a supplier. Pressure could also be applied to a director appointed from an actual or potential competitor given the competitive threat Euroclear could provide. Euroclear's response to such concerns was that the relevant individuals were sufficiently independent in character and judgment not to be subject to such pressures, and furthermore that the nature of user governance meant the presence of such conflicts of interest was inescapable.

The manner in which directors can represent users is also dependent on the relative power of users, shareholders, the board as a whole, and management. There were differences of opinion about this. On the one hand, the board was seen to be representative both of users, given that many directors worked for major users of Euroclear (23 out of the 26 as of year-end 2005), and of shareholders, given that directors from institutions that owned a significant percentage of Euroclear's equity typically served on the board (over 40% as of year-end 2005). It was also seen as the location where the broad strategy for the company was set, where major issues of relevance for the company were decided, and where management was held to account to deliver relevant strategy and decisions, as outlined in the Euroclear annual reports. On the other hand, Euroclear Bank users, together with management, were sometimes seen as dominating decision-making in the group, at the expense of Euroclear CSD users and shareholders. Several factors were put forward to support such a view: the relatively large size of the board, and the force with which opposing opinions were held on it; the way power had devolved to key board committees and to management, which had developed bilateral dialogue with relevant directors; and the belief that Euroclear Bank users had an overrepresentation on key committees relative to their shareholdings.

Euroclear Bank Transparency, 2005

Euroclear Bank used to compete with some of the agent banks in Europe. As a result, it believed that detailed information about its costs and revenues should not be in the public domain, because to publish such information might violate competition law. In contrast, some of Euroclear's users and shareholders were concerned that they did not receive enough information about Euroclear Bank's activities in order to govern and monitor its activities. For example, Euroclear Bank used not to disclose the composition of its billed revenues beyond the one-line "Commissions Received."

In an offering circular to a bond issue in 2005, however, an unaudited breakdown of 2004 revenues was provided, and this is reproduced in table 21.[48] These data show that safekeeping was the largest revenue generator, accounting for €415.3 million or 56% of total Euroclear Bank

TABLE 20
Euroclear SA/NV Board Directors' Firms' Relationships with Euroclear 4/2006

Category	Firm	Board member	Supplier	Competitor
Bank	Société Générale	Alain Closier	Common depository for Luxembourg; subcustodian for France; cash correspondent for France (EUR).	Agent Bank in France
	Fortis	Christian Schaack	Mailbox depository for Belgium; underwriter of bond issue in 2000.	Agent Bank in Netherlands, Belgium
	Credit Suisse	Frank J. DeCongelio	Specialized euro depository for Switzerland; subcustodian for Switzerland and for Luxembourg for investment funds; cash correspondent for Switzerland (CHF); underwriter of bond issue in 2000.	
	UBS	John M. Schofield	Specialized euro depository for` Switzerland; subcustodian for Switzerland; advisor to Euroclear in Euroclear/CRESTCo merger 2002; underwriter of bond issue in 2000.	Global Custody
	HSBC	John S. Gubert	Common depository for Hong Kong and UK; subcustodian for Hong Kong; specialized euro depository for Hong Kong; cash correspondent for Hong Kong (HKD) underwriter of bond issue in 2000.	Global Custody
	State Street	Joseph C. Antonellis	Underwriter of bond issue in 2000.	Global Custody
	Citigroup	Mary M. Fenoglio	Common depository for UK; subcustodian for Argentina, Greece, Philippines; specialized euro depositary for UK; cash correspondent for Greece, (EUR), Argentina (ARS), Hungary (HUF), Philippines (PHP), Slovakia (SKK), United States (USD); underwriter of bond issue in 2000.	Agent bank in France, Netherlands, Belgium, UK; Global Custody
	Deutsche Bank	Richard C. Evans	Common depository for Germany, Hong Kong, UK; subcustodian for Germany, Indonesia, Malaysia; specialized euro depository for Germany, Luxembourg, UK; cash correspondent for Germany (EUR), UK (GBP), Indonesia (IDR), Malaysia (MYR); underwriter of bond issues in 2000 and 2005.	
	Mizuho Intl.	Sabah Zubaida	Common depository; subcustodian for Japan; underwriter of bond issue in 2000.	

TABLE 20 (*cont'd*)

Category	Firm	Board member	Supplier	Competitor
Bank	JP Morgan Chase	Mark S. Garvin	Common depository for Luxembourg; specialized euro depository for Luxembourg; subcustodian for Japan; cash correspondent for Japan (JPY); underwriter of bond issue in 2000 and 2005.	Triparty Repo, Global Custody
	Bank of New York	Paul Bodart	Common depository for UK; specialised euro depository for Belgium, UK: cash correspondent for United States (USD); underwriter of bond issue in 2000.	Triparty Repo, Global Custody
	BNP Paribas	Alain Papiasse	Common depository for Luxembourg; underwriter of bond issue in 2000.	Agent bank in France Netherlands, Belguim, UK; Global Custody
Investment Firm	IXIS Corporate and Investment Bank	Anthony Orsatelli	IXIS is a Group Caisse d'Epargne Company, which is common depository for Luxembourg; specialized euro depository for Luxembourg; underwriter bond issue in 2000.	
	Morgan Stanley	David Nicol	Underwriter of bond issue in 2000.	
	Merrill Lynch	Charles F. Winters	Underwriter of bond issue in 2000	
	Goldman Sachs	Peter Johnston	Underwriter of bond issue in 2000.	
Broker Dealer	Brewin Dolphin Securities Limited	Charlotte Black		
	Halifax Share Dealing Limited	Sue Concannon	Halifax is owned 100% by the HBOS group (Bank of Scotland)— Underwriter of bond issue in 2000.	
Institutional Investor	Fidelity Intl. Limited	Simon S. Haslam		
Stock Exchange	LSE Euronext	Clara Furse Jean-François Théodore	Preferred settlement partner, cross-ownership and board member of LCH.Clearnet.	
Independent	Ernst & Young	Andrew S. Winckler		
Euroclear chairman & deputy chairman	Ex ABN Amro Ex-chairman, CREST	Chris Tupker Sir Nigel Wicks		

TABLE 21

Euroclear's Unaudited Revenue Breakdown, 2004

Revenue item	Millions euros	Proportion of ICSD Income
Safekeeping	415.3	56%
Settlement	65.6	9%
Communication	69.9	9%
Securities lending	40.4	5%
Collateral services	20.6	3%
Money transfer	16.5	2%
Interest on clients' balances	112.7	15%
Subtotal ICSD income	741.0	100%
Rebates to clients	(40.0)	
Other income*	72.3	
Operating income	773.2	

Source: Euroclear Bank (2005, 51).

* Interest income on capital, forex, forex hedging, and "other fees." No information was offered on the nature of €34.1 million of "other fees."

revenues. Settlement fees accounted for 9%, €65.6 million, of the total Euroclear Bank revenues and in absolute terms were less than the fees charged for communication. Banking services (securities lending, collateral services, money transfer, and interest on clients balances) accounted for €190.2 million or 26% of Euroclear Bank revenues. This revenue composition could not have been deduced from the fee schedules available to users.

Some Euroclear Bank users questioned whether a pricing structure that resulted in 56% of revenues coming from safekeeping fees versus 9% coming from settlement fees was equitable between securities holders, who were mainly investors, and securities traders, who were mainly investment banks and brokers. They also argued that Euroclear Bank did not have a commercial incentive to improve the rate of transactions settling on time, because a lower settlement fail rate could reduce a significant source of income for Euroclear Bank, given that revenues from client balances and securities lending accounted for €153.1 million, or 20% of operating revenues.

In contrast, Euroclear argued that the group as a whole, including Euroclear Bank, had a strong incentive both to be as efficient as possible and to set appropriate pricing schedules, given the scrutiny it faced from its board and its user governance model:

> We believe that user shareholder governance ensures that users' interests are properly heeded, not only in terms of tariffs, but also in terms of risk control and assurance that Euroclear remains committed to responding to the needs of clients in all the markets it serves. It is key to making settlement and custody as cost-effective and efficient as possible.[49]

Morals

- Conflict between a market infrastructure institution and its users may make its governance difficult.
- Determining the independence of a board director at a market infrastructure institution may be hard.
- If a market infrastructure institution has different types of users, the nature of user governance may not always be clear.

LCH.CLEARNET: CREATION AND DIFFICULTIES 2003–6

LCH.Clearnet Group Limited (LCH.Clearnet) is a holding company for two operating companies that provide clearing and central counterparty services for major international exchanges and trading platforms primarily based in Europe, as well as a range of OTC markets.[50] On July 5, 2006, Gérard de La Martinière, nonexecutive chairman of LCH.Clearnet since its formation in 2003, and David Hardy, LCH.Clearnet's CEO also since its formation, resigned. The two resignations coincided with a range of serious difficulties that LCH.Clearnet had been facing since its creation. Six linked topics that illustrate how LCH.Clearnet was governed in practice over the period from its creation to the two resignations and briefly afterwards are outlined here: (1) the structure of, and rationale for, the merger between LCH and Clearnet that created LCH.Clearnet; (2) Euronext's role in LCH.Clearnet and conflicts of interest between stakeholders; (3) regulatory issues; (4) technological and financial matters; (5) concerns about the company's board and management; and (6) the restructuring of the ownership of LCH.Clearnet in 2007.

Structure of, and Rationale for, the Clearnet and LCH Merger

The ownership, governance, and profit-model of LCH.Clearnet when it was created, following the merger of London Clearing House (LCH) and Clearnet, was complex. It was owned 45.1% by exchanges—41.5% by Euronext (now NYSE Euronext), 2.7% by London Metal Exchange, and 0.9% by International Petroleum Exchange (now ICE Futures), 45.1% by user-members, and 9.8% by Euroclear.[51] Euronext's 41.5% was divided into 24.9% ordinary shares, with normal voting rights, and 16.6% preference shares, the voting rights of which were vested in an independent third party obliged to vote according to some "Terms of Reference" specified in LCH.Clearnet's constitution. Euronext agreed it would seek to sell its 16.6% preference shares at a later date, at which time the preference shares would convert to ordinary shares, failing which such shares would be redeemed over time (subject to regulatory approval). LCH.Clearnet was valued at 1.2 billion euros when it merged, split evenly between LCH and Clearnet.

For the first five years following the merger, voting caps were imposed on each shareholder (and its associates) as follows: Euronext 24.9%, Euroclear 9.8%, and any member-user 3.0%. In addition, no shareholder (together with its associates), other than Euronext, was allowed to exercise more than 20% of the voting rights. Such voting caps were to continue in force after this initial period if the LCH.Clearnet board considered their extension to be in the best interests of LCH.Clearnet, and shareholders representing at least 25% of votes (excluding votes cast by the independent third party) voted to extend the voting caps. During the initial five-year period, LCH.Clearnet shares could only be held by financial intermediaries or exchanges using LCH.Clearnet, with the exception of Euroclear. These eligibility requirements were to continue after this period, unless the LCH.Clearnet board proposed their termination and shareholders (other than members of the Euronext Group) representing a simple majority of votes voted to approve their termination.

Immediately following the merger, the LCH.Clearnet board had 19 directors: six appointed by exchanges (including four appointed by Euronext, one of which was CEO of the LSE, and one each appointed by the International Petroleum Exchange and the London Metal Exchange), six appointed by users, two appointed by Euroclear, two executive directors, and three independent directors, including the chairman. The four directors appointed by Euronext were required to excuse themselves from any discussions that could give rise to conflicts of interest.[52] As Euronext's preference shareholding percentage was reduced, it was planned to reduce the number of directors Euronext was allowed to appoint from four to two.

On its creation, LCH.Clearnet was mandated to operate on a limited for-profit basis. It sought to reach annual EBIT of at least €150 million from the 2006 financial year onwards. It was also specified that once LCH.Clearnet's EBIT exceeded €150 million in any given year, 70% of this excess would be for the benefit of users, in a manner to be determined by the LCH.Clearnet board. LCH.Clearnet would also pursue a dividend policy of distributing at least 50% of its annual distributable profits in the ordinary course of events, subject to regulatory requirements and after provision was made for payments scheduled to be made on the preference shares.

LCH.Clearnet identified a range of potential benefits from the merger—for users, shareholders, and trading platforms. The key ones may be summarized as follows:[53]

Users

Economies of scale leading to lower clearing fees, via reductions in the operating costs at LCH and Clearnet by using common platforms.

Lower back office operational costs, via standardized procedures and technology with a single interface into clearing services in multiple markets, and harmonized membership criteria.

A *reduction in economic capital requirements* (namely margin collateral), to provide for credit and operational risks at each CCP.

The possibility of cross-margin offsets, across closely correlated products, within and across asset classes, and potentially the adoption of a comprehensive portfolio approach to initial margining.

Faster development of new products and services.

Input onto user committees for each product area, and onto the board via representatives.

Shareholders

Stake in a preeminent CCP group in Europe with scope for growth.

Operation on normal commercial and for-profit basis, with the company seeking to obtain an adequate return on capital invested.

Participation in the direct benefits of the merger, including rationalization of operating costs, and an end to the duplication of investment and technology.

A *valuation of their shareholdings.*

Trading Platforms

Support for their growth and diversification strategies, as a result of LCH.Clearnet's broad international user base.

Opportunity to participate in restructuring the CCP sector, at both a corporate and a product level.

Enhanced liquidity and volume, both because trading was likely to gravitate to trading platforms supported by LCH.Clearnet, and because greater cost transparency for users would likely lead to a fall in all-in transaction costs for users.

Support for new trading platforms and the launch of new products.

The ownership, governance, and for-profit model adopted by LCH.Clearnet was designed to achieve a series of different balances. These included that:

- it be independent of both exchanges and settlement platforms;
- it deliver a balanced representation of exchanges and users-members;
- no shareholder or group, in particular Euronext, have control;
- all its customers, whether exchanges or users, be treated fairly and neutrally;
- it take into account the interests of both shareholders and clients;
- its benefits be shared equitably by users and by shareholders; and,
- it combine the financial discipline of a commercial organisation with extensive ownership and governance rights for users and trading platforms, by mixing the for-profit model operated by Clearnet and the utility model operated by LCH.[54]

There was overwhelming support for the creation of LCH.Clearnet among LCH's owners, as evidenced by a ratification vote of the merger at an Extraordinary General Meeting and Court Meeting held by LCH on November 27, 2003, at which all of LCH's exchange shareholders and 91.2% of its member shareholders voted in favor of the merger. In addition, in order to effect the share ownership structure outlined above, LCH user shareholders subscribed to an offering by Euronext of 7.6% stake in LCH.Clearnet.

Euronext's Role and Conflicts of Interest

Both prior and subsequent to the merger, there was concern that Euronext would have significant influence over LCH.Clearnet as a result of several factors:[55]

- Euronext, together with Euroclear, its strategic partner, had direct control of 34.7% of the equity voting rights in the company (disregarding the preference shares Euronext owned), which in most circumstances would be enough to block any equity voting decisions with which Euronext disagreed;
- Euronext's ability to appoint 4 directors to the board, together with Euroclear's right to appoint 2 directors;

- the eligibility requirements and voting caps imposed on shareholders, which meant that no institution other than Euronext would be allowed, or have an incentive, to hold a large block of shares in LCH.Clearnet;
- Euronext's 50% ownership of Atos Euronext Market Solutions (AEMS), the company that provided most of the technology to LCH.Clearnet SA; and
- the fact that Euronext was the company's single most important customer, accounting for over 60% of LCH.Clearnet's income.[56]

The relationship between Euronext and LCH.Clearnet raised concerns for the LSE, which also used LCH.Clearnet as a clearinghouse.[57] The LSE feared that Euronext would be able to influence LCH.Clearnet to give the Euronext markets a competitive advantage over those operated by the LSE, for example, by gaining confidential competitor information and preferential access to LCH.Clearnet's development resources. Even after having agreed to a contractual arrangement with LCH.Clearnet in which the LSE presumably sought to address such competition issues, they continued to arise. For example, there was a debate at LCH.Clearnet about installing a harmonized equity clearing system, which could deliver significant benefits for users. The aim was to harmonize around the Clearing 21 product, which was owned by AEMS, which in turn was 50% owned by Euronext. LSE disagreed with this approach, however, because it believed that use of Clearing 21 would have added to the cost base for clearing UK equities by transferring it to a less effective legacy platform and also changed the UK clearing model for the purpose of increasing revenues received by Euronext, an exchange with which the LSE competed.

A direct conflict also developed between Euronext and the major users of LCH.Clearnet. Euronext sought to obtain a range of objectives from LCH.Clearnet including most importantly, profit maximization, or at a minimum no impairment of the value of LCH.Clearnet on its books. In contrast, users were concerned about fees, the primary source of LCH.Clearnet's profits, and wanted LCH.Clearnet to charge the minimum necessary. Fundamentally users preferred a not-for-profit utility model, while Euronext wanted a for-profit model. Users saw LCH.Clearnet essentially as a monopoly, and hoped that in time it might become subject to regulatory intervention to limit its profits. Having previously owned LCH, users may also have seen the benefits of owning LCH.Clearnet without influence from Euronext. In order to achieve this, they recognized they might at some stage have to buy out Euronext's shareholding. They were not, however, prepared to buy out Euronext at a valuation determined by the tariffs that LCH.Clearnet was charging that in turn the users believed were unsustainably and unreasonably high.

The profit structure established for LCH.Clearnet on its creation, namely that once its EBIT exceeded €150 million, 70% of the excess would be for the benefit of users, was viewed in different ways by different constituencies. Those shareholders interested in enhancing the valuation of their shares and receiving dividend flows saw it as creating a desired earnings target. Those shareholders who regarded themselves primarily as users saw the structure as a means of controlling the profitability of LCH.Clearnet, given that they wanted fee reductions.

Market participants believed Euronext exerted its influence over LCH.Clearnet in a range of different ways. One example concerned the payment ("retrocession") Euronext received from LCH.Clearnet for every transaction it cleared, a policy that had been established when Euronext owned Clearnet. This fee was set on an ad valorem basis, with a minimum and a maximum amount, and there was a different formula for each market. The policy was not transparent or clear to users, and effectively meant that Euronext was taxing all order flow. The retrocession was, however, important to Euronext as it contributed a significant amount of its earnings before tax.

Euronext consistently rejected claims that it had control over LCH. Clearnet. One clear representation of its viewpoint was presented to the UK Competition Commission, when the commission was examining bids by Euronext and Deutsche Börse for the LSE, and considering Euronext/ LSE's potential influence over LCH.Clearnet should Euronext acquire LSE. After the commission had issued its provisional findings, Euronext maintained that

> *LCH.Clearnet was established to be independent of any individual exchange, including Euronext.* The founding principle that underlies the structure and governance of LCH.Clearnet, agreed at the outset between the London Clearing House and Euronext, was that Euronext should not control LCH.Clearnet. This was seen as essential to secure the necessary approval of the user shareholders of the London Clearing House. The fact that these user shareholders approved the transaction, and purchased nearly 8% of the share capital from Euronext, demonstrates the extent to which the parties most directly concerned were satisfied with the independence of LCH.Clearnet.
> *Euronext does not exercise de jure control over LCH.Clearnet.* Euronext holds only minority shareholding and voting rights in LCH.Clearnet. Accordingly, Euronext lacks the ability to control or otherwise direct LCH.Clearnet to disadvantage or refuse access to a rival exchange.
> *Euronext does not exercise de facto control over LCH.Clearnet.* The Provisional Findings err by over-stating LCH.Clearnet's dependence

on a merged Euronext/LSE and taking insufficient account of Euronext/LSE's dependence on LCH.Clearnet. Euronext has no *de facto* control over LCH.Clearnet because it has no realistic alternative to LCH.Clearnet. In the absence of any alternative clearinghouse provider, Euronext and the LSE have (and will continue to have) no alternative but to use LCH.Clearnet. As a result, Euronext and the LSE are (and will remain) dependent on LCH.Clearnet. Because neither exchange could credibly threaten to switch to an alternative clearing service provider, a merged Euronext/LSE would be unable to leverage its relationship with LCH.Clearnet in the way contemplated in the Provisional Findings.[58]

Given the importance to Euronext of acquiring the LSE, and its concern at the time not to have such a potential takeover be adversely affected by a perception at the Competition Commission that Euronext did have significant influence over LCH.Clearnet, Euronext would have had an incentive not to intervene in LCH.Clearnet's governance in order to minimize the possibility that the Competition Commission might take such a view.

Contrasting views about the influence of Euronext over LCH.Clearnet were provided by two different UK regulators. When the UK's Office of Fair Trading (OFT) examined the LCH.Clearnet merger prior to its completion, it concluded that governance concerns were addressed by the safeguards put in place:

> Euronext may be able to negotiate more favourable clearing terms than its rival exchanges, but this is likely to be as a result of its vertical integration with, and contribution to, LCH.Clearnet's revenue stream rather than any unfair ability to influence LCH.Clearnet strategy.... Notwithstanding third party concerns, there appears to be no strong incentive on the part of the merged entity to allow Euronext to influence strategic decisions in its favour. A complex governance structure also limits Euronext's ability to discriminate against rival exchanges via its shareholding or position on the board. Moreover, the governance structure safeguards users and exchanges interests.[59]

The opposite view was essentially taken by the UK's Competition Commission when it considered whether a hypothetical institution created from a merger of Euronext and the LSE (referred to here as Euronext/LSE) would be likely to be able to influence decisions taken by LCH.Clearnet.[60] The commission recognized that the LSE did not have any material influence over LCH.Clearnet, and noted that Euronext had told the Commission that it had no ability or interest in controlling LCH.Clearnet. The commission also acknowledged the strict governance arrangements that had been put in place at the time of the LCH.Clearnet merger, in response to the possible ongoing influence of Euronext over LCH.Clearnet, and that taken in isolation, these arrangements appeared to be robust. However, taking account of Euronext/LSE's significant shareholding in LCH.Clearnet, its likely four seats on the board of LCH.Clearnet, together with the relatively high proportion of LCH.Clearnet's revenues that would be derived from business transacted on Euronext markets, the commission considered that "on balance, we would expect Euronext/LSE to have the ability to influence LCH.Clearnet's strategic decisions in its favour." While self-evidently the potential Euronext/LSE combination examined by the Competition Commission was not the same as simply Euronext, as examined by the OFT, the reasons for the Competition Commission's opinion would likely also have been applicable had it assessed simply Euronext's influence over LCH.Clearnet—namely Euronext's significant shareholding, its four seats on the board, and its importance as a customer to LCH.Clearnet.

Influence of Regulation

Regulators significantly influenced both the initial governance structure of the merger creating LCH.Clearnet and its ongoing operations. The idea of creating a single CCP with a single legal status was vetoed by the relevant regulators. A year after the merger, a senior LCH.Clearnet official began a speech saying, "Why didn't we immediately proceed to a single clearing house? We could not. The regulators would not let us move to a single clearing house."[61] It appeared unacceptable either that a UK entity could become the dominant CCP for clearing products denominated in euros, or that a Continental entity could become the dominant CCP for clearing products denominated in UK sterling. It was thus insisted that the separate subsidiaries in France and the UK be maintained with their separate legal and regulatory statuses.

This decision had important implications for the ongoing operations of LCH.Clearnet. As the regulators had little jurisdiction over LCH.Clearnet Group Ltd. (the Group) compared with their power over the subsidiary companies (LCH.Clearnet Ltd. and LCH.Clearnet SA), they were wary about granting the subsidiary boards the freedom to let important decisions regarding each subsidiary to be taken by the Group's board. They also required that the boards of both LCH.Clearnet SA and LCH.Clearnet Ltd. be independent. In response, the subsidiary boards put most of their focus on responding to their local regulators, which in turn meant that it was difficult to achieve the Group-wide integration necessary to deliver the intended efficiencies of the merger.

The existence of the "regulatory college" coordinating the supervision of LCH.Clearnet SA also gave difficulties to LCH.Clearnet. Sometimes this college comprised 25 individuals from 10 different regulators, and as a result it apparently proved cumbersome and difficult to reach decisions between so many institutions, which sometimes had competing objectives.

Technological and Financial Issues

A central reason for the creation of LCH.Clearnet was to obtain reductions in costs for users via implementing a technology integration plan. At the core of this plan was the Generic Clearing System project, which was intended to replace the position-keeping systems for lower volume markets such as swaps and repos along with the core CCP functions such as banking and risk management.

The creation of LCH.Clearnet included a timetable to contain and reduce costs in three phases. The first was to be via harmonization of systems and procedures in 2004–5. The second was to be via a rationalization of systems and operations by mid-2006. Although the two CCPs would continue to operate as distinct CCPs over this period, savings would be delivered by using the same technology platform, and realizing other economies of scale in support, risk, and settlement functions. The third phase was to allow users a choice of which CCP to use from 2007. The two CCPs would manage the resultant intersubsidiary balances.

The technology integration plan was pivotal to LCH.Clearnet's goal of delivering cost savings and reducing fees. At the time of its creation in 2003, LCH.Clearnet promised a reduction of 20% in fees, with the additional anticipation that from 2006, when annual earnings before interest and tax were forecast to rise to 150 million euros, any surplus above this level would be distributed, with 70% to customers and 30% to shareholders.[62] This was an ambitious earnings target as the two entities combined had an EBIT of just 76 million euros in 2003.[63] Technology savings as a whole, including those from the Generic Clearing System, were expected to reap annual savings of about 35 million euros by 2007.

Delivery of the technology integration project starting slipping behind schedule close to its inception. The project failed to meet a deadline of going live in October 2004. With EBIT of 77.7 million in 2004 and 86.3 million euros in 2005, LCH.Clearnet did not pay dividends to shareholders or rebates to users in 2004, as it had not achieved the expected costs savings after the merger. In the 2004 annual report, the CEO noted:

> Post-merger, a fuller picture of the underlying state of the two business' infrastructures was understood together with the impact on the expected benefits. As a result, we do not expect to realise all cost savings over the same timeframe as identified at the time of the merger.[64]

In February 2005, when integration testing started in full, it became apparent that the computer system was not working as intended. This was reported at a board meeting in March 2005, and in May 2005 the consultancy firm Accenture was called in to assess the individual components.[65] Accenture reported that some elements would not be able to be used, and accordingly there should be a 20 million euro write-off, while the rest of the components could be used. Several weeks later the CEO said in the interim accounts:

> A key part of the integration programme has been a review of the Group-wide technology strategy. Following the determination that a major software project was unlikely to deliver against original expectations, I reported the position to shareholders in my letter dated 18 May 2005. The review determined that, whilst the software components built or bought in were, in the main, both sound and fit for purpose, the design against which the components were being assembled required simplification. As a result of this review the Group has chosen to focus on the development of common infrastructure in key areas in a modular fashion with less delivery risk. All in all, we concluded that some of the work undertaken and capitalised in the balance sheet will not now be brought into economic use.[66]

In May 2005 LCH.Clearnet suspended work and cut staff on the project from 100 to 40. Hardy said by email to employees that the project had become overcomplicated.[67] At the board there was much concern about this, so much so that at a May 2005 board meeting, the CEO said that he was happy to take accountability for the problem, and the board should consider his position. His offer of resignation was not, however, accepted by the board.

By 2006 the merged company's business model and governance model was being questioned by some users as it became clear the technology and integration timetable would not be met.[68] Major users became concerned over LCH.Clearnet's failure to deliver cheaper fees from merger synergies and were frustrated they had so little influence. Some argued that if LCH.Clearnet had truly been a for-profit company, the IT difficulties would have been tackled earlier through shareholder concern for returns. LCH.Clearnet finally announced a tariff cut in 2006 after lobbying from users, who said it had been difficult to obtain information from the company on how the merger would result in fee cuts.

The failure of the technology integration project was widely reported as being a major contributory factor leading to the resignation of the CEO. The project was formally closed down on July 21, 2006, just over two weeks after the CEO resigned.[69] A further write-off of 47.8 million euros associated with the project was recognized at this time. The write-off was probably recognized then because LCH.Clearnet had been making significant profits, and it was thus an opportune time to realize the impairment.

Different interpretations were put forward for the failure of the technology integration project. On the one hand, LCH.Clearnet may have underestimated the cultural differences in merging the French and British companies. It started out in a difficult position: it was a small company with both a limited talent pool and limited resources, trying to complete an ambitious and complex integration program of two companies' technology systems, right after both companies had separately completed major IT projects.[70] On the other hand, management of the project may have been poor.

Concerns about Relationships among Board, Management, Shareholders, and Users

The conflicts of interest between stakeholders in LCH.Clearnet, the failure of its technology integration program, and various other factors, all combined to give rise to some widely held, and sometimes conflicting, concerns about the relationship between the board, management, shareholders, and users of the company. Noteworthy ones included the following:

- Irrespective of the identity of the chairman, the fact that he devoted just one day a month to the board meant that he could not be effective in overseeing the governance of the company.[71]
- The board was too big to work well, yet at the same time the board made no effort to reduce its size.
- There was a lack of continuity in board members. There were very few consecutive board meetings at which the same people were present, as the user representatives were effectively appointed ex officio to represent their firms, and there was always someone moving jobs inside one of the firms. The core group of board members were the exchange representatives.
- The array of vested interests and the dominant interest of Euronext among stakeholders made it difficult and time-consuming to agree on project priorities.
- Some directors acted so resolutely in their own companies' interests, that it was difficult for the board to pursue the interests of the company.
- It was hard for the board to be effective as it had no secretariat to prepare directors for meetings. When the board did, however, ask for more papers to prepare for meetings and set up operational committees and subcommittees, management began to view this as impinging on its own core competence.

- The IT problems were seen as a failure of management to be sufficiently open with the board.
- The IT problems were also seen as a failure of the board to hold management to account.
- On the one hand, the company's main shareholder, Euronext, was perceived as having too powerful an influence over the management and board of LCH.Clearnet.
- On the other hand, the fact that Euronext was focused on its merger proposal for the LSE during 2004 and 2005, meant it did not supervise management closely enough over the period to tackle technology slippages in good time.
- The split of responsibilities between the Group board and the subsidiary boards was unclear. The two subsidiary boards were composed mainly of independent directors, with no user representation, and subsidiary board directors did not sit on the Group board. Communication between the various boards was therefore difficult. One approach to enhance cooperation was to invite the subsidiary board chairmen as observers to the main board.
- Some user representatives on the board were not present or did not want to enter into a debate between Euronext and the LSE, on both of which they dealt. All the while, the user community criticized management via their main trade association, the London Investment Banking Association (LIBA).
- On the one hand, the independent directors were viewed as not being powerful enough in standing up to the vested interests of particular stakeholders.
- On the other hand, over time some industry and exchange representatives began to view the independent directors as being too supportive of management.
- Management was not strong enough to carry through the merger and juggle the different vested interests either on a day-to-day operational basis, or on a strategic basis, without a proper functioning board.

Ownership Restructuring

On March 12, 2007, the boards of both LCH.Clearnet and Euronext announced that they had reached agreement regarding a repurchase of the majority of the shares of LCH.Clearnet held by Euronext.[72] The key terms of this repurchase included (1) the early redemption of the redeemable convertible preference shares (RCPS) of LCH.Clearnet held by Euronext at their redemption value of approximately €199 million, plus accrued but unpaid dividends;[73] and (2) the subsequent repurchase by

LCH.Clearnet of 26,183,362 ordinary shares of LCH.Clearnet held by Euronext at a price of €10 per ordinary share, the value at which the shares were issued at the time of the LCH/Clearnet merger in 2003. Following the repurchase, users were to hold 73.3% of the outstanding ordinary shares and Euronext was to retain a 5% holding of the ordinary shares of LCH.Clearnet and also one of its four board seats.

The LCH.Clearnet board saw the repurchase as an opportunity both for LCH.Clearnet's customer and shareholder interests to be more closely aligned, and for LCH.Clearnet to be better positioned to respond to ongoing challenges and developments in the clearing sector. It argued that a number of actual and potential developments in the exchange and clearing markets posed significant threats to its clearing volumes and revenue streams. These included "clearing-driven" mergers between exchanges, new or potential new entrants in its market space and the development of alternative trading platforms that could attract liquidity from LCH. Clearnet's customers. Regulatory changes including MiFID and Basel II, together with increasing scrutiny by competition authorities of the sector in which LCH.Clearnet operated, were also seen as posing additional business challenges.

In order to continue prospering as an organization, the LCH.Clearnet board considered that the Group had to seek to minimize or remove the incentive for disintermediation, whatever its source, and that this was best achieved by adjusting its operating model to focus more clearly on delivering benefits to users, in particular by providing an immediate financial benefit to users in the form of substantially lower fees rather than future rebates, or dividends to shareholders of whom users formed a significant part. In order to implement considerably lower tariffs and promote the longer term success of the company, the LCH.Clearnet Board thus considered it necessary to reduce the shareholding of its largest "returns-focused" shareholder, Euronext.

The LCH.Clearnet Group chairman explained:

> In an increasingly competitive environment, the Board concluded that the best way for LCH.Clearnet to overcome the challenges to its revenue streams was to cut tariffs dramatically. As such a move would be inconsistent with the focus on returns of LCH.Clearnet's 41.5% shareholder Euronext, the Proposals seek to accelerate the redemption of the RCPSs and to buy back a large part of the ordinary share capital that Euronext holds in LCH.Clearnet ... the greater alignment between our shareholder and user communities that arises from these Proposals will support a strategy of continuing tariff reductions and, in due course, significant member rebates and allow LCH.Clearnet more effectively to meet the needs of users and shareholders.

Morals

- Both complexity in a market infrastructure institution's governance, and the adoption of contradictory targets for the institution, may make its governance difficult.
- Regulators may seek to promote perceived national interests in their supervision of market infrastructure institutions.
- It may be hard for conflicted board members at a market infrastructure institution to promote the organization's interests rather than those of their own firms.
- The presence of independent directors on a board does not mean that conflicts between board members are easily resolved.

PART IV

Policy Analysis and Recommendations

CHAPTER EIGHT

What Is the Most Efficient Governance Structure?

THE CHOICE OF GOVERNANCE MODEL a market infrastructure institution should adopt is often contentious. This chapter analyzes what is the optimal governance model for market infrastructure institutions using the broad goal of efficiency as the main yardstick to compare different models. Three fundamental elements of governance are examined: an organization's ownership structure, its profit mandate, and its board composition. The analysis draws on the extensive and diverse literature on the governance of different types of organizations, and also on a wide range of context-specific experiences of individual market infrastructure institutions.[1]

The criterion of efficiency as the main benchmark by which to evaluate different governance models is selected for three reasons. First, the reduction of transaction costs is a pivotal goal of most private sector market participants and of most market infrastructure institutions themselves. Second, efficiency is a key economic measure of social welfare. Finally, it is also one of the three core objectives of securities markets regulation identified by IOSCO, namely the protection of investors, ensuring that markets are fair, efficient, and transparent, and the reduction of systemic risk.[2] The use of efficiency here as the key criterion to evaluate different governance models does not mean that the other core IOSCO objectives are of secondary importance. Their significance and the manner in which regulatory intervention in the governance of market infrastructure institutions may promote all the IOSCO objectives are discussed in chapter 10.

The chapter is composed of four sections. In the first three, key issues regarding what governance model a market infrastructure institution should adopt are analyzed. In the first section, the archetypal ownership and mandate models that may be adopted by a market infrastructure institution are outlined. The second section identifies and discusses the pivotal factors that affect the relative efficiency of the different ownership and mandate models. In the third section, two issues of fundamental importance to market infrastructure institutions' boards are discussed: the roles such boards should undertake, and the merits and difficulties of having independent directors or user directors on these boards.

A wide range of arguments are presented in the first three sections of the chapter, many of which are complex in nature, and some of which also conflict with each other. The last section of the chapter seeks to encapsulate these discussions and to present in a simple and accessible manner key lessons about how to choose the optimal ownership structure and mandate for a market infrastructure institution, about the roles that market infrastructure institutions' boards should undertake, and about the merits and difficulties in appointing independent directors and user directors to such boards. In order to do so, twenty general propositions are articulated. Most of the propositions summarize the analysis presented in the first three sections of the chapter; for the few that incorporate new ideas, a justification for their inclusion is presented.

Ownership and Mandate: Archetypal Models and Primary Goals

Five key archetypal governance models that may be adopted by a market infrastructure institution are outlined in this section.[3] They are referred to, respectively, as the *nonprofit*, the *cooperative*, the *for-profit*, the *public,* and the *hybrid* models. These archetypes seek to capture the essence of the main governance models available to market infrastructure institutions. They are highly simplified descriptions, and are not intended to depict the complexity of the governance structures adopted in practice by market infrastructure institutions.

Each model is characterized by the ownership structure and mandate it prescribes for an organization.[4] The basic elements of each model are summarized, and the primary goal or goals that may be imputed to an institution following each model are outlined. Comments on how the actual objectives pursued by market infrastructure institutions adopting the various models may not be those anticipated as their primary goals are presented in subsequent sections.

Nonprofit

The central attribute of a nonprofit firm is that it is restricted from distributing outside the firm any profit or surplus that it earns. In order that any surplus not be appropriated by the firm's management, a nonprofit firm is typically only allowed to pay what is deemed a reasonable compensation to its management. Following Hansmann (1980), most nonprofit market infrastructure institutions may be characterized as "commercial mutual" nonprofits.[5] "Commercial" refers to the fact that such institutions' income derives primarily from providing services for a fee to their customers. "Mutual" refers to the fact that the agents who are the prime source of the institutions' income also control the organization.

Given that a commercial mutual nonprofit firm is controlled by, and run for, the consumers of the firm, that it cannot distribute any profits outside the firm, and that it cannot operate if its cumulative losses exceed its cumulative gains, the primary objective of such a firm may be taken to be, in economic terms, the maximization of consumer surplus subject to breaking even.[6] More informally, this goal may be interpreted as being the advancement of the interests of the firm's users by providing relevant services on a cost-recovery basis. The objectives that nonprofit firms officially follow are reflected in their mission statements.

Although nonprofits are not allowed to distribute any profits they earn outside the firm, they can effect an analogous result by lowering the fees they charge members for the various services that they offer, or by offering rebates to their members.

Cooperative

The governance structure of a consumer cooperative revolves around the notion of membership. A cooperative provides services mainly for the use of its members, and membership is normally limited only to those agents who consume the cooperative's services.[7] The assignment of voting rights at a cooperative is also typically allocated solely to members. Normally each member has only one vote regardless of the number of shares it owns, or the amount of economic activity it brings to the cooperative. Ownership rights are normally not freely tradable or exchangeable, and are often required to be forfeited on cessation of membership. The primary goal of a consumer cooperative may be taken to be the maximization of consumer surplus plus profits, with any profits being distributed to the members of the cooperative. As Baarda (2006, 178) explains:

> The "traditional" cooperative has only one central objective—to provide the greatest returns to its patrons. This is often achieved by focusing primarily on favorable pricing or generating patronage refunds while the member-patrons' investment in the cooperative is regarded only as a means to an end without an independent return-to-equity objective.

Despite there being a difference between consumer cooperatives and commercial mutual nonprofits, namely that the first type of organization may make distributions in cash to its members while the second is only allowed to do so in kind, the two organizational archetypes are very similar. Indeed, most nonprofit market infrastructure institutions are also cooperatives, while many cooperative market infrastructure institutions are also nonprofits. The two types of models are thus often referred to interchangeably. They are sometimes also generically referred to as the "mutual," "membership," or "utility" models.

The primary goal of a cooperative market infrastructure institution to enhance the returns of its members is often complicated by several phenomena. The first is that its membership may not be homogeneous, with different groups of members having varying objectives. Different ownership groups may then attempt to promote their own competing interests via the institution's governance structure. This frequently occurs between members that undertake a large amount of activity on a market infrastructure institution, and accordingly provide most of its income, and the institution's smaller members. The larger members may, for example, seek to obtain volume discounts not available to smaller members. Another source of differences between a market infrastructure institution's members is when some of them compete with the market infrastructure institution. These participants may pursue different goals than the members that do not compete with the market infrastructure institution. In the cash equity markets, for example, some financial intermediaries operate their own internal order-matching systems in competition with exchanges of which they are a member. The progressive movement up the value chain by some CSDs means similarly that they also compete with some of their members.

A second phenomenon that often complicates the goals pursued by a cooperative market infrastructure institution occurs when its members, typically financial intermediaries of one sort or another, have different objectives than their customers, sometimes referred to as the "end-users." These end-users may include investors, issuers, or remote market participants that need to access a market infrastructure via a local intermediary.[8] Members may benefit from inefficiencies in the operation of a market infrastructure institution, while the costs of such inefficiencies are borne by end-users. Even though nonmember end-users have no ownership stakes in a cooperative market infrastructure institution, they may still be able to influence its governance and the goals it pursues.

For-Profit

The fundamental characteristic of a for-profit firm is that it is allowed to distribute profits to equity holders as dividends. For-profit firms typically have no restrictions on who may be their customers, so that anybody may buy their services for the appropriate fee. For-profit firms also typically have no restrictions on who may be their owners, so that anybody including nonusers may own equity, and thus receive dividends and have voting rights at the firm. Access to for-profit market infrastructure institutions' services is thus separable from the ownership rights in such institutions. The primary goal of for-profit firms is taken to be the maximization of profits.

Many nonprofit and cooperative exchanges have transformed themselves into for-profit firms via the process of demutualization. Although this term has been used to mean different things, it is used here to refer to two key phenomena: a change in the ownership structure of an institution from being owned solely by users to being owned by profit-seeking investors, and a change in an institution's mandate from operating on a nonprofit basis to operating on a for-profit basis. The process of demutualization normally takes place in stages and can lead to different outcomes.[9] Typically, cooperative membership rights are converted to common stock ownership rights in a privately owned corporation, via a private placement. Sometimes classes of investors other than the original cooperative's members, such as listed companies, institutional investors, or a strategic partner, are allocated shares in the initial placement. The tradability of the shares may initially be restricted, either partially or fully. The institution may then become a public company via a listing, while still restricting the transfer of its shares. All restrictions on trading may then be lifted, so that anybody may become an owner of the institution, and the shares become widely held.

Although there are significant differences between the for-profit, the nonprofit, and the cooperative archetypes, in certain circumstances they may also have the same goals. The payment of a dividend by a for-profit firm benefits its owners. In contrast, the reduction of fees at a nonprofit or the payment of a rebate at a cooperative benefits the firm's users. The importance of this distinction depends on the extent to which the owners and the users overlap.

Public

The key element of the *public* model of governance is that there is some form of public ownership of the institution in question. Publicly owned market infrastructure institutions may operate on a for-profit or nonprofit basis. The primary goal of the public model for a market infrastructure institution is to ensure that it follows the goals specified for it by government. These typically encompass long-term market development objectives that require major investments in infrastructure, education, and capacity-building that do not have clear payback periods, and may not deliver short-term profits or serve users' immediate needs.

Most developed economies have dismissed the public model as no longer appropriate for infrastructure institutions in their equity markets. It is, however, still used both in some emerging equity markets and for some

CSDs for national government bond markets. It is also the governance model for the TARGET2-Securities (T2S) project to provide a settlement platform for euro-denominated securities under the leadership of the European Central Bank (ECB).[10]

Publicly owned market infrastructure institutions often face two sets of circumstances that complicate the delivery of their stated public interest goals. The first is that these goals may be multiple, broad in nature, and ill-defined, as with some of the other models. This may lead to conflict between the goals.

A second issue faced by public-owned institutions is that they may be subject to political interference that may divert focus away from their stated public interest goals. A description of the National Stock Exchange (NSE) in India in 2001 illustrates this issue:

> The governance of NSE suffers from important vulnerabilities that flow from its being a public sector organisation. Now that NSE is the most important securities exchange in the country, there is likely to be significant interest on the part of political actors to capture NSE and derive rents from it. The constituency which benefits from a well functioning securities exchange (households engaging in saving across the country) has too little at stake to engage in political actions which favour a soundly run NSE.[11]

It is sometimes suggested in contrast, however, that the public model may have an advantage in reconciling the different interests of competing market constituencies in favor of the public interest, as illustrated in the context of the T2S project by the ECB:

> The Eurosystem is well placed to be the neutral, independent authority driving the process of reconciling competing interests in order to achieve very necessary changes.[12]

Hybrid

Hybrid models of governance combine elements of two or more of the archetypal models in a single construct. There are many forms of hybrid models that market infrastructure institutions may adopt, with different combinations of both ownership structures and mandates.[13]

Possible ownership structures include any combination of users, investors, government, other market infrastructure institutions, strategic partners, and other stakeholders such as institutional investors and securities issuers. A key objective of having a broadly based ownership structure for a market infrastructure institution is to ensure that the organization serves the needs of all its shareholders, by internalizing their different interests into its decision-making process.[14] A public-private partnership, for example, where a market infrastructure institution is owned both by relevant government bodies and by private sector market participants, may thus be expected to respond both to the public interest, as specified by government, and to market participants' private interests. A user-investor ownership structure may be intended to deliver the interests of both the users of a market infrastructure institution and investors seeking a rate of return.

The obvious implication of there being more than one type of owner of a market infrastructure institution is that their interests may conflict. In a public-private model, investors' interests may vary from the public interest, for example on the required payback period for investment recovery. In a hybrid model with ownership by users and investors, users may wish to have low levels of fees, while investors may want the opposite, namely high fees that can then be passed through to them via high dividends.

Hybrid models of governance may also contain elements of different types of mandates. A market infrastructure institution may choose to operate on a limited for-profit basis, so that it distributes any profits it earns to its customers up to a certain level, and if profits rise above this level to its investors; or vice versa, so that the first tranche of any profits earned is payable to shareholders, after which any further profits are distributed to customers. Another hybrid model with elements of both the for-profit and nonprofit mandates occurs when a market infrastructure institution operates on a nonprofit basis, while at the same time owning and controlling some for-profit subsidiaries.

OWNERSHIP MODEL AND MANDATE: CRITICAL FACTORS AFFECTING EFFICIENCY

Following Hansmann (1980 and 1996), the optimal governance model for an organization is taken to be the one that minimizes the combined costs to all its *patrons*, where the term "patrons" refers broadly to all agents with any form of economic relationship with the institution in question.[15] These may include, among others, the institution's customers, owners, management, staff, suppliers, and financiers. No priority is given to any particular subset of patrons in seeking to reduce the combined costs they all face.

The critical factors that affect the relative efficiency of the different archetypal governance models are identified and discussed in this section.[16] The factors are examined under the following headings: (1) the profit motive, efficiency, and innovation; (2) market power; (3) multiple objectives, ambiguity, and decision-making; (4) management incentives;

(5) illiquidity; (6) capital-raising; (7) strategic alliances, joint ventures, and partnerships; (8) market development; (9) technology; (10) relationship-specific sunk investments; and (11) information revelation. Key lessons of this discussion are summarized in the last section of the chapter.

It is not possible here to provide an exhaustive list and analysis of all the different costs that all the various governance structures may give rise to for all the different patrons of an organization, let alone to aggregate these costs for each governance structure and then determine which governance structure minimizes them. Instead, this section identifies and examines what are believed to be the most important costs arising from the key different ownership structures and mandates. In order to simplify the analysis, the focus is narrowed in three important ways. First, most of the analysis, though not all, examines the relative merits of the for-profit model on the one hand versus the nonprofit and the cooperative models on the other. Not only are these the most common models, much of the discussion is also relevant for the other types of models. Second, for the most part, the nonprofit and the cooperative models are treated as being the same for the reasons described in the previous section. Finally, when for-profit market infrastructure institutions are examined, attention is focused on discussing those costs of governance that arise as a result of such firms maximizing profits, and having liquid shares and multiple shareholders. Although it is recognized that there are many costs and benefits to a for-profit market infrastructure institution of transforming from a closed firm to a publicly traded listed firm, most of these costs and benefits are similar to those faced by all other types of firms considering such a transformation. They have been widely examined elsewhere, and are therefore not discussed here.

When assessing the efficiency of a particular archetypal governance model, two types of evaluations are required. It is vital first to assess the effects of an institution following the primary goal or goals that may be imputed to it as a result of its adoption of the specified model. In addition, it is crucial to determine whether there are any circumstances in which the institution may not follow these primary goals, and, if so, how this will affect the institution's ability to deliver efficient outcomes. Both these types of analysis are undertaken here.

The Profit Motive, Efficiency, and Innovation

The fundamental benefit of a firm adopting the for-profit model is that in a competitive market the single primary objective of maximizing profits gives the firm a clear incentive to provide the most efficient services: the exploitation of any inefficiency will lead to greater profits. A for-profit market infrastructure institution will thus be responsive to the preferences of all market participants, independent of whether they are members of the institution or not, as long as such preferences can be translated into a demand for the institution's services. Furthermore, as claims to future net earnings can be capitalized and transferred, the financial potential of long-term investments can be appropriately evaluated and obtained by their owners. This implies, as the U.S. General Accounting Office (2002, 9) summarizes in the context of exchanges, that "shareholders of a de-mutualized exchange would be expected to support cost-effective technology that improves customer service and thus the competitiveness of the market, because they would expect it to increase the value of their investments by attracting more business to the exchange." In principle, both cooperative and nonprofit market infrastructure institutions should also maximize profits or surplus, thereby minimizing inefficiencies in competitive markets. Any profits/surplus that such institutions obtained as a result of following this strategy could then be used to deliver their respective primary goals—namely the distribution of profits to cooperative members, or the reduction of the cost of services to nonprofit members. In practice, however, several linked factors may mean that nonprofits and cooperatives do not seek to minimize the inefficiencies faced by all participants in the market.

Both nonprofits and cooperatives may focus excessively on reducing the transactions costs faced by, and enhancing the benefits obtained by, their members, at the expense of considering the interests of other market participants. Members of nonprofits and cooperatives may constrain the introduction of new services that would compete with their businesses, even if the establishment of such services might benefit the market as a whole via greater efficiency. They may worry that changing the way in which a market infrastructure institution operates could destroy their business model. The nonprofit or cooperative structure may thus entrench an industry structure that is obsolete. Many membership exchanges, for example, faced difficulties replacing floor trading with electronic trading because of members' perceived economic interest in floor trading. Similarly a nonprofit or cooperative exchange may not wish to grant access to its system directly to investors without the need for financial intermediation, even when the cost savings to investors, and indirectly to issuers, of doing so could be considerable.[17] To do so would disintermediate, and thus potentially harm the economic interests of, the members who controlled the institution.[18]

A related factor that may limit a nonprofit or cooperative market infrastructure institution from seeking to eliminate inefficiencies or transaction costs faced by market participants other than its members is that its members may not benefit directly from its doing so, given that claims to its future net earnings cannot easily be capitalized and transferred. Nonprofits and cooperatives may thus have a reduced incentive to invest in initiatives with the potential for future growth, as their members can only participate in the financial upside indirectly, through cross-subsidization of charges for services or redistribution of future profits/surplus when they are earned.

In some circumstances, nonprofits' and cooperatives' incentive to manage their costs efficiently may also be limited. As such institutions are typically limited by guarantee, their recourse is normally to assess their members in the event of a financial reversal. Nonprofits and cooperatives may thus not scrutinize their costs rigorously, given that any cost increases they incur can be passed onto their members.

Both public-controlled and hybrid market infrastructure institutions are typically mandated to pursue efficiency and adopt appropriate innovation. Several factors may, however, inhibit their ability to deliver efficient outcomes. In a manner similar to nonprofits and cooperatives, it may be difficult for them to capture the benefits of reducing any inefficiencies in the market. Both types of institutions are also likely to be required to followed other incentives, the pursuit of which may compromise the delivery of efficiency. Public-controlled institutions may in addition be subject to political intervention and bureaucratic inertia.

EMPIRICAL EVIDENCE

A range of empirical analyses have studied the effects of exchanges' demutualizing on three key aspects of their performance: their share price performance, their operating performance, and their market's performance.

Share Price Performance: Mendiola and O'Hara (2004) examine eight demutualized and listed stock exchanges for a period of years following their demutualizations, and find that their share prices generally outperformed both the stocks on their markets and the IPOs listed on their exchanges. The exchanges' share price performance was also positively linked to the fraction of equity the exchange sold to outsiders. While changing governance structure did not overcome the challenges faced by a few exchanges, Mendiola and O'Hara interpret their overall results as providing strong evidence that shifting governance from a cooperative to a corporate structure is value-enhancing for exchanges. Aggarwal and Dahiya (2006) examine the stock price performance of 20 demutualized exchanges that became publicly traded companies.[19] They compare the long-run performance of the exchanges with the performance of relevant stock market indices. Only four exchanges had returns lower than their comparable market index in the postlisting period, and the median excess return of the exchanges as public companies (as of September 30, 2005) was 48.67%.

Operating Performance: Mendiola and O'Hara (2004) also look at various accounting measures of performance of eight demutualized exchanges. They conclude that the evidence is too mixed, or too difficult to interpret, to provide confirmation of whether exchange demutualizations are value-enhancing. Aggarwal and Dahiya (2006) study the operating performance of 20 publicly listed exchanges for the fiscal year 2004, again estimating some widely used accounting measures of operating performance, such as return on equity, return on assets, and operating margin. Most exchanges performed well, with median operating margins of 33.8%. Furthermore, exchanges enjoyed double-digit profit margins and returns growth. The median compounded annual growth rate for the period 2000–4 was 10% for sales and 19% for operating income. There was almost a complete absence of debt, with a median debt-to-total asset ratio of 0.4%. A number of publicly listed exchanges had a fairly high dividend payout (median 42.3%), with a few exchanges paying out more than 100% in dividends.

Serifsoy (2008) examines whether demutualized stock exchanges exhibited stronger operating performance than mutual exchanges over the period 1999–2003 for 28 exchanges.[20] In order to compare the performance of both mutual and demutualized exchanges, efficiency scores are calculated using information on accounting data, staff size, and transaction data, but not share price information. Serifsoy's findings do not support the view that having outsider-owners enhances the efficiency of an exchange. The assumption that demutualization is necessary to install modern trading systems is also not confirmed empirically. On the contrary, the mutual exchanges in the sample had persistently higher proportions of their trading on electronic order books than did the demutualized listed exchanges.

Liquidity and Trading Volume: Mendiola and O'Hara (2004) and Treptow (2006, chap. 4) both find a general improvement in various measures of liquidity at exchanges following their demutualization. Krishnamurti, Sequeira, and Fangjian (2003) compare the market performance of two Indian exchanges, one with a mutual structure, the Bombay Stock Exchange (BSE), and the other with a standard corporate structure, the National Stock Exchange (NSE), for a six-month period in 1997. They find that the NSE had a better quality market than the BSE.[21] The superior governance of NSE appeared to be at least partially responsible for its better market quality. A key factor in the NSE's success was its adoption of new technology, something the BSE was not able to do at the time.

Hazarika (2005) examines trading volumes and costs on the London Stock Exchange (LSE) from 2000 and 2001, and on the Borsa Italiana for various periods from 1996 to 1998. Hazarika maintains that the LSE faced significant competition over these periods, while the Borsa did not. Trading volumes fell on the LSE prior to its demutualization, but increased following demutualization. Trading costs were decreasing before demutualization and continued their fall after demutualization. While the Borsa also regained lost order flow following demutualization, trading costs increased on the Borsa post-demutualization, unlike on the LSE.

Market Power

A critical factor affecting the relative efficiency of different governance models for market infrastructure institutions is the extent to which they face competition. There has been great debate about whether they do in fact have market power, as discussed in chapter 2. If a market infrastructure institution has a dominant position in the provision of some services, it may seek to exploit its market power by acting anticompetitively. Key examples of such behavior include an institution reducing its output and increasing the price of its services above the competitive level, practicing price discrimination, implementing contractual tie-ins, refusing to supply its competitors, or using the dominant position it has in one market to stifle competition in an adjacent market, for example by cross-subsidy or nontransparent pricing. Such anticompetitive activity can be costly to the market as a whole compared to the competitive alternative.

Any single entity or group of agents that has control over a market infrastructure institution with a dominant position may exploit this control to its advantage. A for-profit firm is likely to have a direct incentive to undertake such anticompetitive activity, given that its owners will benefit from any monopolistic profits obtained. Standard corporate governance mechanisms will not stop this behavior. On the contrary, such mechanisms are designed precisely to ensure the promotion of shareholder interests, and shareholders will benefit from any monopolistic profits obtained.

The nonprofit cooperative governance model has a key potential advantage over the other models in the context of a market infrastructure institution with market power: it may restrict such an institution from acting anticompetitively. As Lee (2003b, 300–301) notes, when discussing exchanges:[22]

> The central attribute of a mutual or cooperative securities exchange is that the users of its services are also its owners. A cooperative exchange's customers can therefore control the prices the exchange sets, and ensure that even if it operates effectively as a monopoly, by dint of being the dominant provider of execution facilities, the exchange does not charge anticompetitive prices.

An analogous argument can be used for CCPs and CSDs. User control over a market infrastructure institution with market power will allow the users to determine which activities the institution undertakes, to their advantage.[23]

A range of factors may, however, lessen the potential advantage of the cooperative governance model for a market infrastructure institution with market power over the alternatives. Three are noted here. The first is if a market infrastructure institution has different groups of users, but is controlled by only one group of users. The controlling group may then seek to exploit the dominant position of the market infrastructure institution to its advantage. It may, for example, seek to reduce the fees that it pays at the expense of other users. If the market infrastructure institution offers a range of services, only some of which are provided monopolistically, the controlling group of users may seek to use profits obtained from the services provided monopolistically to subsidize the other services that the market infrastructure institution offers.

The second set of circumstances in which adoption of the cooperative governance model by a market infrastructure institution may not be efficient is if market developments mean that new users could access the institution with overall beneficial economic implications, but to the detriment of the incumbent members of the institution. The incumbent user group may then seek to exploit its monopoly position to restrict the access of new users. This has occurred both when national users of a stock exchange, CCP, or CSD have sought to restrict remote membership by foreign institutions, and when financial intermediaries have sought to restrict direct access by investors to an exchange which the intermediaries owned.

The relative advantage of the cooperative governance model for a market infrastructure institution with market power will also be diminished if there is a regulatory framework that can constrain the institution from acting anticompetitively. Typically this would require a national competition authority that is both legally competent and has the resources and expertise necessary to monitor the institution's behavior, and if necessary impose behavioral or structural remedies to ensure that it does not act anticompetitively.[24] In such circumstances, there would be no need for the internal governance of a market infrastructure to stop it behaving anticompetitively—external regulation would achieve the same effect.

There has been particular controversy about whether exchange ownership of clearing and settlement institutions is optimal. Several key benefits have been identified in separating ownership of the trading, clearing, and settlement functions.[25] A central argument is that such separation may stop an exchange foreclosing competition from other trading systems if it owns a clearing or settlement institution with market power. Trading systems will be able to compete with each other, without such competition being distorted either by inappropriate cross-subsidies coming from the provision of clearing or settlement services, or by any restrictions on access to a CCP or CSD that an exchange owning it may impose. Lee (2002c, xxxix–xl) argues that

> in order for netting to be viable it is necessary that positions can be off-set against each other in a clearing-house, or be fungible with each other. Without such fungibility, no netting is possible. The extent to which market participants will be able to net any positions they take on different trading systems is therefore dependent on whether these trading systems have access to the relevant CCP. If, for example, one exchange owns the CCP on which most clearing is done, and restricts access to this CCP by another competing exchange, market participants will not be able to net any trades they execute on the second exchange through the first exchange's CCP. The ability of the second exchange to compete with the first exchange will therefore be reduced.

Separation of trading, clearing, and settlement services may also allow for different horizontal models at different levels of the industry. For example, while it may be most efficient to centralize clearing services across markets in a single CCP, it may in contrast be more efficient to have competition between multiple trading systems. In addition, integration of ownership may lead to opaque pricing for clearing and settlement services, if the costs of trading, clearing, and settlement are not clearly distinguished.

The central justification for integrated ownership of trading, clearing, and settlement is that it can yield significant efficiencies. Pirrong (2007a, 38) argues that trading, clearing, and settlement each exhibit strong natural monopoly tendencies, and accordingly that "supply of these functions by separate firms can give rise to multi-marginalization problems and opportunistic holdups. Integration of these functions into a single firm—an exchange—can economize on these costs."[26] There may also be economies of scope if the different activities are undertaken by a single institution. Integrated ownership of an exchange and a CCP may, for example, facilitate a trading system to be directly linked with a CCP, with trades being electronically matched and passed through to the CCPs' clearing systems. STP in a single institution may also minimize operational risks. Seifert argues (2001, 18–19):[27]

> The entire value-added chain of securities processing from the initial matching of trades and the determination of prices to the final steps in clearing and settlement has to work with extremely high reliability.

Where new systems are very frequently introduced, and improvement is continuous, only vertically integrated organisations can combine innovation with the level of reliability that customers require.

It has, however, been claimed that such STP between an exchange and a CCP is practical without the need for combined ownership of both institutions.[28]

Integrated ownership of exchanges and CCPs has also been argued as promoting competition, rather than obstructing it, in that it allows exchanges to compete by offering different full-service options. Market participants can thereby compare the full-service offerings of integrated exchanges, namely in trading, clearing, and settlement.[29]

Various additional arguments have been put forward as to why even if exchange ownership of the clearing function is not appropriate for the equities markets, it is optimal for the derivatives markets. Freedberg (2008), for example, comments:

> Although a horizontal clearing model may be suitable for equities, the situation in derivatives is very different. Ordinary shares are standardised instruments issued by the listed company, and clearing and settlement is straightforward and prompt. Exchange traded derivative futures products are different. They are proprietary instruments in the development of which the exchanges make substantial investment. The clearing process is inherently more complex, extends over a far longer period, and is more reliant on proprietary know-how bound up in the product, than is the case for ordinary shares.

The U.S. Department of Justice (DOJ) (2008, 20) identified three principal arguments typically put forward in favor of such control:

> (1) ... sufficient reward to promote innovation can only be assured if replica contracts are kept off the market and ... exchange controlled clearing helps achieve that objective; (2) trading of futures on multiple exchanges could adversely affect traders by fracturing liquidity and diminishing market depth; and (3) the current system minimizes the risk of default.

The DOJ maintained, however, that all three arguments were open to criticism in light of the experience of competition in the equities and options markets. In particular, the DOJ noted that competition between exchanges can spur them to innovate; that the likely effect of competition between futures exchanges would be significantly lower exchange fees, narrower spreads, and greater trading volume, as occurred in the options markets; and that both the options and equities markets, where exchanges do not control the clearing process, have successfully protected investors from default.

There have been few theoretical or empirical analyses that focus specifically on the merits of integrated ownership of the trading, clearing, and settlement functions. On the theoretical side Köppl and Monnet (2003) explore the relative merits of horizontal consolidation for each of the functions of trading, clearing, and settlement, versus "vertical" integration when these functions are provided by a single "vertical silo" firm. They conclude that vertical silos can prevent efficiency gains that are attainable from the horizontal consolidation of trading, clearing, and settlement platforms, if the costs of clearing and settlement are private information. Breaking up such vertical silos, and inducing competition in the areas of clearing and settlement, can realize all the efficiency gains available from consolidation. Tapking and Yang (2004) examine whether integration between trading and settlement is beneficial in a two-country model. They conclude that "complete horizontal integration of CSDs leads to a higher welfare than vertical integration of exchanges and CSDs and vertical integration leads to a higher welfare than complete separation."

On the empirical side, Schmiedel (2001) finds that European exchanges that integrated derivative and settlement activities over the period 1985–99 seemed to manage their overall costs better than those that did not. Serifsoy (2007) examines the effects of vertical integration for 28 stock exchanges for the period 1999–2003. His findings are inconclusive: while technical efficiency seems to be lower for exchanges with a vertical business model, there is some evidence that integrated exchanges had stronger factor productivity growth than exchanges focused solely on the provision of trading services.

Multiple Objectives, Ambiguity, and Decision-Making

Adoption of the for-profit governance model by a market infrastructure institution normally has three critically important implications for the objectives followed by the institution: (1) it pursues one *single* goal above all others, namely maximizing its rate of return; (2) this goal is relatively *clear*, in that it is easily identified and measured; and (3) the goal is widely, if not universally, *accepted* by all the institution's owners—if any do not accept it, they can simply sell their shares. In contrast, adoption of any of the other governance models often leads a market infrastructure institution to have multiple goals, some of which conflict with each other, and some of which are unclear and ambiguous. Such multiplicity, conflict, and ambiguity can lead to difficulties in the decision-making process at an institution and also to inefficient outcomes.

Nonprofit, cooperative, public-controlled, and hybrid firms are all often mandated to pursue many goals, and market infrastructure institutions with such governance models are no exception. The existence of multiple performance benchmarks may lead to conflict between them, especially if different metrics are valued by different constituencies, and there is uncertainty about which are the most important. The objectives mandated for market infrastructure institutions are also frequently ambiguous in nature and difficult to measure.[30] Many exchanges, for example, identify the "integrity" of their markets, "benefits" to members, and "benefits" to the capital markets as a whole, as being key objectives—all quite nebulous concepts.

The lack of a single clear measure of performance at a market infrastructure institution may have several adverse consequences. It may be difficult for the institution to take major business decisions and prioritize initiatives. The decision-making process at nonprofits and cooperatives where voting control is widely dispersed among a large number of members and where different members have different goals may exacerbate this problem. As Holmström (1999, 407) notes,

> Collective decision making is always difficult. But it is more difficult the more the interests of the parties diverge. A group with common interests will have a much easier time to reach a good decision than a group with highly divergent interests. The latter may not reach any decision at all, or reach poor compromises that waste a lot of social surplus.

A range of factors have led to great diversity among market participants over recent years. These include the expansion of securities products and services, the fragmentation of the industry, and the globalization of markets. The situation at the NYSE when it was still a mutual organization provides a telling example of the effects of such diversity, as described by a previous CEO of the exchange:

> Diversity of interest among NYSE members is a continual source of tension and conflict. At times it leads to careful deliberations and consensus judgment. All too often it can lead to cumbersome decision-making and strategic gridlock.[31]

Innovation can also be problematic for the members of a cooperative in this context. As Holmström (1999, 414) argues,

> The biggest dilemma for a cooperative … is that change itself is bound to increase tensions among its members. There are two reasons for this. One is that change upsets established mechanisms for decision making and cooperation. The other is that change tends to cause preferences to diverge … [which] is problematic for ownership.

Conflict and ambiguity between objectives can mean there is no disciplined framework for assessing capital investments. As a result, poor investment decisions may be made, with attendant higher costs for users. It may also lead to goal displacement and a decoupling between the organization's stated mission and the goals it actually follows. Management may thus obtain leeway to pursue its own objectives at the expense of those required of the institution.

The consequences of conflict between the objectives a market infrastructure institution is mandated to follow can be particularly acute at institutions with a hybrid model of governance. One model that has been adopted in various contexts is an ownership structure composed of both users and investors. The hope in adopting this model is that it will lead to an infrastructure that both serves the interests of users and at the same time gains the efficiencies consequent from maximizing profits for investors. Frequently, however, the adoption of such a model simply internalizes the conflict between users who want low fees and any surplus distributed to them, and investors who want high fees and dividends distributed to them. The presence of such a direct conflict between different ownership constituencies means that performance assessment is impossible, because management can justify any outcome that is achieved as satisfying a particular balance of the competing interests.

The decision-making process at a nonprofit or cooperative can be expensive, with multiple competing interests to reconcile. If the members of a cooperative are heterogeneous, one group of them may seek to use the collective choice mechanism operating at the institution to maximize its own welfare by exploiting other groups or customers, to the extent permitted by competition.[32] In such circumstances, there is a strong incentive to form coalitions to capture the available benefits, and many resources may be wasted on internal politics and the creation of coalitions large enough to determine voting outcomes.

The costs associated with collective decision-making need not necessarily be large, however, as Hansmann (1988, 279) notes, even where patrons' interests diverge considerably. If it is easy to account separately for the net benefits bestowed on an organization by each individual patron, and especially if there is a simple and pertinent criterion for balancing their interests, such a procedure may be uncontroversial.

Two theoretical models have been developed to analyze the effects of decision-making at an exchange. Hart and Moore (1996) compare the merits of a cooperative exchange whose members make decisions democratically on a one-member, one-vote basis, with an exchange owned by "outsiders" who maximize profits and do not consume the services offered by the exchange. Collective decision-making in the cooperative structure may be inefficient because the views of the decisive, or median, voter in the exchange, do not represent those of the membership at large, its average voter. When the distribution of traders becomes more skewed, namely when the "distance" between the preferences of the median voter and the average voter increases, the cooperative solution becomes more inefficient.

Outside owners are interested in maximizing exchange profits, and hence decision-making is focused on the marginal user. In the absence of competition, outside owners will act monopolistically, raising prices and restricting supply, and thus excluding too many traders from the exchange compared to the most efficient competitive outcome. An increase in the skewness of the distribution across membership does not affect the incentives facing outside ownership. The introduction of a competing exchange disciplines the pricing policy of the for-profit exchange, increasing its relative efficiency, while having no effect on the pricing policy of the members' cooperative. The model thus predicts that interexchange competition should increase the prevalence of for-profit exchanges. Even if outside ownership is more efficient than the cooperative model, a members' cooperative may not vote in favor of demutualization, however, because the gainers may be unable to compensate the losers.

Pirrong (2000) examines the impact of member heterogeneity on governance structure, with members having varying costs of providing brokerage services, and shows that it has the opposite effect of that in the Hart and Moore model. In particular, greater member heterogeneity allows low-cost members to enforce a nonprofit mutual structure. The reason for this is that low-cost members can credibly threaten to collude and leave the exchange if the high-cost members demand a for-profit structure that would lead to a redistribution of profits away from the low-cost providers. When members are homogeneous, the for-profit model dominates the nonprofit model because a for-profit exchange can exercise market power more effectively than a cartel of members.

As Steil (2002a, 68–71) explains, there are several reasons for the different predictions of the two models. First, Hart and Moore's and Pirrong's governance models are different. Hart and Moore's version of the members' cooperative is one in which all profits are distributed equally among members, whereas Pirrong's version allows no distribution. Hart and Moore's version of the for-profit exchange separates ownership from membership entirely, whereas Pirrong's version does not separate them at all: it merely allows distribution of profits to members. Pirrong's version of a for-profit exchange is thus consistent with Hart and Moore's version of a members' cooperative. A second distinction between the two models is that the source of member heterogeneity in each model differs. Hart and Moore assume that members differ in the quantity of exchange services they demand, whereas Pirrong assumes that they differ in their costs of providing brokerage services. A third difference is that Pirrong's model, unlike Hart and Moore's, allows exchange members to collude and defect from the exchange.

Both models also have fairly restrictive assumptions. Hart and Moore's analysis is dependent on the median-voter theorem. However, if traders have objectives that are not easily collapsible into a single-dimensional measure, the median-voter theorem either breaks down, or only holds under very unintuitive circumstances. Hart and Moore also assume that decision-making at an exchange is based on majority voting by members, with each member having a single vote. As Steil (2002a) notes, however, in an environment with competing trading venues, larger members are likely to have more influence because of their greater ability to migrate their trading activity. Pirrong's model excludes the possibility of exchanges that are not wholly owned by members, and therefore does not capture a central element of demutualization, namely the separation of ownership of an exchange from access to its trading system.

Management Incentives

The for-profit model may offer stronger incentives for enhanced management performance than any of the other models for several reasons. First, in a for-profit firm with the goal of profit maximization, management can be given a compensation package directly linked to the firm's primary objective, namely a share-price-related incentive scheme. This is difficult for market infrastructure institutions following other governance models, and management may thus adopt a bureaucratic mentality in the absence of a profit incentive. Even if a cooperative or nonprofit market infrastructure institution has profit maximization as its primary objective, it will not be able to issue a share-price-based compensation package to its management, given that it has no publicly traded shares. Such firms may, however, be able to create a synthetic compensation package that mirrors what the price of its shares might have been, had they been issued. Typically cooperative, nonprofit, and public-controlled infrastructure institutions have objectives other than profit maximization as their primary goal, such as the promotion of their members' interests, market integrity, market development, or other political goals. It is normally very difficult to obtain performance measures for management that reflect the successful delivery of such goals.

Two other factors may allow a for-profit firm to offer stronger incentives for enhanced management performance than alternative governance models. The objective of a for-profit market infrastructure institution, namely profit maximization, is likely to be more clearly defined than the goals followed by firms with other governance models. This will be to the advantage of for-profit firms, as the more difficult it is to measure an organization's objectives, the more difficult it is likely to be to monitor its management's performance. In addition, if a for-profit firm underperforms, it may be subject to a hostile takeover, with the likely implication that management will be fired. Cooperatives, nonprofits, and public-controlled institutions are generally not subject to such discipline.

Illiquidity

A central attribute of listed for-profit firms, unlike cooperatives, nonprofits, and most closely held and nonpublic for-profit firms, is that their shares can be traded relatively easily and cheaply. In nonprofits, claims to incremental net earnings cannot be bought and sold. In cooperatives, the capitalization and transfer of future net earnings is likely to be only partially effective at best: even though outside equity may be issued, members' equity can normally only be transferred by relinquishing membership rights. It is thus difficult for financially successful cooperatives to recognize appreciation of patrons' equity. A lack of liquidity in the shares of a market infrastructure institution may give rise to different types of costs for its owners.

A horizon problem may arise when an owner's claim on the net cash flow generated by an asset is shorter than the productive life of the asset.[33] When this happens, and when the market for the asset is not competitive, the return to the owner will be less than the return generated by the asset, and there will be underinvestment in such assets compared to the situation where such horizon problems are not present. Members reducing their use of a market infrastructure institution's services will undervalue investment assets compared to the actual cash flow the investments will yield. They will not want to pay more fees now for benefits they may not see in the future. In contrast, those members for whom patronage grows over the life of the investment will overvalue the asset. This may create control problems as investment incentives differ between members, and may again reduce innovation.[34] There may be fewer horizon problems if the owners of a market infrastructure institution are corporations rather than individuals, as corporations may have longer time horizons than individuals.

A further cost may arise in nonprofit or cooperative exchanges because their owners' shares cannot be traded and because a separation of voting from access rights may not be allowed. Any single member of such an institution cannot therefore influence the decisions the institution makes by buying up the votes of other members. Even if firms are allowed to do this, it is also normally expensive to buy up a large enough number of memberships to exert control. The only way to exert pressure, therefore, is via the democratic process that suffers from a "free-rider" problem. Any single member only has one vote, and will only be able to obtain a small part of the gains realized by its actions, even though it will have to incur all the costs necessary to undertake such activities.[35] Costly actions designed to increase the value of a market infrastructure institution may therefore be less likely to be undertaken in cooperative or nonprofits than in for-profit firms, where claims can be concentrated.

This is not true, however, for all nonprofit or cooperative market infrastructure institutions. For example, in some exchanges, an owner of a membership is allowed to lease its membership to somebody else. The owner typically retains the voting rights, while the lessee keeps the trading rights. A single member can thus acquire a number of seats for investment purposes and retain the voting rights associated with those memberships. If votes are allocated on the basis of one per membership owned, rather than one per member, concentration of voting claims will then be possible. Demutualization also allows the large member firms of a market infrastructure institution, which typically pay most of the revenues to the organization, to wield greater power than the exercise of their voting rights would grant them in a cooperative, given the relatively small amount of such rights that they typically own.[36]

Another cost that the owners of a market infrastructure institution may incur if their equity in the institution is illiquid may arise because of the difficulties of diversification. If the owners have a significant proportion of their wealth concentrated in the market infrastructure institution, they may be unable to arrange their investment portfolios so as to reflect their risk preferences. This problem may be exacerbated if it is difficult to use a membership at a market infrastructure institution as collateral for a loan.[37] Members in nonprofit or cooperative market institutions may thus demand a greater return on their investments, or make less of an investment, than their counterparts in for-profit market infrastructure institutions.

The costs to the owners of a market infrastructure institution of not being able to diversify their equity are likely to be higher for individuals or small firms. The wealthier the owners are, the less likely it is that the lack of being able to diversify their equity will be problematic, given that the proportion of their wealth tied up will be smaller. This may lead to different preferences among different classes of owners. A common instance of this has occurred at various mutual exchanges, the members of which may typically be divided into a small group of relatively large firms that provide most of the business on the exchange, and a large group of relatively small firms that each provide only a small proportion of the business of the exchange. It is this second group of members whose votes are normally critical in determining whether an exchange chooses to demutualize or not. A central reason for their voting for such an outcome has been to receive, and be able to sell, the shares in the demutualized exchange, the value of which is likely to be relatively large compared to the size of their firms.[38] Put more bluntly, in the language of a past chairman of the CME, members should consider demutualizing to "get rich."[39]

Capital-Raising

The governance structure of a market infrastructure institution may affect its ability to raise capital to fund growth and technology developments. It is frequently suggested that the cooperative and nonprofit models are disadvantaged in this respect, as their access to capital is believed to be confined to that obtainable from their members. In contrast, the for-profit structure is thought to allow an institution easier and cheaper access to capital, particularly if the institution is listed.

Even if raising capital is cheaper via a public listing, the relative cost advantage does not appear to have been determinative in affecting a choice of governance structure at many institutions. Large expenditures on technology have been undertaken by cooperative and nonprofit CCPs and CSDs, as well as by market infrastructure institutions with a for-profit governance model. Furthermore, as Steil (2002a, 65) explains:

> Exchange officials often maintain publicly that they must sell ownership stakes to outsiders as a means of raising capital for expansion and technology investment. Empirically, however, we find that raising capital is generally a secondary aim, or absent as an aim altogether. Most exchanges that have demutualized have had no immediate need for fresh capital. ... Furthermore, if capital is ... necessary, it can normally be raised from the member firms without having to turn to outsiders.

There are also various ways in which nonprofit and cooperative institutions can raise capital, in addition to seeking it from their members.[40]

Strategic Alliances, Joint Ventures, and Partnerships

The ability of a market infrastructure institution to pursue alliances, acquisitions, and joint ventures is likely to be affected by its governance structure. The adoption of the for-profit model, particularly via a listing, will give an institution a currency with which it can effect such corporate transactions, namely its publicly traded equity, in addition to cash. The many mergers that have occurred between exchanges since their demutualizations illustrate how this can occur. Cooperative and nonprofit institutions do not have the possibility of using publicly issued shares to pursue such opportunities. There have, however, been a few instances both of nonprofit institutions merging,[41] and of nonprofit institutions setting up for-profit joint ventures with other corporations.[42]

The issuance of publicly traded shares by a market infrastructure institution also allows it to form a partnership with key customers by rewarding them with equity, thus giving them a financial incentive to bring business to its trading, clearing, or settlement platform. This may in effect bring a partial "remutualization" of the institution, with its customers becoming its owners. The advantages to customers of such a process is that any equity they obtain in the market infrastructure may appreciate and be liquid—benefits that would not be available if the institution were operated on a nonprofit or a cooperative basis.

Market Development and Institutional Weaknesses

The creation of sustainable market infrastructure institutions necessary for the operation of a financial market is very difficult. In addition, as Lee (2002b, 20–21) notes, "The question of sequencing of development of capital markets is … both controversial, and an area where little research has been undertaken." There is debate about whether, and how, the governance of market infrastructure institutions may affect their growth. Steil (2001, 266) argues that "the development of commercial, for-profit trading system operators should be considered a priority. Mutualized exchanges entrench intermediary control of market development and are less able to innovate and react to the demands of investors and issuers." In contrast, Lee (2003b, 300) maintains that

> the creation of any financial institutions in a developing market is extremely hard, and the development of the institutional investors, who would best be able to benefit from direct access to a stock exchange, is frequently much harder than the creation of the brokers. Any cost savings that a demutualized stock exchange with direct investor access might bring need therefore to balanced against the benefits the presence of brokers, with ownership interests in an exchange, may yield in helping bring the market into existence.

In an African context, Yartey and Adjasi (2007, 21) similarly contend that adoption of the for-profit model should not be a first priority:

> The policy of demutualization should not be of immediate concern to most African exchanges. The reason is that most African exchanges have barely existed for three decades, and are grappling with teething

issues of poor infrastructure and illiquidity. Demutualization would, therefore, be more relevant in the medium to long term when the teething issues have been properly managed. Indeed demutualization should be the step after Africans have consolidated gains on improving liquidity problems and strengthening cooperation.

It is in developing markets where support for the public-owned model has historically been, and continues to be, strongest. Even when public ownership has not been adopted, government influence and control over market infrastructure institutions is not uncommon. There are several reasons for this: (1) governments frequently see the development of an exchange or CSD as part of their national economic strategy to develop their domestic capital markets and financial services industry; (2) there is often a need for collaboration between government and the business community to develop markets; (3) the private sector may be insufficiently mature to organize such a project; and (4) the private sector may not see a viable business case to make the necessary investment in the required market infrastructure institutions.

One particular set of circumstances that may enhance the merits of public ownership of a market infrastructure institution is if a jurisdiction's institutional or regulatory framework is not sufficiently credible or powerful to respond appropriately to market failures. An instance of this may arise when a country's antitrust apparatus is too weak to constrain institutions with market power from acting anticompetitively, or when the private sector is itself hindered in some manner from responding appropriately to the relevant monopoly. Weakness at a regulator may arise due to a lack of expertise, experience, or resources, as sometimes occurs in developing markets and even in more developed ones. It may also occur as a result of overlapping jurisdictions of competing regulators, or when the regulatory process is vulnerable to capture by particular interests, including perceived political or national interests.

The decision by the ECB to establish the T2S project in the EU can be interpreted as an instance of public ownership being proposed in response to these types of institutional weaknesses. The ECB implied that it had little faith in the market being able to deliver an efficient and integrated cross-border settlement system in Europe. A senior ECB executive explained that although the Bank had "a clear preference for the market delivering it" when the euro was launched, "more than seven years after the launch of the euro, the market is still very far from providing a coherent settlement platform for euro-denominated securities, despite the demand of the users who want to benefit from economies of scale allowed by the new currency."[43] Several likely reasons for the market's slow pace in integrating cross-border settlement in the EU were identified by the ECB. Competition between European CSDs was very limited.[44] There were a range of barriers stopping integration, including "different market practices, legal structures and tax procedures, in spite of the work undertaken by ECSDA to develop harmonized market practices and by the European Commission to address the 'Giovannini' barriers."[45] There may also have been "difficulties involved in getting independent and competing organisations to agree on common solutions across multiple countries and many different participants."[46]

Senior ECB executives identified five reasons why the Eurosystem was in a unique position to "drive" T2S:[47] (1) its commitment to efficient and integrated financial markets in the EU; (2) its neutrality as a supranational organization; (3) its role as a possible facilitator in balancing different requirements; (4) its lack of economic interest in T2S, and its ability to operate T2S on a cost-recovery basis; and (5) its experience in successfully creating and implementing Europe-wide infrastructures, including TARGET and TARGET2. Although not stated explicitly, the ECB's decision to launch T2S may also have reflected its belief that other public responses to solve the problem at both a national and an EU level were unlikely to prove successful—otherwise ECB intervention would have been unnecessary.

Various possible weaknesses in the EU's institutional structure may have been identified. The EU competition authorities may have appeared to be relatively powerless to ensure competition between CSDs for several reasons—a lack of jurisdiction, a lack of resources, and the perceived ability of national governments to influence the regulatory process. The possibility of establishing a legal framework that could facilitate competition and consolidation in the provision of clearing and settlement across the EU, in the form of a directive, may in addition have appeared unlikely. In addition, the ECB may have believed that even if a directive on clearing and settlement were to be proposed, it might not ensure the delivery of an efficient pan-European settlement structure within a reasonable time frame for various reasons. The directive might take a long time to be passed into law; its creation might be vulnerable to capture by vested market and national interests, potentially undermining the procompetitive goals anticipated of it; and even if passed in a procompetitive form, the directive might not be enforced properly, due to some member states' political interests in promoting their own national CSDs.

At a national level, the argument that public ownership of a market infrastructure institution may be beneficial if a country's institutional or regulatory framework is not sufficiently credible or powerful to respond appropriately to market failures, may itself have a flaw. If a regulatory or institutional regime over which a government has authority is weak, the ability of government itself to exert efficient control over a market institution may be subject to exactly the same weaknesses as exhibited by the regulatory structure.

Any decision to institute public ownership of a market infrastructure institution due to perceived weaknesses in the private sector, and sometimes even merely the consideration of such a decision, may be self-fulfilling. If government indicates that it may establish a market infrastructure institution in order to reduce inefficiencies, the private sector may respond by deciding that it is not even worth considering whether to provide its own solution to reduce the stated inefficiencies. To do so would require that it compete with the proposed government-sponsored institution. The private sector may be unwilling to do this both because it would find it difficult to compete successfully against the government given the available public resources, and also because there may be other adverse consequences to the private sector were it to choose to compete with government.

Technology

Domowitz and Steil (1999) and Steil (2002a; 2003) argue that the prime determinant of the optimal governance choice for an exchange is the state of trading structure technology.[48] Historically, trading was conducted on the floor of exchanges. In such circumstances, Steil maintains, "A member-owned cooperative is the most logical business structure for an exchange in which investor orders must be represented by human intermediaries transacting verbally within a geographically fixed space … , since there is no 'trading system' distinct from these intermediaries themselves."[49] The development of new technology subsequently allowed investors to send their orders to a trading system without the need for physical intermediation by a broker, and with no limits on either the number of traders that could access the trading system or on their location. This fractured the link between the financial intermediary and the exchange. In such circumstances, Steil argues that

> it should not be surprising that demands from investors (particularly institutional) for disintermediation of the trading process are coming increasingly into conflict with the desires of the Exchange's owners to maintain the profitable aspects of intermediating trades on the floor. If the Exchange were to be transformed from a utility supporting its members' brokerage operations to a self-standing commercial enterprise seeking profits from transactions, rather than brokerage, this endemic conflict of interest would be eliminated.

Relationship-Specific Sunk Investments

If the customers of a firm have to make a sunk investment that is specific to that firm, the firm may seek to exploit its customers once they have made their investment.[50] In order to protect themselves against such a possibility, customers may seek to agree an appropriate contract with the firm before making any relationship-specific investment. This may be difficult, however, if the customers cannot agree a complete contract with the firm, as there may be unanticipated circumstances in which the firm is still able to exploit them. All real contracts are necessarily incomplete for two reasons: because it is costly to specify how a contract should operate under all circumstances, and because not all outcomes can be foreseen in advance. In such circumstances, it may be cost efficient for a firm's customers to seek to govern the firm, via a nonprofit or cooperative model, in order to stop the firm from exploiting them once they have made their sunk investment.[51]

Two situations in the context of market infrastructure institutions may give rise to such a phenomenon. First, financial intermediaries have to incur some costs when using a particular market infrastructure institution. They need, for example, to establish a range of links to all exchanges, CCPs, and CSDs with which they deal. It is unclear, however, whether the costs incurred in such links are now both sunk, and large enough, to warrant their control of the relevant market infrastructure institutions. In the past, financial intermediaries needed to establish expensive trading operations on the floors of any exchanges on which they were members. For the most part, this is no longer necessary. Although financial intermediaries now need automated links to any exchanges on which they trade, the costs to a firm of switching its order flow from one exchange to another do not generally appear to be so high that once it has become a member of the first exchange, it is effectively locked into dealing on that exchange. Relatively cheap alternatives are typically available, either by leasing space on the second exchange if it still operates a trading floor, by hiring electronic capacity to deliver orders to the second exchange if it operates an automated trading system, or by routing orders through a member of the second exchange and paying the required brokerage fees. The issue of whether links to CCPs and CSDs are both sunk and relatively large is more opaque.

A second context in which relationship-specific sunk costs have been argued as being historically relevant for market infrastructure institutions is identified by Macey and O'Hara (1999a). They maintain that listing firms and exchanges used to make reciprocal, firm-specific investments in one another. An exchange provided a range of services for their listed firms (such as the provision of liquidity, monitoring for manipulation and fraud, and a signalling function for investors that issuers' stocks were of high quality), while listing firms provided the shares that the exchange traded. As both parties had nondiversifiable investments in the relationship, Macey and O'Hara claim that each party was vulnerable to being exploited by opportunistic behavior by the other. In order to protect their investments, listed firms wanted a share in governing the exchange. The merits of this model diminished, however, as changes in regulation and technology led exchanges to focus primarily on the provision of liquidity, rather than on listing and other traditional functions.[52] The mutual dependency between companies and exchanges thus broke down, and the need for a cooperative model of governance to stop opportunistic behavior disappeared.

Information Revelation

It has been suggested that the governance of an exchange may affect the nature of the information disclosed about the assets traded on the exchange. Kuan and Diamond (2006, 2) argue in particular that the adoption by an exchange of the nonprofit cooperative model may reduce the costs that investors incur in not being able to determine which issuing companies are truthful in their disclosures.[53]

If investors believe that some companies do not publish accurate information, but cannot distinguish between these companies and those that are truthful, they may accordingly reduce their investments in all companies. Kuan and Diamond suggest that if bankers are the owners of an exchange, then they can act "as gatekeepers to the exchange, screening issuing firms through an extensive 'due diligence' process, [and] providing capital via underwriting." This would create a market in which issuing firms' incentives to disclose were aligned with those of investors, and would also benefit bankers in the long run, who would earn higher banking commissions through new issues. In contrast, Kuan and Diamond claim that a for-profit exchange would benefit primarily from the profits it earns from trades, and only indirectly from the enhanced investor confidence that would result from high quality issuers. A for-profit exchange would thus have less interest in ensuring the quality of listed firms and the quality of information they disclose, and would therefore be unlikely to be as selective as bankers in choosing good issuing firms.

The merits of this argument are questionable. Most nonprofit cooperative exchanges have been owned primarily by the broking community in a particular market, rather than by the relevant banking community, although these communities can overlap. The argument also takes no account of the adverse reputational effect that would accrue to an exchange of being seen to list companies that did not disclose accurate information. Finally, disclosure requirements are normally highly regulated, and exchanges are typically required to ensure that corporate disclosures satisfy the relevant regulatory requirements. Exchanges normally thus have little discretion to sanction insufficient disclosures.

THE BOARD: ROLE AND COMPOSITION

It is widely accepted that an institution's board of directors plays a central role in its governance, but what that role should be and how best to structure a board remain highly controversial. The role of boards of market infrastructure institutions is seen as particularly important, as illustrated by the Group of Thirty's (G30) (2003, 119) description:

> Many strategic decisions require evaluation and weighing of difficult trade-offs, such as balancing the desire to achieve short-term cost savings with the need to invest to achieve innovation and greater savings in the long term, or maintaining a proper balance between the pursuit of potential cost savings and acceptable constraints of safety and risk management. For most such decisions, each of the different stakeholder groups will have different preferences, further complicating matters. Moreover, the requirement to oversee the commercial, operational, and risk management practices of the organization demands a thorough understanding of the mechanics of the business. In aggregate, these challenges go beyond those typically faced by the boards of similarly sized commercial organizations and underscore the strategic importance of clearing and settlement infrastructure to the securities industry as a whole.

Two issues of central importance to market infrastructure institutions' boards are examined in this section: the roles such boards should undertake, and the merits and difficulties of having independent directors and user directors on such boards.[54] The following sets of issues and theories relating to how boards operate are analyzed: (1) the fundamental corporate principal-agent problem, managerial hegemony, and monitoring; (2) user representation on nonprofit and cooperative boards; (3) stakeholder representation on boards; (4) resource dependency theory; and (5) stewardship theory.[55] Given the enormity and diversity of the literature on corporate governance, only the most important elements of it are summarized. Key lessons of the discussion are presented in the last section of the chapter.

The Principal-Agent Problem, Managerial Hegemony, and Monitoring

A fundamental principal-agent problem arises in the context of a for-profit corporation because the management of the institution, the *agent*, may advance its own interests at the expense of those of the institution's owners, the *principals*.[56] Two factors may exacerbate the principal-agent problem. The first is if there is asymmetric information between management and owners. In such circumstances owners will be unable to monitor directly the performance of management, and thus cannot evaluate fully whether self-interested actions by their agent are occurring. The second is if management is so strong that it can dominate the board. A range of studies indicate that control of a corporation normally rests with management rather than the board, except during crises.[57] As Cornforth (2004, 18) summaries, this means that "the board ends up as little more than a 'rubber stamp' for management's decisions. Its function is essentially symbolic to give legitimacy to managerial actions."

There are many pivotal ways in which the corporate principal-agent problem may be alleviated. First, an incentive scheme for management may be established in order to align its interests with those of the firm's owners. This typically involves paying the management a salary dependent on the returns earned by the firm. Second, greater disclosure about the company and management's actions may make it easier for owners to assess management's performance. Third, competition for the goods or services that the company provides is likely to reduce the possibility of management acting in its interests at the expense of shareholders. To do so would make the company inefficient, which in turn would make the company less competitive. Fourth, the existence of a market for corporate control of the company may similarly restrict management from sacrificing efficiency to promote its own interests. If it did this, a predator could take over the firm, install new management to maximize value, and thereby realize an arbitrage profit.

Another way of alleviating the principal-agent problem gives a central role to a company's board, and provides the main justification for the appointment of independent directors, sometimes referred to as outsiders. It is to use the board of directors as an internal control mechanism to monitor management so as to ensure that management acts in the best interests of shareholders.[58] The effectiveness of a board as a monitor is often assumed to be a function of the board's independence from management—the less independent it is, the more likely will it acquiesce to, rather than question, management's decisions.[59] The presence of independent directors on a board is also hoped to mitigate the problem of managerial domination of the board over weak and dispersed shareholders.

Notwithstanding the potential importance of independent directors as monitors of management in for profit corporations, there are a range of reasons why they may not be effective in this role. First, it is difficult to create a formal definition of "independence" that ensures that directors satisfying the definition are truly independent of the management they are meant to monitor. True independence requires, as Clarke (2007,

84–85) notes, that a director be "one who has no need or inclination to stay in the good graces of management, and who will be able to speak out, inside and outside the boardroom, in the face of management's misdeeds in order to protect the interests of shareholders." As Gordon (2007, 1499) argues, such "independence is more a disposition, a state of mind, rather than a concrete fact," and is thus normally not directly observable. The notion of an "independent director" has been used to mean many different things for different reasons.[60] Among the key criteria that have been used to assess a director's independence are employment and employment-like relationships with the firm, including different types of advisory positions; other financial relationships with the firm; donor relationships; and family or social relationships with management. Some legal jurisdictions choose explicitly not to provide an *ex ante* definition of independence, but rather seek only to determine *ex post* whether a director is independent if a conflict arises in a particular transaction and if this transaction is challenged.[61] The specifics of the situation are then assessed in order to evaluate the relevant directors' independence. Despite the merits of these approaches, they have all faced difficulties in ensuring that nominally independent directors have been independent from management in reality.

Various other factors may also make directors open to pressure from management.[62] As Bebchuk and Fried (2004) argue, and summarized by DeMott (2005, 3–4):

> Directors depend on the CEO for their initial selection as directors and their continued presence on the board, as well as for their compensation for service as directors. As a consequence, directors do not occupy a stance of arm's-length negotiation with either the corporation's incumbent CEO or with his or her successor, given directors' incentives to establish a collegial relationship with a new CEO.
>
> Reforms that made the nominating committee independent were designed to avoid the old sense of beholdenness to insiders for board seats, and the trend toward granting directors stock options or restricted stock was designed to align outside directors with shareholders. The success of these measures is debatable, at best.

In the context of market infrastructure institutions, the management of a particular institution may in addition be able to exert influence over individual directors as a result of the relationships a director's company has with the infrastructure institution. These may include if the company is a user of the market infrastructure institution's services, a supplier to the institution, a competitor of the institution, or a firm regulated by it. All these relationships may be leveraged by management to ensure a board director's support for management's policies.

A second reason why independent directors may not be effective in monitoring management is that they may not have the time or financial motivation to do so. As Bainbridge (2002) explains,

> most outside directors have full-time employment elsewhere, which commands the bulk of their attention and provides the bulk of their pecuniary and psychic income. Independent directors therefore may prefer leisure or working on their primary vocation to monitoring management.

Hermalin and Weisbach (2003, 10) identify another motivational problem for independent directors. While they accept that independent directors have incentives to build a reputation as an expert monitor,[63] they also note that "a reputation as a director who does not make trouble for CEOs is potentially valuable to the director as well."

A third critical factor that may impede independent directors from monitoring management successfully is that they rely on management for information about the corporation to do so, but management has an incentive to present information that promotes its self-interest.[64] Independent directors may thus simply not have the information necessary to undertake appropriate monitoring. Adams and Ferreira (2005) analyze theoretically the consequences of the board's dual role as an advisor as well as a monitor of management. As a result of this dual role, the CEO faces a trade-off in disclosing information to the board. On the one hand, the more information the manager provides and the better the manager synthesizes the information, the better is the board's advice. On the other hand, a more informed board will monitor the CEO more intensively, potentially to the CEO's disadvantage. Since an independent board is a tougher monitor, the CEO may be reluctant to share information with it. In some contexts, however, management-friendly boards can be optimal.

A fourth reason why independent directors may not be able to undertake a monitoring role concerns their expertise. Reiser (2007, 809) stresses their merits, in the context of nonprofits, arguing that

> independent director requirements arguably can contribute to more efficient direction and management by nonprofit boards. The credentials that mark directors as independent are intended to afford them some greater level of objectivity as to the organization's internal affairs than their non-independent colleagues. They can use this "outsider" perspective to challenge conventional wisdom, ask more probing questions, "think outside the box," and offer the other benefits of objectivity touted by auditors, management consultants, and other professional outsiders.

However, an independent director may not have the relevant expertise or skills to add significantly to a board's work, precisely because of his independence.[65] There are very few experts in the fields of clearing and settlement, for example, who are also independent of the major clearing and settlement institutions, however independence is defined.

A final factor why independent directors' effectiveness in monitoring management may be limited is that even if such directors are not biased in favor of management, they may still defer to management's views and seek to avoid criticizing them.[66] Morck (2004, 21–22) notes, for example, that

> experiments in social psychology show that human nature includes a reflexive subservience to people perceived to be legitimate authorities, like corporate chief executive officers. This reflex disposes directors to fall into line behind their CEO. ... Other behavioral factors, such as cognitive dissonance, reciprocal favor trading, and group conformity, may significantly reinforce this subservience.

It is not just at for-profit market infrastructure institutions that management may promote its own interests at the expense of the interests of its owners, or more generally the primary objectives anticipated of the institution. This may occur at organizations with any of the other main governance models, and for similar reasons.[67] Dispersed ownership at a mutual organization, for example, may give rise to a collective action problem among members, giving management leeway to pursue its own interests. The problem of managerial hegemony is also common in cooperatives, as Itkonen (1996, 20) notes:[68]

> Power and decision-making in co-operatives are all too often concentrated at the top in too few hands. Co-operative performance has for a long time been characterized by a lack of participation and sense of involvement. Statutory governing bodies exist to review past performance and to endorse management decisions rather than to challenge policies and strategies.

At first sight the potential role of independent directors in limiting self-interested rent-seeking behavior by powerful managers at market infrastructure institutions with one of the cooperative, nonprofit, public-controlled, or hybrid governance models, may appear to be even more important than at for-profit market infrastructure institutions.[69] This is because the four other main ways of alleviating the adverse affects of the principal-agent problem used in for-profit firms may be limited or unavailable.

In particular, granting management a compensation package or incentive scheme aligned with the interests of a market infrastructure institution's owners, or more generally the primary objectives anticipated of such an institution, may be neither possible nor appropriate. Management may not be allowed to share in the residual earnings of nonprofit firms by law, for example. More generally, if the anticipated goals of a market infrastructure institution do not readily translate into traditional measures of business performance, it may be hard to construct an appropriate incentive scheme for management.

The other main ways used to reduce the adverse effects of the principal-agent problem in for-profit firms also appear ineffective. If a market infrastructure institution's shares are not readily tradable, as is typically the case with nonprofit or cooperative firms, its owners will have less external information available to them to evaluate the performance of the firm's management than would the owners of a similar but listed for-profit institution. Such firms will thus not be subject to the same external scrutiny. Market infrastructure institutions may face little competition for the services they provide. Finally, the market for control of nonprofit, cooperative, public controlled, and hybrid firms is normally limited, given again that their shares are normally not freely tradable, and that any potential purchasers of such firms may not be able to reap the benefits of any efficiencies achievable as a result of a takeover.

There are, however, two reasons that may mean that the use of independent directors to monitor management performance at a market infrastructure institution with a governance model other than the listed for-profit model is neither as important nor as effective a mechanism as might initially be considered. The first reason is that the other main ways of alleviating the principal-agent problem may actually be viable, despite at first sight being ineffectual. So, even if a nonprofit market infrastructure institution is not allowed by law to distribute its profits to management, a shadow share price of the relevant institution may be calculated, and the compensation package of management may be linked to this. Similarly, even if the shares of a market infrastructure institution are not freely tradable and thus cannot reveal publicly information about the institution, its customers may have better information about management performance than would any outside owners or independent directors, given that they monitor the quality of the services it provides and other aspects of its operations on an ongoing basis. Finally, even if a market infrastructure institution's shares are not freely tradable and if the rewards of improved efficiency at such an organization cannot be reaped via enhanced earnings, as is likely to occur at nonprofit and cooperative firms, this does not necessarily mean that there is no market for control of such a firm. If an institution's customers are able to gain the benefits of any efficiencies that could be effected by a takeover, via lower fees for example, they will have an incentive to encourage such a corporate transaction.

The second factor that may render ineffective the use of independent directors on a market infrastructure institution's board to monitor management performance arises from the fundamental problem of identifying what the goals of such an institution are. The duty of good faith for directors of a cooperative, for example, appears similar to that placed on directors of for-profit institutions. Cooperatives[UK], the Union of Co-Operative Enterprises in the UK, summarizes it as requiring directors

> act[] at all times in the best interests of the society [i.e. cooperative]—this means ensuring that the society's interests always come first, and that a director never uses their position to obtain a benefit or advantage for themselves, for other people or other organisations; [and] avoid[] conflicts of interest—a director should avoid putting themselves in a position where their duties and responsibilities as a director conflicts with other personal interests. Where a conflict arises, they must comply with the society's rules.[70]

However, and as discussed above, the goals of a nonprofit, cooperative, public-controlled or hybrid market infrastructure institution may often be both ambiguous and multifaceted. This may place an impossible legal obligation on independent directors in pursuing their fiduciary responsibilities towards the company, because, as Boozang (2007, 4) notes in the context of nonprofits,

> scholars, attorneys general, and corporate counsel do not even agree on the answer to a most basic corporate law question—to whom is the non-profit board accountable? ... nonprofit boards have multiple constituencies and operate with few guiding principles as to how to prioritize competing claims for their resources.

If the independent directors on the board of a market infrastructure institution cannot identify what are the goals management should follow, then no amount of monitoring will allow them to determine whether the goals are in fact not being followed.

A large body of literature has investigated the impact of board independence, as measured typically by the ratio of insiders to outsiders or independent directors on a board, on for-profit companies' performance. Even given the methodological difficulties complicating such empirical work,[71] the results have been noticeably mixed.[72] A summary of this literature is beyond the scope of this chapter, but two stylized findings are noteworthy. First, as summarized by Duchin, Matsusaka, and Ozbas (2008, 1), "Empirically, it is notoriously difficult to find reliable evidence that outside directors matter at all for performance, with most studies finding small, statistically insignificant correlations."[73] Second, and similarly, while the composition of a board is found to affect how it completes particular tasks, the overall evidence on the benefits of greater board independence is again equivocal at best.[74] Contrary to a central tenet of principal-agency theory, therefore, there is no conclusive evidence that independent directors monitor management to the benefit of shareholders in for-profit firms. There has been little analysis of the effects of independent directors' monitoring of management at firms with other types of governance models.

The importance of independent directors on corporate boards is now widely accepted, both in the many codes for good corporate governance that have been developed at a national and an international level, and indeed more widely.[75] As Beecher-Monas (2007, 375) notes, "Independence as the solution for director dereliction in corporate governance now appears as a mantra in government regulation, stock exchange listing requirements, corporate best-practice standards, and legal commentary." Even ignoring both the lack of evidence to support the appointment of independent directors in for-profit corporations, and the possibility that the widely accepted codes of corporate governance were created primarily to respond to one particular group of capital market participants, namely active institutional investors[76]—and thus not necessarily in the interests of the many other types of participants in the capital markets—the argument that independent directors should be appointed to the boards of cooperatives and nonprofits is questionable. Boozang (2007, 2) concludes that "there is no convincing articulation of *why* nonprofit boards should be independent," arguing that:

> Precisely because the research in the for-profit sector remains inconclusive, and because of the paucity of empirical work in the nonprofit sector, best practices promoters should pause before aggressively pursuing governance reform that rests on an independent board. Nonprofits should experiment with a mix of inside and outside directors, including monitoring directors as well as other directors solicited for their particular expertise and stakeholder status, until it becomes clear what combination works best for each nonprofit.[77]

This conclusion is mirrored in one code of best practices for corporate governance that has been created specifically for the cooperative sector by Cooperatives[UK].[78] The code was initially developed solely for consumer cooperative societies, and subsequently modified for use by other cooperative sectors. Although it is debatable whether market infrastructure institutions would satisfy all the requirements of being a cooperative, as discussed in the code,[79] two of its recommendations are noteworthy in this context. First, contrary to most of the standard codes of corporate governance, this code makes no recommendations for any minimum number of independent directors. Instead it stresses that directors should be elected by, and from, the membership, although it does allow for a board to co-opt "professional external directors," if this is believed beneficial to the cooperative. Second, the code recommends that "in order to safeguard the democratic status of the board a society should ensure that professional external directors are always in the minority."[80]

User Representation on Nonprofit and Cooperative Boards

The role of user directors on the board of a cooperative or nonprofit market infrastructure institution is fundamental. They are appointed in order to ensure that user interests are represented on the board, and thus shape its decisions and policies, which in turn should ensure that the infrastructure institution delivers *its* primary goal, namely serving precisely these user interests. Notwithstanding the apparent simplicity and clarity of this role, however, there are various factors that may complicate both how user-directors behave in practice and the relationship between their interests and those of the institution on whose board they sit. Some of these factors can undermine the ability of a cooperative or nonprofit market infrastructure institution to deliver its primary goal.

A central difficulty arises if there is tension between the fiduciary duty that a user director owes to the institution on whose board the director sits, and the director's role as representative of user interests. At first sight, such a tension should never arise, given that the primary goal of a cooperative or nonprofit market infrastructure institution is precisely to serve its user interests. How could the interests of a user, as represented by a user director, conflict with the goal of the institution, namely serving user interests? This congruency may, however, be broken in several ways.[81]

If the membership of a mutual or nonprofit market infrastructure institution is heterogeneous in some important manner, it may be difficult to represent the full diversity of membership on the institution's board, given that there are always only a limited number of board seats available. More importantly, diversity among users will mean there is no single user viewpoint on key issues. In such circumstances, the interests of some users are bound to conflict with the goals of the institution, however these are chosen. The congruency between user interests and those of the infrastructure institution will thus be broken.

Another factor that may complicate the representation of user interests on a board is if the identity of the users of a market infrastructure institution change. If representation on the board is dependent on shareholding and there is not a one-to-one relationship between shareholders and users, the board may represent shareholders rather than users. In some market infrastructure institutions, for example, shareholding may be based on historical capital contributions to the institution, rather than ongoing usage.[82]

Even if all the users of a market infrastructure institution are homogeneous, its management may pursue goals that conflict with users' interests. This may arise as a result of a regulatory obligation imposed on the institution, such as delivering market efficiency. While the market as a whole may benefit from the introduction of enhanced efficiencies, users may benefit from existing inefficiencies, and may not wish to change their existing business practices. Conflicts of interest between user directors and the market infrastructure institution on whose board they sit may be particularly acute when the institution seeks to compete with its users. Such a conflict may arise at an exchange when board directors come from financial intermediaries that seek either to internalize order flow or to sponsor trading systems that compete with the exchange. Similarly, a conflict may arise at a CSD if board directors come from banks that provide custody services in competition with services provided by the CSD.

If there are differences between competing user viewpoints on the board of a market infrastructure institution, and if its mandated goal is to promote user interests, by construction its mandate will not be clear, and some method for resolving conflicts between its various users' interests will be necessary. This role could be, and indeed often is, undertaken by management. However, this may allow management to pursue its own interests at the expense of those of its users and, as discussed above, exacerbate the corporate principal-agent problem.

The role of resolving competing user viewpoints on a market infrastructure institution's board could also be undertaken by independent directors. Their presence is, however, neither necessary to resolve differences of opinion, nor a guarantee that such differences will be resolved in any particular manner—for example either in minimizing inefficiencies, or more generally in promoting the public good, however this is defined. The nature of the individuals involved may in these circumstances take on extra significance: directors with previous high-level regulatory or public policy experience are sometimes expected to assume such a role.

The very concept of what user representation on a board means is also controversial. It contravenes a key notion put forward by the OECD in its widely accepted principles of corporate governance. In particular, the OECD (2004, 59–60) states:

> In carrying out its duties, the board should not be viewed, or act, as an assembly of individual representatives for various constituencies. While specific board members may indeed be nominated or elected by certain shareholders (and sometimes contested by others) it is an important feature of the board's work that board members when they assume their responsibilities carry out their duties in an even-handed manner with respect to all shareholders.

It is in addition not clear how a particular director is meant to gauge users' views or to represent them on the board. Sometimes, the election of user directors onto the board of a cooperative is viewed as a democratic process, which requires potential directors to seek the votes necessary for election on the basis of a manifesto on key issues affecting the cooperative.[83] In practice, however, user directors are not elected to the boards of market infrastructure institutions on this basis. Rather a nominating committee at such institutions proposes potential directors, who are then elected by the general membership. As in all firms, control of the nominating committee critically affects the nature of the board, and the interests that it follows.

Once on a market infrastructure institution's board, the manner in which directors should represent users is also contentious. A user director may seek to present the viewpoint of all users, of just that user constituency from which the director's firm comes, or of just the director's firm itself. These three viewpoints may differ. The Group of Thirty (G30) (2003, 50) has argued that directors have a duty of care in such circumstances, so that:

> If a director's employer engages in a line of business that profits from processing inefficiencies while other users could benefit from introduction of a more efficient service, the duty of that director is to exercise his or her authority in the interest of the clearing and settlement entity and all of its users and to disclose conflicts of interest before the board acts.

The reality is that user directors may seek to promote their own interests on the board. As Seifert (2001, 19) notes, when discussing the ownership by intermediaries of what he defines as Providers of the Securities Process Chain (PSPCs), in this context exchanges, CCPs, and CSDs:

> A representative of a large bank ... stated in a board meeting that he is not sitting there to safeguard the value of this company, but to make sure that his own back-office can benefit most from the decisions being taken. Most owners of today's PSPCs tolerate inefficient management to keep up their influence over corporate governance.

It may even be difficult for a user director to determine what the view of the director's own firm is regarding particular issues. Most user directors on market infrastructure institutions' boards work in large investment or commercial banks. Such firms are typically composed of many different departments, each of which may have different views about how a particular market infrastructure institution should operate. In addition, even if a user director worked for a firm that had a consistent view about what should be done at a particular infrastructure institution, the director may not be aware of this view, and indeed may legally not be permitted to discover it. Like most firms, market infrastructure institutions require their directors to keep confidential any information that they obtain as a result of being directors. Typically directors are thus not allowed to share relevant board documents or information with colleagues at their firms. Directors may thus be unable to determine what view their firm has on relevant issues.

Limits on directors' ability to consult within their own firm regarding issues concerning the operation of a market infrastructure institution on whose board they sit may also affect the expertise available to the infrastructure institution. This is especially important for clearing and settlement institutions, given that both are complicated activities in which there are few experts, and may give rise to a difficult choice for CCPs and CSDs wishing to have user representation on their boards. As G30 recommends, clearing and settlement institutions may seek to appoint senior managers from their users who have proven managerial experience, wide industry expertise, and an ability to assess complex situations and make key strategic decisions.[84] G30 justifies this recommendation as follows:

> Boards of institutions that form the clearing and settlement infrastructure face complex challenges and demands from many sources: the owners of the institutions, the users of the services the institutions provide, and other important stakeholders, including public authorities. Addressing these challenges and meeting the needs of the varied stakeholders requires board members to have an appropriate level of seniority and a broad range of capabilities to exercise sound judgments over often opaque and occasionally intractable problems.[85]

Senior executives at user firms may not, however, have the technical experience or knowledge to assess the recommendations put to them by a market infrastructure institution's management. If, however, a market infrastructure institution appoints people to its board who do have the direct experience of clearing and settlement functions, they are likely to be operationally focused, to be less senior in their respective firms, and not to have the experience in taking the types of strategic decisions that a board should be taking.

Stakeholder Representation

Market infrastructure institutions are frequently considered to have many types of stakeholders besides their shareholders, and it is often argued that their boards, and particularly those of clearing and settlement organizations, should contain representatives of the different stakeholder groups.

Although the definition of what constitutes a stakeholder in such considerations is not normally examined in depth, if at all, the direct users of such institutions are almost always viewed as an important group of stakeholders, and not just at cooperatives and nonprofits. In the EU, for example, various trade associations of financial intermediaries sought in 2005 to ensure that their members' interests, as users, were given top priority alongside shareholders at for-profit exchanges and clearing and settlement organizations.[86] On the assumption that consolidation would occur to create some pan-European clearing and settlement organizations, these associations also recommended that a majority of user directors be appointed to the boards of such institutions.[87] Other types of institutions and interests sometimes deemed stakeholders include issuers, end-users or investors, and also the public interest. Russo et al. (2004, 4) provide an example of a particularly expansive view of the range of interests that should be considered:

> The governance structure of a clearing and settlement system should address not only the needs and interests of the different stakeholders in the system, but also the national, transnational and Community interests in the operation of the system and the public interest in the minimisation of systemic risk. It should also ensure that the ongoing reorganisation of the financial infrastructure does not increase the overall risk in the financial system as a whole.

The fundamental question of who should be classified as a stakeholder in a market infrastructure institution is both difficult to answer and typically ignored.[88] The notion of what a stakeholder is may be derived from the concept of a firm, itself a very ambiguous notion.[89] Following Jensen and Meckling (1976), a firm can be considered as a "nexus of contracts" between different parties, which are all in some way related to one legal entity called "the firm." Each of the different contracting parties obtains certain benefits from being associated with the firm in some way, and each makes its own specific contributions to the firm. Some provide equity, others credit, others labor of various kinds, still others money that they use to pay for the products or services produced by the firm. All of these contributions are required for the economic survival of a firm. A stakeholder may be defined as a party in the nexus of contracts whose future well-being depends in an important way on how the firm develops over time, and how it performs. Such a party has "something at stake" in the continuing existence of the firm. Classes of contracting parties that are often considered stakeholders include shareholders, employees, creditors, and some types of long-term suppliers. Those who contribute to the firm but can easily and without significant economic losses terminate their cooperation with the firm and walk away are not stakeholders. In many, but not all, circumstances, for example, a firm's clients are not considered stakeholders of the firm.

Using this definition of a stakeholder, the future well-being of many types of both direct and indirect market participants, and indeed many other constituencies in an economy, could all be viewed as depending in an important way on how a market infrastructure institution develops over time, and how it performs. The wider the group of stakeholders, however, the more difficult it is to ensure an appropriate representation of them on the board of a market infrastructure institution.

It is sometimes recognized that the importance and nature of stakeholders at a market infrastructure institution can change, and that this might give rise to a need for changes in their relative representation. The Group of Thirty (2003, 54) argues, for example, that "provision should be made for regular review of, and for changes as necessary in, board composition to ensure continuing balanced representation of varying stakeholder groups, including users."

The importance of representing stakeholder interests in the governance of clearing and settlement institutions has been stressed in various private sector and public sector recommendations on the topic, although the extent to which this should imply board representation has not always been clear. CPSS and IOSCO (2001b, 19) recommend that "governance arrangements for CSDs and CCPs should be designed to fulfil public interest requirements and to promote the objectives of owners and users."[90] While they stress that "no single set of governance arrangements is appropriate for all institutions within the various securities markets and regulatory schemes," they also note that key questions that need to be addressed in assessing the implementation of their recommendation include the following:

> How is the composition of the board determined? What steps are taken to ensure that board members have the necessary skills, and represent or take into account in their deliberations the full range of shareholder and user interests as well as the public interest?

CPSS and IOSCO (2004, 5) make a similar recommendation solely for CCPs:[91]

> The board should contain suitable expertise and take account of all relevant interests. One means for the board to take account of the objectives of participants is through their representation on the board or through participant committees.

The private sector Group of Thirty (2003, 11 and 121) recommends that securities clearing and settlement providers' boards should "ensure equitable and effective attention to stakeholder interests," and then clarifies that this means that "*board participation* should represent different stakeholders' interests fairly and equitably."[92]

Several justifications are typically put forward to support stakeholder representation on the board of a market infrastructure institution.[93] Most importantly it is believed that this may ensure that the interests and needs of different stakeholders are considered and addressed in the institution's internal decision-making processes, particularly regarding its strategy, its allocation of resources, and how it distributes any surplus or profits it earns. Blair (2004, 183–84) explains this rationale in the more general corporate context as follows:

> Corporations are more likely to be managed in ways that maximize social value if those who monitor and control firms receive (at least some of) the residual gain and bear (some of) the residual risk, and, conversely, if those who share in the residual gains and risks are given the access and authority they need to monitor. Put more simply, corporate resources should be used to enhance the goals and serve the purposes of all those who truly have something invested and at risk in the enterprise. Those parties, in turn, should be given enough of the control rights to ensure that corporate resources are used to those ends. If control rights could be allocated in this way, all of the participants would have an incentive to see that the total size of the pie is maximized, and any one stakeholder group would have trouble increasing the value of its stake simply by pushing costs and risks onto other stakeholders.

Stakeholder representation has also been thought important in limiting the possibility that a clearing and settlement organization might abuse a dominant position, in delivering appropriate risk management and fair treatment of users at the organization, and in allowing the institution's performance to be properly monitored.

It is self-evident that the placement of multiple stakeholder interests on a board creates the possibility of conflict between them. A key goal of good governance in a stakeholder model is thus taken to be the minimization and resolution of conflicts of interest between different stakeholders.[94] While the outcome of this political function may lead to the minimization of costs at the institution, there are many factors that may mean that it does not lead to the most efficient outcomes. Most importantly, the management of an infrastructure institution with a board composed of competing stakeholder interests may be able to gain power at the expense of its board, by dividing and ruling among the various constituencies. The typical principal-agent problem may thus arise.

Independent directors are sometimes seen as a mechanism to minimize conflicts of interest on board. The role of the independent director as a mediator between potentially conflicting stakeholder interests, particularly in for-profit corporations, has not been universally accepted, however. Clarke (2007, 85) notes in the United States, for example, that this

> view of the role of the independent director—one who is independent of profit-seeking shareholders as well as independent of management—has not . . . found fertile soil in American corporate law scholarship or practice. The dominant view has been that directors who are responsible to many constituencies are in effect responsible to none, and that while many of those who deal with the firm, such as customers, workers, and suppliers, can protect themselves through contract and the threat of terminating their association with the firm, the shareholders are uniquely unable to do so because their investment is sunk and cannot be withdrawn.

The difficulties with the notion of representation, as discussed above in the context of user representation on the board of nonprofits and cooperatives, are also relevant in the context of broader stakeholder representation. In particular, it is unclear how a director could represent a particular stakeholder group on a board when he or she also has a fiduciary duty to the organization on whose board he or she sits. Stakeholder representation could reasonably be expected to ensure that the viewpoints of different stakeholders are represented on a board. If ever there were a conflict between a stakeholder's viewpoint and the organization's interest, however, the stakeholder director would be obliged to fulfill his or her fiduciary duty towards the organization rather than that of his or her constituency.

A key criticism of requiring different constituencies to be represented on the board of an institution is that it may give rise to multiple performance measures, rather than simply having profit as the sole criterion of success. As Blair (2004, 180) summarizes, this may in turn allow "corporate executives and directors carte blanche to do whatever they want . . . because almost any decision can be justified on the grounds that it benefits or protects some constituency."[95] The establishment of a stakeholder board may, in principle, be allied with any ownership structure or governance mandate. If, however, the interests represented on the board of a market infrastructure institution are not consistent with those of the institution's ownership structure or mandate, the likelihood of conflict may be exacerbated. The most common instance where this may arise is at a for-profit firm, where the shareholders wish the firm to maximize and distribute profits, but where various stakeholder-appointed directors may either seek to restrain the institution from maximizing profits, or on the contrary seek just that, but try to ensure that any profits obtained are handed back to stakeholder constituencies other than shareholders, such as users.

Resource Dependency

According to resource dependency theory, developed by Pfeffer and Salancik (1978), organizations are interdependent with their environment, and boards are a key mechanism they can use to manage their relationship with this environment.[96] Cornforth (2004, 16) summarizes the theory as follows:

> Organisations depend crucially for their survival on other organisations and actors for resources. As a result they need to find ways of managing this dependence and ensuring they get the resources and information they need ... the board is seen as one means of ... creating influential links between organisations through for example interlocking directorates. The main functions of the board are to maintain good relations with key external stakeholders in order to ensure the flow of resources into and from the organisation, and to help the organisation respond to external change.

In order to deliver such functions, the key criteria for selecting board members are the relevant influence they can wield outside a firm and knowledge they can bring to the institution. The independence of a director is of no relevance in this context.

The issue of whether it is in the interest of market infrastructure institutions to appoint board directors to cultivate particular resources outside their organizations is an empirical question. It may be more efficient to hire targeted contacts or external expertise whenever it is needed, rather than place a director on the board with specific characteristics that may only be needed in rare circumstances.[97] For the most part, market infrastructure institutions do not appear to have appointed board directors with the aim of managing their external relationships, except for one notable type of exception. In particular, all market infrastructure institutions recognize that the relationships they have with their regulators are critical to their ongoing existence, and as a result many have appointed board directors who previously had senior positions at these regulators. Such directors are typically appointed to exploit their specific knowledge about how the relevant regulators work, and more generally to maintain credibility, a high reputation, and good contacts with the regulators, which can be useful, particularly in times of crisis.

Stewardship

Not all theories of how boards operate assume that management is self-interested and seeks solely to enhance its own rewards. Stewardship theory acknowledges "a larger range of human motives including orientations towards achievement, altruism, ... the commitment to meaningful work,"[98] and the intrinsic satisfaction of successful performance and recognition. Accordingly the theory posits that management will act as an effective steward of an organization's resources, and not seek to misappropriate corporate resources for its own benefit.[99]

In such circumstances, there is no need for the board to act as a monitor of management. Instead, its role is to act as a partner to management in order to improve strategy and organizational performance, and to add value to key decisions. The board is best composed of management insiders, given that they have the best interests of the company at heart, and other participants who can complement the work of management. Independence from management is not only of no value, it may even be harmful in such circumstances. As Langevoort (2000) argues,

> Too much true independence in the boardroom has unintended consequences: by reducing the level of trust that comes from closer or less adversarial relationships, it chills communication, leads to a variety of influence activities by insiders, and produces more complicated (and less useful) agendas and debates. It interferes with the board as a productive team in all its capacities, including monitoring.

CONCLUDING DISCUSSION AND GENERAL PROPOSITIONS

The question of what is the most efficient governance model for a market infrastructure institution to adopt is explored in this chapter. In order to encapsulate the discussions presented here and to summarize key lessons in a simple and accessible manner, twenty general propositions are articulated. They address how to choose the optimal ownership structure and mandate for a market infrastructure institution, the roles that market infrastructure institutions' boards should undertake, and the merits and difficulties in appointing independent directors and user directors to such boards. Most of the propositions summarize the analysis presented in the first three sections of the chapter; for the few that incorporate new ideas, a justification for their inclusion is presented.

Several implications and aspects of the approach of using a series of simple and accessible propositions to summarize the analysis and present key lessons are important to note. First, there is a risk in doing so of oversimplifying a complex reality. Second, the propositions are not intended to address how any particular market infrastructure institution should be governed. Third, no single proposition is intended to be definitive. Notwithstanding these comments and concerns, taken together the propositions provide a useful and compact aid in choosing the most efficient governance model for any market infrastructure institution.

> **Proposition 1:** To evaluate the relative efficiency of a governance model for an institution, all the costs and benefits arising from adopting the model in the relevant context must be assessed.

Five key types of governance models may be adopted by a market infrastructure institution: the nonprofit, cooperative, for-profit, public, and hybrid models. Each model is characterized by the ownership structure and mandate it prescribes for an organization. In many contexts, the cooperative and nonprofit models are very similar.

> **Proposition 2:** The for-profit governance model has a range of potential benefits for a market infrastructure institution:
>
> 1. Profit maximization yields a strong incentive to provide efficient services by ensuring resources are allocated to initiatives that enhance shareholder value.
> 2. Decision-making is relatively agile, flexible, streamlined, and swift.
> 3. The model delivers a single primary goal for an institution, namely profit maximization, that is both easily measured and widely accepted by its owners.
> 4. The financial potential of investments can be appropriately evaluated and obtained by an institution's owners, as claims to future net earnings can be capitalized and transferred.
> 5. The model may provide a good incentive for management to perform well, and may also impose market discipline on poorly performing management.
> 6. The model facilitates relatively cheap and easy access to capital.
> 7. Separation of ownership and membership is possible, allowing optimal diversification of ownership risk.
> 8. A for-profit market infrastructure institution will respond to the demands of all market participants, independent of whether they are members of the institution or not.
> 9. Shares in a market infrastructure institution can be used to effect alliances, acquisitions, and joint ventures, and reward market participants for bringing business to the institution.

There is now a widespread presumption that the for-profit listed model is the best governance structure for an exchange, as evidenced both by the global trend to adopt such a governance model and by empirical and theoretical analyses.[100] Many factors have contributed to this view: the need for exchanges to adopt new technology; the transition from a predominantly individual-based membership at most exchanges to one dominated by corporations; globalization in its many forms, including greater cross-border investment and greater direct involvement by the global financial intermediaries in most markets; perceived or actual competition between trading systems; the growing divergence of members' interests; reductions in the cost of switching between trading systems; and in some contexts, the exceptional share price performance of many exchanges that have demutualized.[101]

Although excellent share price performance of demutualized exchanges has self-evidently been value-enhancing for the exchanges, it is not necessarily evidence that the adoption of the for-profit governance model has delivered more efficiencies than the previous nonprofit or cooperative models would have effected. Many factors may have contributed to demutualized exchanges' good financial performance that are independent of any efficiencies obtained. These include the exploitation of a dominant position by an exchange; robust growth in transaction activity and revenues, associated with relatively high fixed costs; the removal of regulatory restrictions on trading, such as transaction taxes, restrictions on access, restrictions on remote membership; and major privatizations.[102] While prices for trading services at demutualized exchanges have been reduced in many instances, it is unclear whether such reductions have matched declines in the average cost per-trade.

Notwithstanding the potential benefits of the for-profit model for a market infrastructure institution, several factors may reduce its ability to deliver an efficient outcome. In particular, the anticipated benefits of the for-profit model may not materialize, they may not be relevant, and there may be costs associated with the model that other models can mitigate. The most important such cost can arise when a market infrastructure institution has a dominant position in the provision of one or more of its services, and exploits this market power to act anticompetitively.

> **Proposition 3:** A for-profit market infrastructure institution with a dominant position may exploit its market power to benefit its shareholders at the expense of its users.

In fact, any institution or group of agents that has control over a market infrastructure institution with a dominant position may seek to exploit such control to its advantage. The cooperative and nonprofit models may, however, have an important advantage over the other governance models in this context.

> **Proposition 4:** The cooperative and nonprofit models can allow users to stop themselves from being exploited by a market infrastructure institution with market power.

User control of a market infrastructure institution via the cooperative or nonprofit models may let them determine the fees the institution charges, and also restrain the institution from being inefficient at their expense.

There are four particularly important conditions regarding a market infrastructure institution, that if satisfied, will significantly enhance the relative merits of the institution adopting the cooperative or nonprofit governance models: (1) the institution has market power; (2) all its users are its owners; (3) its user base is homogeneous; and (4) its user base is stable in response to market developments, such as changes in products, services, clients, technology, and regulation. Given that clearing and settlement infrastructure institutions may well have market power, and that the costs of a market infrastructure exploiting a dominant position are potentially high, the cooperative/nonprofit governance models may be optimal for such institutions—assuming that other costs arising from these forms of governance structures are not too high. If an exchange has market power, the for-profit model may also not be the most efficient governance model for it either.

> Proposition 5: The cooperative and nonprofit governance models may, however, give rise to various costs when adopted by a market infrastructure institution:
>
> 1. The institution is likely to promote the interests of its member-users at the expense of other interests, including other groups of actual or potential users.
> 2. It may be difficult for users to evaluate the financial potential of investments, or to obtain their benefits, as claims to future net earnings cannot easily be capitalized and transferred.
> 3. Nonprofits and cooperatives may not manage their costs efficiently, given that any cost increases they incur can typically be passed directly onto their members.
> 4. The existence of different types of users may give rise to conflict between them, with a range of adverse consequences:
>
>   • It may be difficult to identify the goals of the infrastructure institution;
>   • decision-making may be cumbersome and expensive;
>   • It may be hard to measure and assess management's performance;
>   • it may be hard to incentivize management to perform well;
>   • Management may be able to pursue its own interests by dividing and ruling among the various user interests.
>
> 5. Access to relatively cheap capital may be restricted.
> 6. Ownership of the institution may not be sufficiently diversified.

Proposition 6: Public-owned firms will likely face the same types of costs faced by cooperatives and nonprofits, as well as costs arising from government intervention and bureaucratic inertia.

Proposition 7: The public-owned model may, however, yield efficient outcomes in certain specific contexts, including:

1. markets where the private sector is insufficiently mature, or does not see a viable business case, to support the required market infrastructure institutions; or,
2. jurisdictions where the institutional/regulatory framework is not sufficiently credible or powerful to respond appropriately to market failures.

Proposition 8: Hybrid institutions will likely face the same types of costs faced by cooperatives and nonprofits, particularly from any conflict between rival objectives they are asked to follow.

Given the range of costs and benefits that affect an evaluation of what is the best governance model to adopt, and the diversity among market infrastructure institutions and the markets and jurisdictions in which they operate, no single governance model is optimal for all types of market infrastructure institutions in all contexts. It is important, however, not to draw from this conclusion the additional false conclusion that the current choice of governance model for each market infrastructure institution is optimal.

Proposition 9: No one governance model is globally optimal for all market infrastructure institutions.

The roles undertaken by, and the composition of, a board of a market infrastructure institution can have a critical effect on its governance.

Proposition 10: Different roles for the board of a market infrastructure institution may be appropriate at different times including:

1. monitoring management;
2. limiting managerial domination of the board;
3. partnering and assisting management; and
4. providing access to external resources for the company.

If a board focuses on just a single role, it is likely to prove too inflexible to respond to varying circumstances. In particular, too confrontational an approach between board and management as a result of the board's need to monitor management may undermine trust between the two, while too close a partnership between board and management may undermine the board's ability to monitor management rigorously.[103]

Proposition 11: Independent directors on for-profit market infrastructure institutions' boards may be able to monitor managerial performance and mitigate managerial domination.

This is indeed the central justification for the widely followed trend to appoint independent directors onto the boards of for-profit companies.

Proposition 12: Independent directors may not be effective in monitoring management in for-profit and other types of market infrastructure institutions for various reasons:

1. It is difficult to define "independence" to ensure that directors satisfying the definition are truly independent of the management they are meant to monitor.
2. Management may be able to exert influence over directors via the nomination process.
3. Management may be able to exert influence over individual directors as a result of the relationships their companies have with the market infrastructure institution.
4. Independent directors may not have the time or financial motivation to monitor management effectively.
5. Independent directors may have an incentive to build a reputation as people who do not make trouble for management.
6. Independent directors rely on management for information to monitor management, but management may present information that promotes its self-interest.
7. Independent directors may lack the expertise necessary to monitor management.
8. All directors, including the independent ones, may defer to management's views and seek to avoid criticizing them.

Notwithstanding the almost universal consensus about the merits of appointing independent directors as monitors of management, however, there is no conclusive evidence that independent directors do in fact monitor management to the benefit of shareholders in for-profit firms.

Proposition 13: Independent directors may have a key role in monitoring managerial performance in cooperatives/nonprofits, given the difficulties with other methods of doing so.

Proposition 14: However, independent directors in a cooperative or nonprofit may face two specific fundamental difficulties that undermine their role as potential monitors of management:

1. Uncertainty about what the institution's goals are.
2. Uncertainty about to whom they owe their directorial fiduciary duty.

Proposition 15: The hope that independent directors may act as mediators between conflicting interests on a market infrastructure institution's board is often problematic for two reasons:

1. The difficulty independent directors face in determining what is in the institution's interest, given precisely that there is conflict between different stakeholders' interests.
2. The fact that their legal position is normally no different from that of other directors, and they thus have no formal mandate to act as a mediator between competing interests.

Proposition 16: The role of user directors on the board of a cooperative or nonprofit market infrastructure institution is fundamental to ensure users' interests are pursued.

Proposition 17: The presence of user directors does not ensure that users' interests are broadly served, or even that they are served at all for various reasons:

1. There may be tension about which interests a user director should represent: those of all users, of just that user constituency from which the director's firm comes, or of just the director's firm itself.
2. There may be conflict between the fiduciary duty that a user director owes to the institution and the director's role as representative of user interests.
3. Diversity among users may lead to conflict between user directors on key issues, with the same adverse effects noted above, namely:

   - it may be difficult to identify the goals of the infrastructure institution;
   - decision-making may be cumbersome and expensive;
   - it may be hard to measure and assess management's performance;
   - it may be hard to incentivize management to perform well; and,
   - management may be able to pursue its own interests by dividing and ruling among the various user directors' interests.

Proposition 18: Stakeholder representation on the board of a market infrastructure institution may bring several benefits, particularly if it has market power:

1. It may ensure that the interests of different stakeholders are considered in the institution's decision-making, so that participants at risk from dealing with the institution help control it.

2. It may stop the organization from abusing a dominant position.
3. It may enhance the monitoring of management performance.

If a market infrastructure institution operates in a competitive environment, there is less need for stakeholders to have representation on the institution's board to ensure that their demands are met. If any one infrastructure institution does not meet the demands of a particular stakeholder group, competition will ensure that another organization does.

> **Proposition 19:** Various related factors may, however, mean that stakeholder representation on the board of a market infrastructure institution does not lead to efficient outcomes:
>
> 1. Board decisions may result from a political bargaining process between stakeholder representatives rather than a search to minimize costs.
> 2. Tension may arise between the fiduciary duty that a stakeholder director owes to the institution and the director's role as representative of a particular stakeholder constituency.
> 3. Conflict between different stakeholder interests may give rise to the same problems noted above, namely:
>
> - it may be difficult to identify the goals of the infrastructure institution;
>   - decision-making may be cumbersome and expensive;
>   - it may be hard to measure and assess management's performance;
>   - it may be hard to incentivize management to perform well; and,
>   - management may be able to pursue its own interests by dividing and ruling among the various stakeholders' interests.

> **Proposition 20:** Conflict between the incentives faced by an institution as a result of its board representation, and as determined by its ownership structure and mandate, can be costly.

CHAPTER NINE

Who Should Regulate What?

THE QUESTION OF what regulatory authority over securities markets, if any, should be assigned to exchanges, CCPs, and CSDs has long been controversial.[1] This issue is explored here in the broader context of examining how regulatory powers should be allocated between government regulators, SROs, and other types of regulatory institutions.

The discussion is limited in several ways. First, a full specification of how regulatory powers should be allocated in any single jurisdiction is not presented. Second, the discussion does not provide a history of regulation, either generally or in any specific jurisdiction.[2] Third, although setting and enforcing regulatory standards in the securities markets may be undertaken by litigation and arbitration, as well as by different forms of private and public regulatory agencies, the relative merits of courts or arbitrators in undertaking such roles are not examined.[3] Finally, although a few comments are made about the role of CCPs and CSDs as potential regulators, most of the analysis of self-regulation focuses on exchanges. It is they that have historically undertaken most self-regulatory activity in the securities markets, and their role that has given rise to most controversy.

The chapter is composed of three sections. In the first, the complexity of the decision as to how to allocate regulatory powers in a jurisdiction is discussed. The second section lists and analyzes crucial factors and constraints that affect the relative merits of allocating regulatory powers to different types of institutions. The last section of the chapter encapsulates these discussions and presents in a simple and accessible manner key lessons about how best to allocate regulatory powers in the securities markets. In order to do so, nine general propositions are articulated. Most of the propositions summarize the analysis presented in the first sections of the chapter; for the few that incorporate new ideas, a justification for their inclusion is presented.

COMPLEXITY

A determination of which institutions in a particular jurisdiction should be granted what regulatory powers over the securities markets is complex for many reasons. There is great debate about the nature of regulation,

with different conceptions having differing implications for how regulatory powers both can, and should be, allocated.[4] A previously widely
held view that regulation was an activity essentially undertaken by the
state and its agencies is progressively being replaced by a wider view
that different types of actors may undertake different types of regulatory roles. The importance of the relationships between all these actors is
also stressed to a greater extent than before.[5] Commenting on the implications of these developments for the financial markets, Black (2003,
3) notes:

> Most commonly, regulatory systems are analysed by the tools that are
> deployed (are they legal, economic, social, etc), and by who is deploy-
> ing them (is it government, the market, the community). It is important
> to stress that any of the regulatory tools may be used by the state, the
> market, the community, association, networks, organisations or indi-
> vidual actors (including firms) (with the obvious exception within ...
> a liberal democracy that the use of force and imprisonment are con-
> fined to the state), and that complex sets of relationships between
> these actors may exist. All too often debates about the appropriate
> structure of regulation, particularly in the financial services context,
> take the black or white, state or self-regulatory form. The reality is
> that these are but two examples of a far wider range of possible con-
> figurations and roles.

There is also great debate about the nature of self-regulation both generally, and specifically in the securities markets.[6] No attempt here is made
to give a precise definition of an SRO. Instead, the term is employed to
refer at the broadest level to an institution that typically has three characteristics: (1) it undertakes some form of regulatory activity; (2) it is a
private or nongovernmental institution; and (3) the market participants
it regulates have some form of influence over its activity. Many categories of self-regulation have been identified. Black (2003, 9), for example,
notes the following types:[7]

> *mandated self-regulation*, in which a collective group is required or
>   designated by the government to formulate and enhance norms
>   within a broad framework set by government (e.g., the old structure
>   of self-regulatory organisations);
> *sanctioned self-regulation* in which the collective group formulates
>   rules which are then approved by government;
> *coerced self-regulation*, in which the industry formulates and imposes
>   regulation but only in response to the threat of statutory regulation;
> *co-regulation* in which government may take backstop statutory pow-
>   ers to impose regulation;

voluntary self-regulation, where there is no government involvement, direct or indirect, in promoting or mandating self-regulation;

"stakeholder" self-regulation, in which there is involvement by consumer or community representatives on rulemaking or disciplinary panels, or agreements with local communities;

"verified" self-regulation, in which third parties are responsible for monitoring compliance (such as auditors and others); and,

"accredited" self-regulation, in which rules and compliance are accredited by another non-government body (e.g. a standards council or technical committee).

Given the diversity of institutional configurations of different types of private bodies undertaking varying regulatory duties in securities markets across the world, it is unsurprising that the term "self-regulation" has been used to mean many different things in the securities markets.[8]

A general theory of regulation is not presented here. Instead, a simple approach for how to determine an optimal allocation of regulatory powers over the securities markets in any jurisdiction is discussed. The approach comprises three core activities: an identification of the regulatory objectives in the securities markets that a jurisdiction seeks to pursue; a determination of the constraints that limit how regulatory authority can be allocated and exercised; and an evaluation of how regulatory powers should be allocated in the jurisdiction in order to best deliver the desired objectives, subject to the relevant constraints. Any such regulatory allocation requires, in turn, addressing a further question composed of three linked elements: *Which* functions in the regulatory process, governing *which* areas of activity and types of participants in the markets, should be allocated to *which* institutions? When seeking to determine an optimal allocation of regulatory powers in any one jurisdiction, the absolute merits of any single allocation are not important; rather, the relative merits of all the available options need to be compared.[9]

In order to illustrate the complexity of making a regulatory allocation decision, brief comments are now provided on the regulatory objectives that jurisdictions adopt, and on the types of regulatory allocations that are possible.

Regulatory Objectives

The choice of regulatory objectives pursued in a jurisdiction can have a significant effect on the optimal allocation of regulatory powers in the jurisdiction. The "public interest," a term used here to refer generically to the aggregate of all the regulatory objectives followed by a particular jurisdiction, typically serves as the justification for government or regulatory intervention. The broader the notion of the public interest, the greater is the scope, often, for government regulatory intervention, and the narrower is the scope for self-regulation.

Three core objectives of securities regulation, as developed by IOSCO, are globally accepted as being important: the protection of investors; ensuring that markets are fair, efficient and transparent; and the reduction of systemic risk.[10] It is, however, not always easy to determine what regulatory objectives are actually pursued in a jurisdiction. Such objectives are only sometimes made explicit in legislation, and even then, the objectives pursued in reality may differ from those specified in legislation.

The unanimity apparent in the global acceptance of the IOSCO objectives masks a wide diversity among jurisdictions over the regulatory objectives they follow in practice. There are several reasons for this. First, regulators and jurisdictions sometimes interpret the three objectives in different ways. For example, in some jurisdictions "the protection of investors" is taken to mean placing the interests of retail investors over those of wholesale market participants in determining appropriate regulation, while greater emphasis on protecting wholesale markets is placed in other jurisdictions. Similarly, some governments have intervened in markets when there has been a price collapse in the belief that this is necessary to reduce systemic risk, while other jurisdictions are resolutely opposed to official intervention to support markets.

Diversity among the regulatory objectives pursued in different jurisdictions may also arise if there are conflicts between the three IOSCO objectives, and different regulators and jurisdictions place varying priorities over which should take precedence. In some emerging markets, for example, priority is placed on market development and on the promotion of investor protection and market efficiency, at the expense of the reduction of systemic risk.

In addition, some regulators may choose not to follow all the core IOSCO objectives. The notion that transparency should be a core objective of securities market regulation, for example, has been particularly controversial. Some regulators believe both that transparency is only a means to deliver the other core regulatory objectives, and that in some contexts greater transparency may actually harm the realization of the other objectives.[11]

Finally, there are a range of objectives, in addition to the three identified by IOSCO, that regulators and jurisdictions follow that differ across jurisdictions. One of the most important is the promotion of the perceived national interest. This objective can clash with the three IOSCO objectives.

Possible Allocation Structures

There are many possible ways of allocating regulatory powers in a jurisdiction. Each of the three key elements of the question that needs to be answered in making such an allocation—namely specifying *which* functions in the regulatory process, should govern *which* areas of activity and types of participants in the markets, and to *which* institutions the regulatory functions should be allocated—themselves can be addressed in many ways. The complexity inherent in all three elements is briefly illustrated here.

At the broadest level, many jurisdictions seek to regulate the following activities and types of participants in the securities markets:

1. Initial listing, prospectus issuance, and ongoing disclosure
2. Securities distribution
3. Corporate governance
4. Secondary markets
5. Fraud and market manipulation
6. Broker-dealers
7. Investment management firms
8. Clearing and settlement

This list is not comprehensive. Furthermore, each of the categories covers a multitude of activities. For example, the regulation of broker-dealers may include supervising their dealings both with each other and with their customers, sales practices, markups, research, financial responsibility, cross-market trading, front running, training, supervision, and recordkeeping.

A fundamental question concerning any regulation is whether it is necessary, or conversely whether market forces can deliver the desired objectives without regulatory intervention. An answer to this question for any particular area of regulation of the securities markets, let alone for all of them, is beyond the scope of the analysis here. Nevertheless, two simple characteristics of the types of responses to the question are important to note in the context of examining how best to allocate regulatory powers. First, there are some areas where it is widely agreed that market forces may reduce the need for regulation, and others where it is widely agreed that some form of regulation is more appropriate. In most contexts, for example, competition is normally accepted as a better mechanism for price-setting than government rate regulation. Second, in many areas of regulation there is great controversy about whether market forces or regulatory intervention can best deliver the desired objectives. This has occurred, for example, regarding access to exchange trading facilities, the sale of stock exchange data by exchanges,[12] the dissemination of price and quote information,[13] and whether issuers and investors should be allowed to contract privately for desired levels of disclosure and fraud protection.[14]

The process of regulation in the securities markets is typically thought of as being composed of five key functions:[15]

1. Standard setting/rulemaking
2. Licensing/authorizing
3. Monitoring compliance with rules
4. Enforcement
5. Prosecution of rule violations

Each of these different functions, for each of the various types of market participants or activities being regulated, may be allocated to different institutions. There is also a wide of range of institutions that could, and indeed do, undertake different regulatory activities. Black (2003, 10–11), for example, identifies the following types of institutions relevant for UK regulatory policy:

> *International financial institutions* (such as the World Bank and IMF);
> *International government standard-setting and policy bodies* (such as the BIS and IOSCO);
> *International nongovernmental issue and standard-setting bodies* (such as ICMA and ISDA);
> *EU institutions* (such as the EU Commission and the Committee of European Securities Regulators);
> *National regulators in other countries* (including central banks, agencies and government departments);
> *UK national-level statutory regulators and departments* (such as FSA and HMT);
> *UK national level organisations* (including recognised exchanges, clearinghouses, professional bodies, trade associations and other action and pressure groups);
> *Market actors* including *Gatekeepers* (such as credit ratings agencies, insurers, and auditors); *Advisors* (such as legal, management consulting and accounting firms); *Competitors and professional counterparties*; *Consumers*; *Regulated Firms*; and *Individuals within firms*;
> *Influential individuals*; and,
> *Courts*.

The discussion in this chapter focuses mainly on four types of organizations that could undertake regulation in the securities markets: (1) an exchange (an "exchange SRO"), (2) an entity owned and controlled by the industry (meaning broker-dealers) that is independent of market infrastructure institutions (an "industry SRO"), (3) a private entity not owned or controlled by the industry (an "independent private regulatory organization"), and (4) a statutory regulator. Even this short list, however, masks several important subcategories and definitional ambiguities in the types of institutions that can undertake regulation. In particular, exchanges may have different governance structures. The provision of regulatory services at an exchange may also be organized in different ways, for example, by being provided by a division that is separate from the commercial divisions of the exchange, or by having a separate holding company dedicated solely to regulation. Finally, advances in technology have meant that the classification of what constitutes an exchange is in many contexts not easy to determine.[16]

The diversity of decision variables for each of the three elements of a regulatory allocation means that there is a very wide spectrum of possible allocations of regulatory powers in the securities markets.[17] At one extreme no regulation is undertaken at all; at the other, a single public regulator undertakes all the regulatory functions, governing all the activities and types of participants in the securities markets. In between there are many possible configurations in which differing combinations of different types of private and public institutions undertake differing regulatory functions supervising different combinations of securities market activities and types of market participants. Even without specifying all aspects of the regulatory allocations, these include having:

- single exchange SRO with minimal government/regulatory oversight;
- single exchange SRO with statutory regulatory oversight of its effectiveness and judicial review;
- single exchange SRO that investigates cases of fraud and manipulation, with a statutory regulator to decide penalties;
- competing exchange SROs that regulate matters solely related to the operation of their individual markets (such as listing and market-specific trading), together with a single industry SRO supervising cross-market issues and broker-dealers; and,
- single nonindustry SRO consolidating all self-regulation regarding market-related and broker-dealer issues.

A full list of all possible regulatory allocations is not presented here.[18]

FACTORS AND CONSTRAINTS AFFECTING RELATIVE MERITS OF DIFFERENT ALLOCATION STRUCTURES

The crucial factors and constraints affecting the relative merits of different allocations of regulatory powers are listed and examined in this section. The most important issue is whether an institution allocated regulatory powers faces a conflict of interest between its private incentives and its public regulatory duties. Some comments on this topic are presented first. Nine other sets of factors affecting the relative merits of different regulatory allocations are also discussed: (2) completeness—which refers here to the extent to which a regulatory institution takes account of *all* the costs and benefits of its actions; (3) competition; (4) fairness; (5) the expertise, knowledge, and experience of a regulatory institution; (6) the flexibility and responsiveness of different types of regulatory institutions; (7) efficiency and funding; (8) compliance and enforcement; (9) a jurisdiction's politics, history, business culture, and legal system; and (10) internationalization. Some of these factors are closely linked with each other and are thus explored in several different contexts. Key lessons of this discussion are summarized in the last section of the chapter.

Conflicts of Interest

The most important factor determining whether an institution allocated regulatory powers will be successful in delivering its public interest mandate is whether the incentives the institution faces support the delivery of such a mandate. If the private interest of an institution granted regulatory powers is congruent with the public interest, the institution will have a direct incentive to deliver the public interest. The presence of a conflict between the private interest of an institution charged with undertaking regulation and the public interest, however, may put into question whether the institution will pursue this public interest at the expense of its private interest. It has long been recognized that such conflicts of interest are inherent in self-regulation.[19] For this reason it is often suggested that regulation should be undertaken by a government agency, or an SRO independent of particular private sector constituencies, both of which it is hoped could shield the regulatory process from undue private sector influence.[20] Conflicts between public and private interests may also arise, however, at such institutions.

It is sometimes difficult to determine whether a conflict between public and private interests does exist at a regulatory institution, and if so, under what circumstances the conflict would stop the institution from delivering the public interest. Such difficulties have led to controversy about the merits of self-regulation. Assessing whether a conflict between public and private interests exists at a regulatory institution depends on many factors including the institution's mandate, the activities and market participants it regulates, the types of regulatory functions it undertakes, the character of the institution itself, the context in which it operates, and a range of factors that may mitigate any conflicts of interest that arise. A single institution can be conflicted in some areas but not in others, and may correspondingly perform some areas of regulation well and others poorly.[21]

Various mechanisms may be used to ensure that SROs deliver their public interest mandates, rather than their private interests, in the presence of conflicts between the two. To the extent that any of these are successful in reducing the adverse effects of such conflicts of interest, they clearly affect the relative merits of different ways of allocating regulatory power. One approach for exchange SROs, commented on below, is to separate their regulatory from their commercial functions. Some other mechanisms used to mitigate the adverse effects of conflicts of interest are discussed in the next chapter in the context of regulatory intervention in exchanges' governance structures.

EXCHANGE SROS

The traditional justification for self-regulation by member-controlled mutual exchanges is that they have a powerful private incentive to pursue the public interest. This arises because an exchange, and the market participants who both trade on the exchange and control it, have an economic interest in maintaining the integrity of the markets on which they trade. The quality of an exchange's regulatory environment is believed likely to contribute to its reputation as both a listing and a trading location. Conversely, as explained by Cameron (2002, 8), "The members of a mutual exchange [also] share the financial and reputational risks of a failure to regulate appropriately."

A similar justification is offered to support self-regulation by demutualized exchanges. As Ketchum (2006), then CEO of NYSE Regulation Inc. (part of the demutualized NYSE group), maintains, self-regulation "provides a great economic incentive to ensure that a market's reputation is enhanced through strong regulation and enforcing the highest standards of ethical conduct."[22] Markman (2002, 192) similarly argues that "demutualized exchanges have a vested interest in preserving their reputations for providing fair and efficient markets. They ultimately bear a heavy price in sacrificing good will and their reputations in the interest of short-term profits." The key difference between the justifications for self-regulation to be undertaken by a mutual versus a demutualized exchange, is that while the former focuses on the incentives faced by both market participants and the exchange, the latter focuses on the incentives faced primarily by the exchange.

The economic self-interest of both types of exchanges can manifest itself in exactly the same way to promote the desired regulatory goals. In particular, all exchanges have a strong incentive to maximize trading on their platforms, whatever their corporate status or governance structure, and this incentive may be taken to be congruent with the public interest. As Mahoney (2003, 2–3) notes:

The traditional nonprofit exchange is owned by its members, who typically are brokers. Higher trading volumes on the exchange generate greater profits for brokers. A for-profit exchange can be owned by dispersed investors, many of whom may not be brokers. Such exchanges earn profits from fees paid by listed companies and brokers and by selling market data. More transactions mean more fees and more data that the exchange can sell. Anything, then, that increases the public's eagerness to trade in listed securities is good for exchanges, whether nonprofit or for-profit, mutual or publicly owned.

Notwithstanding these justifications for self-regulation, there are many ways in which private interests may undermine an exchange SRO from delivering the public interest. There have indeed been many instances when exchange SROs have pursued their private interests at the expense of their public obligations.[23] In examining the US SEC's performance over its first 70 years, Seligman (2004, 2) makes a claim that reflects a common viewpoint held globally over the entire history of self-regulation in the securities markets: "SRO conflicts of interest have been a serious and unrelenting problem for the stock exchanges and NASD. These have all too frequently called into question the ability of the SROs to regulate themselves or the SEC to supervise the SROs." One approach to mitigating the adverse effects of the conflicts of interest inherent in self-regulation by an exchange SRO is to separate the exchange's commercial activities from its regulatory functions, without handing them to another distinct regulator.[24] This may be effected in various ways, for example by a functional separation within a single legal entity, or by establishing a holding company and two subsidiaries, one for running market services and the other dedicated solely to regulation. It is hoped that the existence of separate personnel, cultures, and a clear division of missions between the commercial and the regulatory arms, will reduce the adverse effects of relevant conflicts of interest.

There are, however, several difficulties with this separation approach. First, it is not always easy to distinguish between the commercial and the regulatory functions undertaken by exchanges. Second, as the aim is not to separate completely the commercial activities from the regulatory activities of an exchange, relevant conflicts of interest may still remain, given that both activities will still be under common management. Third, and as NASDAQ (2005, 12) notes, such a separation may "result in an unwieldy and excessively bureaucratic decision-making process that is ill-suited to a public company." Finally, too rigid a separation between the regulatory and commercial functions at an exchange may mean both that the benefits of self-regulation disappear, as the "self" is taken out of regulation, and that the costs associated with having a distinct regulator also rise.

Conflicts between public and private interests at exchange SROs may be categorized in different ways. Following Carson (2003), six broad types of conflicts are identified and briefly discussed here:[25] (1) conflicts between business and regulation mandates; (2) conflicts in specific regulatory functions; (3) conflicts in the administration of rules and programs; (4) conflicts in funding regulation; (5) conflicts in regulating competitors or business partners; and (6) the self-listing conflict. Although Carson identified and discussed these categories of conflicts of interest in the context of demutualized securities exchanges, the first five of them are also relevant for mutual exchanges. The sixth category, the self-listing conflict, is the exception, given that mutual exchanges are not listed. The fourth and fifth categories, regarding funding and competition respectively, are also discussed at greater length in subsequent sections.

1. *Conflicts between Business and Regulation Mandates:* At a demutualized exchange SRO, such a conflict may arise when the exchange acts in its shareholders' interest by maximizing shareholder value at the expense of undertaking its regulatory duties in the public interest.[26] For-profit exchanges place high emphasis on the revenues that customers who are regulated entities bring in the form of listing fees, trading fees, and other charges. A loss of revenue may have more immediate consequences for a profit-maximizing exchange than a threatened diminution of the exchange's reputation, which is harder to quantify, may not materialize, and may also only have a longer-term effect.[27] For-profit exchanges may thus be more sensitive to the needs of their customers than membership organizations, less willing to establish strong regulatory standards, and less willing to enforce their rules rigorously against their customers. As discussed in the previous chapter, however, even if a mutual exchange operates on a nonprofit basis, it may seek to maximize its surplus, namely its revenues minus its costs. This is economically equivalent to maximizing profits, and thus mutual exchange SROs may in principle face the same conflict of interest in this context as demutualized exchange SROs. A mutual exchange's members will also seek to maximize their own profits, which may be another source of conflict with the regulation mandates of the exchange.

The fact that demutualized exchanges are for the most part also listed may exacerbate the conflict between business and regulation mandates at such exchanges. The public listing of any corporation may put pressure on the corporation to deliver short-term financial results.[28] Listed exchanges may be no exception. The conflict of interest they face to improve financial performance at the expense of their regulatory duties, may therefore be more intense than that faced by mutual exchanges.

Most of the concern about conflicts of interest at exchange SROs has been to ensure that private interests do not inappropriately interfere with their regulatory duties. It is critical to recognize as well, however, following Carson (2003, 2), that "it is possible for regulators and exchanges to conclude that the conflicts can be managed from a regulatory point of view, but for some exchanges to conclude that they are not manageable from a business point of view." This is likely to occur if an exchange views having responsibility for regulation as not being consistent with its business strategy, and as not being a core asset. The wider an exchange's regulatory responsibilities, the more difficult it will be for an exchange to reconcile them with its business mandate and objectives, whether the exchange is demutualized or not. There are, however, many exchanges that believe that regulation is part of their brand, and accordingly want some control over both rulemaking and enforcement activity.

2. *Conflicts in Specific Regulatory Functions:* These may occur in all the key functions undertaken by exchanges, including listing, operating a trading system, market surveillance, member regulation, clearing, and settlement. The manner in which such conflicts arise and their intensity varies for the different functions.

A central conflict of interest that may arise when an exchange SRO undertakes member regulation is that it may not wish to punish its trading members severely. Accordingly, it may fail to identify systemic weaknesses, to prosecute widespread practices that are financially beneficial to members although harmful to investors, or to implement necessary regulatory reforms.[29] As B. S. Black (2001, 5) argues:

> It is difficult for an exchange to regulate its broker-dealers more strongly than the broker-dealers want. If the exchange is controlled by broker-dealer members this is almost a tautology. If the members don't face external pressure to behave well, they won't want strong exchange regulation that constrains how they behave toward their customers. What they don't want, they won't get. Even with the government supervising the exchange's self-regulation, and prodding the exchange to do more, there is only so much that an organization run by broker-dealers will do to discipline errant members.

There is, however, some evidence that exchange SROs may facilitate enforcement that is stronger than it would be without their intervention.[30] Industry members of disciplinary committees are frequently tougher on miscreants than outsiders, and may also have a better sense of which infractions are serious than people who have no firsthand knowledge of the industry. There is also controversy about whether in fact exchanges will not undertake appropriate self-regulation of their members. Exchange

SROs may have a strong incentive to police how brokers act toward each other: all sides want quick, efficient settlement of trades and resolution of trade disputes. The US DOJ noted that while

> self-regulation can be a useful supplement to government regulation in disciplining members for fraud and dishonest commercial activities since in such cases the interests of almost all of the members [of an exchange] are likely to be coincident with the public interest, [the same coincidence of interest] is not likely to exist with respect to situations involving economic conflicts between members or with non-members.[31]

Exchange SROs may face different incentives in regulating insider trading and manipulation. On the one hand, such activities are likely to increase the total volume of trading, and therefore exchanges and market participants may not wish to jeopardize such trading volume by regulating these activities too rigorously. On the other hand, as Macey and O'Hara (2005, 589) argue:

> Insider trading and manipulation have an important characteristic in common: they increase the risks and the transaction costs associated with trading. The more that one transacts in the securities subject to manipulation and insider trading, the costlier trading becomes. Since market makers and exchange specialists engage in more transactions than most other traders, they are the groups with the strongest incentives to regulate manipulation and insider trading.

Conflicts of interest may also arise in the listing function. An exchange may ease up on the scrutiny of new listings, or grant listing rule waivers more readily than the pursuit of the public interest might warrant, so as not to antagonize its listed company customers. Pritchard (2003, 36) notes "the concern that exchanges will be reluctant to require full disclosure and impose sanctions on companies and their officers for fear that they will discourage listings."

The intensity of conflicts of interest in specific regulatory functions at an exchange SRO may vary depending on the governance structure of the exchange. B. S. Black (2001, 16) argues that

> exchanges, as long as they are controlled by their members, will not do a good job of policing moderate overcharging and other ways that brokers take advantage of customers. This situation changes dramatically if the exchange is owned by investors. The exchange must then address both the needs of brokers, who must be persuaded to use the exchange instead of a competitor, and the needs of investors, who must be persuaded to trade on the exchange instead of one of its competitors.

Stronger self-regulation by exchanges of brokers becomes possible, in part because the exchange is not so directly regulating itself—its members.

More generally, as the IOSCO Technical Committee (2001, 7) summarizes,

Demutualization may lessen some of the self-regulatory organization conflicts. Where demutualization leads to a separation of the owners of an exchange from its members, the interests of the owners may act as a constraint on actions that would benefit only the interests of the member firms. Where a reputation as a fair and efficient market is seen to be a competitive advantage, a for-profit exchange may have more resources available and greater incentives to devote those resources to activities that enhance that reputation.

3. *Conflicts in the Administration of Rules and Programs*: These may occur when an exchange SRO uses its authority in making administrative decisions about specific cases, for example in deciding whether to investigate or discipline a major customer, or what sanction to apply in a particular case. An exchange SRO may promote its own interests against an individual market participant, even if the exchange's business and regulatory goals are generally aligned. For example, an exchange SRO may use its regulatory powers to silence criticism against its rules or practices, by individual firms it regulates.[32] Given the confidential nature of many aspects of individual cases, it is difficult to find documented instances of this type of conflict occurring, although a few particular instances are frequently discussed off-the-record. One such instance concerned an exchange using its regulatory powers to sanction a member inappropriately for using a competing trading system.

4. *Conflicts in Funding Regulation*: These may occur when an exchange's focus on financial performance undermines its willingness to devote sufficient resources to regulatory functions, or gives it an incentive to fine regulatory infractions too much.[33]

5. *Conflicts in Regulating Competitors or Business Partners*. These may arise when an exchange shows inappropriate severity in regulating a competitor or customer of one of its competitors, or shows inappropriate favor in regulating a partner or customer.

6. *The Self-Listing Conflict*: This can occur when an exchange is required both to follow the relevant listing rules and simultaneously to enforce its compliance with these rules. Self-listing has been widely accepted as being too direct a conflict for a demutualized exchange.[34] Typically, the relevant national securities regulator takes all the powers and functions that an exchange has in relation to listed issuers regarding the exchange's own listing, except for the exchange's power to make listing rules.

INDUSTRY SROS AND INDEPENDENT PRIVATE REGULATORY ORGANIZATIONS

The term "industry SRO" is used here to refer to a broker-dealer owned and controlled organization that is independent of any exchange or other market infrastructure institution. There are few such organizations in the world.[35] They may regulate either markets, intermediaries, or both, and are typically membership and nonprofit organizations, which are governed and funded by the industry. The level of industry input into the governance of such institutions has been diluted in various contexts. Indeed, this has occurred to such an extent at the Financial Industry Regulatory Authority (FINRA) in the United States that the question of whether it should best be considered a government agency has been mooted.[36] Although some industry SROs evolved from industry associations, most now separate their self-regulatory activity from their industry advocacy, in light of the direct conflict of interest between regulating members and acting as their advocate. At least one industry SRO, namely the Japan Securities Dealers Association, still acted as a trade association as of 2009, although it had taken steps to separate the governance and operation of SRO from industry association functions.[37]

The term "independent private regulatory organization" is used to refer to a private organization not owned or controlled by industry that is thus independent of both the broker-dealer industry and any exchange. The model for an independent private regulatory organization is the Public Company Accounting Oversight Board, created to regulate auditing by accountants for public companies in the United States. It is a private-sector, nonprofit corporation, governed by independent commissioners, and funded by both listed companies and the accounting profession. No similar organization has been created to date in the securities market.

The primary benefit of employing either an industry SRO or an independent private regulatory organization is that both their structures eliminate the conflicts of interest between the business and regulatory functions in exchange SROs. In particular, the potential for exchanges to use their regulatory powers to promote their own market's interests at the expense of their regulatory obligations is minimized. The inherent conflict in self-regulation, namely when industry members regulate their own conduct, remains in industry SROs, but may be mitigated through governance structures that provide for significant independence at the board level. By construction, independent private regulatory organizations should not face this conflict of interest. The independence of such institutions from government, however, may be less than anticipated. Their boards, composed of directors independent of the securities industry, will necessarily be dependent on their staff for information and direction. If an independent private regulatory organization is under tight control by, and accountable to, a government regulator, the attitudes and operational methods of its staff may become similar to that of its regulator.

Both industry SROs and independent private regulatory organizations may enhance the competitiveness and business focus of exchanges by relieving them of key regulatory responsibilities. By providing what is hoped to be a neutral industry regulator that can oversee multiple markets based on a uniform rulebook, such institutions can facilitate competition among exchanges and other trading systems.

STATUTORY REGULATORS

All statutory regulators are mandated to pursue the public interest. This is the essence of their role, the goal they are required to follow in all their decisions and actions, and the standard to which they are usually held to account under relevant legislation. Furthermore, while fraud and corruption are possible in any institution, only in rare circumstances do regulatory agencies benefit commercially from their activities, or from the redistributive consequences of any rules they establish.[38] Statutory regulators therefore typically do not face the same conflicts of interest in undertaking regulation that private sector entities face, and indeed, by construction, their private interest should in principle be exactly the same as the public interest.

Such institutions may, however, face different conflicts of interest that mean that they too sometimes have an incentive not to deliver the public interest. Two important instances of this are noted here. The first arises because statutory regulators always operate in a political environment. Whatever the formal mandate a statutory regulator is given, it is a common experience over history and across jurisdictions that regulators and governments face most opprobrium when financial crises and scandals occur.[39] For this reason, a key implicit goal statutory regulators often follow is the avoidance of such crises and scandals. As Mahoney (2003, 3) notes:

> The incentives facing political actors [including regulators] are considerably more one-sided than those facing market actors. Exchanges and brokers gain when trading volumes are high and lose when volumes are low. By contrast, the political harm that elected officials [and regulatory officials] suffer when a market decline occurs on their watch is typically much greater than the credit they receive when markets are healthy. When markets are rising, the public typically judges its political leaders on some other set of issues. . . . The stock market is politically important only when it is in sharp decline.

Regulators may have another incentive to avoid crises. As Fisch (2005, 625) notes, "Crises create instability not just within interest group competition but [also] within the balance of authority among competing institutional regulators." A regulator may therefore seek to establish an environment that reduces the likelihood of crisis, for fear of losing regulatory powers in any reorganization that would be likely to occur subsequent to a crisis.

A desire on the part of government regulators to avoid crises and scandals has an important implication for regulatory outcomes. At the most general level, it means that a statutory regulator may assign less priority than other types of regulators to the efficiency of markets than to the protection of investors or the reduction of systemic risk, among the three core IOSCO objectives, as the last two objectives are likely to be compromised by a financial scandal or crisis.

A second context in which a statutory regulator may face a conflict of interest impeding it from delivering the public interest is if it is subject to undue influence from the private sector. At the extreme, a statutory agency may be "captured" by a particular constituency.[40] There have been many instances where this has been thought to arise, some of which have significantly undermined confidence in the affected regulator.[41] Pritchard (2003, 35) describes the similarity between the conflicts of interest that SROs and statutory regulators may face as follows:

> The forces demanding less stringent regulation from exchanges will demand the same from government. The forces of rent seeking do not recognize any boundary between the public and private spheres. Exchanges respond to the preferences of broker-dealers and executives of listing companies because they do not want to lose market share in listings and trading volume. Governments respond to those same groups because they are well organized, well financed, and have a strong interest in lobbying politicians. The only difference is that the rent seeking will be in the form of efforts to influence political decision-making as opposed to being mediated through the forces of competition.

SROs may in fact be less susceptible to political influence than public regulators, given that statutory regulators are normally both appointed by, and directly accountable to, government. This does not normally occur at SROs.

Completeness

One important context in which a regulator may not fully deliver the public interest, even if there is no direct conflict between its private interest and the public interest, is if its private interest is not completely congruent with the public interest. Macey and O'Hara (2005, 581) empha-size that an exchange should be entrusted with the task of self-regulation when, and only when, it internalizes all the costs and benefits of the rules it promulgates. This criterion is relevant for any regulator: any institution that incurs all the costs of providing regulatory services but captures only part of the benefits may underprovide such services, as it will not take all their benefits into account.

In the context of exchange SROs in the United States, Macey and O'Hara suggest that an appropriate policy is to "allocate to firms [i.e. ex-changes] decisions regarding the internal operations of securities trading and assign to the SEC [i.e. the national statutory regulator] decisions re-lating to the overall market."[42] Their justification is that while exchanges have an incentive to enforce trading rules for their own markets, market-wide standards need to be developed by a market-wide regulator, be it a statutory regulator, an industry SRO, or an independent private regula-tory organization.

Determining what are the areas of regulation where an exchange would internalize all the relevant costs and benefits is, however, controversial. In the US context, Macey and O'Hara (2005, 599) suggest that the "reg-ulation of listing and delisting, which define access to the U.S. capital markets, are better handled by the SEC [namely the statutory regulator], while decisions regarding trading system capacity are handled more ef-fectively by the market itself." The regulation of listed firms is thought to create a significant public good since it benefits entities besides the listed companies that pay for it, including all the traders in the listed compa-nies' shares. Conversely, it is believed that exchanges have sufficient pri-vate incentive to determine a socially optimal level of investment in their internal systems, such as capacity and reliability.

Although neither of these views is examined in depth here, both are debatable. As noted above, an exchange SRO is likely to have an incen-tive to require companies to disclose just that amount of information that maximizes trading in its listed companies' shares. Such a level of disclosure could be viewed as the socially optimal level. Conversely, an exchange may not have an incentive to invest in sufficient capacity in its internal systems from a regulatory perspective. In most markets, there is a single exchange that dominates trading, particularly at times of crisis. Such periods occur very infrequently, but when they do, they are accom-panied by very large volumes of trading. In this situation an exchange may actually not have an incentive to maximize trading, but rather to maximize profits (or surplus). The marginal investment that would be necessary to pay for the capacity sufficient to handle the unusually large trading spikes during a crisis may not be compensated by the marginal revenue the exchange would receive from such trading, given that they would occur so infrequently. In contrast, the public interest may be best served by ensuring that the dominant trading system in a jurisdiction can handle any unusually large trading volumes that do occur.

The importance of a regulator internalizing all the costs and benefits of its regulation is also relevant for statutory agencies, although in a different way from exchanges. Unlike an exchange SRO that may not take account of all the benefits of their regulation, a statutory regulator may not take account of all the costs of its regulation, given that many such costs are borne by market participants and not by the regulator itself. Government regulators may therefore be excessively bureaucratic, intrusive, and rigid in their approach, and not sufficiently responsive to the costs of regulation imposed on market participants. As Pritchard (2003, 35) argues:

> If a rule makes an incremental contribution to the avoidance of a future crisis, government regulators may be quick to see the rule's wisdom, discounting its costs. Those costs will be borne by investors generally, in the form of small reductions in their investment returns and disclosure documents that bury important information in a sea of minutia. Those costs are sufficiently diffuse that they are unlikely to generate a groundswell for regulatory reform. Thus, the cumulative effect of regulation in response to crisis is a ratchet effect pushing toward greater, more intrusive regulation.

Self-regulation is likely to have a comparative advantage over regulation by a statutory agency in this context. As the SRO Consultative Committee to IOSCO (2000, 12) maintains: "Since SROs are close to their markets and market users, they are ... in a good position to balance the benefits of their regulation relative to the costs and avoid unnecessary regulatory costs."

There has been a great emphasis in the EU and elsewhere on an agenda to achieve *better regulation*.[43] Three important elements of this agenda may help regulators take account of all the costs and benefits of their regulation: they are typically required to consult publicly on their proposals; to undertake cost-benefit analyses, sometimes called regulatory impact assessments, on such proposals; and to publish justifications for any regulatory proposals adopted. Notwithstanding the hopes of this *better regulation* agenda, however, there are several reasons why it may not ensure that regulators do take account of all the costs and benefits of their regulation. First, market participants may fear reprisals if they identify relevant costs of regulation and by doing so are seen as criticizing their regulator. Second, while cost-benefit analyses of some regulatory proposals are possible, there are many aspects of regulation for which undertaking a cost-benefit analysis may be very difficult or even impossible—for example, on enforcement cases. Third, even if all the relevant costs and benefits are identified via public consultation and cost-benefit analyses, and even if a regulator's decisions must be publicly justified and therefore subject to public scrutiny, all the relevant costs and benefits may still not be internalized by the regulator. The regulator's private incentives may still mean that it does not give sufficient weight to relevant costs or benefits in making its decisions, as doing so will harm its private interests.

Competition

The intensity of competition in a market can affect the relative merits of different allocations of regulatory powers; and conversely, different allocations of regulatory powers can also affect the intensity of competition in a market. Four aspects of the relationship between competition and how regulatory powers are allocated are noted here.

1. Self-regulation can be used for anticompetitive activity. If an exchange SRO is controlled by its members, it may use its regulatory powers to promote their commercial interests, particularly when the exchange is the only provider of a service required by nonmember market participants.[44] There has been a long history in the United States, and elsewhere, of anticompetitive practices by exchanges seeking to exploit their market power for their members' interests.[45]

An exchange SRO may use regulation to exclude or limit the influence of its competitors, such as large brokerage houses or firms operating ATSs.[46] This can manifest itself in many ways, as the U.S. General Accounting Office (2002, 7) notes:

> SROs could adopt rules that unfairly impede the ability of members to compete against the SROs—for example, by adopting rules that give preference to noncompetitors' orders . . . an SRO might sanction a competing member more severely than other members by, for instance, inappropriately concluding that the member had failed to satisfy its best-execution obligation when it routed an order to a competing market for execution rather than to the SRO . . . an SRO, in its regulatory capacity, could obtain proprietary information from a member and, in its capacity as a market operator, inappropriately use the information. For example, an SRO might obtain proprietary information about its members' customers and then use that information to market its services to the customers.

An exchange SRO may also seek to exploit its listing rules against any competitors listed on the exchange.[47]

2. If competition to an exchange exists, it may not internalize all the benefits of any self-regulatory activity it undertakes as an SRO, most importantly ignoring any benefits that accrue to its competitors. As discussed above, it may then underprovide regulatory services, making a statutory regulator more likely to deliver better regulatory outcomes in such a situation.

3. Macey and O'Hara (2005, 570) argue that one of the key factors justifying self-regulation historically was that an exchange SRO was able to use its market power for regulatory purposes, mainly by threatening individual members and listed issuers with termination of their contractual arrangements in case of noncompliance with its rules. They note that the advent of competition for the provision of both trading and listing services reduced the force of such a threat, thus undermining self-regulation. This argument depends, however, on the fact that equivalent regulatory standards are not required on the alternative trading or listing venues that compete with an exchange SRO.

4. The question of whether competition between securities markets regulators is beneficial has long been, and remains, controversial.[48] An examination of the merits of such competition is beyond the scope of this chapter. Nevertheless a few comments on the topic, with particular focus on its implications for how regulatory authority should be allocated, are noted here.

Various arguments have been put forward for why regulatory competition may be undesirable. The most prominent is that competition between regulators will lead to a "race to the bottom." An exchange SRO, for example, may misuse its regulatory powers, or not be diligent in enforcing securities laws or its own rules, in order to enhance its competitive position.[49] In order to increase the number of its listed companies, a stock exchange may adopt corporate governance rules that promote management rather than shareholder interests, given that the listing decision is a responsibility of management. Similarly, an exchange SRO may not enforce its rules stringently against either listed companies or trading participants, for fear that they might move, respectively, to another listing or trading venue.

Competition between regulators has also been argued as having a range of merits. It may yield the standard benefits of competition: lower costs, greater efficiency, and a wider range of regulatory services offered.[50] It may reduce the likelihood of protectionist regulation or regulatory capture. Increased competition may also create an incentive for exchanges to police themselves better, if investors prefer to trade on well-regulated environments.[51]

In practice, the possibility of having multiple regulators in a single national jurisdiction has only occurred in the largest markets. In the United States there has been a progressive centralization of various regulatory activities away from competing exchange SROs, in favor of the SEC and a single industry SRO, namely FINRA. Broker-dealer regulation was centralized in FINRA, via a merger of the member regulation divisions of the NASD and NYSE in 2007, while competing exchange SROs continued to retain responsibility for market regulation. It was hoped that the creation of FINRA would deliver a range of benefits: eliminate inefficient and inconsistent rulemaking; avoid duplication of examinations; preserve the synergy between markets and market-specific oversight; foster competition between markets; ensure greater independence for member regulation; and remove concerns associated with potentially anticompetitive behavior of SROs against members that offered alternative trading services.[52]

In the international context, there has been no centralization of regulation away from national regulators. Even in the EU, a single supranational jurisdiction, there has been little support to date for the creation of a single centralized supranational securities markets regulator to replace the various national regulators.[53] Various European institutions have, however, been given the power to undertake what might be considered regulatory activities. The European Commission proposes EU-wide laws; the European Parliament and the Council of Ministers pass such laws; and the Committee of European Securities Regulators has several relevant roles, including to "improve co-ordination among securities regulators," to "act as an advisory group to assist the EU Commission, in particular in its preparation of draft implementing measures of EU framework directives," and to "work to ensure more consistent and timely day-to-day implementation of community legislation in the Member States."[54]

Whether competition between regulators is viewed as desirable or not need not necessarily affect the decision about how regulatory powers should be allocated. If, for example, it is believed that competition would not be desirable for a certain regulatory area, the single institution designated to undertake regulation could in principle be any of the main types discussed above, namely an exchange SRO, an industry SRO, an independent private regulatory organization, or a statutory regulator. If competition between regulators were believed desirable in a single jurisdiction, however, this would likely imply that regulatory powers should be allocated to competing exchange SROs. It is hard to conceive of a jurisdiction in which more than one statutory regulator for the securities markets could exist—although the SEC and the Commodity Futures Trading Commission in the United States have at times regulated similar products. Similarly, unless the securities market industry is disaggregated into several different components, the existence of more than one industry SRO is difficult to imagine. At an international level, where market participants have a choice of jurisdiction in which to conduct the same business, competition between national regulators can self-evidently exist.

Fairness

Many different aspects of the notion of fairness may influence what is deemed an optimal allocation of regulatory powers. Two important ones are noted here.

The first is economic in nature: particular constituencies of market participants may believe that the actions of a regulator are unfair if it takes decisions that they believe unreasonably undermine their ability to pursue their economic objectives. Three examples illustrate when this may be thought to occur. First, an exchange SRO may design its trading rules to promote the interests of certain groups trading on the exchange, at the expense of other groups or investors.[55] This has sometimes occurred when a particular group controls the governance of an exchange. Second, an exchange SRO may supervise traders who have no interest in the markets that the exchange operates, and the exchange may seek to create rules that favor participants trading on its market over nonparticipants. Third, if the users of an exchange SRO also control it, they may seek to restrict the types of activities that the exchange can undertake, particularly if such activities might compete with services that they are already providing. This may happen even if the activities the exchange were proposing to undertake would benefit the market as a whole.

Several aspects of this economic notion of fairness are noteworthy. First, any constituency of market participants that finds a situation to its economic disadvantage is likely to argue that the situation is unfair to them, whatever the merits of the situation, including if they simply have been outcompeted. Second, if an SRO provides services that can be provided by other institutions, then the question of whether a particular SRO is being unfair becomes much less important, given that customers can obtain the same services elsewhere. Third, perceptions about what is fair often depend on a particular market model. Changing circumstances, such as product or technology developments, may change perceptions of what is fair. Previously, for example, it was necessary for an investor to access a stock exchange via a financial intermediary, given the physical nature of intermediation on the floor of exchanges. Now that it is relatively easy for investors to have direct computerized access to a trading system, it is harder to justify any access or information privileges granted to particular membership constituencies at an exchange. Finally, statutory regulators are less likely to be open to the criticism of being unfair than exchange SROs or industry SROs, given that statutory regulators are not controlled by one particular type of market participant, except in unusually adverse circumstances.

A second aspect of fairness that may influence what is deemed an optimal allocation of regulatory powers concerns the decision-making processes followed by a regulator. In particular, market participants need to believe that any regulatory procedures to which they are subject are just. Statutory regulators are typically required to follow a series of administrative law processes, which are themselves defined as part of the law and legal framework in the jurisdiction in which they operate. Even if the decision-making processes at exchange SROs, industry SROs, and independent private regulatory organizations are different from those at statutory regulators, market participants will still require that such processes are seen to be just.

Expertise, Knowledge, and Experience

The expertise, knowledge, and experience of a regulator about the markets it regulates are crucial in determining its effectiveness. One of the main historical justifications for employing self-regulation is that it may produce better rules than the alternatives, as industry participation in the regulatory process is likely to bring more expertise, knowledge, and experience than is available to a statutory regulator or an independent private regulatory organization.[56] Exchange SROs have a particular advantage in market regulation as trading is conducted through their facilities, and their regulatory staff are exclusively engaged with overseeing their systems.[57] Industry participation in self-regulation is beneficial, as Kaswell (2004) notes, because "industry professionals 'know where the bodies are buried,' and can determine quickly whether an activity is unfair to investors or is appropriate and consistent with industry norms."

Four factors may, however, reduce the comparative advantage SROs have in this context. First, statutory regulators can and do hire people with relevant experience.[58] Second, most statutory regulators are increasingly employing consultation procedures in many of their activities in order precisely to access the expertise, knowledge, and experience of market participants. A third factor reducing the comparative advantage SROs have is that they are becoming increasingly bureaucratized, especially in the larger markets such as the United States, with their increasing size and the great specialization of their staff. This has meant that industry representation is largely becoming confined to board oversight and to member participation in SROs' committee structures and disciplinary proceedings.[59] The extent to which market participants have influence over regulatory activity is therefore being reduced in SROs. Finally, when an SRO's regulatory powers expand to areas beyond its specialist knowledge and experience, such as for example if an exchange SRO seeks to review the accuracy of financial statements or corporate governance requirements, its comparative advantage over other regulatory bodies regarding expertise is likely to be reduced.[60]

There is one area of regulation that it is widely agreed exchange SROs should undertake, notwithstanding the presence of any conflicts of interest in undertaking such a function, namely real-time market surveillance of the trading on their systems. It is viewed as impractical to delink an exchange from market surveillance, not only from an operational point of view, but also because to separate the two would be to lose significant expertise.[61] The extent to which an exchange SRO should share such responsibility with a statutory regulator is, however, more debatable. Similarly, there is disagreement about whether a single exchange SRO could, or should, undertake surveillance of all trading. In order to do so, trading data from other competing systems would need to be accessed, and it is frequently viewed as more appropriate that a central statutory regulator act as a neutral institution to regulate trading across multiple markets.

Grajzl and Murrell (2007) present a theoretical model analyzing the optimal allocation of regulatory authority, based on two key assumptions: producers (in this context financial intermediaries) have better knowledge than government about regulatory issues, and regulatory contracts are incomplete. The source of potential welfare gains in delegating rulemaking powers to producers, namely in establishing self-regulation, is their greater adaptability to changing institutional conditions. The source of potential welfare losses is the participation of producers, namely regulated market participants, in the regulatory process. When there is a great uncertainty about the results of institutional construction, or little divergence between producer and consumer interests, the benefits of self-regulation outweigh its costs. In the opposite case, the regulatory arrangement that yields higher social welfare depends on the extent to which the government's motives are populist or aligned with those of producers.

Flexibility and Responsiveness

Self-regulation may be more flexible and responsive than the alternatives for several reasons, three of which are noted here.[62]

1. SROs may be free of some limitations faced by government agencies. Statutory regulators' jurisdictions, for example, are normally clearly delimited in relevant legislation, while such limitations are normally not

placed on SROs.[63] Government enforcement actions may also be subject to tighter due process requirements and other procedural restrictions than those of SROs. In the United States, for example, there are many laws that apply to government agencies that would make broker-dealer regulation cumbersome.[64] In addition, securities industry professionals may be entitled to claim a privilege against self-incrimination in any agency investigation, or be otherwise protected in ways that would make statutory agency investigations and disciplinary proceedings less flexible than SRO actions.[65]

2. The scope of self-regulation can be wider than government regulation. In particular, self-regulation may be able to monitor many types of conduct and activity that lie beyond the reach of the law, such as enforcing ethical standards and best practices.[66]

3. Given that SROs are close to their markets and market users, they may be able to modify their rules and surveillance techniques more quickly to respond to market changes than statutory agencies.

Efficiency and Funding

A complicated relationship exists between how regulatory authority is allocated, how regulation is funded, and the delivery of the core IOSCO objectives.[67] It is a difficult balance to ensure that an SRO has sufficient funds to be an effective regulator, that such funds are paid for on a fair basis among public companies, member firms, investors, and other market participants who benefit from securities regulation, and that there is accountability by the SRO to all of these groups, as well as to the government regulator charged with its oversight. Five key aspects of the relationship between how regulatory authority is allocated, how regulation is funded, and the delivery of the core IOSCO objectives, are noted here.

1. SROs are almost always funded directly by the industry they regulate, whereas regulation by a public body is typically, though not always, funded by some form of tax.[68] Industry financing has a range of benefits. It can, first, supplement available governmental resources by reducing the need for large government bureaucracies. Second, the resources of an SRO will be independent of the government budget, and the political considerations that surround it.[69] Third, industry financing may be considered fairer than requiring the nontrading taxpayer to finance a government agency.[70] A fourth benefit may arise if the securities industry that finances an SRO also controls how it is operated: the industry will then have both the incentive and the power to ensure that any money spent on regulation is not wasted. Self-regulation may thus be cheaper than the alternatives, including having a government regulator.[71]

Allowing the securities industry to fund regulation and also have some control over how a regulator is operated, such as in an SRO, does, however, have a major drawback. It creates a direct conflict of interest, in that it may give the industry influence over the regulator whose key duty is to monitor and supervise the industry.

It is generally difficult to find evidence about which type of regulatory allocation is cheaper, as to do so normally requires comparing a real situation with one or more hypothetical alternatives. One context where a comparison between two existing alternatives was possible occurred in the United States between 1964 and 1983, where brokers were given the opportunity to choose to be regulated either by an SRO, namely the NASD, or directly by the government regulator, namely the SEC, via what was called the SEC Only program. The SEC Only program was not successful, however, and convinced both the SEC and market participants that such direct regulation was not a feasible approach. A range of reasons were put forward at the time, and subsequently, for its failure.[72] These included that the program was unnecessarily costly, that it diverted the SEC's limited resources away from areas of major concern merely to duplicate the functions of the NASD, that SROs were better able to maintain ethical standards for the industry and to perform certain detailed oversight functions, and that the SEC faced limitations in enforcement and compliance remedies in comparison to those available to the NASD. It was also believed impractical for the SEC to regulate directly the several thousand broker-dealers and business corporations subject to its jurisdiction, given its limited capacity, and that to do so properly would require significant extra expenditures by the SEC.

2. If an SRO undertakes commercial activities in addition to its regulatory duties, as exchange SROs do, it may seek to enhance its commercial performance in two inappropriate ways. First, such an SRO may cut resources for regulation excessively in order to reduce costs. Assessing what is an adequate level of spending on regulation is, however, extremely difficult. As noted by the IOSCO Technical Committee (2006a, 7), it is necessary "to distinguish between cuts in regulatory budgets that increase the risk of a regulatory failure and cost reductions that an exchange achieves by increasing efficiency." An SRO with a commercial arm may also seek to enhance its revenues inappropriately, by charging too much for its regulatory services or other regulatory receipts, such as fines or penalties. Irrespective of whether an SRO has a commercial arm, the use of fines and other penalties to fund a regulatory organization may give a regulator a perverse incentive to pursue and prosecute disciplinary cases too severely.[73]

3. Two adverse effects on competition may arise if a single institution undertakes both regulatory activities and commercial activities, and also competes with entities that do not undertake similar regulatory activities. If such an SRO is required to fund its regulatory activities from its commercial revenues, it is likely to be at an unfair competitive disadvantage to other competing systems not subject to similar requirements.[74] Exchange SROs' regulatory activities have, for example, traditionally been funded primarily through transaction fees, listing fees, and quote and trade data revenues. The provision of all these services is now, however, subject to competitive threat, which may mean such cross-subsidization is no longer feasible. There is competition for the provision of trading systems between exchanges, and between exchanges and ATSs. In the competition for listings, listed companies may decide it is not worthwhile for them to pay high listing fees that subsidize regulatory activities. Industry members are also objecting to the utilization of market data fees to subsidize general exchange activities.[75]

Competition between an institution undertaking both regulatory activities and commercial activities, and entities that do not undertake similar regulatory activities, may also be adversely affected if the first institution is able to cross-subsidize its commercial activities with its regulatory income. This would give it an unfair competitive advantage.

4. It may be difficult for statutory regulators to pay the same wages, or attract the same calibre of people, as private regulators are able to do. Sometimes, however, statutory regulators are able to attract and hire highly qualified staff, given the credibility, knowledge, and experience, that working for such institutions bring.

5. The existence of multiple regulators, of whatever nature, in a single jurisdiction may be relatively expensive if it entails duplication of regulatory efforts and leads to a lack of coordination among different regulators with overlapping spheres of competence. By construction a single regulator would eliminate duplicative regulatory inefficiencies. However, competition between regulators may also lead to efficiencies in the delivery of regulation.

Compliance and Enforcement

The manner in which regulatory authority is allocated can affect both the compliance with, and the enforcement of, regulation in various ways. Seven instances of this are noted here.

1. Market practitioners may learn about the regulatory process by participating in an SRO, and thereby enhance their firms' internal compliance with their regulatory duties.

2. Rules imposed by industry peers may carry more legitimacy with market participants than those imposed by an external regulator, and thus market participants may be more willing to comply with such rules.

3. As member representation is reduced, there is less "self" in self-regulation.[76] This may make a regulatory system more adversarial, and discourage voluntary compliance.

4. SROs may face limits in their ability to enforce regulation. For example, exchange SROs often lack the investigatory powers that government entities may possess, such as subpoena powers to obtain records from nonmembers. In such circumstances, government assistance or enforcement may be necessary.[77] Attempting to resolve this issue by allocating rulemaking powers to an SRO, and enforcement powers to a government regulator, may have its own problems. As Dombalagian (2007, 345) argues, "Any separation of rulemaking and enforcement powers would raise concerns about inconsistent interpretation, underallocation or overallocation of enforcement resources to particular rules."

5. The regulatory sanctions available to exchange SROs may be limited.[78] If an exchange's regulatory power is based on contract, its sanctioning abilities will typically depend on the contracts it agrees. Discontinuation of a contract and consequent expulsion from the exchange, therefore, often constitute the harshest measure an exchange SRO may impose on a regulated entity, be it a trading member or a listed firm. Given the adverse effects expulsion would have on an exchange's revenues, however, it is likely that such a measure would only be used in very rare circumstances.[79] A statutory regulator may be more willing to implement severe sanctions.

6. There may be types of market participants or activities that do not fall within the remit of an SRO.[80] The intervention of a statutory regulator, with a wider jurisdiction, may therefore be necessary to supervise such market participants or activities.

7. Whether an SRO is a for-profit company or a mutual organization may influence its enforcement policy. As noted above, there is wide concern that a for-profit exchange SRO may not devote sufficient resources to its regulatory obligations, including enforcement policies. As well as being disputed, unsurprisingly, by for-profit exchange SROs, however, there is also little empirical evidence to support this concern. In addition, at least one theoretical model, presented in Reiffen and Robe (2007), describes a context in which for-profit exchange SROs have a greater incentive to enforce rules than do mutual exchange SROs.[81]

Politics, History, Business Culture, and Legal System

A simple model for choosing how to allocate regulatory powers in a jurisdiction is to employ the following three-stage optimization process:

identify the objectives of regulation; determine the constraints that limit how regulatory authority can be allocated and exercised; and evaluate how regulatory powers should be allocated in order to best deliver the desired objectives, subject to the relevant constraints. The logic of this process masks, however, the fundamental fact that regulation exists to serve the goals of a society. Both the feasibility, and the desirability, of how regulatory powers are allocated to different kinds of institutions, is thus not just a formulaic activity, but also critically dependent on the politics, history, business culture, and legal system of the jurisdiction in which it operates. Although these four attributes of a jurisdiction are all distinct from each other, they are also closely linked in many contexts, and for this reason are discussed together here.[82] Eight examples of their potential influence are noted.

1. Financial markets and their regulation are intimately intertwined with the political systems in which they operate.[83] An SRO may be created for politically expedient reasons, quite independent of the merits of allocating regulatory powers to such an institution. An example occurred in Russia, as described by Frye (1997), where brokers faced a series of problems typical in a relatively new market with little legal or regulatory protection—such as endemic reneging on contracts. In response, the brokers "tried to create a self-governing organization (SGO) [or an SRO in the terminology used here] that would define standard contracts, write trading rules, and ensure contract compliance without an external enforcer." Frye (1997, 4) describes its creation, noting:

> The decision to help brokers create an SGO on this market was linked in large part to the short-term political interests of the Federal Commission on Securities and the Capital Market. Locked in a bureaucratic struggle with the Russian Central [Bank] and the Ministry of Finance, the Federal Commission sought to create an SGO to help entrench its position within the state. By creating an interest group to help bolster its position, the Federal Commission sought to strengthen itself against rivals within the state, and by doing so, helped to create a functioning SGO.

2. The adoption of self-regulation in the United States has been portrayed as a "historical anachronism"[84] or a "historical accident."[85] According to this account, it was convenient for Congress to assign regulatory powers to exchanges when it first did so, as they already had significant regulatory infrastructure in place at the time.

3. Self-regulation may act as a substitute for a statutory regulator where political factors impede government regulation. Canada's political inability to create a federal securities regulator to date, for example, has

meant that a number of other entities, some endowed with self-regulatory authority, have filled the gap.[86]

4. Some political systems either do not recognize the concept of SROs, or face constitutional or administrative law hurdles to their recognition. While self-regulation has been employed at different times in the UK, and by extension in the Commonwealth and the United States, it has for the most part not been used in Continental European countries.[87] The United States has its own constraints over what types of regulatory bodies are acceptable. For example, the creation of the Public Company Accounting Oversight Board as an independent private regulatory organization, namely a nonstate actor, has been challenged.[88]

5. Various cultural factors may enhance the effectiveness of self-regulation. These include the existence of a relatively small number of market participants bound together by a community of interest, a jurisdiction with a small population and high visibility of market functions and participants, and the normative force of "reputational" consequences. Davies (2004) argues that

> self-regulation works best if there is an identifiable community of participants in a well-defined marketplace. Where that is so, those participants know that their reputations are bound up with each others. They therefore have a strong incentive to police the behaviour of their colleagues, and to come down hard on those who break the rules, and damage the reputation of the market as a whole. Indeed in those circumstances there is some evidence that self-regulators can be tougher than statutory regulators.[89]

If new participants enter a marketplace that was previously composed of relatively homogeneous participants, as may occur, for example, when new foreign participants enter into a previously solely domestic marketplace, the community of interest that existed formerly can break down. This may lead to a failure in self-regulation as reputational effects diminish.[90]

6. If a country is at a relatively low state of economic development, the relative merits of self-regulation over statutory regulation may be enhanced, particularly if a government and its agencies are relatively ineffective. The personnel and resources available to different sorts of institutions vary widely across countries. Carson (2003, 3) maintains, for example:

> Emerging markets may ... be less able to sustain the injury caused by regulatory problems and scandals because the basic conditions required to establish market integrity, such as effective legal and regulatory systems, effective institutions, sound corporate governance and disclosure

may not be in place. The exchanges' roles [for example, as SROs] are crucial to building institutional capacity and effective systems.

7. The extent to which the rule of law is viable in a country can affect how regulatory authority is allocated. Zhang (2001) discusses the example of China, where

> a 2000-year old history coloured by feudalism and dictatorship has contributed to the cultivation of a deep-rooted legal culture centred on the rule by people (or, in other words, rule by administration). The imprint and effects of tradition will stay for some time to come. In terms of regulation in the securities market, the culture of rule by administration makes it impossible to carry out regulation in accordance with law.

8. Demutualization may lead to inconsistencies between regulatory governance requirements and a for-profit corporation's governance requirements.[91] For example, a regulator may require that the governing board of an exchange SRO include meaningful representation of a variety of market users in order to promote the public interest in the self-regulatory process, as well as foster integrity and impartiality in the boards' decision-making. In contrast, the board of a for-profit corporation, including an exchange SRO, may be required to represent only the interests of the corporation and its shareholders.

Internationalization

There are many ways in which markets, their participants, and their regulators interact with each other across national borders. Different facets of the internationalization of markets can have a range of consequences for the optimal balance between self-regulation and government regulation. Seven are noted here.

1. The internationalization of markets has led to greater cooperation between regulators internationally. A central vehicle to promote this is the Multilateral Memorandum of Understanding developed by IOSCO.[92] This document, and other bilateral and multilateral approaches to international regulatory cooperation, need to be signed by government regulatory bodies. This may lead regulation to become more centralized in government agencies within national jurisdictions, and may reduce the feasibility of self-regulation.

2. Internationalization may lead to conflicts between regulatory approaches. Divergent views surfaced, for example, in 2006 between UK and US regulators as to the relative merits of "principles based" regulation and "rules based" regulation. Governments may react to the poten-

tial implications of regulatory "spillover" from a foreign jurisdiction by intervening to insulate their markets from foreign regulation.[93] This may again lead to greater reliance on statutory regulators, given that governments have more direct control of such institutions than SROs.

3. Some national jurisdictions operate within broad supranational legal frameworks that affect how regulatory authority may be allocated in their jurisdictions. The members states of the EU are prominent examples. Various EU directives have increasingly limited the discretion over how regulatory powers in the securities markets may be allocated between governments, regulators, market infrastructure institutions, and SROs in the EU.[94]

4. There is a growing awareness in many jurisdictions about how regulatory issues are approached in other jurisdictions across the world. This, together with a series of technical assistance programs provided by various national and international agencies,[95] has led a range of countries to copy regulatory approaches employed in other countries.[96] For example, self-regulatory concepts have been introduced into some financial systems where previously they were not employed.[97]

5. Greater internationalization of the markets led to the development of IOSCO's core objectives and principles. These have served both as a model for the development of national regulatory systems and as an informal measure of the performance of such systems, via the IMF and World Bank's Financial Sector Assessment Program. Although the IOSCO objectives and principles seek to be neutral with regards the use of self-regulation, they do sanction its "appropriate" use, depending on a market's size and complexity.[98]

Following the revision of the IOSCO objectives and principles, which was still in process in mid-2010, it is possible that less emphasis might be placed on the recommended role of self-regulation for several reasons. The original standards were developed in the late 1990s, and it was only after this period that many of the major exchanges demutualized, bringing in turn greater regulatory concern about whether for-profit exchanges should act as SROs. The use of self-regulation has also progressively been reduced in many major markets, including especially the UK and the United States. Such a change in the IOSCO objectives and principles would likely reduce the adoption of self-regulation more generally across the world.

6. Exchanges, CCPs, and CSDs have enjoyed a central position in many countries' financial systems, and sometimes also a role as a national political symbol. This may lead national governments to oppose international mergers or alliances, or to diminish the self-regulatory powers of market infrastructure institutions, in order to maintain influence over the key policy decisions such institutions take.[99]

7. International consolidation of market infrastructure institutions may make self-regulation more attractive, especially where there is no supranational legal framework to provide guidance or regulatory authority.[100] Self-regulation relies on contractual relationships, and is thus not dependent on the existence of national or supranational frameworks targeted specifically at securities markets, which may be difficult to create.[101] As the cross-border market infrastructure institutions will be small in number, highly visible, and *sui generis* to a large degree, their prominence may also enhance the effectiveness of the "reputational" element of self-regulation.

Both national and supranational law may, however, undermine the use of self-regulation, for example if it contravenes competition law.[102] National regulators may also be cautious about relying on exchange and industry SROs from other jurisdictions over which they have little control, and which may be less tied to the interests of any single national market or jurisdiction. To date, the regulatory frameworks that have been developed to accommodate international mergers between market infrastructure institutions have not relied on self-regulation. There is a growing consensus that the appropriate model to regulate such institutions is to create a regulatory "college" composed of all the relevant national government regulators.[103]

Concluding Discussion and General Propositions

The question of what regulatory powers in the securities markets should be allocated to exchanges, CCPs, and CSDs is explored in this chapter. It is examined in the context of the broader issue of how regulatory powers should be allocated between government regulators, SROs, and other types of regulatory institutions. In order to encapsulate the discussions presented in the chapter and to present key lessons in a simple and accessible manner, eight general propositions are articulated. They address how best to allocate regulatory powers in the securities markets. Most of the propositions summarize the analysis presented in the first sections of the chapter; for the few that incorporate new ideas, a justification for their inclusion is presented.

Several implications and aspects of the approach of using a series of simple and accessible propositions to summarize the analysis and present key lessons are important to note. First, the propositions are not intended to be a comprehensive set of rules for deciding how best to allocate regulatory power over the securities markets in any single jurisdiction. The general nature of the propositions necessarily means that they cannot address the specific details relevant for evaluating any particular jurisdiction. By construction the propositions also aim to abstract the most important aspects of the decision-making process, rather than capture its full complexity. Second, the simplicity of the propositions does not mean that they have been widely accepted in the past: indeed many of their implications have proven controversial, and have also frequently not been followed in practice. Third, the propositions ignore the critical question of how conflicts of interest may be mitigated by regulatory intervention in SRO governance—this topic is examined in the next chapter. Finally, no single proposition is intended to be definitive. Notwithstanding these comments and concerns, taken together the propositions provide a useful and compact aid in deciding how best to allocate regulatory power over the securities markets in any jurisdiction.

> **Proposition 1:** A simple model for choosing how to allocate regulatory powers in a jurisdiction is to employ the following three-stage optimization process:
>
> 1. Identify the objectives of regulation;
> 2. Determine the constraints that limit how regulatory authority can be allocated and exercised;
> 3. Evaluate how regulatory powers should be allocated in order to best deliver the desired objectives, subject to the relevant constraints.
>
> **Proposition 2:** An allocation of regulatory powers in a jurisdiction requires addressing the following three-part question: *Which* functions in the regulatory process, governing *which* areas of activity and types of participants in the markets, should be allocated to *which* institutions?

The view that the determination of how to allocate regulatory powers is solely a binary decision between statutory regulation on the one hand and self-regulation on the other is no longer valid. Given the multiplicity of regulatory functions that need to be undertaken, the many areas of activity and types of participants in the markets that are regulated, and the many categories of institutions that could assume regulatory responsibilities,

> **Proposition 3:** Many different ways of allocating regulatory powers in the securities markets are possible.

Choosing an optimal allocation of regulatory powers is complex.

> **Proposition 4:** The decision of how best to allocate regulatory powers in a single jurisdiction requires evaluating many factors, including the following:

1. whether the private incentives a regulator faces support the delivery of its public interest mandate, or conversely whether it faces a conflict between its private interests and public duties;
2. whether a regulator internalizes all the costs and benefits of the regulation it undertakes;
3. the presence of competition between regulators;
4. whether the actions of a regulator are believed fair or not;
5. the expertise, knowledge, and experience, of a regulator;
6. the flexibility and responsiveness of a regulator;
7. the manner in which a regulator is funded;
8. the efficiency of a regulator;
9. how market compliance and regulatory enforcement is affected by different potential regulatory allocations;
10. the politics, history, business culture, and legal system of the jurisdiction;
11. the manner in which markets, market participants, and regulators interact with each other internationally.

Given the many ways of allocating regulatory powers, the numerous variables that affect how best to make such an allocation, and the diversity among jurisdictions,[104]

Proposition 5: No single optimal structure for allocating regulatory powers in the securities markets is applicable globally.

This does not imply, however, that the current diversity of regulatory allocation models adopted in the world is optimal. As summarized by the IOSCO Technical Committee, many different models have been adopted around the world, and these choices "have tended to be customized and pragmatic, based on an assessment of the particular circumstances in a jurisdiction."[105] An assessment of whether any of these models is optimal in its context would require evaluating all the relevant factors in all the jurisdictions under consideration. Thus no single factor, including even the presence of a conflict between the private interest and public duties of a regulator, should determine the decision of the optimal allocation.

Any decision about the allocation of regulatory powers to be made in any specific jurisdiction also requires an assessment and judgment about the relative merits of the available options. The benefits of accepting the possibility of potentially acute conflicts of interest at an SRO have been accepted in some circumstances. In the U.S. derivatives markets, for example, it is accepted that a director of a futures exchange may vote on significant self-regulatory issues, even when facing a direct conflict of interest in doing so, as long as the director does not act in "bad faith."[106]

Proposition 6: No single factor should determine how best to allocate regulatory powers.

Proposition 7: The choice of what allocation of regulatory powers should be adopted can only be made by comparing the relative merits of the available options.

There has been a gradual decline of self-regulation in many jurisdictions and over a long period, in favor of greater direct government oversight and statutory regulatory intervention.[107] There are many reasons for this including: lapses of fiduciary duty on the part of exchange and industry SROs, leading to market and customer abuses and scandals; the perceived self-interest of exchange SROs in maximizing shareholder returns and of industry SROs in maximizing benefits to the industry, both at the expense of the public interest; anticompetitive conduct by SROs; the centralization of statutory regulation into a single regulator in many jurisdictions; the difficulty of extending the concept of self-regulation internationally; and the need for greater international regulatory cooperation, which may be easier for statutory regulators than for other types of institutions.

Some of these problems are not new. In 1973, for example, a US Senate committee examining self-regulation in the securities markets explained:

> The inherent limitations in allowing an industry to regulate itself are well known: the natural lack of enthusiasm for regulation on the part of the group to be regulated, the temptation to use a facade of industry regulation as a shield to ward off more meaningful regulation, the tendency for businessmen to use collective action to advance their interests through the imposition of purely anti-competitive restraints as opposed to those justified by regulatory needs, and a resistance to changes in the regulatory pattern because of vested economic interests in its preservation.[108]

Probably the most important factor seen as reducing the attractiveness of self-regulation is the perceived adverse effect that the conflicts of interest endemic to self-regulation have on the delivery of the public interest. Such a perception is not, however, always appropriate. As Oliver (2005), a previous president of the IDA, argues:

> In the tension between independence and expertise, independence is increasingly the winner. It shouldn't always be. But that depends, of course, on the depth of the conflict and how it has been managed historically, that is whether the track record demonstrates integrity or regulatory capture.

For all its weaknesses, however, self-regulation retains several comparative advantages over alternative models of allocating regulatory responsibility: it can save the government money; it can be more flexible, responsive, and have a wider reach, extending beyond the scope of the law; it may be better placed to bring industry expertise, knowledge, and experience into the regulatory process; statutory regulation may face its own conflicts of interest, inhibiting the delivery of the public interest, and may also prove inefficient and impractical. Given these various advantages, it is concluded here that there are likely to be contexts where self-regulation may still be the optimal regulatory solution.[109]

> **Proposition 8:** Although there has been a gradual decline of self-regulation in many jurisdictions over a long period, it may still be an optimal solution in particular contexts.

CHAPTER TEN

How Should Market Infrastructure Institution Governance Be Regulated?

THE GOVERNANCE OF market infrastructure institutions is now seen as a fundamental factor determining whether such organizations deliver the public interest, and as a result regulatory interest and intervention in their governance has been growing.[1] This chapter explores what regulatory intervention in the governance of market infrastructure institutions, if any, is optimal. Attention is focused on how such intervention can enhance the realization of the three core objectives of securities markets regulation identified by IOSCO, namely the protection of investors, ensuring that markets are fair, efficient, and transparent, and the reduction of systemic risk.

The chapter is divided into five sections. In the first, some preliminary comments are presented. In the next three sections, the manner in which regulatory intervention in the governance of market infrastructure institutions may promote each of the IOSCO core objectives in turn is examined. The last section of the chapter seeks to encapsulate these discussions and also to present in a simple and accessible manner key lessons about how best to regulate the governance of market infrastructure institutions. In order to do so, 16 general propositions are articulated. Most of the propositions summarize the analysis presented in the first sections of the chapter; for the few that incorporate new ideas, a justification for their inclusion is presented.

PRELIMINARY COMMENTS

At a conceptual level, there is no need in most jurisdictions for any special regulatory intervention in the governance of market infrastructure institutions in order for regulators to have substantial power over such institutions. Most regulators have the authority to approve, or disapprove, all decisions made and rules promulgated by market infrastructure institutions in their jurisdiction, and many regulators also have the right to initiate rule changes at such institutions. In theory, therefore, most regulators could force all market infrastructure institutions under their jurisdiction to follow whatever strategies the regulators deemed appropriate for the furtherance of the public interest.

There are, however, a range of reasons why the ability of a regulator to ensure that a market infrastructure institution successfully delivers the public interest by intervening in specific decisions of the institution may be limited.[2] First, a regulator may not have sufficient information to decide what policy a market infrastructure institution should follow in order to deliver the public good. Second, even if a regulator does have sufficient information, it may not have the appropriate expertise or experience to know what is the correct policy for a market infrastructure institution to follow in order to best realize the public interest. Third, a regulator may not have the resources to monitor and control all market infrastructure institutions within its jurisdiction. Fourth, despite any general powers a regulator may have concerning the operations, decisions, and rules of market infrastructure institutions, there may be legal limitations on the extent to which the regulator is allowed to intervene in such institutions' specific decisions. Fifth, whatever powers regulatory agencies may have over market infrastructure institutions, they are normally constrained from imposing measures on such institutions that would jeopardize the continuous operation of the markets for which these institutions provide key services. Sixth, if a regulator takes direct responsibility for the decisions taken by a market infrastructure institution, it is likely to be required to assume any liability that may arise as a result of such decisions, whether by force of law or as a result of political pressure, and this in turn is likely to weaken market discipline and exacerbate moral hazard problems. Finally, for market infrastructure institutions that operate across multiple jurisdictions, it may be difficult for all the relevant regulatory authorities to coordinate their actions, and their powers of enforcement over such institutions may also be limited.

Given these difficulties, a universal way in which jurisdictions and regulators seek to ensure that market infrastructure institutions deliver the public interest is to try to create an environment in which such institutions have a private incentive to do so. This chapter analyzes how regulatory intervention in the governance of market infrastructure institutions may enhance their incentives to deliver the public interest. The key areas of regulatory intervention examined are those affecting the ownership, mandate, board structure, management, and some other corporate governance processes of market infrastructure institutions. This is only a limited subset of the entire supervisory apparatus that is employed to regulate market infrastructure institutions. Direct regulatory intervention into specific operational decisions or rules of market infrastructure institutions is ignored, as are a range of other broad areas of regulation, including competition policy.

The reason for focusing attention on how regulatory intervention in the governance of market infrastructure institutions can assist the realization of the three core IOSCO objectives is that these are, as of mid-2010, globally accepted as being the appropriate standards jurisdictions should promote. There is, however, a wide diversity among jurisdictions over the regulatory objectives they actually follow in practice. Differences in the objectives that regulators choose to follow across jurisdictions are likely to mean that the optimal form of regulatory intervention in the governance of market infrastructure institutions also differs across jurisdictions.

Sometimes the distinction between the core IOSCO objectives is blurred. A pivotal instance of this concerns the difficulty of distinguishing between efficiency and investor protection in some circumstances. This blurring of the efficiency and investor protection objectives has two key implications for the analysis here. From a definitional viewpoint, it makes categorizing the different forms of regulatory intervention by the objectives they deliver difficult, and the allocation of the topics analyzed here into the different sections of the chapter is therefore somewhat arbitrary in places.

More substantively, the blurring of the two objectives of efficiency and investor protection also means that the commercial activities of a market infrastructure institution cannot always be easily distinguished from its regulatory activities. Some market infrastructure institutions, and particularly exchanges, do provide self-regulatory services as well as trading, clearing, and settlement services, where self-regulatory services in this context means more than simply enforcing their rules of operations. An example of such a regulatory service is the regulation of broker-dealer conduct. However, not all market infrastructure institutions, and indeed not all exchanges, do provide such regulatory services, despite the fact that in some jurisdictions all exchanges are defined in the law as being SROs.[3] It is argued here that it is useful to distinguish between the provision of trading, clearing, and settlement services, on the one hand, and the provision of regulatory services, on the other. Different types of regulatory intervention may be appropriate in the governance of market infrastructure institutions that are also SROs and those that are not.

A central element of all regulation is its scope. If it is believed that regulatory intervention in the governance of market infrastructure institutions is necessary, it is then critical to specify which institutions should be subject to such regulation. This is particularly important where different forms of regulatory intervention may be tailored to promote the different IOSCO core objectives. All the IOSCO objectives are relevant to all the types of market infrastructure institutions examined here: it is critical that exchanges, CCPs, and CSDs all protect investors, are efficient, fair, and transparent, and reduce systemic risk. Nevertheless, some of the IOSCO objectives have a special relevance for particular types of institutions, and this informs the discussion here in two specific ways. First, the goal of investor protection is taken to be particularly critical in the context of exchanges, and any self-regulatory activity they undertake. Second, the goal of reducing systemic risk is thought especially important for CCPs.

It is hard both to define and to measure the realization of, each of the IOSCO objectives, except possibly that of efficiency. Self-evidently, there is no single yardstick to assess the second IOSCO objective, which is composed of three different elements—fairness, efficiency, and transparency. As a result of these and other difficulties, there has been little analysis of what types of regulatory intervention in market infrastructure institutions' governance best help deliver the IOSCO objectives. Any such analysis, including the one undertaken here, is therefore necessarily more a matter of judgment than of formally balancing the costs and benefits of the available regulatory options.

INVESTOR PROTECTION

The central problem that market infrastructure institutions, and particularly exchanges, face in seeking to promote the first IOSCO core objective, namely investor protection, is that doing so may conflict with their own interests, or those of their owners or other controlling participants. This is particularly important when an exchange is also an SRO—for example, if it supervises the conduct of its members with regards their clients, or if it supervises the listing process and listed companies. Attention in this section is thus focused, though not exclusively, on exchange SROs.

Many mechanisms have been employed to try to ensure that exchange SROs protect investors, given the presence of conflicts of interest between their private interests and public duties.[4] These include the following:

1. Enhanced external regulatory oversight;
2. The reinforcement of exchanges' public interest mandates;
3. Specific conflict management processes tailored to the needs of the various regulatory functions performed by exchanges;
4. The establishment of internal controls and processes at exchanges to identify and manage conflicts of interest;
5. The disclosure of conflicts of interest at exchanges, and of how exchanges address these conflicts, such as via an annual regulatory report;

6. Corporate governance requirements, including appointing "independent," public, stakeholder, or other types of directors to their boards, and requiring fair representation;
7. Restrictions on exchanges' ownership;
8. The management of exchanges' self-listing by the supervising regulator;
9. Making the disciplinary decisions of an exchange be subject to due process, with appropriate appeals procedures[5;]
10. Ensuring the rulemaking process of an exchange is transparent, with public consultation, solicitation of comments, and justification of any decisions made;
11. Separating the regulatory functions and finances from the commercial activities and finances at exchanges;
12. The transfer of specified regulatory functions from exchanges to a statutory regulator or other independent body.

While all the above regulatory responses may be considered intervention in the governance of an institution, in that they all seek to influence how power is exercised at the institution, attention here is focused on three areas: the appointment of board directors and senior management, mandate and ownership restrictions, and some additional corporate governance measures. These three areas are chosen for two reasons: they are among the most controversial areas of regulatory intervention, and while they are important in managing conflicts of interest at an SRO, they have important, and sometimes adverse, effects on the management of market infrastructure institutions.

Directors and Management

Three types of regulatory intervention regarding the boards and management of market infrastructure institutions have been thought particularly important in enhancing investor protection. The first reflects a central concern of all regulators to ensure the quality of the board directors, and sometimes also of the management, appointed or elected to control market infrastructure institutions. In order to effect this, almost all regulators apply a "fit and proper" test to check that board directors, and sometimes also senior officers, have the levels of skill, experience, and integrity believed necessary to govern and manage a licensed market infrastructure institution with public interest responsibilities. The purpose of such a test is not to substitute the choice of the regulator for that of the shareholders, nominating committee, or other bodies that appoint board directors or senior management. These "fit and proper" tests are uncontroversial, in the sense that they are widely accepted. They are also, however, untested in the sense that there is little evidence to support the notion that without them, directors appointed to the boards of market infrastructure institutions would not have sufficient levels of skill, experience, and integrity.

A second form of regulatory intervention in the governance of market infrastructure institutions that is widely used to promote investor protection is to require such institutions to appoint specific types of directors to their boards. These may include "independent" directors, "public" directors, or directors appointed by government or a regulator. Despite the differences in nature between these classes of directors, the fundamental reason for mandating the appointment of all of them is the same: it is believed that they all may have a greater incentive to promote investor protection than industry representatives or directors seeking to maximize the profits of a market infrastructure institution. The appointment of such specific types of directors is viewed as particularly important if the institution is an SRO, as it is believed critical to ensure that regulated firms do not have an excessive degree of control over an organization that is responsible for adopting the rules and setting the policies that regulate them. In order to temper the conflicts of interests that are an inescapable consequence of self-regulation, the appointment of independent directors may, as Martin (1971, 7) explains regarding "public representation" on the NYSE board, "answer the prevalent criticism that member firms ... cannot be expected to discipline themselves."

The nature of different classes of directors, and the implications of appointing them, may differ. The appointment of *independent directors* to the board of a market infrastructure institution SRO is undertaken typically to ensure that the board is not conflicted by pursuing both private and public interests simultaneously. In order to effect this, such directors need to be independent both of the market infrastructure institution on whose board they sit, and of other relevant parties, including participants using the facilities of the market infrastructure institution, and issuers listed or traded on the exchange.[6] Given this, it is not unusual that in many jurisdictions there are few people who are both knowledgeable about the securities market and also independent, as so defined.

Independent directors are also placed on the boards of market infrastructure institutions for reasons other than simply to promote investor protection. They are often appointed to enhance the institution's incentives to promote all the core IOSCO objectives, rather than solely investor protection. For market infrastructure institutions that are public listed companies, the main perceived role of independent directors is to act as an internal control mechanism to monitor management and ensure that it acts in the best interests of shareholders. Self-evidently these different roles may conflict.[7]

The requirement to appoint independent directors to the boards of market infrastructure institutions has not always been applied with the same intensity to clearing and settlement institutions as it has to exchanges.[8] While the promotion of investor protection is a key concern of both CCPs and CSDs, it is believed to be best effected by ensuring the sound operation of such institutions. They are normally not confronted with the same direct conflicts of interest that exchange SROs face, and therefore have less need for independent directors to mitigate such conflicts.

The appointment of *public* directors is only sanctioned in some jurisdictions. As IOSCO's Emerging Markets Committee (2005, 22) notes, the concept of a public director is often more stringent than that of an independent director. Three different ways of defining a public director are typically employed. In particular, a public director may be defined as: (1) a director appointed by a public institution, typically a government or a regulator; (2) a director who satisfies certain personal criteria, typically being both independent of particular, and sometimes all, relevant market constituencies, and sometimes with a proven record of serving the public interest, for example by having had senior public service or regulatory employment; and (3) a director who has certain specific legal obligations to promote the public interest. These three definitions may be applied concurrently or implemented separately.

The most interventionist regulatory approach regarding the boards of market infrastructure institutions is for their directors or senior management to be directly *appointed by a government or a regulator*.[9] Self-evidently this strategy allows the government or regulator a direct voice in how such institutions are governed. It may also, however, lead to a range of problems. The approach may expose a market infrastructure institution to political interference in its governance and operations. In addition, it is likely to give rise to a conflict of interest between a regulator's participation in the market infrastructure institution's governance and the regulator's oversight functions, which require the regulator to make an independent assessment of the institution's governance and performance. Furthermore, as discussed by Allen, Christodoulou, and Millard (2006, 20) in the context of CCPs,

> It can create moral hazard by providing a false comfort. It also risks the overseer/regulators losing their advantage of objectivity if they become closely associated with any successes and failures of the infrastructure. Finally, it leaves open the potential for conflicts of interest between the board member's responsibility to promote the good of the company and any responsibility he might have to the overseer.

Indeed a central problem with appointing directors onto the board of a market infrastructure institution specifically in order to ensure investor protection, and more generally to uphold any of the IOSCO core objectives, is that the legal duties of such directors are normally no different from those of other directors. All directors are typically obliged to act in the best interests of the institution on whose board they sit, in accordance with relevant corporate and securities law, with due weight given to promoting the public interest. All directors also face the same sanctions if they do not act in this manner. It is certainly likely that both the nature of an organization or body that appoints a director to the board of a market infrastructure institution, and the personal and professional characteristics, expertise, affiliations, and experience of a director, are important influences on how the director behaves regarding the promotion of the public interest at the institution. However, the most important determinant of how board directors behave is likely to be the legal obligations and liability to which they are subject. Given that all directors normally have the same legal obligations, the probability that any of the special types of directors examined here will promote investor protection, and indeed more broadly the public interest, in a manner different from the directors appointed in the normal manner, for example via a shareholder vote or nominations process, may therefore not be high.[10]

It is conceivable that an environment could be structured in which different types of directors on the board of market infrastructure institutions could be given different legal obligations—with some being required to focus on the delivery of the public interest, including investor protection. This approach would, however, give rise to two significant problems. First, different bodies of jurisprudence would be required to assess the performance of the different classes of directors. Second, the board of an institution with different classes of directors would by construction not have the single goal of acting in the best interests of the institution, subject to appropriate corporate and securities law constraints. Conflict would thus be embedded into the board, with the likely consequences that it would be difficult for the board to act in a unified manner, and that management might be able to exploit such conflict to its own advantage.

A third type of regulatory intervention in the boards of market infrastructure institutions that is sometimes used to promote investor protection is to require that different types of market constituencies be given fair representation on such institutions' boards. This approach is commented on below.

Mandate and Ownership

There is no evidence that any one of the main governance models a market infrastructure institution can adopt best delivers investor protection. Conflicts of interest between the promotion of investor protection and a market infrastructure's private interests, or those of its owners or controllers, may arise in all the cooperative, nonprofit, for-profit, public, and hybrid models. There are, however, two types of regulatory intervention in the mandate of market infrastructure institutions that are sometimes thought to enhance investor protection. The first is simply to specify clearly what public interest obligations such institutions have, including investor protection. Greater clarity in these obligations may make it more difficult for market infrastructure institutions to pursue their own goals, or those of their owners or controllers, at the expense of the public interest. Given the broad nature of the IOSCO objectives, however, it is impossible to define them too tightly. There will thus always be room for interpretation as to how they should be implemented, and whether what is in a market infrastructure institution's private interest is in the public interest or not.

The second form of regulatory intervention in the mandate of a market infrastructure institution that may enhance investor protection is to require that if there is a conflict between the public interest and the private interests of such an institution, the public interest, including that of investor protection, should prevail.[11] While such an approach may constrain self-interested actions by a market infrastructure institution in some circumstances, its effects in changing the incentives faced by such institutions may also be limited, given that they often argue that their private interests are congruent with those of the public interest.

Three types of regulatory controls over the ownership of market infrastructure institutions are sometimes employed to enhance investor protection. The first is to require regulatory notification and public disclosure when the percentage of a market infrastructure institution owned by a single party exceeds certain prespecified thresholds. The second is to require major or controlling shareholders to satisfy a "fit and proper" test in order to ensure that such agents are unlikely to act against the public interest. The third is to impose maximum limits on the percentage any single party may own of a market infrastructure institution.[12] All these forms of regulation essentially seek to prevent a single firm, and sometimes more broadly a single market constituency, from exercising significant and undue influence over a market institution that is also an SRO.

Additional Corporate Governance Measures

There are a range of additional corporate governance measures that an exchange SRO may be required to adopt to help respond to conflicts of interest. These include the following:

1. The creation of a board-level Regulatory Oversight Committee (ROC), the functions of which are to ensure the independence and effectiveness of the exchange's regulatory and surveillance programs, and to assess its regulatory performance. The composition

of a ROC, and in particular the extent to which it is composed of exchange executives or independent directors, may itself affect whether conflicts of interest arise.

2. The appointment of a chief regulatory officer who reports directly to a ROC.[13]

3. The establishment of a "conflicts committee" to address conflicts between an exchange SRO and the listed companies that it regulates. The prime mandate of such a committee is typically to review the exchange's dealings with any of its listed companies that the exchange either competes with, or has business dealings with, in order to ensure that the exchange's listing rules are administered in an unbiased manner.

4. The creation of a code of conduct for directors to ensure that directors facing a conflict on an issue respond appropriately, for example either by recusing themselves from the discussion and decision on the matter, or disclosing appropriately the conflict while still participating in the decision.

Two points about these and other corporate governance measures aimed at responding to conflicts between an exchange SRO's private interests and its public obligations are important to note. First, while they may be required by regulation, they may also be implemented by an exchange SRO without any regulatory requirement to do so. Second, the merits of adopting many of these measures depend in large part upon the view taken as to what is the best solution to the potential presence of conflicts of interest. There are two basic approaches. The first is to seek to eliminate such conflicts by ensuring that whoever has to take a regulatory decision is not conflicted. The second approach is to accept the existence of conflicts of interest, but to manage them by requiring appropriate disclosure by relevant conflicted parties, by obliging such parties to justify any decisions they make, and by *ex post* regulatory or judicial monitoring of their decisions. The relative merits of these two approaches are dependent on the costs and benefits of applying each approach to the specific contexts under consideration.

EFFICIENCY, FAIRNESS, AND TRANSPARENCY

IOSCO's second core objective is composed of three distinct elements: efficiency, fairness, and transparency. The way in which regulatory intervention in the governance of market infrastructure institutions may promote each of them is examined in turn.

Efficiency

Even though efficiency is a core IOSCO objective, regulators themselves may not have the best incentive to determine how best to realize this goal. They may focus more on the protection of investors and the reduction of systemic risk than on efficiency, as the first two objectives are likely to be compromised by a financial scandal or crisis, and the prevention of such scandals or crises is normally a top priority of most regulators. Furthermore, unlike the private sector, regulators do not directly incur the costs of inefficiency.

If the provision of trading, clearing, or settlement services is competitive, there is normally no need for regulatory intervention in the governance of market infrastructure institutions to promote efficiency. If any particular provider of trading, clearing, or settlement services is inefficient, users will simply move to an alternative provider. Furthermore, even if a provider of trading, clearing, or settlement services has market power, the private sector may have both the best incentive and means to stop the anticompetitive exploitation of such market power via an appropriate governance structure.

There are, however, situations where the private sector cannot stop dominant market infrastructure institutions from acting anticompetitively. Intervention in the governance of such institutions is only a small part of the full regulatory approach that is typically employed to address this problem. Nevertheless, two types of regulatory intervention in the governance of market infrastructure institutions are noteworthy in this context. One is a requirement that a national exchange demutualize.[14] Such a decision is typically taken to promote the efficiency of the exchange in the face of an exchange membership that is reluctant to sanction both automated trading and remote access by foreign trading participants out of fear that both would jeopardize their privileged status. Although the experience of such demutualizations has widely been seen as positive both for the exchanges that were demutualized and for the markets they run, many other factors contributed to these developmental successes. No similar policy of demutualization has been imposed on national CCPs or CSDs where they have not been owned by a stock exchange.

The second form of regulatory intervention in the governance of market infrastructure institutions aimed at enhancing efficiency is to require the appointment of user or stakeholder directors to the boards of such institutions. It is hoped that giving a voice to these types of market participants in the governance of a market infrastructure institution might limit the extent to which the institution is able to exploit them anticompetitively.

All forms of regulatory intervention have direct costs that themselves reduce efficiency. Furthermore, and often more significantly, regulatory intervention in the governance of market infrastructure institutions may adversely affect private sector incentives to promote efficiency. Two instances of this are particularly important. The first concerns ownership restrictions. The issue of whether it is in the national interest to permit foreign ownership of key market infrastructure institutions is frequently a matter of national economic and political debate. Historically, many jurisdictions have seen their national exchange as being central both to the development of their national financial markets and their country's economic strategy.[15] This remains true in many jurisdictions, but not in all, as illustrated by Ladekarl's (2000, 77) description of the Danish context:

> Up until 1996, there was this very strong feeling in political circles ... that we needed a local stock exchange because a country has to have a local stock exchange. So, it was sort of a part of being a country. We've done away with that. The politicians are not very worried about the stock exchange moving, and it actually allows for regional integration, which brings many efficiency benefits.

Ownership caps and restrictions on voting rights may have various costs and disadvantages, especially for listed exchanges. Low caps limit the value and liquidity of a listed exchange's shares because the cap reduces demand for the shares. They may also reduce the premium a buyer might pay for a significant stake or control. Some exchanges believe ownership limits also set a negative example for their markets because exchanges generally favor open markets, including markets for corporate control. Ownership limits may also reduce the accountability of the board and management to shareholders because there is less threat of a takeover if the company's performance is unsatisfactory.

A second way in which regulatory intervention in the governance of market infrastructure institutions may adversely affect efficiency concerns the appointment of particular directors mandated specifically to promote the core IOSCO objectives other than efficiency, particularly investor protection, fairness, and the reduction of systemic risk. Such directors are unlikely to have a strong incentive to promote efficiency, and may thus place insufficient weight on its delivery.

Fairness

Although there are many possible interpretations of what the notion of fairness implies in the context of how a market infrastructure institution should be governed, probably the most commonly held view is that no single organization or market constituency should be able to control such an institution primarily for its own interests. This is particularly important if the market infrastructure institution is an SRO, as it is widely believed vital to prevent one market segment from dominating the decisions an SRO takes.

Three types of regulatory intervention in a market infrastructure institution's governance structure are often employed to enhance fairness. The first is to place a cap on the percentage of shares any single market participant can own of such an institution. The second is to appoint independent or public directors to its board in order to ensure it is responsive to all stakeholders, and not simply those market constituencies the other directors represent. The third is to require the board of a market infrastructure institution to have a fair representation of different types of market participants, including typically all the classes of members or users of the institution, and sometimes also other key stakeholders.

There are many ways in which the fair representation requirement may be implemented. It is in the United States that the requirement has been established for the longest period, and there, a securities exchange is obliged to "assure a fair representation of its members in the selection of its directors and administration of its affairs and provide that one or more directors shall be representative of issuers and investors and not be associated with a member of the exchange, broker, or dealer."[16] CCPs and CSDs have a similar obligation.[17] The SEC is responsible for deciding whether the fair representation requirement has been satisfactorily implemented in any particular context, and it has accepted a wide range of governance mechanisms as satisfying the requirement. These include, among others, the following:[18]

1. Direct participation of participants in the election of directors;
2. Solicitation of director nominations from all participants;
3. Selection of candidates for election to the board of directors by a nominating committee composed of, and selected by, participants;
4. Enabling participants to select a slate of nominees, and then requiring shareholders to select from those nominees;
5. Affording participants a reasonable opportunity to acquire voting stock of the institution, directly or indirectly, in reasonable proportion to their use of the institution;
6. Allowing participants to select a small minority of the directors, together with the representation of participants on key committees.

Two important general points about implementing the goal of fairness in the context of the governance of market infrastructure institutions are important to note. The existence of competition between market infrastructure institutions should mean that any organization or market constituency that believes itself to be unfairly disadvantaged by the operation or governance of any particular market infrastructure institution can simply seek another provider of relevant services. The ability to access alternative providers of trading, clearing, or settlement services does not, however, mean that market participants or indeed regulators are always happy to sanction competition for the provision of regulatory services, such as the prevention of fraud or manipulation. It is often believed that providers of regulatory services should be held to high and absolute standards that should not be determined by competition. The notions of fairness applicable to market infrastructure institutions that provide solely commercial services may therefore be different from those applicable to institutions that also provide regulatory services.

The second important point to note about the goal of fairness in the context of the governance of market infrastructure institutions is that a decision as to what is fair always requires a judgment about what is an appropriate allocation of resources or assets between different firms or market constituencies. In the context of the fair representation requirement, this means specifying which groups of market participants are to be represented on the board of a particular market infrastructure institution. Groups of market participants that are so represented may, however, use their board positions to protect themselves against economic competition. One example of this occurring is when new technology disintermediates a particular class of market participants who, by dint of history, are represented on a market infrastructure institution's board. They may seek to restrict access to the institution without continued intermediation through their facilities.

Transparency

Transparency is often seen both as an end in itself, and also as a means to achieve the other core IOSCO objectives. In order to assess the merits of transparency as a means, it is necessary to identify what information might be made public, and then analyze the costs and benefits of doing so. It is quite possible that the costs of publishing particular information may be assessed to be greater than the benefits of releasing it. In such circumstances, a conflict arises between the goal of transparency as an end, which always requires publishing more information, and the use of transparency as a means of achieving the other core objectives.

When a market infrastructure institution acts as an SRO, it is widely accepted that transparency plays a vital role in its delivery of investor protection, as well as some of the other IOSCO core objectives. At the most general level, and as Brandeis (1914, 92) explained: "Publicity is justly commended as a remedy for social and industrial diseases. Sunlight is said to be the best of disinfectants; electric light the most efficient policeman."

An analysis of the fundamental role that transparency should play in any legal, judicial, or indeed regulatory process is beyond the scope of the analysis here.[19] Nevertheless, in the context of securities market regulation it is noteworthy that transparency is vital to enhance investor confidence in, and the perceived legitimacy and fairness of, the regulatory process. There are many ways in which transparency can effect these results. For example, disclosure about disciplinary cases allows the public and industry to check whether members of an SRO are being treated fairly and equally. A public process for issuing proposed new regulations allows for comment and other input concerning such regulations. The publication of regulatory revenues and expenses contributes to the perception that the costs of regulation are being appropriately shared. The publication of regulatory conflicts and the manner in which they are addressed makes self-interested regulatory activity less likely. All these, and other, benefits of transparency at SROs have led to a body of regulations in many jurisdictions requiring appropriate levels of transparency at such institutions.

The costs and benefits of transparency in the context of providing trading, clearing, and settlement services are, however, quite different from those arising from transparency in the provision of self-regulatory functions. Two examples illustrate contexts where greater publication may not be beneficial. The first concerns the publication of prices and quotes at an exchange. The publication of this information is vital for enhancing investor protection, as it allows investors to compare the price of any trades undertaken on their behalf with comparable prices and quotes available at the same time. The merits of transparency for the delivery of efficiency, however, have been highly controversial. The growth of so-called dark pools, namely trading systems that publish only very limited information about the quotes submitted to them and about trades executed on them, attest to the growing belief that less transparency may in fact enhance efficiency in some contexts. A second example of how transparency is not always believed beneficial concerns the publication of information about board discussions and decisions at exchanges, CCPs, and CSDs. To do so may prejudice directors' willingness to speak frankly in board meetings, and may also hamper the ability of market infrastructure institutions to compete, given that their competitors may be able to see their key strategic decisions and respond accordingly.

Systemic Risk Reduction

The governance of market infrastructure institutions affects both their preferences towards incurring risks in their operations, and the way in which these risks are managed. Even though there is no consensus about how to measure or even define systemic risk, it is widely accepted that the failure of a market infrastructure institution can have significant and adverse systemic effects.[20] At a minimum, the closure of an exchange, a CCP, or a CSD may lead to a stop in trading, especially if the relevant institution operates a monopoly. This in turn will have the attendant socially harmful consequences of a lack of liquidity in the assets being traded and a lack of price discovery. The failure of a CCP may have particularly severe systemic effects, given the novation of contracts that transfers the obligation to settle all transactions to the CCP. In the event of a CCP's insolvency, trading firms are exposed to replacement cost risk of their trades, and may face liquidity risk due to the margin and collateral given to the CCP being frozen during the winding-up process. It may also lead to a subsequent contagion among associated financial institutions, and, at the extreme, a threat to the financial stability of an economy or even a wider region. Given CCPs' potential importance to systemic stability, attention is focused here on how regulatory intervention in their governance may best reduce systemic risk.

Two key aspects of governance are seen as critical in enhancing the adequacy of a CCP's prudential safeguards. The first concerns the incentives faced by those in control of a CCP. In particular, and as the Bank for International Settlements (1990, 3) recommends in the context of multilateral netting systems, it is widely accepted that both netting providers and market participants should have "the incentives and the capabilities to manage and contain each of the risks they bear."[21] The mutual model of governance for a CCP appears at first sight able to deliver this goal directly, as explained by Dale (1998, 35) in the context of examining clearinghouses (i.e. CCPs) in the derivatives markets:

> The clearing house is typically owned by its members who have the incentive and capability to monitor and control its risk procedures. The clearing house has a reciprocal incentive and capability to monitor and control risks incurred by its members. The members have some incentive to monitor each other based on mutualisation of losses through loss-sharing rules.

In contrast, the for-profit model may not provide a CCP's owners with the same incentive to monitor risks. As a for-profit CCP's owners will typically not be its customers, they will not bear the direct costs of a large-scale clearing failure.[22] Shareholders may therefore not have as strong an incentive to ensure the financial stability of such an institution compared with user-owners.

The governance model a CCP adopts may affect the extent to which it is innovative, which in turn may influence the manner in which its operations affect systemic risk. Different effects are possible. On the one hand, a for-profit firm may adopt a business strategy characterized by greater innovation, and greater associated commercial and operational risks, than cooperative, nonprofit, or other governance models.[23] On the other hand, such innovation can enhance a CCP's risk management process, for example by improving systems that accelerate information flow, by establishing an early warning system, or by implementing real-time risk management.

Whatever the perceived weaknesses of the for-profit model for a CCP in ensuring adequate protection against systemic risk, no evidence has been put forward to show that for-profit CCPs do in fact provide less protection against systemic risk than those with other governance structures. Indeed, there is a growing number of CCPs that are operated on a for-profit basis, primarily as part of integrated exchanges. Such institutions typically argue that they have a strong incentive to ensure the safety and soundness of their clearing function in order to differentiate themselves from their competitors.[24] They also stress that they place the highest priority on maintaining the financial integrity of their clearing operations.[25] In addition, as Hills et al. (1999, 130) note, there is another way of seeking to ensure that those at risk of loss if a CCP faces a default are able to monitor and control the CCP to assure that its risk mitigation procedures are sufficient, apart from a establishing mutual governance structure. It is to establish an appropriate incentive structure for management to make it accountable to those at risk of loss. Logically, there is no reason why a for-profit governance model may not be able to accommodate such an incentive package, although it may be difficult to enforce accountability on managers if they leave a CCP when losses occur.

The second aspect of a CCP's governance structure that is widely accepted as being fundamental to ensure that it does not take excessive risks is that its risk-management policies and procedures, and especially its policies for handling defaults and allocating the burden of losses from defaults, should be transparent to market participants.[26] As Dale (1998, 35) summarizes,

> The idea … is that good practice guidelines on operating procedures coupled with disclosure of prudential risks and financial safeguards will encourage market participants to choose the best regulated—or self-regulated—exchanges and clearing houses to conduct their business.[27]

Notwithstanding the widespread acceptance that the above two aspects of governance are critical in seeking to ensure that a CCP protects itself adequately against systemic risk from a public policy perspective, there are a range of reasons why CCPs may still not do so, even if they satisfy both requirements.[28] The first is that the reduction of systemic risk is precisely a systemic or public good. While a CCP has an incentive to take account of any costs that are likely to be incurred by its owners, it is unlikely to take into account the costs that would be incurred by all other market participants were it to fail. The pressure on a CCP to reduce the amount it spends on prudential safeguards may be particularly intense if it operates in a competitive environment: any savings it can make by reducing the amount it spends on risk mitigation will allow it to provide cheaper clearing services.

The difficulty for a CCP, and for those market participants that control such an institution, in taking account of the costs incurred by all market participants arising from the CCP's operations, rather than simply their own, may lead to other problems in addition to insufficient investment by the CCP in risk mitigation safeguards. Köppl and Monnet (2006) provide a theoretical model in which a user-owned CCP may choose to shut down trade in order to avoid the cost of a default that will be incurred by its members, even if overall there would be net gains for all users by allowing trading to continue. Under the same circumstances, Köppl and Monnet maintain, a for-profit CCP may still allow trade to continue, given that it would continue receiving revenues and that its users, rather than its owners, would bear the costs of the default. This theoretical possibility is, however, dismissed by LCH.Clearnet (2006a, 8) as not representing how CCPs operate in practice:

> Rather than "shut down trade," a CCP is likely to have other more appropriate powers at its disposal that it could employ to limit losses. In particular, it is likely to have powers ... to forcibly close out the positions of a defaulter through the creation of offsetting contracts without the need to interfere with the proper functioning of the rest of the market. Indeed, for a CCP to "shut down trade" would run counter to the raison d'être of a CCP which is to cap the potential costs that would be incurred by non-defaulting members.

A second reason why a CCP may provide a socially insufficient level of risk-mitigation is, as explained by Jenkinson in the context of a user-owned CCP, that its owners "may place insufficient value on systemic stability because material operational failures are low-probability events and difficult to anticipate. Their assessment horizon may also be shorter than the social optimum."[29] Jenkinson (2007) also notes a third factor that may limit a mutual CCP, but not a for-profit one, from taking sufficient steps to reduce systemic risk, namely that there may be coordination problems among the owners of the mutual CCP:

> Users of a particular infrastructure, many of whom may compete in underlying markets, need to coordinate their actions if they are to influ-

ence decisions on the future strategy of the infrastructure provider. Investment in the reduction of operational risk will be one such decision. Difficulties in organising effective bargaining among users may leave them unable to coordinate, particularly in the face of differences in their information, expectations or preferences. Potential welfare-increasing actions may, therefore, not be carried out.

In order to respond to the difficulties of ensuring that CCPs take adequate account of the public interest in monitoring and mitigating systemic risk, there is a growing tendency by regulators to seek to influence the governance of CCPs by appointments to their boards. One approach is to appoint regulatory representatives directly onto the board of a CCP. Another more common strategy is to appoint independent or public directors to act as "guardians" of the public interest of systemic risk reduction. Both these approaches are likely to give rise to the problems noted above with regulatory intervention regarding the appointment of directors to market infrastructure institutions' boards.

CONCLUDING DISCUSSION AND GENERAL PROPOSITIONS

This chapter explores the question of what regulatory intervention in the governance of market infrastructure institutions, if any, is optimal. In order to encapsulate the discussions and to present key lessons in a simple and accessible manner, 16 general propositions are articulated here. They address how best to regulate the governance of market infrastructure institutions. Most of the propositions summarize the analysis presented in the first sections of the chapter; for the few that incorporate new ideas, a justification for their inclusion is presented.

The propositions are not intended to be a comprehensive set of rules for deciding how regulators should intervene in the governance of market infrastructure institutions; nor are they intended to specify how any particular jurisdiction should regulate the governance of market infrastructure institutions; nor indeed is any single proposition intended to be definitive. Taken together, however, the propositions provide a useful and compact aid for choosing what regulatory intervention in the governance of market infrastructure institutions, if any, is optimal in any jurisdiction.

> **Proposition 1:** A four-stage analysis is required in order to answer how best to regulate the governance of a market infrastructure institution:
>
> 1. Identify the functions undertaken by the institution;
> 2. Specify the goals of regulation;

3. Evaluate whether the institution has an incentive to deliver the specified regulatory objectives for each of the functions it undertakes; and, if not,

4. Assess which, if any, types of regulatory intervention in the institution's governance will best further the specified regulatory objectives for each function the institution undertakes.

Many factors may complicate this analysis. A market infrastructure institution may provide any combination of the three core market services—trading, clearing, and settlement. The provision of each service has different risks, affects the delivery of the desired regulatory objectives in different ways, and may thus require different forms of regulatory intervention. Some market infrastructure institutions, primarily exchanges, may also undertake regulatory functions in addition to providing market services. Such SROs are likely to require particular forms of regulatory intervention.

> **Proposition 2:** If a market infrastructure institution is also an SRO, greater regulatory intervention in its governance is likely to be needed in response to the conflicts of interest it faces.

> **Proposition 3:** The choice of what regulatory measures to adopt to respond to conflicts of interest at an SRO depends on whether it is seen best to eliminate such conflicts or to manage them.

Regulators typically seek to deliver the three core IOSCO objectives. Some regulators, however, follow other goals, in addition to, or that replace, these core objectives. The most important of these is the promotion of what is believed to be in the national interest. The existence of multiple regulatory objectives is likely to lead to trade-offs in their simultaneous delivery.

> **Proposition 4:** Of all the IOSCO objectives, it is hardest for regulatory intervention in a market infrastructure institution's governance to promote efficiency.

There are two reasons for this. First, any regulatory intervention in the governance of a market infrastructure institution is likely to give rise to direct costs, and may also indirectly reduce the incentives that the institution has to promote efficiency. Second, regulators may sometimes face incentives to promote the other IOSCO objectives, and particularly investor protection and the reduction of systemic risk, at the expense of efficiency.

The main forms of regulation of a market infrastructure institution's governance are interventions in the institution's ownership, mandate, board structure, management, and other corporate governance processes.

Each of these different forms of regulatory intervention may give rise to different costs and benefits.

Proposition 5: A requirement for a market infrastructure institution to appoint independent directors, public directors, or accept directors appointed by a regulator, may further the IOSCO objectives in two main ways:

1. Such directors may promote investor protection, fairness, transparency, and systemic risk reduction, more than industry-appointed or profit-maximizing directors—although these latter types of directors may also promote the desired regulatory objectives appropriately.
2. Such directors may mitigate the conflicts of interests that are an inescapable consequence of self-regulation, again promoting both investor protection and fairness.

Proposition 6: The mandatory appointment of independent directors, public directors, or directors selected by a regulator, may, however, lead to several problems:

1. If they are required specifically to advance the IOSCO objectives, this is likely to conflict with the requirement that all directors act in the best interests of the institution on whose board they sit, subject to relevant corporate and securities law.
2. If they are required specifically to advance the IOSCO objectives, this is likely to conflict with the role typically placed on independent directors, namely to ensure management acts in the best interests of all shareholders.
3. Such directors may have insufficient incentive to promote efficiency.
4. In many jurisdictions there are few people who are both knowledgeable about the securities markets and also independent in an appropriate way.

Proposition 7: There is no evidence that any one of the main governance models a market infrastructure institution may adopt best delivers investor protection.

Proposition 8: There is no evidence that any one of the main governance models a market infrastructure institution, and particularly a CCP, may adopt best reduces systemic risk.

Proposition 9: Mandatory fair representation on the board of a market infrastructure institution may promote fairness, but may also entrench incumbent interests, reducing efficiency.

Proposition 10: While demutualization has been associated with enhanced efficiency at some market infrastructure institutions, there is no evidence that mandatory demutualization will enhance the efficiency of such institutions.

Proposition 11: Mandatory user or stakeholder representation on the board of a monopolistic market infrastructure institution may restrict it from acting anticompetitively, but may entrench incumbent interests, reducing efficiency.

Proposition 12: Mandatory ownership constraints may prevent a single firm from exercising undue influence over a market institution that is also an SRO, but may reduce efficiency.

Proposition 13: Mandatory transparency at an SRO plays a vital role in its delivery of investor protection, but may reduce efficiency.

Proposition 14: Transparency of a CCP's risk-management policies and procedures is likely to provide both it and its market participants an incentive to protect against systemic risk—but this transparency may be delivered by a CCP without a regulatory requirement to do so.

Some jurisdictions and regulators have recommended that market infrastructure institutions follow the same codes of conduct that have been promoted for the corporate sector in their country, and that are also often required of listed companies. In the UK, for example, the FSA has encouraged market infrastructure institutions to consider and apply as appropriate the principles set out in the UK's Combined Code on Corporate Governance for public companies, although the FSA does accept that this may not always be appropriate.[30] Given that the primary goal of these codes is to promote shareholder interests, however, there is no reason to expect that their imposition on market infrastructure institutions would enhance the delivery of the three core IOSCO objectives. As the Bond Market Association (Gross 2005, 9) argues, "SROs [and market infrastructure institutions] should be held to a governance standard that is tailored to reflect [their] … unique role, not a standard that is a cookie-cutter application of the listing standards to a new and different context."

Proposition 15. A requirement for a market infrastructure institution to follow a national code of corporate governance is unlikely to mean the institution delivers the core IOSCO regulatory objectives, whether or not it is an SRO.

Regulatory interest and intervention in the governance of market infrastructure institutions has grown to a high level for three main reasons:

the governance of a market infrastructure institution is seen as critical in determining whether the incentives it faces enhance the core IOSCO regulatory objectives; the private interests of a market infrastructure institution are often believed insufficient to deliver the public interest, and sometimes even thought directly opposed to it; and regulatory intervention in the governance of market infrastructure institutions is believed more beneficial than direct intervention in their specific decisions. There are, however, many reasons why regulation of market infrastructure institutions' governance may not achieve its intended effects.

> **Proposition 16:** Expectations about the extent to which regulatory intervention in market infrastructure institutions' governance will enhance the delivery of the IOSCO core objectives should not be too high.

Authorities

Canada Business Corporations Act (R.S. 1985, c. C-44)

Directive 90/387/EEC of June 28, 1990, on the establishment of the internal market for telecommunications services through the implementation of open network provision (OJ L 192, 24/07/1990, pp. 1–9) (EU)

Directive 96/92/EC of the European Parliament and of the Council of December 19, 1996, concerning common rules for the internal market in electricity (OJ L 27, 30/1/1997, pp. 20–29) (EU)

Directive 98/26/EC of the European Parliament and of the Council of May 19, 1998, on settlement finality in payment and securities settlement systems (OJ L 166, 11/06/1998, pp. 45–50) (EU)

Directive 2003/6/EC of the European Parliament and of the Council of January 28, 2003, on insider dealing and market manipulation (market abuse) (OJ L 96, 12/4/2003, pp. 16–25) (EU)

Directive 2003/71/EC of the European Parliament and of the Council of November 4, 2003, on the prospectus to be published when securities are offered to the public or admitted to trading and amending Directive 2001/34/EC (OJ L 345, 31/12/2003, pp. 64–89) (EU)

Directive 2004/39/EC of the European Parliament and of the Council of April 21, 2004, on markets in financial instruments amending Council Directives 85/611/EEC and 93/6/EEC and Directive 2000/12/EC of the European Parliament and of the Council and repealing Council Directive 93/22/EEC (OJ L 145, 30/4/2004, pp. 1–44) (EU)

Directive 2004/109/EC of the European Parliament and of the Council of December 15, 2004, on the harmonization of transparency requirements in relation to information about issuers whose securities are admitted to trading on a regulated market and amending Directive 2001/34/EC (OJ L 390, 31/12/2004, pp. 38–57) (EU)

Financial Services and Markets Act 2000 (Recognition Requirements for Investment Exchanges and Clearing Houses) Regulations 2001 (S.I.2001/995) (United Kingdom)

Financial Supervision Act of September 28, 2006 (Wet op het financieel toezicht) (Netherlands)

Freedom of Information Act of 1966 (P.L. 89-554, 80 Stat. 383) (United States)

Government in the Sunshine Act of 1976 (P.L. 94-409, 90 Stat. 1241) (United States)

Investment Exchanges and Clearing Houses Act 2006 (c.55) (United Kingdom)

Regulatory Flexibility Act of 1980 (P.L. 96-354, 94 Stat. 1164–70) (United States)

Securities and Futures Ordinance (Cap. 571), 2003 (Hong Kong)

Securities Exchange Act of 1934 (P.L. 73-291, 48 Stat. 881) (United States)

Cases and Decisions

Aspen Skiing Co. v. Aspen Highlands Skiing Corp., 472 U.S. 585 (1985)

Associated Press v. United States, 326 U.S. 1 (1945)

Business Roundtable v. SEC, 905 F.2d 406 (D.C. Cir. 1990)

EU Commission Decision 94/19/EC relating to a proceeding pursuant to art. 86 of the EC Treaty (IV/34.689-*Sea Containers v. Stena Sealink—Interim measures*) [1994] OJ L15/8

EU Commission Decision of 11 June 1992 [1992] 5 CMLR 255

Gordon v. New York Stock Exch., 422 U.S. 659 (1975)

IMS Health GmbH & Co OHG v. NDC Health GmbH & Co KG (C-418/01) [2004] ECR I-5039

Istituto Chemioterapico Italiano SpA v. Commission of the European Communities (Commercial Solvents) (6/73 & 7/73) [1974] ECR 223; [1974] 1 CMLR 309

MCI Communicators Corp v. American Tel. & Tel. Co, 708 F. 2d 1081 (7th Cir. 1983)

In re *New York Stock Exchange/Archipelago Merger Litigation* (N.Y. Sup. Ct. December 5, 2005) filed under index number 6016461/05 is a consolidation of two former actions: *William J. Higgins v. the New York Stock Exchange, Inc., et al.*, filed under index number 601646/05 and *William J. Caldwell, Jr. v. the New York Stock Exchange, Inc., et al.* filed under index number n106717/05. Consolidation was ordered on September 9, 2005

Oscar Bronner GmbH & Co KG v. Mediaprint Zeitungs- und Zeitschriftenverlag GmbH & Co KG (C-7/97) [1998] ECR I-7791

Otter Tail Power Co. v. United States, 410 U.S. 366 (1973)

People v. Grasso, Index No. 120, 2008 NY Slip Op. 5770 (N.Y. June 25, 2008)

People v. Grasso, Index No. 401620/04, NY Slip Op. 5970 (App. Div. 1st Dep't July 1, 2008)

Radio Telefis Eireann v. Commission of the European Communities (C-241/91 P) [1995] ECR I-743; Sub nom. *Independent Television Publications (ITP) v. Commission of the European Communities* (C-242/91 P) *("Magill")* [1995] ECR I-743

Sarabex, Eighth Report on Competition Policy, points 35–37; 1979-2 CMLR 262

Silver v. New York Stock Exchange, 373 U.S. 341 (1963)

Tiercé Ladbroke SA v. Commission, Case T-504/93 [1997] ECR II 923

United States v. Terminal RR Association, 224 U.S. 383 (1912)

United States v. Solomon, 528 F.2d 88, 90 (9th Cir. 1975)

Verizon Communications, Inc. v. Law Offices of Curtis V. Trinko 540 U.S. 398 (2004)

Volbroker (Deutsche Bank/UBS/Goldman Sachs/Citibank/JP Morgan/Natwest), Case 38.866, Commission Press Release IP(00)806, July 31, 2000; [2000] 5 CMLR 405

Notes

CHAPTER 1
DEFINITIONS

1. Payment systems are ignored here.

2. A detailed analysis of the nature and identification of exchanges is presented in Lee (1998).

3. *American Heritage Dictionary*; *Webster's Third New International Dictionary*, 1161, as noted in Frischmann (2005, 923–24); *Wikipedia*: "infrastructure" (visited February 12, 2007); and Jacobson and Tarr (1995, 3).

4. Alexander and Mayer (1997, 1); *Wikipedia*: "public utility" (visited February 12, 2007), and Gómez-Ibáñez (2003, 4).

5. *Black's Law Dictionary*, 784, as noted in Frischmann (2005); Levine (2007, 141); Congressional Budget Office (U.S.) (1983, 1), as reported in Moteff and Parfomak (2004, 2).

6. Chen (2004), and Waller and Frischmann (2007, 12–13).

7. Gómez-Ibáñez (2003, 4); and Jacobson and Tarr (1995, 3).

8. National Council on Public Works Improvement (1988, 33), as reported in Moteff and Parfomak (2004, 3).

9. Gómez-Ibáñez 2003, 4.

10. *Wikipedia*: "public utility" (visited February 12, 2007); Jacobson and Tarr (1995, 3); and Gómez-Ibáñez (2003).

11. Jacobson and Tarr (1995, 3), and Frischmann 2005, (923–24).

12. Jacobson and Tarr (1995, 3); National Council on Public Works Improvement (1988, 33), as reported in Moteff and Parfomak (2004, 3); Vaughan and Pollard (1984, 1–2), as reported in Moteff and Parfomak 2004, 2; and Levine (2007, 141).

13. In addition to the above references, see Estache and Goicoechea (2005) and Estache (2004).

14. Kauko (2005, 7); Reece (2001); Schmiedel and Schönenberger (2005, 5); and IOSCO, Technical Committee (2006b, 5).

15. See, for example, use of the term by the central bank of Sweden (Riksbank—http://www.riksbank.com/templates/Page.aspx?id=9401).

16. Financial Services Authority (2000, 5).

17. Reuters (2007).

18. CPSS and IOSCO (2001b, 1). In the EU, the Committee of European Securities Regulators and the European System of Central Banks (2009, 4) have put forward recommendations regarding clearing and settlement institutions with similar language.

19. CPSS and IOSCO (2004, iii).

20. Kazarian (2006).

21. http://www.ecb.int/paym/groups/cogesi/html/index.en.html. The term "infrastructure" has been used similarly elsewhere by the ECB—see http://www.ecb.int/paym/market/secmar/integr/html/index.en.html.

22. See, for example, European Parliamentary Financial Services Forum (2006); Steil (2005), Tessler (2006), and Moskow (2006).

23. http://ec.europa.eu/internal_market/financial-markets/index_en.htm.

24. Committee on Economic and Monetary Affairs, European Parliament 2005.

25. Waller and Frischmann (2006); Pitofsky, Patterson, and Hooks (2002); and *United States v. Terminal Railroad Assn.*, referred to by Justice Douglas in his concurring opinion on *Associated Press v. United States*, cited in Areeda and Kaplow (1999, 351).

26. *MCI Communications Corp. v. AT&T.*

27. *United States v. Terminal Railroad Assn.*

28. *Associated Press v. United States.*

29. *Otter Tail Power Co. v. United States.*

30. *MCI Communications Corp. v. AT&T.*

31. *Aspen Skiing Co. v. Aspen Highlands Skiing Corp.*

32. *Verizon Communications, Inc. v. Law Offices of Curtis V. Trinko*, for this and the next quote. For an analysis of the decision, see Geradin 2004.

33. Waller and Frischmann (2006, 9–12).

34. See, for example, Temple Lang (1994); Shin (undated); Turney (2005); and Brinker and Loest (2004).

35. EU Commission Decision 11 June 1992, and EU Commission Decision 94/19/EC.

36. http://ec.europa.eu/comm/competition/general_info/e_en.html#t69.

37. See, for example, Directive 90/387/EEC on the establishment of the internal market for telecommunication services through the implementation of open network provision, and Directive 96/92/EC concerning common rules for the internal market in electricity.

38. See *Sarabex*, *Volbroker*, and Georges and Senkovic (undated, 34).

39. See, for example, *Tiercé Ladbroke SA v. Commission*; *Oscar Bronner GmbH & Co KG v. Mediaprint Zeitungs- und Zeitschriftenverlag GmbH & Co KG*; *Radio Telefis Eireann v. Commission of the European Communities*; *Istituto Chemioterapico Italiano SpA v. Commission of the European Communities (Commercial Solvents)*; *IMS Health GmbH & Co OHG v. NDC Health GmbH & Co KG*. For an analysis of most of these decisions, see the opinion of Mr. Advocate General Jacobs in *Bronner*, delivered on May 28, 1998, Case C-7/97, p. I-07791. See also Temple Lang 2005. Almost identical conditions are noted in Van Cayseele (2004, 17).

40. *Oscar Bronner GmbH & Co KG v. Mediaprint Zeitungs- und Zeitschriftenverlag GmbH & Co KG.*

41. *Radio Telefis Eireann v. Commission of the European Communities*; and *Istituto Chemioterapico Italiano SpA v Commission of the European Communities (Commercial Solvents)*.

42. *IMS Health GmbH & Co OHG v. NDC Health GmbH & Co KG*, judgment of April 29, 2004.

43. See generally Economides (1996) and Rochet and Tirole (2003).

44. Rochet and Tirole (2005) and references therein.

45. Shy (2001, 5).

46. Klemperer (1995) and references therein.

47. For a review of the economics of standards with reference to the clearing and settlement industry, see Milne (2005a).

48. When there was a high level of demand for railway services, such as in the railway boom of the nineteenth century, private firms were able to impose sufficiently high customer charges to cover the costs of investment in railway track. Nowadays, however, demand may be limited due to competition from other transport facilities, and it may be difficult to pay for the required fixed investments.

49. For an analysis of contestable markets, see Baumol, Panzer, and Willig 1982.

50. See, for example, Shy (2001, 7).

51. Other exchange, CCP, and CSD associations include the Africa and Middle East Depositories Association, the African Stock Exchanges Association, the Asian and Oceanian Stock Exchanges Federation), the Asia-Pacific Central Securities Depository Group, the Association of Futures Markets, the Association of Eurasian Central Securities Depositories, the Central and Eastern European CSD Association, the European Central Securities Depositories Association, the Federation of Euro-Asian Stock Exchanges, Federation of European Securities Exchanges), the Ibero-American Federation of Exchanges, the International Association of Exchanges of the Commonwealth of Independent States, the International Options Markets Association, and the South Asian Federation of Exchanges.

52. This draws on Lee (1998, chap.1).

53. Securities Exchange Act § 3(a)(1).

54. SEC Rule 3b-16, under Securities Exchange Act 1934.

55. This is a slightly modified version of the definition in CPSS and IOSCO 2004, 6.

56. For descriptions of the development of CCPs in derivatives markets, see Kroszner (1999) and Moser (1998).

57. See, for example, Bliss and Papathanassiou (2006) and McPartland (2005).

58. Certificated securities means in physical paper form. Such physical securities are now normally immobilized at a CSD. "Dematerialized" means that the securities exist only as electronic records.

59. See, for example, CPSS and IOSCO 2001b, p. 2, para. 1.7 and *Wikipedia*: "Central Securities Depository" (visited March 3, 2007).

60. And indeed Market Oriented New Systems for Terrifying Exchanges and Regulators—(MONSTERs).

61. See, for example, Domowitz and Lee (2001); and Lee (1998, chap. 12).

62. CPSS and IOSCO (2001b, 2); and Committee of European Securities Regulators and European System of Central Banks (2004, 3–7).

63. In the EU, "listing" refers only to admission to trading on a regulated market that is an Official List. In the UK, however, many rules and regulations still refer to "listing" as a synonym for admission to trading.

64. See, for example, Foucault and Parlour (2004) and Pagano et al. (2001).

65. Deutsche Börse, for example, estimated that for small and medium-sized firms, they could amount to 5–7% of the issue volume—see Deutsche Börse AG (2003, 30). The LSE provided a similar range with 4–8%—see London Stock Exchange (2002a, 24).

66. In UK, the LSE established the Alternative Investment Market, which significantly lowered minimum requirements, for example concerning free float, firm size, and track record of the firm, and also demanded substantially lower fees from issuers. Deutsche Börse closed its initially highly successful Neuer Markt segment after eight years of existence due to a series of accounting scandals. Swiss Exchange shut down a similar segment after three years.

67. In the case of stock options, the most important criteria for the selection process of appropriate underlying securities for listing are trading volume, volatility, and market capitalization. See Mayhew and Mihov (2004).

68. A comprehensive account of the different types of trading systems is presented in Harris (2003), and a theoretical survey on market microstructure is provided by Madhavan (2000).

69. Floor trading does still exist in some markets, however. For example, the regional German exchanges, including the Frankfurt Stock Exchange, operated by Deutsche Börse, still offer floor-trading services for their customers.

70. Domowitz and Steil (1999).

71. Venkataraman (2001).

72. There is usually a difference between the quoted and the effective spread on markets. Due to bargaining with market makers, investors can receive bid and ask prices that may lie within the boundaries of the quoted spread. See, for example, Lee and Ready (1991) and Venkataraman (2001).

73. Formally, they license the use of their data, rather than sell them.

74. This list is reproduced from Lee (1998), itself enlarging on the lists in Domowitz (1993), and IOSCO (1990).

75. For an overview, see Sutcliffe, Board, and Wells 2002.

76. Several studies confirm this, including Balsam, Bartov, and Marquardt (2002), El-Gazzar (1998), and Walther (1997).

77. See, for example, Depository Trust and Clearing Corporation (2006).

78. Confirmation is usually an automated process on an electronic exchange, and may thus be considered the last step in "trading" rather than the first step in "clearing," as the exchange typically has its record of the trade as the definitive record of what the terms are (in case of disagreement between the parties in an open outcry market). However, from the perspective of work organization, the confirmation is not done in the "front office." It is one of the postexecution tasks done in the mid- and back office, so it may be classified under clearing and settlement.

79. This is not a difficulty in the day-to-day conduct of business, however, as market participants are clear what such terms mean in any given context.

80. EU Commission (2005a, 2005b, and 2005c).

81. EU Commission (2005c, 9).

82. Committee on Economic and Monetary Affairs, European Parliament 2005.

83. This was also raised in CPSS and IOSCO (2004, 6).

84. EU Commission (2005c, 12).

85. Not all exchanges provide clearing and settlement services, but this is not reflected in the aggregated global data presented in the "Services" category.

86. Macey and O'Hara (2002).

87. This is particularly the case on US markets. According to the respective exchange websites, NASDAQ had approximately 20% in NYSE-listed stocks in terms of share volume, whereas NYSE-Archipelago possessed approximately 17% in NASDAQ-listed shares in December 2005.

88. Macey and O'Hara (2002).

CHAPTER 2
MARKET POWER

1. For an understanding of the type of analysis that would be required, see, for example, National Economic Research Associates (2001) and Office of Fair Trading (2004a and 2004b).

2. Office of Fair Trading (2004b, 2). The quotes below come from this page, and then pp. 9–10.

3. He sources Cournot (1838).

4. This text has been marginally amended, and italics have been added.

5. See, for example, Directorate General Internal Market and Services (2006a) and Schmiedel and Schönenberger (2005, 28–31). Attempts to measure revenue and cost elasticities for stock exchanges in Europe have been undertaken by Andersén (2005) and Voth (2005).

6. Leinonen (2003).

7. Blanc 2007 and Lee (1998, chap. 11).

8. See, for example, Henry (undated, 19).

9. See, for example, Deutsche Börse AG (2005b, § 1.40); Harris (2003, 528); Pagano (1989); and Schwartz and Pagano (2005, 7).

10. Directorate General Competition Services (2006, 17).

11. Financial Services and Markets Act 2000; regulations 2001.

12. One part of the conditions necessary for cross-border regulatory recognition is the ability for national regulators to share information with each other. Efforts to enhance such information sharing have been growing—see IOSCO, Technical Committee (2007).

13. For an assessment of the implications of this law, see Davies, Dufour, and Scott-Quinn (2006).

14. Tafara and Peterson (2007).

15. Lee (1998, chap. 6).

16. See, for example, Competition Commission (2005, 58).

17. Pagano and Padilla (2005, 32).

18. See, for example, Harris (2006).

19. Donohue 2006.

20. On the topic of this section, factors enhancing competition and reducing market power, see, for example, Competition Commission (2005, 53), and Lee (2007).

21. Foucault and Menkveld (2006).

22. As reportedly occurred when trading moved from LIFFE to DTB in Stuchfield (2005).

23. See, for example, Steil (2007).

24. Competition Commission (2005, 64).

25. Stuchfield (2005). A theoretical backing to this argument is provided in Baglioni (2006).

26. This idea was suggested by Larry Harris.

27. For an analysis of its anticipated effects, see Gray (2007).

28. Harris (2003, 526).

29. See, for example, Advent Software Inc. (2006).

30. Overviews of how competition and consolidation has developed in different regions are provided in Angel (1998), Schmiedel and Schönenberger (2005), Steil (1996), and Trombly (2007).

31. See Millman (2002).

32. For a list of the marketplaces that Market Regulation Services Inc. (RS) regulates in Canada, see http://www.rs.ca/en/about/markets.asp?printVersion=no&loc1=about&loc2=markets. For a discussion about facilitating competition in trading services in Australia, see Australian Securities and Investments Commission (2007) and Swan and Bowen (2009). Competition in Japan is noted in Thomson Reuters (2009).

33. Competition Commission (2005), appendix H, "History of Entry and Expansion in Europe from 1995."

34. Pirrong (2005). DTB is now called Eurex. The National Stock Exchange in India is not the same as the National Stock Exchange in the United States.

35. Shah and Thomas (2000).

36. Weber (2006).

37. As shown in figure 4, Petrella (2009).

38. A formal definition of the FFI is presented on the Fidessa Fragmentation website.

39. NASDAQ and ArcaVision both provide data on NASDAQ's market shares over time, and the figures they provide are not always equal, as shown in the first two columns of table 6 in Lee (2009).

40. Cruickshank (2002a).

41. Deutsche Börse AG (2006, 4).

42. Competition Commission (2005, 35).

43. Competition Commission (2005, 5).

44. US Department of Justice 2007.

45. Chicago Mercantile Exchange (2007) and Nystedt (2004).

46. Bartram and Fehle (2006).

47. Freedberg (2006). The first quote is marginally modified.

48. For statements to this effect from market participants, see Hardy (2006) and Competition Commission (2005, 40).

49. A CCP monitors only its members' creditworthiness, but not all market participants will be members of a CCP. So market participants will still need to monitor the creditworthiness of other market participants that are not members of the CCP.

50. Moser (1994).

51. Russo, Hart, and Schönenberger (2002, 29); and Moser (1994).

52. Kazarian (2006, 6).

53. Competition Commission (2005, 61–62).

54. The extensive variety of such rules in European posttrade processing are illustrated in London Economics (2005, table 1, pp. xii–xvi).

55. LCH.Clearnet (2006a, 6).

56. These two arguments are drawn from Russo, Hart, and Schönenberger (2002, 34).

57. EU Commission (2004).

58. Federation of European Securities Exchanges, European Association of Central Counterparty Clearing Houses, and European Central Securities Depositories Association 2006.

59. On potential competition see, for example, Directorate General Competition Services (2006, 8).

60. Citigroup (2004, 11–12).

61. The notion of interoperability has been discussed in Group of Thirty (2003, 27).

62. See the discussion in Committee on Payment and Settlement Systems (1997, 41–42).

63. BNP Paribas Securities Services (2004, 15); Euroclear (2006b, 5); Henry, (undated, 19); London Stock Exchange (2002b, 12–13); and Malkamäki and Topi (1999, 30).

64. See, for example, European Banking Federation (2006, 3); and Deutsche Börse AG (2006, 10).

65. Citigroup (2004, 11).

66. LCH.Clearnet (2006a, 4).

67. Citigroup (2006, 3).

68. SIS x-Clear (2006).

69. These arguments draw on Moskow (2006).

70. This occurs, for example, at CLS, the global foreign exchange market's payment versus payment system, which nets multilaterally without a CCP.

71. Historical information about Europe is presented in London Economics (2005, xi).

72. The author is unaware of any derivatives exchanges that do not have a CCP, or of any that have more than one.

73. See, for example, Associazione Bancaria Italiana (2006); Directorate General Competition Services (2006, 9); and Citigroup (2004, 11–12).

74. Deutsche Börse AG (2005a, 21).

75. McPartland (2002) and http://www.cme.com/clearing/clr/spec/mos.html.

76. virt-x (2003); virt-x, SIS x-clear, and LCH.Clearnet (2004); and Federation of European Securities Exchanges (2006).

77. virt-x (2005, 1).

78. LCH.Clearnet (2005c).

79. Chi-X 2007 and Trade News (2007).

80. EuroCCP (2007 and 2008b).

81. See, for example, Chi-X (2009); European Multilateral Clearing Facility (2009b); London Stock Exchange (2006 and 2008); LCH.Clearnet (2009c, 2009d, 2009e, 2009f, and 2009g); NASDAQ OMX et al. (2009); SIS x-Clear

(2009a and 2009b); SIX x-clear and European Multilateral Clearing Facility (2009); and SWX, SIS x-clear, and LCH.Clearnet (2006, 2).

82. See European Multilateral Clearing Facility (2009a); EuroCCP (2009b, LCH.Clearnet (2009b and 2009h); and SIS x-Clear (2008).

83. Trade News (2009a).

84. See, for example, Blair and Gerding (2009); Deutsche Börse AG (2009c); Glass (2009); and Squam Lake Working Group on Financial Regulation (2009).

85. US Treasury (2009).

86. EU Commission (2009a, 2009b, and 2009c).

87. See Chicago Mercantile Exchange (2008, 2009a, and 2009b); Deutsche Börse AG (2009a and 2009b); and LCH.Clearnet (2009a).

88. Depository Trust and Clearing Corporation (2009).

89. This summary is drawn from Considine (2006); Depository Trust Corporation (1998); European Securities Forum (2000, 3–4); and Russo, Hart, and Schönenberger (2002).

90. NASDAQ OMX (2008).

91. Trade News (2009b).

92. See, for example, Leinonen and Soramäki (2003, 32).

93. See, for example, Kauko (2002, 8); and Jenkinson (2007, 7).

94. See, for example, Citigroup (2004, 13); and CPSS and IOSCO (2001b, 20).

95. Oxford Economic Research Associates (2004, 72–73).

96. The extensive variety of such rules in European posttrade processing as of 2005 is documented in London Economics (2005, table 1, pp. xii–xvi).

97. Directorate General Competition Services (2006, 10).

98. Linciano, Siciliano, and Trovatore (2005, 15–16).

99. Citigroup (2004, 12).

100. Kauko (2002) and Citigroup (2004, 14).

101. A variation of this model is to allow the establishment of "shadow securities" in a domestic CSD that mirror the securities held in the foreign issuer CSD. See, for example, Niels, Barnes, and van Dijk (2003, 637).

102. Henry (undated, 19) estimates the cost of such a link at between $100,000 and $400,000.

103. See, respectively, European Central Securities Depositories Association (1997 and 2002).

104. Milne (2005b, 22).

105. Milne (2004).

106. Linciano, Siciliano, and Trovatore (2005, 13–14).

107. Citigroup (2003a, 11); Euroclear (2005a); and State Street (2006, 4). For a different viewpoint see Lo Guidice (2007). Internalization of settlement is not the same as internalization of trading.

108. Euroclear (2005a, 6).

109. Citigroup (2003a, 11).

110. Holthausen and Tapking (2004).

111. Citigroup (2004, 53–54); and Directorate General Internal Market and Services (2006b, 20).

112. Directive 98/26/EC (EU).

113. Citigroup (2004, 10).

114. Malkamäki and Topi (1999, figure 4, p. 24). The data are taken from Thomas Murray (1999).

115. The Group of Thirty (1989, Recommendation III) states, "Each country should have in place an effective and fully developed central securities depository, organized and managed to encourage the broadest possible direct and indirect industry participation."

116. See, for example, Holthausen and Tapking (2004, 5).

117. Citigroup (2004, 13 n. 13).

118. It has also occurred in India, where there are two CSDs for the same securities.

119. Euroclear (2005a, 3).

120. Committee of European Banking Supervisors (2009, para. 12).

121. See also Freiss and Greenaway (2006, 183); and Directorate General Competition Services (2006, 9).

122. See also Van Cayseele (2004, 14).

123. Euroclear (2006b, 7).

CHAPTER 3
THE ALLOCATION OF REGULATORY POWERS OVER SECURITIES MARKETS

1. The results reported here are reproduced with the permission of the WFE.

2. World Federation of Exchanges 2005. All quotes in this section come from the survey.

3. The respondents were the American Stock Exchange, Australian Stock Exchange, BME Spanish Exchanges, Bolsa de Comercio de Santiago, Bolsa de Valores de Lima, Bolsa de Valores do São Paulo, Bolsa Mexicana de Valores, Bourse de Luxembourg, Bourse de Montréal, Budapest Stock Exchange Ltd., Bursa Malaysia, Chicago Board Options Exchange, Colombo Stock Exchange, Copenhagen Stock Exchange, Deutsche Börse AG, Euronext, Hong Kong Exchanges and Clearing, Irish Stock Exchange, Istanbul Stock Exchange, JSE Securities Exchange–South Africa, Korea Stock Exchange, Ljubljana Stock Exchange, London Stock Exchange, Malta Stock Exchange, National Association of Securities Dealers, National Stock Exchange of India Ltd., New York Stock Exchange, Philippine Stock Exchange, Shanghai Stock Exchange, Shenzhen Stock Exchange, Singapore Exchange, Stock Exchange of Tehran, Stock Exchange of Thailand, SWX Swiss Exchange, Taiwan Stock Exchange Corp., Tokyo Stock Exchange, TSX Group, Warsaw Stock Exchange, and Wiener Börse AG.

4. The results reported here are reproduced with the permission of ICSA. ICSA's members are the Association of Capital Market Intermediary Institutions of Turkey, Australian Financial Markets Association, Bond Exchange of South Africa, French Association of Investment Firms, International Capital Market Association, Investment Dealers Association of Canada, Italian Association of Financial Intermediaries, Japan Securities Dealers Association, Korea Securities Dealers Association, London Investment Banking Association, National Association of Securities Dealers, Securities and Financial Markets Association, Swedish Securities Dealers Association, and Taiwan Securities Association.

5. International Council of Securities Associations, Secretariat (2006). The respondents were the ASX, Bond Exchange of South Africa, ICMA, IDA, Japan Securities Dealers Association, Korea Securities Dealers Association, NASD, Naional Futures Association, NYSE, and TSE. All quotes in this section come from the survey.

6. This section has benefited from comments by Jane Welch.

7. A copy of the questionnaire is reproduced in Gadinis and Jackson (2007).

8. Full details of results of the survey for each jurisdiction are provided in Gadinis and Jackson (2007).

9. "Marketplace oversight" refers to oversight of market institutions themselves (for example, who licenses the stock exchange, who reviews the suitability of their management, etc.) or, where no such institutions are established, who has oversight of relevant OTC markets.

10. In the public debate in the US surrounding the SEC's adoption of Regulation NMS, NYSE CEO John Thain (2004) warned the SEC that it should avoid turning the US market into an immense central limit-order book.

11. Autorité des Marchés Financiers, undated, 1.

12. http://www.bafin.de/cgi-bin/bafin.pl?verz=0101010000&sprache=1&filter=&ntick=0.

13. Japan is a good example.

14. This is the case in France.

15. International Monetary Fund (2004a, 39).

16. The "government commissioner" has a seat on all of the AMF's bodies (board, Enforcement Committee, and specialized committees) but is not entitled to vote. The representative may, however, request a second deliberation. http://www.amf-france.org/affiche_page.asp?urldoc=college.htm&lang=en&Id_Tab=0.

17. Cha (2000).

18. Australian Stock Exchange and Australian Securities and Investments Commission (2004). A history of the ASX is presented on its website—see http://www.asx.com.au/research/market_info/history/history_ASX.htm.

19. Australian Stock Exchange (2000) and Hockey (2000).

20. Swan and Bowen (2009).

21. In Australia, the Department of Treasury does, however, maintain the right to disallow certain ASX rules changes that refer to the regulation of the marketplace itself.

22. In this respect, guidance is different from no-action letters issued by the SEC. Moreover, guidance represents the official view of the agency, as opposed to no-action letters that do not represent the official view of the SEC.

23. In the Government-Led jurisdictions, however, agencies will also typically have to obtain the approval of a central government entity before their rules enter into force.

24. Mahoney (2001).

25. See http://www.finra.org/AboutFINRA/CorporateInformation/index.htm.

26. http://www.rs.ca/en/about/history.asp?printVersion=no&loc1=about, visited September (2006).

27. http://www.iiroc.ca/English/Pages/home.aspx, visited September (2009).

28. For example, U.S. administrative law restricts the President from dismissing an independent agency chairman merely on the grounds of disagreement with the chairman's policies.

29. UK Government, Investment Exchanges and Clearing Houses Act (2006).

30. HM Treasury (2001).

31. These may be summarized as maintaining market confidence in the financial system, promoting public understanding of the financial system, securing the appropriate degree of protection for consumers, and reducing financial crime by regulated persons or bodies.

32. See, for example, Schooner and Taylor (2003); Markham (2003); and Mistry (2007).

33. See Jackson (2007).

34. Tiner (2006).

35. Balls (2006a).

36. Balls (2006b).

37. McCarthy (2007).

38. Directive 2003/71/EC art. 21.

39. Directive 2004/109/EC.

40. Directive 2004/109/EC arts. 24(4)(f), 21(1) & 21(2).

41. Directive 2004/39/EC art. 40(1).

42. Directive 2004/39/EC art. 40(3).

43. Directive 2003/6/EC.

44. Directive 2003/6/EC art. 11.

45. Directive 2004/39/EC art. 14(1).

46. Directive 2004/39/EC art. 43(1) for this and next quote.

47. Directive 2004/39/EC art. 43.

48. Directive 2004/39/EC art. 36(2).

49. Directive 2004/39/EC arts. 37, 38, and 39.

50. Directive 2004/39/EC art. 38(3).

51. Directive 2004/39/EC arts. 50(2), 41(2) and 14(7).

CHAPTER 4
REGULATION AND GOVERNANCE OF MARKET INFRASTRUCTURE:
GLOBAL PERSPECTIVE

1. Use is also made of a limited amount of other data culled from technical assistance work done in various countries.

2. The Financial Sector Assessment Program is different from the EU's Financial Services Action Plan, although both have the same acronym.

3. G7 Finance Ministers (1998, point 17).

4. http://www.imf.org/external/np/fsap/fsap.asp.

5. World Bank, Independent Evaluation Group (2006, xiii).

6. See, for example, http://www.imf.org/external/np/fsap/fsap.asp; International Monetary Fund and World Bank Staff (2005, 4); and Marcus (2000).

7. International Monetary Fund, Independent Evaluation Office (2006, 15 n. 2). See also Hilbers (2001).

8. Detailed information about ROSCs is available at http://www.imf.org/external/np/rosc/rosc.asp.

9. International Monetary Fund and World Bank Staff (2005, 4).

10. International Monetary Fund and World Bank Staff (2003).

11. See respectively IOSCO (2003a) and CPSS and IOSCO (2001b).

12. The term "securities" includes derivatives in this context, and the term "investors" includes customers. IOSCO (2003a).

13. CPSS and IOSCO (2001b, 7).

14. CPSS and IOSCO (2001b, 2).

15. IOSCO (2003b, 3).

16. See, for example, World Bank, Independent Evaluation Group (2006, vii).

17. IOSCO (2003b).

18. World Bank, Independent Evaluation Group (2006, vii–viii).

19. IOSCO (2003b, 5).

20. World Bank, Independent Evaluation Group (2006, 20–21).

21. International Monetary Fund, Independent Evaluation Office (2006, 37).

22. International Monetary Fund, Independent Evaluation Office (2006, 43).

23. International Monetary Fund, Independent Evaluation Office (2006, 11).

24. This has been done by Bermuda, the Cayman Islands, Czech Republic, the Philippines, Portugal, and Sweden. See International Monetary Fund 2005a and 2005b; International Monetary Fund, Monetary and Exchange Affairs Department and World Bank, Financial Sector Vice Presidency 2001 and 2002; International Monetary Fund, Monetary and Capital Markets Department 2006; and International Monetary Fund, Monetary and Exchange Affairs Department 2002.

25. As of August 2007, there were 185 countries that were members of the two global international financial institutions, the IMF and the World Bank.

26. IMF and World Bank definitions of different country's income levels are used here. The IMF and the World Bank used the World Bank's World Development Indicators to classify countries by per capita gross national income. The categories were low income, $825 or less; lower middle income, $826 to $3,255; upper middle income, $3,256 to $10,065; and high income, $10,066 or more. The terms "developing country," "emerging market country," and "developed country," are used here to describe, respectively, low- and lower-middle-income countries, upper-middle-income countries, and high-income countries.

27. International Monetary Fund and World Bank (2002 and 2006).

28. International Monetary Fund (2004b, 15).

29. Five years later, however, the PSE was still struggling to meet the legislative requirement that brokers own less than 20% of the exchange.

30. International Monetary Fund (2004b, 15).

31. International Monetary Fund, Monetary and Exchange Affairs Department (2002, 85).

32. International Monetary Fund, Monetary and Exchange Affairs Department (2002, 108).

CHAPTER 5
GOVERNANCE OF MARKET INFRASTRUCTURE INSTITUTIONS: A SNAPSHOT

1. See, for example, Aggarwal (2002); Chesini (2001); IOSCO, Emerging Markets Committee (2005); Karmel (2002) and (2003b); Mendiola and O'Hara (2004); Lee (2003b); Ramos (2006); Serifsoy (2008); and Treptow (2006).

2. Formally the exchange was "companized" rather than demutualized, but the effect was the same.

3. World Federation of Exchanges (2008, 9).

4. The full database is reproduced in table 16 in Lee (2009).

5. Verification of compliance with WFE membership requirements is made by a team of visiting member exchange managers, who check an applicant exchange against a formalized set of membership criteria, which have gained recognition for public investment and fiscal authorities in some jurisdictions.

6. A number of highly developed futures exchanges are corresponding members.

7. The figures differ from those on the website of the WFE in September 2006 for two reasons. First, the analysis only covers stock exchanges, whereas the WFE includes 15 exchanges that do not trade ordinary shares, four clearing corporations, and one regulator (NASD—which is different from NASDAQ). Second, the WFE includes four members for Euronext and two for OMX. The analysis here treats Euronext and OMX as single entities.

8. For example, the *Handbook of World Stock, Derivative and Commodity Exchanges* lists some 158 stock exchanges. See http://www.exchange-handbook.co.uk/index.cfm?section=home.

9. Including the *Handbook of World Stock, Derivative and Commodity Exchanges*, International Securities Services Association (ISSA), various newspapers and on one occasion *Wikipedia*.

10. The rules by which markets are categorized by FTSE International are shown in table 21 in Lee (2009).

11. Lee (2009, table 23), lists the full 90 stock exchanges by level of development.

12. MarketWatch (2009).

13. Korea Exchange (2009, 3).

CHAPTER 6
EXCHANGES

1. See Deutsche Börse AG and London Stock Exchange (2000) and Zenina (2001).

2. For this, and the next quotes about the benefits, see Deutsche Börse AG and London Stock Exchange (2000, 6–9). Italics added.

3. See also the discussion in Hilton and Lascelles (2000).

4. Lee (2000).

5. *Financial News* (2000a).

6. Lloyd-Smith (2000).

7. Financial Services Authority, Bundesaufsichtsamt für den Wertpapierhandel, and Hessisches Ministerium für Wirtschaft, and Hessisches Ministerium für Wirtschaft, Verkehr und Landesentwicklung (2000).

8. Davies (2000a).

9. For this and the next quote, see Davies (2000b).

10. Moore (2000).

11. Garfield (2000).

12. Quoted in Zenina (2001, 16–17).

13. Wright (2000).

14. *Financial News* (2000c).

15. BBC News (2000a).

16. *Business Week* (2000).

17. Reuters (2000a).

18. BBC News (2000f).

19. BBC News (2000e).

20. BBC News (2000d).

21. BBC News (2000a).

22. Huber (2000).

23. BBC News (2000f).

24. BBC News (2000g).

25. *Computer Business Review* (2000).

26. BBC News (2000h).

27. BBC News (2001a).

28. *Financial News* (2000b).

29. Reuters (2000b).

30. House of Commons, Treasury Select Committee (2002a).

31. *Sunday Telegraph* (2001).

32. *Sunday Times* (2001a).

33. Evening News, Scotland (2001).

34. BBC News (2001b).

35. *Sunday Times* (2001b).

36. House of Commons, Treasury Select Committee (2002b).

37. Reuters (2001).

38. House of Commons, Treasury Select Committee (2002b).

39. Ranson (2005, 28).

40. For a summary of the approach, see Kotewall and Kwong (2002, chap. 3), and Chow (2004).

41. Securities and Futures Commission (2002a).

42. Securities and Futures Commission (2002b, 27), and Low (2004, 84).

43. Securities and Futures Commission (2002b, 28).

44. Hong Kong Exchanges and Clearing (2002).

45. Lee (2002).

46. Kotewall and Kwong (2002, chap. 6).

47. Lee (2002).

48. Hong Kong Exchanges and Clearing (2002, 1).

49. See Moiseiwitsch (2003) and Webb (2002).

50. This was raised at a luncheon meeting between the Secretary for Financial Services, the chairman of HKEx, and brokers. See Kotewall and Kwong (2002, para 9.10, p. 105).

51. Kotewall and Kwong (2002, annex 7.1).

52. Yiu (2002).

53. This list is drawn from Kotewall and Kwong (2002, annex 7.1), and Kwong (2002).

54. Kotewall and Kwong (2002, 2–3).

55. Kotewall and Kwong (2002, 122).

56. Webb (2002).

57. Sources for this and the next seven paragraphs are Kotewall and Kwong (2002, 120–21, 134, 169, 178, 178, 179, and 14).

58. BBC (2004).

59. BBC (2005a).

60. BBC (2005f).

61. BBC (2005e).

62. BBC (2006a).

63. BBC (2006f).

64. NASDAQ (2006).

65. BBC (2006b).

66. BBC (2006d) and Walsh (2006a).

67. BBC (2006d).

68. BBC (2006c) and Walsh (2006b).

69. BBC (2006g).

70. Kennedy (2006).

71. BBC (2006h).

72. Office of Fair Trading (2007).

73. Quinn (2007).

74. Peston (2007).

75. The initial deadline had been extended to this date.

76. London Stock Exchange (2007a).

77. See also Perrin (2006).

78. Balls (2006c).

79. Investment Exchanges and Clearing Houses Act (2006, chap. 55).

80. BBC (2007a).

81. BBC (2007b).

82. Finansinspektionen (2007a and 2007b).

83. *Evening Standard* (2007).

84. McGhie (2007).

85. NASDAQ (2007a) and Magnusson and McSheehy (2007).

86. NASDAQ also agreed to subscribe for 50% of any additional capital contribution calls made by DIFX, subject to a maximum aggregate additional commitment of up to $25 million.

87. Cohen (2007).

88. London Stock Exchange (2007b).

89. NASDAQ (2007b). The Committee on Foreign Investment in the United States is an interagency committee authorized to review transactions that could result in control of a US business by a foreign person, in order to determine the effect of such transactions on the national security of the United States.

90. Associated Press (2008).

91. A detailed history of Grasso's tenure at, and resignation from, the NYSE is presented in Gasparino (2007).

92. Gasparino (2003).

93. Gasparino, Kelly, and Craig (2003).

94. Anderson (2003a).

95. New York Stock Exchange (2003a).

96. New York Stock Exchange (2003b).

97. Donaldson (2003).

98. Anderson (2003b) and English (2003a).

99. English (2003b).

100. White (2003).

101. Lublin (2003).

102. Mann (2003).

103. Glassman (2003).

104. Angelides (2003).

105. CalPERS subsequently instituted a lawsuit against the NYSE and its specialists in December (2003). See NYSE Group (2006, 134).

106. This draws on New York Stock Exchange (2006, 61–62).

107. NYSE Group (2006, 135).

108. Reuters (2004).

109. David and Keaveny (2004).

110. Anderson (2004).

111. These are summarized in Bachelder (2008).

112. *People v. Grasso*, No. 120, 2008 N.Y. LEXIS 1821 (N.Y. June 25, 2008), and *People v. Grasso*, No. 401620/04, 2008 N.Y. App. Div. LEXIS 5853 (N.Y. App. Div. 2008).

113. Anderson (2008).

114. Reuters 2008 and Anderson 2008. Spitzer had been replaced as Attorney General by this time.

115. This section draws, with permission, on Osaki (2005).

116. The "Hercules" market was created after NASDAQ decided to pull out of its joint venture NASDAQ-Japan in December 2002.

117. Chaired by Professor Shigeru Morimoto, dean, Graduate School of Law, Kyoto University.

118. SEL (2000, art. 106-4, para.1).

119. Kyodo News International (2005).

CHAPTER 7
CCPs AND CSDs

1. There was in fact also a fourth pillar consisting of insurance companies.

2. Review Committee on Canadian Depository for Securities (1974, 11).

3. Institutions allocated preferred shares were the Canadian Investor Protection Fund, the Trust Companies Association of Canada Inc., the Investment Funds Institute of Canada, Guaranty Trust Company of Canada, the Bank of Nova Scotia, the Canada Trust Company, Canada Permanent Trust Company, Crown Trust Company, Montreal Trust Company of Canada, Royal Trust Corporation of Canada, and the Canadian Life and Health Insurance Association

4. Toronto Stock Exchange (2006).

5. The quorum rule was present in the by-laws formulated in 1980.

6. Canadian Depository for Securities (2002)

7. Marley (2005).

8. Marley (2005), Canadian Depository for Securities (2005, 6).

9. Dow Jones (2000).

10. Jones (2000).

11. Greensted (2003).

12. European Securities Forum (2000). Some text is marginally revised from the original.

13. Dow Jones (2001a).

14. *Global Investor Magazine* (2001).

15. Dow Jones (2001a).

16. Greensted (2001).

17. Maguire (2001a).

18. The source for this paragraph and the next is Strickberger (2002).

19. As well as the specific references identified below, the account in this section draws on Global Custodian (1989); Hobson (1999a, 1999b, and 2001); and Norman (2007, chap. 12).

20. Date of foundation drawn from http://en.wikipedia.org/wiki/Cedel.

21. The shareholding cap was in the articles of incorporation of Cedel International in early 2000. The author could not confirm, however, whether such a provision was in the articles of incorporation of Cedel in the 1970s.

22. Euroclear (1999).

23. Reuters (1999).

24. Kentouris (2000).

25. Hobson (2000).

26. Fairlamb (2001).

27. Dow Jones (2001b).

28. Greensted (2002).

29. Dow Jones (2002).

30. Boer (2001).

31. Wright (2001).

32. *Financial News* (2002).

33. Euroclear (2006a, 60).

34. A detailed history of Euroclear is presented in Norman (2007).

35. Date of foundation drawn from http://en.wikipedia.org/wiki/Cedel, visited February 25, 2006.

36. The author is unsure about whether this and the next sentence are accurate.

37. Sicovam Holding represented Sicovam SA users, after they bought the Banque de France's 40% stake in Sicovam SA.

38. This was validated by the Euroclear plc board on July 8, 2004, and implemented on January 1, 2005.

39. Euroclear subsequently purchased the CSDs of Finland and Sweden, formerly known as Suomen Arvopaperikeskus Oy and VPC AB, respectively, in November 2008.

40. http://www.fairandclear.org/index.html, visited August 2006.

41. If shareholders believed that rebates created user loyalty, thereby leading to increased business and profits, they might, however, have supported them.

42. Euroclear (2006a, 7).
43. Euroclear (2005b).
44. Euroclear (2006a, 60).
45. Euroclear (2006a, 70).
46. Financial Reporting Council (2008, § 1.A.3.2).
47. Euroclear (2006a, 60–61).
48. Euroclear Bank (2005).
49. Euroclear (2006a, 55).

50. In addition to the specific references noted in subsequent notes, the following references also provided background information: Annesley (2006a and 2006b); Banker (2006); Brodie (2006); Central Banking (2006); Cohen and Hughes (2006); Finextra (2004 and 2006); Grainger (2006); ICFA News (2006); Manifest (2006); McCue (2006); Waters magazine (2006); and Wright (2006).

51. Clearnet and London Clearing House (2003) and LCH.Clearnet (2003).
52. Cohen (2006a).
53. These are drawn from Clearnet and London Clearing House (2003).
54. Greensted (2000).
55. Hobson (2003); Lee (2003a).
56. Competition Commission (2005, 6).·
57. Cohen (2006a).
58. Euronext NV (2005).
59. Office of Fair Trading (2003).
60. Competition Commission (2005, 6–7).·
61. Lamb (2004).
62. Greensted (2000).
63. Deloitte Securities (2003).·
64. LCH.Clearnet (2005a, 5).·
65. *Computerweekly.com* (2005).
66. LCH.Clearnet (2005b).
67. *Computerweekly.com* (2005).·
68. Cohen (2006b).
69. LCH.Clearnet (2006b).
70. Colyer (2003).

71. Prior to his resignation, the chairman had himself informed the board early in 2006 that his commitments elsewhere made it impossible for him to meet the growing time requirements of LCH.Clearnet, and that he wished to stand down when a successor had been identified. LCH.Clearnet (2006c, 8).

72. LCH.Clearnet (2007).
73. These were redeemable in December 2008 under their then-existing terms.

CHAPTER 8
WHAT IS THE MOST EFFICIENT GOVERNANCE STRUCTURE?

1. As discussed, for example, in the case studies in chapters 6 and 7.
2. IOSCO (2002a, 5). Although IOSCO was in the process of revising these objectives as of 2010, efficiency will still continue to be a fundamental regulatory goal whatever the outcome of this process.

3. This section draws on, and extends, the analysis in Lee (1998, chap. 2, 2002b, and 2003b). See also BTA Consulting (2001); Karmel (2002 and 2003b).

4. Complications arising from ambiguities surrounding the nature of ownership are, for the most part, ignored. See Honoré (1961).

5. See also Chambers and Carter 1990. Exceptions to this include nonprofit market infrastructure institutions subsidized by governments.

6. Consumer surplus is defined as the difference between the amount consumers are prepared to pay for something minus the amount they actually pay.

7. Packel (1970), quoted in Sedo (1987, 378 n. 6).

8. Van Cauwenberge (2003, 95–96).

9. A summary of the listing process for various exchanges is presented in Chesini (2001, 19–24).

10. Godeffroy (2006). T2S will settle non-euro-denominated securities as well, provided the central bank of that currency agrees entries in its cash accounts can be made in the T2S environment.

11. Shah and Thomas (2001, 22–23).

12. European Central Bank (2007, 2).

13. Chaddad and Cook (2003) produce a typology of organizational models, in which the traditional cooperative structure and the investor-oriented firm are characterized as polar forms. See also Pellervo (2000, 21), and Baarda (2006, chap. VI).

14. For a discussion of the merits of "stakeholder mutuals," defined as companies owned and controlled by their employees, customers, and suppliers, see (Turnbull 2000).

15. For general descriptions of the transaction cost methodology, see Coase (1937); Williamson (1990 and 1996).

16. For discussions of some of these issues concerning particular exchange demutualizations, see Securities and Exchange Commission of Pakistan, Expert Committee (2004); Fok (2001); Humphry (1998); International Securities Consultancy, Aries Group, and HB Consultants (2006); Na-Ranong (2002); and Sydney Futures Exchange (2000).

17. Domowitz and Steil (1999 and 2002).

18. See, for example, General Accounting Office (2002, 9); Oesterle, Winslow, and Anderson (1992); and Shah and Thomas (2001, 22–23).

19. This extends an earlier analysis presented in Aggarwal (2002).

20. Some institutions typically not thought of as exchanges, such as Instinet, were included in the calculations.

21. Using a market quality measure derived in Hasbrouck (1993).

22. See also Di Noia (1999).

23. Holmström (1999, 406–7).

24. The promotion of competition might also be undertaken by a national securities market regulator, or a supranational authority, like the European Commission in the EU.

25. The ideas presented here extend those initiated in chapter 2. See also Competition Commission (2005, 58–63); U.S. Department of Justice (2008); Deutsche Börse AG (2006, 4–6); and Lee (2001).

26. See also Pirrong (2007b).

27. Seifert was previously CEO of Deutsche Börse.

28. Hardy (2001).

29. This appeared to be occurring in the EU in (2008).

30. Kanter and Summers (1987).

31. Grasso 1999. For a description of a similar problem at LIFFE, see Hodson (2002a).

32. See, for example, Ben-Ner (1986).

33. Porter and Scully (1987).

34. Holmström (1999, 415).

35. See, for example, Pellervo (2000, 13).

36. Humphry (1998) and Steil (2002b, 33).

37. Davidson (1994).

38. Schrader (1989).

39. Lambert (2008).

40. Chaddad and Cook (2003); and Co-operative Action (undated).

41. As occurred in the creation of DTCC.

42. As occurred in the creation of Omgeo by DTCC and Thomson Financial.

43. Godeffroy (2006).

44. Godeffroy (2006).

45. Tumpel-Gugerell (2006).

46. Tumpel-Gugerell (2007).

47. Godeffroy and Bayle (2007).

48. See also Corcoran (2006, 243).

49. Steil (2003) for this and the next quote.

50. This discussion draws on transactions costs theory. See Holmström and Tirole (1989, 68–69); Klein, Crawford, and Alchian (1978); and Williamson (1975, 1979, and 1985).

51. Hart (1991).

52. Macey and O'Hara (2002).

53. The idea extends the "lemons" concept presented in Akerlof (1970).

54. A range of other questions relevant for deciding an optimal board composition are not examined. These include the following: Should there be a single or a dual board structure? How homogeneous or diverse should a board be? What is the optimal board size? What is the optimal length of service, age, and capacity for a director? and, Should the CEO and the chairman positions be separated? For a discussion about the optimal size of a board, see Hermalin and Weisbach (2003, 8), who note that one of the most consistent empirical relationships regarding boards of directors is that board size is negatively related to firm profitability. For analyses of the optimal diversity or homogeneity of a board see, for example, Dallas (2001) and Goodstein, Gautam, and Boeker (1994). In the context of a market infrastructure institution's board, diversity refers to the extent to which different groups of stakeholders are represented, rather than to gender, race, or ethnic diversity.

55. The discussion draws on, and extends, the literature surveys presented in Clarke (2004a) and Cornforth (2004). For widely accepted commercial views of what boards do in the UK and United States, see, respectively, Financial Reporting Council (2008, 5), and Business Roundtable (2005, 5–10).

56. For a summary of the literature on principal agent problems, see Holmström and Tirole (1989).

57. Lorsch and MacIver (1989 and Mace 1971).

58. Fama and Jensen (1983).

59. See also, for example, Sale (2006, 1), and Millstein and MacAvoy (1998, 1291).

60. *Harvard Law Review* Note (2006, 1555).

61. Such as the state of Delaware in the United States. See, for example, Rodrigues (2007, 5); and Clarke (2007, 80–83).

62. Shivdasani and Yermack (1999).

63. As per the analysis in Fama (1980) and Fama and Jensen (1983).

64. See, for example, Mitchell (2005).

65. See, for example, Pellervo (2000, 17).

66. Rodrigues (2007, 18–19).

67. For discussions of how this has occurred at cooperatives, see Cuevas and Fischer (2006, 10); and Shaw (2006, 33).

68. Quoted in Cornforth (2004, 19).

69. See, for example, Reiser (2007, 811).

70. Cooperatives[UK] (2005b, 31).

71. Such difficulties include (1) assessing whether the definitions of director "independence" employed are sufficiently robust to ensure that any directors who satisfy them are in fact independent of management (see Rodrigues 2007, 21); (2) evaluating whether share price performance or other accounting measures of firm performance best capture the interests of shareholders; (3) the endogeneity of almost all the variables of interest (see Hermalin and Weisbach 2003, 8, and Bhagat and Bolton 2007); (4) the difficulty of distinguishing between equilibrium and out-of-equilibrium phenomena; (5) the likelihood that the effects of increased numbers of outside directors will not have a uniform impact across firms (see Duchin, Matsusaka, and Ozbas 2008, 2); and (6) the possibility that the effectiveness of independent directors has changed over time as a result of exogenous factors.

72. Relevant literature surveys include Bhagat and Black 1999; Dalton et al. (1998); Fields and Keys (2003); and Hermalin and Weisbach (2003).

73. Studies finding a positive correlation between board independence and share price performance include Baysinger and Butler (1985), Rosenstein and Wyatt (1997), and Millstein and MacAvoy (1998). The lack of a link between board independence and firm performance is found, for example, in Bhagat and Black (2002).

74. Specific issues that have been studied include whether boards with higher proportions of outside directors are more likely to remove a CEO as a result of poor performance, to prevent management from paying greenmail, to be involved in restructuring decisions, to distinguish between good and bad acquisitions, to spend more on R&D, to establish golden parachute agreements, and to adopt poison pills.

75. See, for example, Gregory (2002), Financial Reporting Council (2008), and Organisation for Economic Co-operation and Development (2004 and 2005). For a list of such guides, see http://www.ecgi.org/codes/all_codes.php.

76. See, for example, Gordon (2007, 1540); and Hertig (2005).

77. Boozang (2007, 17–18).

78. Cooperatives[UK] (2005a).

79. As specified in International Co-operative Alliance (1995). For example, the ICA states that cooperatives are based "on the values of self-help, self-re-

sponsibility, democracy, equality, equity and solidarity. In the tradition of their founders, co-operative members believe in the ethical values of honesty, openness, social responsibility and caring for others."

80. Cooperatives[UK] (2005a, 11).

81. See, for example, Hodson (2002b).

82. See, for example, Citigroup (2003b).

83. See, for example, Cornforth (2004, 24).

84. Group of Thirty (2003, recommendation 17, p. 10).

85. Group of Thirty (2003, 119).

86. See, for example, London Investment Banking Association et al. (2005, 5).

87. French Association of Investment Firms et al. (2006, 9).

88. A skeptical view of the potentially unlimited nature of who, or indeed what, might be considered stakeholders in a clearing and settlement institution, is provided by Hobson (2008): "And who exactly are the 'stakeholders'? The shareholders, obviously. The management, obviously. The staff, obviously. But who else? The suppliers? The customers? The creditors? The competitors? The pensioners? The rain forests? The fish in the sea?"

89. For a discussion of what a stakeholder is, see Clarke (2004b, 195).

90. The two subsequent quotes are on pp. 20 and 31 respectively.

91. Subsequent quote is on p. 45.

92. Italics added.

93. See, for example, Group of Thirty (2003, 122); and French Association of Investment Firms et al. (2006, 9).

94. See, for example, Cornforth (2004, 17); and Russo et al. (2004, 4).

95. Hobson (2008) characterizes the problem provocatively in the context of clearing and settlement organizations: "Stakeholding gives arrogant and unresponsive managements free rein to build empires, over-invest in prestige projects, make senseless mergers and acquisitions, and line their own pockets through extravagant pay and perks."

96. Hillman, Cannella, and Paetzold (2000).

97. See, for example, Clarke (2007, 81).

98. Clarke (2004a, 117); and Levrau and Van den Berghe (2007, 6–7).

99. Davis, Schoorman, and Donaldson 1997 and Muth and Donaldson (1998).

100. See, for example, Cha (1999); Cameron (2002); and Mendiola and O'Hara (2004, 8–9).

101. For analyses of why exchanges have demutualized, see Ramos (2006) and Treptow (2006).

102. See, for example, Ho (2002).

103. See, for example, Sundaramurthy and Lewis (2003).

CHAPTER 9
WHO SHOULD REGULATE WHAT?

1. For relatively recent discussions concerning self-regulation in the U.S., see Lipton (1983); Keaveny (2005); Loss and Seligman (1990, 2787–94); National Association of Securities Dealers (1995, §§ II-5 to II-21); and Securities and Exchange Commission, Division of Market Regulation (1994, study VI).

2. Histories of the regulation of the US securities and commodities markets are presented, respectively, in Seligman (2003) and Markham (1987).

3. Xu and Pistor (2005).

4. See, for example, Morgan and Yeung (2007); Black (2002, and 2005).

5. See also Hutter (2006) and (Scott 2004).

6. See, for example, J. Black (2001).

7. Italics added, and text and punctuation marginally changed.

8. See, for example, B. S. Black (2001, 3); International Council of Securities Associations (2006, 1–2); and Ogus (2000).

9. Keaveny 2005, (1420–21); and Prentice (2006, 799–800).

10. As previously noted, these objectives were in the process of being revised as of mid-2010.

11. For a discussion of how transparency may compromise the delivery of efficiency, see Lee (2002a).

12. See, for example, Karmel (2002) and Advisory Committee on Market Information (2001). See McTague (2006).

13. See, for example, Lee (2002a and 1998, chap. 11).

14. See, for example, Coffee (1999); Prentice (2002 and 2005); and Romano (1998).

15. Quite generally regulation is often viewed as being composed of three activities: standard setting, information gathering, and behavior modification—see Black (2002, 18–20).

16. Lee (1998, chap. 12); and O'Hara (2004). Canada and the United States have developed specific rules to regulate the activities of ATSs. In the United States, ATSs are governed by the SEC (Securities and Exchange Commission 1998b). In Canada, ATSs are subject to the Canadian Securities Associations (Canadian Securities Administrators 2001).

17. See, for example, B. S. Black (2001, 5); Ahdieh (2004, 285–86); International Council of Securities Associations, Secretariat (2006, 9); Securities and Exchange Commission 2004f; and Securities Industry Association (2003).

18. For other structural options, see Fleckner (2006); Dombalagian (2007); and Hunter (2005).

19. For example, see Miller (1985) and Securities and Exchange Commission, Division of Market Regulation (1994, VI-3).

20. Securities and Exchange Commission (2004f).

21. B. S. Black (2001, 3).

22. Ketchum (2006).

23. For two examples that have occurred in Canada and the Philippines, see, respectively, Ontario Securities Commission 2000a; and Lim and Pascual, (undated, 32–34). Two relatively recent instances include Securities and Exchange Commission 1996 and 2005. For a listing of SEC actions against U.S. SROs between October 1990 and October 2005, see Ramphal (2007, 154–57).

24. As proposed, for example, in Securities and Exchange Commission (2004e).

25. See also Holthouse (2002, 146).

26. See, for example, General Accounting Office (2002, 8–9).

27. IOSCO, Technical Committee (2001, 7).

28. See, for example, Tonello (2006).

29. Kahan (1997, 1517); and Securities and Exchange Commission (2004f).

30. Kondo (2006) provides empirical evidence that NASD involvement in the resolution of disputes by arbitration between investors and brokers enhanced the strength and efficiency of enforcement against broker misbehavior.

31. Quoted in National Association of Securities Dealers (1995, II-14).

32. Peake and Mendelson (1994, 463).

33. See, for example, World Bank and International Monetary Fund (2005, 150).

34. See, for example, Fleckner (2006) and Pearson (2002, 98).

35. Not least because there is controversy about what constitutes an SRO. The existence of industry SROs in Canada, Jordan, the Philippines, and the United States, is noted in chap. 6. ICSA has 14 members, some of which could also be considered industry SROs, in addition to those already noted.

36. http://www.finra.org/AboutFINRA/CorporateInformation/index.htm and Karmel (2007).

37. See http://www.jsda.or.jp/html/eigo/about_act.html.

38. See, for example, Macey and O'Hara (2005, 583).

39. See generally Banner (1998).

40. See, for example, Levine and Forrence (1990).

41. This was said to have occurred in the Philippines, as discussed in chap. 6, and also in Alberta, Canada. See Auditor General Alberta (2005).

42. Macey and O'Hara (2005, 599).

43. See, for example, EU Commission (2006) and http://bre.berr.gov.uk/regulation/.

44. See, for example, IOSCO, Technical Committee (2001, 7–8).

45. For U.S. examples, see *Silver v. NYSE* (1963) and *Gordon v. NYSE* (1975).

46. See, for example, Russo and Wang (1972) and Karmel (2002, 401).

47. Erickson (2000).

48. Coffee (2002), General Accounting Office (2002); Mahoney (1997); and Securities Industry Association (2003, pt. III.D.2).

49. General Accounting Office (2002, 2).

50. Macey and O'Hara (1999b, 22).

51. Keaveny (2005, 1422).

52. See, for example, Securities Industry Association (2003, pt. III.D).

53. For a discussion about the factors affecting the creation of a European SEC, see Hertig and Lee (2003).

54. See generally Moloney (2008). See www.cesr-eu.org about the Committee of European Securities Regulators.

55. Miller (1985, 864).

56. This argument has been supported by SROs and the securities industry. See, for example, International Council of Securities Associations 2006, 1; Lackritz (2005, 9–10); and Salman (2003). See also Securities and Exchange Commission (2004f).

57. Lipton (1983, 545).

58. Mahoney (2003, 2).

59. Dombalagian (2007, 329).

60. Macey and Haddock (1985, 319).

61. See, for example, Elliott (2002, 21).

62. International Council of Securities Associations (2006, 1).

63. *Business Roundtable v. SEC* (1990).

64. These include Government in the Sunshine Act (1976), Freedom of Information Act (1966), and Regulatory Flexibility Act (1980).

65. Courts have rather consistently held that SROs are not state actors for purposes of the Fifth Amendment's Due Process Clause and Self-Incrimination Clause. See, for example, *United States v. Solomon* (1975) and Karmel 2003a.

66. Douglas (1940, 82); Glauber (2006); U.S. Senate (1975, 22); and Mahoney (1997, 1458).

67. See, for example, IOSCO, Technical Committee (2001, 12).

68. Coffee and Seligman (2003, 673). Some statutory regulators, such as the SEC in the United States and the FSA in the UK are funded by the industry.

69. Miller (1985, 855).

70. Hunter (2005, 639).

71. See, for example, Lackritz (2005, 9–10).

72. Securities and Exchange Commission (2004f).

73. For this reason, many SROs are not funded this way. For example, the NYSE may not use any regulatory fees, fines, or penalties for commercial purposes, including distributions to shareholders. See New York Stock Exchange LLC (2007, § 4.05).

74. See, for example, Cox (2000, 18), and NYSE comment letter to the SEC Market 2000 study, quoted in Peake and Mendelson (1994, 462).

75. Securities Industry Association (2005, 16–18).

76. Aggarwal, Ferrell, and Katz (2006, 26).

77. Badway and Busch (2005, 1355).

78. See, for example, Kahan (1997, 1517).

79. Macey, O'Hara, and Pompilio (2005).

80. Edwards (1983, 194–95).

81. See also DeMarzo, Fishman, and Hagerty (2005).

82. See, for example, Schlag (2007).

83. See, for example, Rajan and Zingales (2001), and Roe (2003 and 2005).

84. Peake and Mendelson (1994, 444).

85. Dombalagian (2005, 8).

86. Including at different times, the Canadian Securities Administrators, IDA, Market Regulation Services, and TSX.

87. See, for example, Drezner (2002, 17–18) and Jordan (2005, 1009).

88. Nagy (2005).

89. Mahoney (1997, 1458), also notes that exchange SROs have often imposed upon the entities they regulate stricter standards than those required by the federal securities laws.

90. Macey and O'Hara (2005, 571).

91. Erickson (2000).

92. IOSCO (2002b).

93. Osborne (2006); Grant (2006); and Posner (2006).

94. As discussed in chapter 3.

95. Relevant agencies include the Asian Development Bank, Canadian International Development Agency, Department For International Development in the

UK, Deutsche Gesellschaft für Technische Zusammenarbeit (German Corporation for Technical Assistance to Developing Countries), Inter-American Development Bank, International Finance Corporation, IMF, OECD, the EU's Poland and Hungary: Assistance for Restructuring Their Economies, and Technical Aid to the Commonwealth of Independent States programs, United States Agency for International Development, and World Bank.

96. See, for example, Pistor, Berkowitz, and Richard (1999). These are sometimes called "me too reforms," a phrase attributed to Hertig (2005).

97. See, for example, Jandosov (1998).

98. IOSCO (2003a, principle 6).

99. Elliott (2002, 17).

100. Karmel (2002, 401).

101. IOSCO, SRO Consultative Committee (2000, 12).

102. Bradley (2002, 29).

103. The weaknesses of this approach are discussed in Hertig, Lee, and McCahery (2009).

104. See, for example, International Council of Securities Associations, Working Group on the Governance of Market Infrastructures (2006); IOSCO, Emerging Markets Committee 2005, 26; and IOSCO, Technical Committee (2001, 15).

105. IOSCO, Technical Committee (2006b, 30).

106. Lee (1998, 201–13).

107. IOSCO, Technical Committee (2006b, 11).

108. U.S. Senate Subcommittee on Securities, Committee on Banking, Housing and Urban Affairs (1973, 145).

109. This view was upheld by the Securities and Exchange Commission (2004f).

CHAPTER 10
HOW SHOULD MARKET INFRASTRUCTURE INSTITUTION
GOVERNANCE BE REGULATED?

1. See, for example, IOSCO, Technical Committee (2006b, 12); and CPSS and IOSCO (2001b, 20).

2. See, for example, Allen, Christodoulou, and Millard (2006, 17).

3. As occurs, for example, in the United States.

4. See, for example, Carson (2003, 3); IOSCO, Emerging Markets Committee (2005, 23); IOSCO, Technical Committee (2001, 9); and Lee (2003c, 7).

5. Such a review process is frequently utilized in the United States. See, for example, Rubin and Cannon (2006).

6. See, for example, Securities and Exchange Commission (2004e).

7. Even among jurisdictions that require independent directors to be appointed to the board of a market infrastructure institution, there are differing views about the optimal number of such directors. The SEC has advocated that the boards of SROs, including exchanges, have a majority of independent directors. See Securities and Exchange Commission (2004e). The UK's FSA has taken a flexible approach to the appointment of independent directors, encouraging "consideration of a balance between company executives, independents and users"

on governing boards, without requiring specific percentages for each category. See Evans (2004, 2). The FSA has, however, generally favored a minimum of two independent nonexecutive directors, and believes recognized bodies should consider having at least half their board, excluding the chairman, be independent, and having many directors with no connection with the company. In Canada, there has been a trend towards market infrastructure institution boards where at least half of the directors are independent. See, for example, regarding the Toronto Stock Exchange, Ontario Securities Commission (2000b).

8. In Canada, for example, CDS has four independent directors on a board of 15, even though its regulator, the Ontario Securities Commission, views CDS as an SRO, and believes that public interest considerations require fair representation of a broad group of stakeholders and the perspective of directors who are independent of participant-owners. In the United States, the DTCC had no independent directors until 2010.

9. In Hong Kong, for example, the government appoints several directors to the board of the HKEx, and also has a veto on the appointment of its CEO. See Securities and Futures Ordinance (Hong Kong), cap. 571, §26 and §77(1).

10. See, for example, Clarke (2007, 82–83).

11. This is required, for example, in Hong Kong concerning the governance of exchanges. Securities and Futures Ordinance (Hong Kong), cap. 571, §21(2)(b).

12. Examples of ownership restrictions are set out in IOSCO, Technical Committee (2006a, pp. 16–18, table 2).

13. Securities and Exchange Commission (2004e).

14. Many jurisdictions have done this. See, for example, Committee on the Governance of the Exchanges, Monetary Authority of Singapore 1999; Ho 2002; and Securities and Exchange Board of India 2003 and 2005.

15. See, for example, Hellenic Exchanges Holding S.A. 1999, 185; IOSCO, Technical Committee (2006a, 6); and Committee on the Governance of the Exchanges, Monetary Authority of Singapore (1999, 4).

16. Securities Exchange Act (1934, §6(b)(3)).

17. Securities Exchange Act (1934, §17A(b)(3)(C)).

18. For a general discussion, see Lee (1998, 192–98). For a range of specific rulings with relevance to the fair representation requirement, see Securities and Exchange Commission (1980, 1988, 1989a, 1989b, 1998a, 1998b, 2004a, 2004b, 2004c, and 2004d).

19. For a summary listing of its many benefits, and the issues involved with it, see, for example, Henderson et al. (2003).

20. See De Bandt and Hartmann (2000); Dow (2000); Kaufman and Scott (2003); and Schwarcz (2008).

21. See also Kroszner (2006).

22. Allen, Christodoulou, and Millard (2006, 4–5); and Goldberg et al. (2002, 5).

23. See, for example, Lee (2002c).

24. See the statement by the CME, a for-profit listed company and owner of CME Clearing, the world's largest derivatives clearing organization at http://www.cme.com/clearing/fm/fs/ (visited July 2008).

25. See, for example, Eurex Clearing AG (2008).

26. Kroszner (2006).

27. For policy recommendations to this effect, see Authorities, The (1995); CPSS and IOSCO (2004, 4–5), recommendations 6 and 14; and Futures Industry Association Global Task Force on Financial Integrity (1995, recommendations 6–8).

28. Jenkinson (2007). See also Kroszner 1999, and for a similar discussion in the context of payments systems, see Bank of England (2005, 51).

29. See also Kroszner (1999) for a discussion of how market infrastructure institutions do take sufficient account of risk. For a similar discussion in the context of payments systems, see Bank of England (2005, 51).

30. Formally the suggestion is for "recognised bodies," which include exchanges and clearing and settlement organizations. See Evans (2004, 3).

References

Adams, R. B., and D. Ferreira. 2005. A theory of friendly boards. ECGI Finance Working Paper No. 100/2005. October.

Advent Software Inc. 2006. The buyside and the three phase evolution of electronic trading.

Advisory Committee on Market Information. 2001. Report: a blueprint for responsible change. Prepared for US SEC. September 14.

Aggarwal, R. 2002. Demutualization and corporate governance of stock exchanges. *Journal of Applied Corporate Finance* 15 (1): 105–13. Spring.

Aggarwal, R., and S. Dahiya. 2006. Demutualization and public offerings of financial exchanges. *Journal of Applied Corporate Finance* 18 (3): 96–106. Summer.

Aggarwal, R., A. Ferrell, and J. Katz. 2006. U.S. securities regulation in a world of global exchanges. Harvard Law School, John M. Olin Discussion Paper Series No. 569. December.

Ahdieh, R. B. 2004. Law's signal: a cueing theory of law in market transition. *Southern California Law Review* 77 (2): 215–306.

Akerlof, G. A. 1970. The market for "lemons": quality uncertainty and the market mechanism. *Quarterly Journal of Economics* 84 (3): 488–500. August.

Alexander, I., and C. Mayer. 1997. Incentives on private infrastructure companies. Prepared for the Private Sector Development Department, Private Participation in Infrastructure Group, World Bank. January 1.

Allen, H., G. Christodoulou, and S. Millard. 2006. Financial infrastructure and corporate governance. Bank of England Working Paper No. 316. December.

Andersén, A. 2005. Essays on stock exchange competition and pricing. Dissertation, Helsinki School of Economics.

Anderson, J. 2003a. Spitzer: we're keeping an eye on governance at NYSE. *New York Post*. May 22.

———. 2003b. Target: Grasso–anti-management protest memo hits NYSE floor. *New York Post*. September 9.

———. 2004. Dick's new demand: $48m or apology. *New York Post*. May 10.

———. 2008. Stock exchange's ex-chief wins battle to keep pay. *New York Times*. July 2.

Angel, J. J. 1998. Consolidation in the global equity market: an historical perspective. Working paper, Georgetown University. February 19.

Angelides, P. (California State Treasurer). 2003. California treasurer Angelides, chiefs of California's pension funds, call on NYSE's chairman Grasso to resign. Press release. September 16.

Annesley, C. 2006a. Clearing house chief resigns in wake of debacle. *Computerweekly.com*. July 6.

———. 2006b. Did lack of IT involvement at outset doom LCH.Clearnet's grand vision? *Computerweekly.com*. July 18.

Areeda, P., and L. Kaplow. 1999. *Antitrust Analysis, Problems, Text, and Cases.* New York: Aspen Publishing. 5th ed.

Associated Press. 2008. Borse Dubai completes planned sale of OMX to Nasdaq. February 27.

Associazione Bancaria Italiana. 2006. ABI comment on the European Commission issues paper "Competition in EU securities trading and post-trading". June.

Auditor General, Alberta (Canada). 2005. Report of the auditor general on the Alberta Securities Commission's enforcement system. October.

Australian Securities and Investments Commission. 2007. Competition for market services—trading in listed securities and related data. Consultation Paper 86. July.

Australian Stock Exchange. 2000. ASX's supervisory arrangements. Media release. November 9.

Australian Stock Exchange and Australian Securities and Investments Commission. 2004. Memorandum of understanding, Australian Securities and Investments Commission and Australian Stock Exchange Limited. ACN 008 624 691. June 30.

Authorities, The. 1995. Windsor Declaration. May 16–17.

Autorité des Marchés Financiers (France). Undated. Creation of the Autorité des Marchés Financiers.

Baarda, J. R. 2006. Current issues in cooperative finance and governance. Cooperative Programs, Rural Development, U.S. Department of Agriculture. April.

Bachelder, J. E., III. 2008. New York courts dismiss "Grasso" compensation case. *New York Law Journal.* August 27.

Badway, E. E., and J. M. Busch. 2005. Ending securities industry self-regulation as we know it. *Rutgers Law Review* 57 (4): 1351–76. Spring.

Baglioni, A. 2006. Entry into a network industry: consumers' expectations and firms' pricing policies. Università Cattolica del Sacro Cuore, Dipartimenti e Istituti di Scienze Economiche (DISCE), Working Paper IEF-69. November.

Bainbridge, S. M. 2002. A critique of the NYSE's director independence listing standards. UCLA School of Law, Research Paper No. 02-15. June.

Balls, E. (Economic Secretary to the Treasury, UK). 2006a. Remarks. Chief Regulatory Officers' International Symposium, Tokyo Stock Exchange. November 6.

———. 2006b. The City as the global financial centre: risks and opportunities. Bloomberg. June 14.

———. 2006c. Financial services: a UK perspective. Speech at the Hong Kong General Chamber of Commerce and the British Chamber of Commerce. September 13.

Balsam, S., E. Bartov, and C. Marquardt. 2002. Accruals management, investor sophistication, and equity valuation: evidence from 10-Q filings. *Journal of Accounting Research* 40: 987–1012. September.

Bank for International Settlements. 1990. Report of the committee on interbank netting schemes of the central banks of the Group of Ten countries. Lamfalussy Report. November.

Bank of England. 2005. Payment systems oversight report 2004. Issue No. 1. January.

Banker, The. 2006. Tough IT challenge of forging a single European clearing house. August 7.

Banner, S. 1998. *Anglo-American Securities Regulation: Cultural and Political Roots, 1690–1860.* Cambridge: Cambridge University Press.

Bartram, S. M., and F. Fehle. 2006. Competition without fungibility: evidence from alternative market structures for derivatives. February 6.

Baumol, W. J., J. Panzer, and R. D. Willig. 1982. *Contestable Markets and the Theory of Industry Structure.* New York: Harcourt Brace Jovanovich.

Baysinger, B., and H. N. Butler. 1985. Corporate governance and the board of directors: performance effects of changes in board composition. *Journal of Law, Economics, and Organization* 1 (1): 101–24. Spring.

BBC News. 2000a. Analysis: a marriage of equals. May 3.

———. 2000b. Doubts over market merger. May 17.

———. 2000c. More trouble for Exchange merger. August 14.

———. 2000d. Exchange of views. August 21.

———. 2000e. German "threat" to stock market merger. August 25.

———. 2000f. Boost for stock market merger plan. August 31.

———. 2000h. Stock exchange head quits. September 15.

———. 2001a. London exchange battle hots up. September 30.

———. 2001b. Deutsche Börse "in Liffe bid." October 18.

———. 2004. LSE rejects German takeover bid. December 13.

———. 2005a. Euronext trumpets LSE bid savings. February 9.

———. 2005b. Deutsche Boerse ditches LSE bid plans. March 7.

———. 2005c. LSE rejects "derisory" takeover. December 9.

———. 2006a. Macquarie signals end to LSE bid. February 20.

———. 2006b. Nasdaq hails "attractive" LSE bid. March 10.

———. 2006c. Nasdaq withdraws LSE takeover bid. March 30.

———. 2006d. Nasdaq snaps up 15% stake in LSE. April 11.

———. 2006e. Nasdaq holding in LSE nears 25%. May 10.

———. 2006f. LSE rejects £2.7bn Nasdaq offer. November 20.

———. 2006g. Nasdaq unveils hostile LSE offer. December 12.

———. 2006h. LSE dubs Nasdaq bid "inadequate." December 19.

———. 2007a. Nasdaq bids $3.7bn for Nordic OMX. May 25.

———. 2007b. Dubai in $4bn bid for Nordic OMX. August 17.

Bebchuk, L., and J. Fried. 2004. *Pay without Performance: The Unfulfilled Promise of Executive Compensation.* Cambridge, Mass.: Harvard University Press.

Beecher-Monas, E. 2007. Marrying diversity and independence in the boardroom: Just how far have you come, baby? *Oregon Law Review* 86 (2): 373–411.

Ben-Ner, A. 1986. Nonprofit organizations: Why do they exist in market economies? In *The Economics of Nonprofit Institutions: Studies in Structure and Policy.* Edited by S. Rose-Ackermann. Oxford: Oxford University Press.

Bhagat, S., and B. Black. 1999. The uncertain relationship between board composition and firm performance. *Business Lawyer* 54: 921–63.

———. 2002. The non-correlation between board independence and long-term firm performance. *Journal of Corporation Law* 27: 231–74. Winter.

Bhagat, S., and B. Bolton. 2007. Corporate governance and firm performance. University of Colorado at Boulder, Department of Finance; and University of New Hampshire. June.

Black, B. S. 2001. The role of self-regulation in supporting Korea's securities markets. Self-Regulatory Institutions in the Korean Securities Markets, Korea Stock Exchange. Speech. December 7.

Black, J. 2001. Decentring regulation: understanding the role of regulation and self-regulation in a "post-regulatory" world. *Current Legal Problems* 54: 103–46. November.

———. 2002. Critical reflections on regulation. Discussion Paper No. 4, Centre for the Analysis of Risk and Regulation (CARR), London School of Economics. January.

———. 2003. Mapping the contours of contemporary financial services regulation. Discussion Paper No. 17, Centre for the Analysis of Risk and Regulation (CARR), London School of Economics. October.

———. 2005. Proceduralisation and polycentric regulation. *Revista DireitoGV*, Especial 1.

Blair, M. M. 2004 (1995). Ownership and control: rethinking corporate governance for the 21st century. In *Theories of Corporate Governance: The Philosophical Foundations of Corporate Governance*. Edited by T. Clarke, pp. 174–88. London: Routledge.

Blair, M. M., and E. F. Gerding. 2009. Sometimes Too Great a Notional: Measuring the "Systemic Significance" of OTC Credit Derivatives. Working Paper No. 09-22. Vanderbilt University Law School, Law and Economics.

Blanc, R. D. 2007. Intermarket competition and monopoly power in the U.S. stock markets. *Brooklyn Journal of Corporate, Financial and Commercial Law* 1 (2): 273–300. Spring.

Bliss, R., and C. Papathanassiou. 2006. Derivatives clearing, central counterparties and novation: the economic implications. Working paper. March 8.

BNP Paribas Securities Services. 2004. Clearing and settlement in the European Union—the way forward. Contribution to the European Commission Communication to the Council and the European Parliament. September.

Boer, M. 2001. Clearstream shareholders push Euroclear deal. *Wall Street Journal Europe*. June 8.

Boozang, K. M. 2007. Does an independent board improve nonprofit corporate governance? Seton Hall Public Law Research Paper No. 1002421. July.

Bradley, C. 2002. Technology, demutualisation and stock exchanges: the case for co-regulation. Working paper, University of Miami School of Law. February 5.

Brandeis, L. D. 1914. *Other People's Money and How the Bankers Use It*. http://library.louisville.edu/law/brandeis/opm-ch5.html.

Brinker, I., and T. Loest. 2004. *Essential Facility Doctrine and Intellectual Property Law: Where Does Europe Stand in the Aftermath of the IMS Health Case?* Gleiss Lutz Rechtanwälte.

Brodie, S. 2006. Speedy clearance for Liddell to leap into LCH's top slot. *Daily Telegraph*. Business diary. July 21.

BTA Consulting. 2001. To be or not to be: demutualization survey. February.

Business Roundtable. 2005. Principles of corporate governance—2005.

Business Week. 2000. Deutsche Börse on the prowl: With the LSE deal dead, what will CEO Werner G. Seifert do next? September 25.

Cameron, A. 2002. Demystifying demutualization.

Canadian Depository for Securities Ltd., The. 2001. Response to ISSA's recommendations 2000. August.

———. 2002. CDS section 3.01, by-law No. 11: A by-law relating generally to the transaction of the business and affairs of the Canadian Depository for Securities. January 8.

———. 2005. Report on internal controls and safeguards. October 15.

Canadian Securities Administrators. 2001. National instrument 21-101—marketplace operation (NI 21-101). December 1.

Carson, J. W. 2003. Conflicts of interest in self-regulation: Can demutualized exchanges successfully manage them? World Bank Policy Research Working Paper 3183. December.

Central Banking. 2006. Europe's clearing needs better governance. July 13.

Cha, L. (Deputy Chair, Securities and Futures Commission, Hong Kong). 1999. Regulatory framework after the merger of the exchanges. HKSI Seminar. October 21.

———. 2000. Securities markets reform: the Hong Kong experience. Speech, Commonwealth Club of California. June 6.

Chaddad, F. R., and M. L. Cook. 2003. The emergence of non-traditional cooperative structures: public and private policy issues. NCR-194 Research on Cooperatives Annual Meeting, Kansas City, Missouri. October 29.

Chambers, S., and C. A. Carter. 1990. US futures exchanges as nonprofit entities. *Journal of Futures Markets* 10 (1): 79–88. February.

Chen, J. 2004. The nature of the public utility: infrastructure, the market and the law. *Northwestern University Law Review* 98 (4): 1617–1708. Review essay.

Chesini, G. 2001. Changes in the ownership structure of stock exchanges: from demutualisation to self-listing. X International "Tor Vergata" Conference on Banking and Finance, Rome. December 5–6.

Chicago Mercantile Exchange Group Inc. 2007. Myths versus realities.

———. 2008. CFTC and Federal Reserve Bank of New York determine CME Group meets regulatory requirements to clear credit default swaps—CME Group Risk Committee approves CDS clearing using combined guarantee pool. Chicago. Press release. December 23.

———. 2009a. CME Group appoints Andrew Lamb to lead European clearing venture—experienced European clearing and risk management executive named CEO, CME Clearing Europe Limited. London. Press release. July 28.

———. 2009b. CME Group opens credit default swaps initiative to additional partners and focuses solution on clearing services—buy and sell-side firms joining as founding members. Chicago. Press release. September 18.

Chi-X. 2007. Chi-X commences services with EMCF N.V. Trading Notice 0001. March 26.

———. 2009. Chi-X Europe to become first MTF to offer participants choice through CCP interoperability. London. February 3.

Chow, P. (CEO, HKEx). 2004. Implementation and enforcement in corporate governance—the case of Hong Kong. OECD—6th Asian Roundtable on Corporate Governance. November 2.

Citigroup. 2003a. Citigroup's response to ESCB-CESR consultative report on the standards for securities clearing and settlement systems in the European Union. Supporting document. October.

———. 2003b. Creating a safe and level playing field. White paper on issues relating to settlement of securities in Europe. July.

———. 2004. The optimal market structure for clearing and settlement in the EU. Citigroup Response to the Communication on Clearing and Settlement from the European Commission. July.

———. 2006. CCPs: a user's perspective. Joint Conference of the ECB and the FRBC on Issues related to Central Counterparty Clearing. Discussion paper. April.

Clarke, D. C. 2007. Three concepts of the independent director. *Delaware Journal of Corporate Law* 32 (1): 73–111.

Clarke, T., editor. 2004a. *Theories of Corporate Governance: The Philosophical Foundations of Corporate Governance*. London: Routledge.

———. 2004b. The stakeholder corporation: a business philosophy for the information age. In *Theories of Corporate Governance: The Philosophical Foundations of Corporate Governance*. Edited by T. Clarke, pp. 189–201. London: Routledge. Reprinted from Clarke 1998.

Clearnet and London Clearing House. 2003. Clearnet and LCH to merge to form the LCH.Clearnet Group, Europe's leading independent group of central counterparty clearing houses. Announcement. June 25.

Coase, R. H. 1937. The nature of the firm. *Economica* 4 (16): 386–405. November.

Coffee, J. C., Jr. 1999. The future as history: the prospects for global convergence in corporate governance and its implications. *Northwestern University Law Review* 93 (3): 641–708. Spring.

———. 2002. Racing towards the top? the impact of cross-listings and stock market competition on international corporate governance. *Columbia Law Review* 102 (7): 1757–1831. November.

Coffee, J. C., Jr., and J. Seligman. 2003. *Securities regulation: cases and materials*. 9th ed., Foundation Press.

Cohen, N. 2006a. LCH.Clearnet: a relationship that causes some disquiet—a question of control. *Financial Times*. July 7.

———. 2006b. Chairman resigns from LCH.Clearnet. *Financial Times*. May 13.

———. 2007. LSE faces fresh bidding war. *Financial Times*. September 20.

Cohen, N., and C. Hughes. 2006. LCH.Clearnet chief resigns following rift with board. *Financial Times*. July 6.

Colyer, T. 2003. European clearing survey: double or nothing. *GlobalInvestormagazine.com*. July–August.

Committee of European Banking Supervisors. 2009. Report on the outcome of CEBS's call for evidence on custodian banks' internalisation of settlement and CCP-like activities. April 17.

Committee of European Securities Regulators and European System of Central Banks. 2004. Summary of responses on the European System of Central Banks

(ESCB) and Committee of European Securities Regulators (CESR) joint consultation on standards for securities clearing and settlement systems in the European Union. January 12.

———. 2009. Recommendations for securities settlement systems and recommendations for central counterparties in the European Union. May.

Committee on Economic and Monetary Affairs (European Parliament). 2005. Clearing and settlement in the European Union. Final Report A6-0000/2005 (2004/2185(INI)). Rapporteur—Piia-Noora Kauppi. May 24.

Committee on Payment and Settlement Systems, Bank for International Settlements. 1997. Clearing arrangements for exchange traded derivatives. March.

Committee on Payment and Settlement Systems, Bank for International Settlements, and Technical Committee, International Organization of Securities Commissions (CPSS and IOSCO). 2001a. Recommendations for securities settlement systems. Consultative report. January.

———. 2001b. Recommendations for securities settlement systems. Report of the CPSS IOSCO Joint Task Force on Securities Settlement Systems. November.

———. 2004. Recommendations for central counterparties. November.

Committee on the Governance of the Exchanges, Monetary Authority of Singapore. 1999. Report of the committee on governance of the exchanges. January 18.

Competition Commission (UK). 2005. Deutsche Börse AG, Euronext NV and London Stock Exchange plc. A report on the proposed acquisition of London Stock Exchange plc by Deutsche Börse AG or Euronext NV. November.

Computer Business Review. 2000. LSE courts public disaster. October 1.

Computerweekly.com. 2005. Rescue bid launched for City integration project. May 17.

Congressional Budget Office (US). 1983. Public works infrastructure: policy considerations for the 1980s. April.

Considine, J. (CEO/Chairman, DTCC). 2006. Remarks. Joint Conference of the European Central Bank / Federal Reserve Bank of Chicago, on Issues Related to Central Counterparty Clearing, Frankfurt. April 3–4.

Co-operative Action. Undated. Co-operative capital: a new approach to investment in co-operatives and other forms of social enterprise.

Cooperatives[UK]—The Union of Co-Operative Enterprises. 2005a. *Corporate Governance.* Vol. 1: *The Code of Best Practice.* For Consumer Co-operative Societies in Membership of Cooperatives[UK]. April.

———. 2005b. *Corporate Governance.* Vol. 2: *Appendices to the Code of Best Practice.* For Consumer Co-operative Societies in Membership of Co-operatives[UK].

Corcoran, A. 2006. Self-regulation and operational controls: reflections on the oversight of exchange-traded derivatives. *Revue d'Économie Financière* 82: 241–59 Special Edition on The Future of Financial Exchanges. April.

Cornforth, C. 2004. The governance of cooperatives and mutual associations: a paradox perspective. *Annals of Public and Cooperative Economics* 75 (1): 11–32. March.

Council of Institutional Investors. 2003. Private entity with a public purpose: governance of the New York Stock Exchange. An overview. July.

Cournot, A. 1838. *Research into the Mathematical Principles of the Theory of Wealth.*

Cox, J. D. 2000. Brands v. generics: self-regulation by competitors. *Columbia Business Law Review* 2000 (1): 15–22.

Cruickshank, D. (Chairman, LSE). 2002a. Clearing and settling European securities: where competition works (and where it doesn't). European Harmonisation of Cross-Border Settlement Conference. March 21.

———. 2002b. The evolution of EU securities markets: next steps for clearing and settlement. World Federation of Exchanges Conference, Madrid. October 18.

Cuevas, C. E., and K. P. Fischer. 2006. Cooperative financial institutions: issues in governance, regulation, and supervision. World Bank Working Paper No. 82.

Dale, R. 1998. Risk management in U.S. derivative clearing houses. Essays in International Financial & Economic Law, No. 14, London Institute of International Banking, Finance & Development Law, in cooperation with International Financial Law Unit, Centre for Commercial Law Studies, Queen Mary & Westfield College, University of London, and SMU Institute of International Banking and Finance.

Dallas, L. L. 2001. Developments in U.S. boards of directors and the multiple roles of corporate boards. University of San Diego School of Law, Public Law and Legal Theory Research Paper No. 48 and Law and Economics Research Paper No. 1.

Dalton, D. R., C. M. Daily, A. E. Ellstrand, and J. L. Johnson. 1998. Meta-analytic reviews of board composition, leadership structure, and financial performance. *Strategic Management Journal* 19 (3): 269–90.

David, J., and J. Keaveny. 2004. Spitzer sues former NYSE head Grasso over pay. Reuters. May 24.

Davidson, J. P., III. 1994. Disintermediated, disaggregated and dissatisfied: a financial intermediary's perspective on unbundling. 17th Chicago Kent Conference, Chicago. November 3.

Davies, H. 2000a. Global markets, global regulation IOSCO Annual Conference Sydney. speech. May 17.

———. 2000b. Speech. London Chamber of Commerce Conference, London. June 13.

———. 2004. What's left for self-regulation? Speech, Hong Kong. March.

Davies, R., A. Dufour, and B. Scott-Quinn. 2006. The MiFID: Competition in a New European Equity Market Regulatory Structure. In *Investor Protection in Europe Corporate Law Making, The MiFID and Beyond.* Edited by G. Ferrarini and E. Wymeersch. Oxford: Oxford University Press. Chap. 6.

Davis, J. H., F. D. Schoorman, and L. Donaldson. 1997. Toward a stewardship theory of management. *Academy of Management Review* 22 (1): 20–47. January.

De Bandt, O., and P. Hartmann. 2000. Systemic risk: a survey. European Central Bank, Working Paper Series, No. 35. November.

Deloitte Securities. 2003. Securities and banking update. November.

DeMarzo, P. M., M. J. Fishman, and K. M. Hagerty. 2005. Self-regulation and government oversight. *Review of Economic Studies* 72 (3): 687–706. July.

DeMott, D. A. 2005. The texture of loyalty. Duke Law School of Law, Legal Studies Research Paper Series, No. 64. March.

Depository Trust and Clearing Corporation (U.S.). 2006. Following a trade: a guide to DTCC's pivotal roles in how securities change hands.

———. 2009. NYSE Euronext and DTCC to create joint venture for more efficient clearing of U.S. fixed income securities and derivatives. New York. Press release. June 18.

Depository Trust Corporation (US). 1998. A quarter century of trust: a short history of the Depository Trust Corporation.

Deutsche Börse AG. 2003. Your IPO—a guide to your IPO and life as a public company.

———. 2005a. The European post-trade market: an introduction. White paper. February.

———. 2005b. Memorandum of Deutsche Börse in reply to the Competition Commission's letter of 29 March 2005 Reference to the Competition of the Possible Acquisition of the London Stock Exchange plc by Deutsche Börse AG. April 18.

———. 2006. Deutsche Börse AG's observations on the Commission's issues paper: Competition in EU securities trading and post-trading. June.

———. 2008. Just value: annual report 2007. March.

———. 2009a. Eurex Credit Clear successfully starts CDS clearing—first credit default swap transaction cleared on 30 July/Eurex Credit Clear major step to improve market safety and integrity for OTC derivatives. Press release. July 31.

———. 2009b. CFTC recognizes Eurex Clearing as Multilateral Clearing Organization (MCO)—CFTC order permits Eurex Clearing to expand its OTC facilities in the U.S. press release. August 4.

———. 2009c. The global derivatives market: a blueprint for market safety and integrity. White paper. September.

Deutsche Börse AG (Germany), and London Stock Exchange. 2000. iX—international exchanges merger of Deutsche Börse and London Stock Exchange. Information document. May.

Devasabai, K. 2006. Hardy quits LCH.Clearnet *International Custody and Fund Administration News*. July 10.

Directorate General Competition Services, EU Commission (Financial services: banking and insurance). 2006. Competition in EU securities trading and post-trading: issues paper. Working document of the Commission Services. May 24.

Directorate General Internal Market and Services, EU Commission (Financial services). 2006a. Analysis of studies examining European post-trading costs. Annex 1 to Report: Draft Working Document on Post-Trading Services. Working document of the Commission Services, Work in Progress. May 23.

———. 2006b. Draft working document on post-trading services. May 23.

Di Noia, C. 1999. The stock-exchange industry: network effects, implicit mergers, and corporate governance. Quaderni di Finanza, No. 33. CONSOB Commissione Nazionale per la Società e la Borsa. March.

Dombalagian, O. H. 2005. Demythologizing the stock exchange: reconciling self-regulation and the national market system. *University of Richmond Law Review* 39 (4): 1069–1154. May.

———. 2007. Self and self-regulation: resolving the SRO identity crisis. *Brooklyn Journal of Corporate, Financial and Commercial Law* 1 (2): 317–53. Spring.

Domowitz, I. 1993. A taxonomy of automated trade execution systems. *Journal of International Money and Finance* 12 (6): 607–31.

Domowitz, I. and R. Lee. 2001. On the Road to Reg ATS: A Critical History of the Regulation of Automated Trading Systems. *International Finance* 4 (2): 279–302, Summer.

Domowitz, I., and B. Steil. 1999. Automation, trading costs, and the structure of the securities trading industry. In *Brookings-Wharton Papers on Financial Services 1999*. Edited by R. E. Litan and A. M. Santomero, pp. 33–81. Washington, D.C.: Brookings Institution Press.

———. 2002. Securities trading, in *Technological Innovation and Economic Performance*. Edited by B. Steil, D. G. Victor, and R. R. Nelson. Princeton: Princeton University Press. Chap. 12. A Council on Foreign Relations Book.

Donaldson, W. H. (Chairman, SEC). 2003. Letter to NYSE regarding NYSE executive compensation. September 2.

Donohue, C. S. (CEO, CME). 2006. Efficient clearing and settlement systems: a case for market-driven solutions. 10th European Financial Markets Convention, Zurich. June 8.

Douglas, W. O. 1940. *Democracy and Finance*. New Haven: Yale University Press.

Dow, J. 2000. What is systemic risk? Moral hazard, initial shocks, and propagation. *Monetary and Economic Studies, Bank of Japan* 18 (2): 1–24. December.

Dow Jones. 2000. European Sec Forum calls for single CCP body for Europe. June 19.

———. 2001a. ESF ends plan to build own European central counterparty. July 17.

———. 2001b. Clearstream takeover battle seen prolonged over price. December 6.

———. 2002. Deutsche Boerse Agrees to Buy Remaining 50% of Clearstream. February 3.

Drezner, D. W. 2002. Who rules? The regulation of globalization. University of Chicago. August.

Duchin, R., J. G. Matsusaka, and O. Ozbas. 2008. When are outside directors effective? USC Center in Law, Economics and Organization, Gould School of Law, Research Paper No. C07-13. February.

Economides, N. 1996. The economics of networks. *International Journal of Industrial Organization* 14 (6): 673–99. October.

Edwards, F. R. 1983. Futures markets in transition: the uneasy balance between government and self-regulation. *Journal of Futures Markets* 3 (2): 191–205.

El-Gazzar, S. M. 1998. Predisclosure information and institutional ownership: a cross-sectional examination of market revaluations during earnings announcement periods. *Accounting Review* 73 (1): 119–29. January.

Elliott, J. 2002. Demutualization of securities exchanges: a regulatory perspective. IMF Working Paper WP/02/119.

English, S. 2003a. Traders petition for Grasso to pay or go. *Telegraph*. September 12.

———. 2003b. Grasso forgoes $48m to quell storm. *Telegraph*. September 10.

Erickson, T. J. (Commissioner, CFTC). 2000. Futures exchange demutualization. Brooklyn Law School and New York Stock Exchange Breakfast Roundtable, New York. April 18.

Estache, A. 2004. Emerging infrastructure policy issues in developing countries: a survey of the recent economic literature. POVNET Infrastructure Working Group, Berlin. INFVP, World Bank. Background paper. October.

Estache, A., and A. Goicoechea. 2005. A "research" database on infrastructure economic performance. (INFVP) World Bank Policy Research Working Paper 3643. June.

EU Commission. 2004. Clearing and settlement in the European Union—the way forward. Communication from the Commission to the Council and the European Parliament. COM (2004) 312 final. April 28.

———. 2005a. EU clearing and settlement. CESAME, Definitions Sub-Group. I Meeting. January.

———. 2005b. EU clearing and settlement. CESAME, Definitions Sub-Group. I Meeting. MARKT/G2/SLG D(2005). May 11.

———. 2005c. Commission services working document on definitions of post-trading activities. Working document/MARKT/SLG/G2(2005)D15283. CESAME Sub-Group on Definitions. October.

———. 2006. Better regulation—simply explained.

———. 2009a. Commission staff working paper accompanying the Commission Communication: Ensuring efficient, safe and sound derivatives markets [COM(2009) 332 final] [SEC(2009) 914 final]. SEC(2009) 905 final. Brussels. July 3.

———. 2009b. Ensuring efficient, safe and sound derivatives markets. Communication from the Commission, COM(2009) 332 final [SEC(2009) 905 final] [SEC(2009) 914 final], Brussels. July 3.

———. 2009c. Ensuring efficient, safe and sound derivatives markets: future policy actions. Communication from the Commission to the European Parliament, the Council, the European Economic and Social Committee, the Committee of the Regions and the European Central Bank. Brussels, COM(2009) 563/4 Provisional Version. October 20.

Eurex Clearing AG. 2008. We set the standards that make a stronger market. And keep them. C5E-001-0508.

EuroCCP. 2007. DTCC's European subsidiary chosen as clearance and settlement provider for Project Turquoise. Citi's global transaction services to serve as EuroCCP's settlement agent. Press release, London. April 18.

———. 2008a. The clearing industry in Europe: cost comparison. July 1.

———. 2008b. EuroCCP to launch clearing & settlement system Friday: will support Turquoise's limited live launch of trading platform. London. August 13.

———. 2009a. EuroCCP proposes European convention on interoperability. Standard agreement would ensure transparency in risk management. London. June 17.

———. 2009b. EuroCCP sets new low clearing price benchmark for European equity trades, with highest volume users to pay just 0.2 euro cents per side. London. September 15.

Euroclear. 1999. The hub and spokes clearance and settlement model: the pan-European settlement solution for efficient and competitive capital markets. May.

Euroclear. 2004. Clearing and settlement in the European Union: the way forward. Euroclear's response to the European Commission's communication. July.

———. 2005a. Internalisation of settlement. September.

———. 2005b. Euroclear response to London Economics report (February 2004). addressed to Ms. Rosalind Buxton, DG Competition, European Commission. EU8209IKG65. June 29.

———. 2006a. Annual report 2005.

———. 2006b. Response to the issues paper of DG Competition. July.

Euroclear Bank. 2005. Offering circular for €300 million bond issue by Euroclear Finance 2 SA irrevocably guaranteed on a subordinated basis by Euroclear Bank SA/NV. June 8.

Euronext NV. 2005. Comments on the Competition Commission's provisional findings. Cleary Gottlieb Steen & Hamilton LLP. August 16.

European Banking Federation. 2006. Response: DG Competition issue paper—Competition in EU securities trading and post-trading. R6112EER, SF/DH. July 4.

European Central Bank, Eurosystem. 2007. Editorial. *Target2-Securities Newsletter* 1. June.

European Central Securities Depositories Association. 1997. Eurolinks: delivering the future.

———. 2002. ECSDA cross-border settlement. Prepared by the ECSDA Working Group on cross-border settlement (WG3). Version 1.2. February.

———. 2005. Survey on ECSDA members' services.

———. 2006. ECSDA response to DG Competition issues paper "Competition in EU securities trading and post trading". July 1.

European Multilateral Clearing Facility N.V.. 2009a. EMCF cuts UK clearing fees to 3 Euro cents. Amsterdam. April 7.

———. 2009b. EMCF signs MOU with LCH Clearnet Ltd. on interoperability. Amsterdam. May 19.

European Parliamentary Financial Services Forum. 2006. Unblocking the plumbing—clearing and settlement. June 21.

European Securities Forum. 2000. EuroCCP: ESF's blueprint for a single pan-European central counterparty. December 6.

Evans, G. H. (Director, Markets Division, FSA) 2004. Letter to chief executives of all recognised bodies (concerning corporate governance of recognised bodies). March 31.

Evening News, Scotland. 2001. LSE set to launch 400m pounds Liffe bid. July 31.

Evening Standard. 2007. LSE surges as Nasdaq sells stake. August 20.

Fairlamb, D. 2001. Commentary: Europe needs an independent settlement system. *Business Week*. June 4.

Fama, E. F. 1980. Agency problems and the theory of the firm. *Journal of Political Economy* 88 (2): 288–307. April.

Fama, E. F., and M. C. Jensen. 1983. Separation of ownership and control. *Journal of Law and Economics* 26 (2): 301–25. June.

Federation of European Securities Exchanges. 2006. Position paper on clearing and settlement. May 19.

———. 2009. European exchange report 2008. August.

Federation of European Securities Exchanges, European Association of Central Counterparty Clearing Houses, and European Central Securities Depositories Association. 2006. European code of conduct for clearing and settlement.

Fields, M. A., and P. Y. Keys. 2003. The emergence of corporate governance from Wall Street to Main Street: outside directors, board diversity, earnings management, and managerial incentives to bear risk. *Financial Review* 38 (1): 1–24. February.

Financial News. 2000a. LSE faces struggle to win merger support. August 28.

———. 2000b. Liffe takes its first step towards IPO. October 2.

———. 2000c. iX alliance provokes uncertainty. May 22.

———. 2002. Top Cedel investors set to share e720m. February 4.

Financial Reporting Council (UK). 2008. The combined code on corporate governance. June.

Financial Services Authority (UK). 2000. The FSA's approach to regulation of the market infrastructure. January.

Financial Services Authority (UK), Bundesaufsichtsamt für den Wertpapierhandel (Germany), and Hessisches Ministerium für Wirtschaft, Verkehr und Landesentwicklung (Germany). 2000. iX-international exchanges—joint statement. August 21.

Finansinspektionen (Sweden). 2007a. Finansinspektionen's decision. FI D No. 07-7095. August 23.

———. 2007b. Borse Dubai's press release was a public takeover bid. Press release. August 23.

Finextra. 2004. Merger-related IT costs eat into LCH.Clearnet gains. *www.finextra.com*. September 1.

———. 2006. LCH.Clearnet ditches IT integration project. *www.finextra.com*. July 21.

Fisch, J. E. 2005. Institutional competition to regulate corporations: a comment on Macey. *Case Western Reserve Law Review* 55 (3): 617–25.

Fleckner, A. M. 2006. Stock exchanges at the crossroads. *Fordham Law Review* 74 (5): 2541–2620, April.

Fok, L. (Deputy CEO, Hong Kong Exchanges and Clearing Ltd). 2001. Demutualisation, merger and listing: the Hong Kong experience. APEC Financial Regulators Training Initiative, Regional Seminar—Demutualization of Exchanges, Asian Development Bank, Manila, Philippines. August 13–14.

Foucault, T., and A. Menkveld. 2006. Competition for order flow and smart order routing systems. Working paper, HEC School of Management, Paris, and Vrije Universiteit Amsterdam. January.

Foucault, T., and C. Parlour. 2004. Competition for listings. *Rand Journal of Economics* 35 (2): 329–55. Summer.

Freedberg, H. (Chief Executive, Euronext.LIFFE). 2006. Letter to *Financial Times*. *Financial Times*. November 9.

———. 2008. Horizontal model does not meet Liffe's needs. *Ft.com*. April 18.

Freiss, B., and S. Greenaway. 2006. Competition in EU trading and post-trading service markets. *Competition Policy International* 2 (1): 157–85. Spring.

French Association of Investment Firms, Italian Association of Financial Intermediaries, French Banking Federation, and London Investment Banking Association. 2006. Post-trading in Europe: calls for consolidation. February.

Frischmann, B. M. 2005. An economic theory of infrastructure and commons management. *Minnesota Law Review* 89: 917–1030, April.

Frye, T. 1997. Governing the Russian equities market. *Post-Soviet Affairs* 13 (4): 366–95. Working paper (August) published October 12.

Futures Industry Association, Global Task Force on Financial Integrity. 1995. Financial integrity recommendations for futures and options markets and market participants. June.

G7 Finance Ministers. 1998. Strengthening the architecture of the global financial system. Report of G7 Finance Ministers to G7 Heads of State or Government for their meeting in Birmingham. May 15.

Gadinis, S., and H. E. Jackson. 2007. Markets as regulators: a survey. *Southern California Law Review* 80 (6): 1239–1378. September.

Garfield, A. 2000. iX deal in disarray as OM Gruppen launches £822m hostile bid for LSE. *Independent*. August 30.

Gasparino, C. 2003. Grasso is NYSE's $10 million man—chairman's pay package in 2002 came amid slump in stocks, big board profit. *Wall Street Journal*. May 8.

———. 2007. *King of the Club: Richard Grasso and the Survival of the New York Stock Exchange*. New York: HarperCollins.

Gasparino, C., K. Kelly, and S. Craig. 2003. Dick Grasso is $10 million man for the NYSE, in terms of pay. *Wall Street Journal*. May 7.

General Accounting Office (US). 2002. Securities markets: competition and multiple regulators heighten concerns about self-regulation. GAO-02-362. May.

Georges, A., and P. Senkovic. Undated. Places de marché électronique B2B et droit de la concurrence Décideurs Juridiques et Financiers No. 21.

Gerardin, D. 2004. Limiting the scope of Article 82 of the EC Treaty: What can the EU learn from the U.S. Supreme Court's judgment in Trinko in the wake of Microsoft, IMS and Deutsche Telekom? *Common Market Law Review* 41: 1519–53.

Giovannini Group, The. 2001. Cross-border clearing and settlement arrangements in the European Union. November.

———. 2003. Second report on EU clearing and settlement arrangements. April.

Glass, A. W. 2009. The regulatory drive towards central counterparty clearing of OTC credit derivatives and the necessary limits on this. *Capital Markets Law Journal* 4 (S1): S79–S98.

Glassman, J. 2003. Grasso's greed is not the issue for the NYSE. *Financial Times*. September 16.

Glauber, R. (Chairman and CEO, NASD) 2006. Self-regulatory organizations: hearing before the Senate Committee on Banking, Housing and Urban Affairs. 109th Cong. testimony. March 9.

Global Custodian. 1989. The intermediary dilemma. December.

Global Investor Magazine. 2001. ESF acknowledges EuroCCP setback. July 1.

Godeffroy, J.-M. (Director General, Payment Systems and Market Infrastructure, ECB). 2006. Ten frequently asked questions about TARGET2-Securities. Speech, British Bankers Association, London. September 20.

Godeffroy, J.-M. (Director General, Payment Systems and Market Infrastructure, ECB), and M. Bayle (T2S Programme Manager, ECB). 2007. TARGET2-securities. Presentation, Tokyo. October 10.

Goldberg, L., J. Kambhu, J. M. Mahoney, L. Radecki, and A. Sarkar. 2002. Securities trading and settlement in Europe: issues and outlook. *Federal Reserve Bank of New York, Current Issues in Economics and Finance* 8 (4). April.

Gómez-Ibáñez, J. A. 2003. *Regulating Infrastructure, Monopoly, Contracts, and Discretion.* Cambridge, Mass.: Harvard University Press.

Goodstein, J., K. Gautam, and W. Boeker. 1994. The effects of board size and diversity on strategic change. *Strategic Management Journal* 15 (3): 241–50. March.

Gordon, J. N. 2007. The rise of independent directors in the United States, 1950–2005: Of shareholder value and stock market prices. *Stanford Law Review* 59 (6): 1465–1568. June.

Grainger, A. 2006. LCH-Clearnet loses CEO. *FOW Futures and Options World.* July 10.

Grajzl, P., and P. Murrell. 2007. Allocating lawmaking powers: self-regulation vs. government regulation. *Journal of Comparative Economics* 35 (3): 520–45.

Grant, J. 2006. Ex-SEC chief hits out at "turf protection." *Financial Times.* 16–17. September.

Grasso, R. A. (Chairman and CEO, NYSE). 1999. Testimony. Senate Banking Committee: Hearing on Public Ownership of the U.S. Stock Markets. September 28.

Gray, D. M. 2007. The essential role of regulation in promoting equity market competition. *Brooklyn Journal of Corporate, Financial and Commercial Law* 1 (2): 395–407. Spring.

Greensted, R. 2000. It's my (counter) party and I'll cry if I want to. *Scrip Issue.* October 23.

———. 2001. ESF needs to break vested interests. *Financial News.* December 10.

———. 2002. ESF sell-out on Deutsche Boerse deal. February 4.

———. 2003. DTCC needs to stay at home more. *Financial News.* June 1.

Gregory, H. J. 2002. *International Comparison of Selected Corporate Governance Guidelines and Codes of Best Practice.* New York: Weil, Gotshal & Manges.

Gross, M. (Senior Vice President and Regulatory Counsel, Bond Market Association) 2005. Letter to SEC re SRO governance and transparency proposal-file No. S7-39-04; SRO concept release-file No. S7-40-04 SEC. March 8.

Group of Thirty. 1989. Clearance and settlement in the world's securities markets.

———. 2003. Global clearing and settlement: a plan of action.

Handbook of World Stock, Derivative and Commodity Exchanges. 1998. London: Mondo Visione.

Hansmann, H. B. 1980. The role of nonprofit enterprise. *Yale Law Journal* 89 (5): 835–901. April.

———. 1988. Ownership of the firm. *Journal of Law, Economics and Organization* 4 (2): 267–304. Fall.

Hansmann, H. B.. 1996. *The Ownership of Enterprise*. Cambridge, Mass.: Harvard University Press.

Hardy, D. (CEO, London Clearing House). 2001. CCP urgently needs co-operation. *Financial News*. August 20.

———. (CEO, LCH.Clearnet). 2006. The need to remove structural barriers to consolidation of CCP clearing. Joint Conference of the European Central Bank/Federal Reserve Bank of Chicago, on Issues Related to Central Counterparty Clearing, Frankfurt. April 3–4.

Harris, L. 2003. *Trading and Exchanges. Market Microstructure for Practitioners*. Oxford: Oxford University Press.

———. 2006. Breaking the futures monopoly. Commentary. *Forbes.com*. June 11.

Hart, O. 1991. Incomplete contracts and the theory of the firm. In *The Nature of the Firm: Origins, Evolution, and Development*. Edited by O. Williamson and S. Winter. New York: Oxford University Press.

Hart, O., and J. Moore. 1996. The governance of exchanges: members' cooperatives versus outside ownership. *Oxford Review of Economic Policy* 12 (4): 53–69. Winter.

Harvard Law Review. Note. 2006. Beyond "independent" directors: a functional approach to board independence. *Harvard Law Review* 119 (5): 1553–75. March.

Hasan, I., and M. Malkamäki. 2001. Are expansions cost effective for stock exchanges? a global perspective. *Journal of Banking and Finance* 25 (12): 2339–66. December.

Hasbrouck, J. 1993. Assessing the quality of a security market: a new approach to transaction-cost measurement. *Review of Financial Studies* 6 (1): 191–212. Spring.

Hazarika, S. 2005. Governance change in stock exchanges. Working paper, Baruch College, City University of New York.

Hellenic Exchanges Holding S.A. 1999. Prospectus.

Henderson, K., V. Autheman, S. Elena, L. Ramirez-Daza, and C. Hinojosa. 2003. Judicial transparency checklist: key transparency issues and indicators to promote judicial independence and accountability reforms. International Foundation for Electoral Systems. Summer.

Henry, D. undated. Clarifying and settling access to clearing and settlement in the EU. Working paper, Institute for European Legal Studies, University of Liège, Belgium.

Hermalin, B. E., and M. S. Weisbach. 2003. Boards of directors as an endogenously determined institution: a survey of the economic literature. *Federal Reserve Bank of New York, Economic Policy Review* 9 (1): 7–26. April.

Hertig, G. 2005. On-going board reforms: one-size-fits-all and regulatory capture. *Oxford Review of Economic Policy* 21 (2): 269–82. Summer.

Hertig, G., and R. Lee. 2003. Four predictions about the future of EU securities regulation. *Journal of Comparative Law Studies* 3 (Part 2): 359–77. October.

Hertig, G., R. Lee, and J. A. McCahery. 2009. Empowering the ECB to Supervise Banks: A Choice-Based Approach. TILEC Discussion Paper No. 2009-001, Amsterdam Center for Law & Economics Working Paper No. 2009-01. August.

Hilbers, P. (Deputy Division Chief, Financial Systems Surveillance I Division, Monetary and Exchange Affairs Department, IMF). 2001. The IMF/World Bank Financial Sector Assessment Program: economic perspectives. February.

Hillman, A. J., A. A. Cannella Jr., and R. L. Paetzold. 2000. The resource dependence role of corporate directors: strategic adaptation of board composition in response to environmental change. *Journal of Management Studies* 37 (2): 235–56. March.

Hills, B., D. Rule, S. Parkinson, and C. Young. 1999. Central counterparty clearing houses and financial stability. *Financial Stability Review, Bank of England* 6: 122–34. June.

Hilton, A., and D. Lascelles. 2000. iX: Better or just bigger? CSFI No. 46. August.

HM Treasury (UK). 2001. An independent and accountable FSA. Press Notice 144/01. December 13.

Ho, B. M. 2002. Demutualization of organized securities exchanges in Hong Kong: the great leap forward. *Law and Policy in International Business* 33 (2): 283–368. Winter.

Hobson, D. 1999a. Cedel's shotgun wedding. *Global Custodian*. Summer.

———. 1999b. The French kiss-off. *Global Custodian*. Winter.

———. 2000. Islands in the Clearstream. *Global Custodian*. Spring.

———. 2001. Lussi falls. *Global Custodian*. Summer.

———. 2003. Stench of the smoke-filled room lingers over LCH-Clearnet deal. *Global Custodian*. June 30.

———. 2008. What is the right mechanism for governance in clearing and settlement? What is the role of public authorities in the post-trade arena? European Clearing & Settlement Conference, ICBI. May 20.

Hockey, J. (Minister for Financial Services and Regulation). 2000. Corporate watchdog to watch exchanges. Media release. November 9.

Hodson, D. 2002a. Governance: the board. Gresham Professor of Commerce, Lecture. October 9.

———. 2002b. The non-executive director. Gresham Professor of Commerce, Lecture. December 14.

Holmström, B. 1999. Futures of cooperatives: a corporate perspective. *Finnish Journal of Business Economics* 48 (4): 404–17.

Holmström, B. R., and J. Tirole. 1989. The theory of the firm. In *Handbook of Industrial Organization*. Edited by R. Schmalansee and R. Willig. Amsterdam: North Holland.

Holthausen, C., and J. Tapking. 2004. Raising rival's costs in the securities settlement industry. ECB Working Paper Series No. 376. July.

Holthouse, D. 2002. Demutualization of exchanges—the conflicts of interest (an Australian perspective). In *Demutualization of Stock Exchanges: Problems, Solutions and Case Studies*. Edited by S. Akhtar. Asian Development Bank. Chap. 6.

Hong Kong Exchanges and Clearing Ltd. 2002. Consultation paper on proposed amendments to the listing rules relating to initial listing and continuing listing eligibility and cancellation of listing procedures. July.

Honoré, A. M. 1961. Ownership. In *Oxford Essays in Jurisprudence*. Edited by A. G. Guest. Oxford: Clarendon Press.

House of Commons, Treasury Select Committee. 2002a. Memorandum submitted by the London Stock Exchange Minutes of Evidence. January 14.

———. 2002b. Letter from Sir Brian Williamson (chairman of LIFFE) and M. Jean François Théodore (chairman of the Managing Board of Euronext N.V. and CEO) and submission by LIFFE. Minutes of Evidence. January 11.

Huber, N. 2000. IT conversion costs hit exchange merger plans. *Computerweekly .com*. July 27.

Humphry, R. (Managing Director, Australian Stock Exchange). 1998. ASX demutualisation: cause and effect. Speech, Association of Superannuation Funds of Australia, Sydney. December 9.

Hunter, J. D. 2005. "No crying in baseball"—and no more crying in the stock markets: an alternate-hybrid approach to self-regulation. *University of Cincinnati Law Review* 74 (2): 639–62.

Hutter, B. M. 2006. The role of non-state actors in regulation. In *Global Governance and The Role of Non State Actors*. Edited by G. F. Schuppert, pp. 63–79. Berlin: Nomos Verlagsgesellschaft. Also discussion paper No. 37, Centre for Analysis of Risk and Regulation (CARR), London School of Economics. April 2006.

International Co-operative Alliance. 1995. Statement of co-operative identity.

International Council of Securities Associations. 2006. Best practices for self regulatory organizations. September.

International Council of Securities Associations, Secretariat. 2006. Self-regulation in financial markets: an exploratory survey. September.

International Council of Securities Associations, Working Group on the Governance of Market Infrastructures. 2006. Draft principles for the governance of market infrastructures. May.

International Monetary Fund. 2004a. France: financial system stability assessment, including reports on the observance of standards and codes on the following topics: monetary and financial policy transparency, banking supervision, securities regulation, insurance regulation, payment systems, securities settlement, and anti-money laundering and combating the financing of terrorism. IMF Country Report No. 04/344. November.

———. 2004b. Philippines: Financial Sector Assessment Program—IOSCO objectives and principles of securities regulation assessment. IMF Country Report No. 04/62. March.

———. 2005a. Bermuda: assessment of the supervision and regulation of the financial sector. Volume 2—detailed assessment of observance of standards and codes. January.

———. 2005b. Cayman Islands: assessment of the supervision and regulation of the financial sector. Volume 2—detailed assessment of observance of standards and codes. March.

International Monetary Fund, Independent Evaluation Office. 2006. Report on the evaluation of the Financial Sector Assessment Program. January 5.

International Monetary Fund, Monetary and Capital Markets Department. 2006. Financial Sector Assessment Program Portugal. IOSCO objectives and principles of securities regulation: detailed assessment of observance. December.

International Monetary Fund, Monetary and Exchange Affairs Department. 2002. Financial Sector Assessment Program. FSAP: detailed assessment of observance of standards and codes. Sweden. July.

International Monetary Fund, Monetary and Exchange Affairs Department, and World Bank, Financial Sector Vice Presidency. 2001. Financial Sector Assessment Program Czech Republic. Volume III: assessment of observance with six key international standards and codes. July.

———. 2002. Financial Sector Assessment Program Philippines. IOSCO objectives and principles of securities regulation. July.

International Monetary Fund and World Bank. 2002. Experience with the assessments of the IOSCO objectives and principles of securities regulation under the Financial Sector Assessment Program. April 18.

———. 2006. Implementation of the IOSCO principles. Internal document. May.

International Monetary Fund and World Bank Staff. 2003. Development issues in the FSAP. February 24.

———. 2005. Financial Sector Assessment Program—review, lessons and issues going forward. Approved by Tomás J. T. Baliño and Cesare Calari. February 22.

International Organization of Securities Commissions (IOSCO). 1990. Screen-based trading systems for derivative products. June.

———. 2002a. Objectives and principles of securities regulation. February.

———. 2002b. Multilateral memorandum of understanding concerning consultation and cooperation and the exchange of information. May.

———. 2003a. Objectives and principles of securities regulation. May.

———. 2003b. Methodology for assessing implementation of the IOSCO objectives and principles of securities regulation. Madrid. October.

International Organization of Securities Commissions (IOSCO), Emerging Markets Committee. 2005. Exchange demutualisation in emerging markets. April.

International Organization of Securities Commissions (IOSCO), SRO Consultative Committee. 2000. Model for effective regulation. May.

International Organization of Securities Commissions (IOSCO), Technical Committee. 2001. Issues paper on exchange demutualization. June.

———. 2006a. Regulatory issues arising from exchange evolution. Consultation report. March.

———. 2006b. Regulatory issues arising from exchange evolution. Final report. November.

———. 2007. Multi-jurisdictional information sharing for market oversight—final report. April.

International Securities Consultancy Ltd., Singapore, Aries Group Ltd., USA, and HB Consultants Ltd., Bangladesh. 2006. Demutualization and merger of the Dhaka and Chittagong stock exchanges. Final Report. Prepared for Finance Division, Ministry of Finance, Government of Bangladesh. Asian Development Bank Project on Preparing the Financial Markets Governance Program. Technical Assistance Number 4246-BAN. April.

Itkonen, R. 1996. My views on co-operative corporate governance. *Review of International Co-operation* 89 (4): 20–24.

Jackson, H. E. 2007. Variation in the intensity of financial regulation: preliminary evidence and potential implications. *Yale Journal on Regulation* 24 (2): 101–39. July.

Jacobson, C. D., and J. A. Tarr. 1995. Ownership and financing of infrastructure: historical perspectives. A background paper for the *1994 World Development Report*. World Bank Policy Research Working Paper 1466. June.

Jandosov, O. (First Deputy Prime Minister, Republic of Kazakhstan). 1998. Development, prospects and challenges of financial system in Kazakhstan. Speech, International Conference in Honor of the Fifth Anniversary of the Kyrgyz Som: Challenges to Economies in Transition: Stabilization, Growth, and Governance. Cosponsors: Kyrgyz Republic and the IMF. May 27.

Jenkinson, N. (Executive Director, Financial Stability, Bank of England). 2007. Promoting financial system resilience in modern global capital markets: some issues. Conference on Law and Economics of Systemic Risk in Finance, University of St. Gallen, Switzerland. Speech. June 29.

Jensen, M. C., and W. H. Meckling. 1976. Theory of the firm: managerial behavior, agency costs and ownership structure. *Journal of Financial Economics* 3 (4): 305–60 October.

Jones, H. 2000. Europe's top banks seek one central counterparty. Reuters. June 19.

Jordan, C. 2005. The conundrum of corporate governance. *Brooklyn Journal of International Law* 30 (3): 983–1027.

Kahan, M. 1997. Some problems with stock exchange-based securities regulation: a comment on Mahoney "The exchange as regulator." *Virginia Law Review* 83 (7): 1509–19. October.

Kanter, E. M., and D. V. Summers. 1987. Doing well while doing good: dilemmas of performance measurement in nonprofit organizations and the need for a multiple-constituency approach. In *The Nonprofit Sector: A Research Handbook*. Edited by W. Powell. New Haven: Yale University Press.

Karmel, R. S. 2002. Turning seats into shares: causes and implications of demutualization of stock and futures exchanges *Hastings Law Journal* 53 (2): 367–430.

———. 2003a. Reconciling federal and state interests in securities regulation in the United States and Europe. *Brooklyn Journal of International Law* 28 (2): 495–548.

———. 2003b. Demutualization of exchanges as a strategy for capital market regulatory reform. In *Focus on Capital: New Approaches to Developing Latin American Capital Markets*. Edited by K. Dowers and P. Masci, pp. 269–94. Washington, D.C.: Inter-American Development Bank. Chap. 9.

———. 2007. Is the Financial Industry Regulatory Authority a government agency? Brooklyn Law School, Legal Studies Paper No. 86. October 1.

Kaswell, S. 2004. Self-regulation and the securities market: a renewed effort. *Futures Industry Magazine*. January–February.

Kaufman, G. G., and K. E. Scott. 2003. What is systemic risk, and do bank regulators retard or contribute to it? *Independent Review* 7 (3): 371–91. Winter.

Kauko, K. 2002. Links between securities settlement systems: an oligopoly theoretic approach. Bank of Finland Discussion Papers No. 27-2002. October 22.

———. 2005. Interlinking securities settlement systems: A strategic commitment? Bank of Finland. February.

Kazarian, E. 2006. Integration of the securities market infrastructure in the European Union: policy and regulatory issues. IMF Working Paper, Monetary and Capital Markets WP/06/241. October.

Keaveny, J. 2005. In defence of market self-regulation: an analysis of the history of futures regulation and the trend toward demutualization. *Brooklyn Law Journal* 70 (4): 1419–52. Summer.

Kennedy, S. 2006. London Stock Exchange short of options in fending off Nasdaq. *MarketWatch*. December 13.

Kentouris, C. 2000. Clearstream gets serious about merger. *Securities Industry News*. March 13.

Ketchum, R. G. (CEO, NYSE Regulation, Inc.). 2006. Self-regulation in the modern era. Chief Regulatory Officers International Symposium, Tokyo. Speech. November 6.

Klein, B., R. G. Crawford, and A. A. Alchian. 1978. Vertical integration, appropriable rents, and the competitive contracting process. *Journal of Law and Economics* 21 (2): 297–326. October.

Klemperer, P. 1995. Competition when consumers have switching costs. *Review of Economic Studies* 62 (4): 515–39. October.

Kobayashi, B. H. 2005. Does economics provide a reliable guide to regulating commodity bundling by firms? A survey of the economic literature. *Journal of Competition Law & Economics* 1 (4): 707–46. December.

Kondo, J. E. 2006. Self-regulation and enforcement in financial markets: evidence from investor-broker disputes at the NASD. Working paper, MIT Sloan School of Management. July 27.

Köppl, T. V., and C. Monnet. 2003. Guess what: it's the settlements! European Central Bank, Directorate General Research. November.

———. 2006. Central counterparties. Working paper, Department of Economics, Queen's University, and DG Research, European Central Bank. March 10.

Korea Exchange. 2009. Business Report 2008.1.1-12.31.

Kotewall, R. G., and G.C.K. Kwong. 2002. Report of the panel of inquiry on the Penny Stock Incident ("PIPSI Report"). September.

Krishnamurti, C., J. M. Sequeira, and F. Fangjian. 2003. Stock exchange governance and market quality. *Journal of Banking and Finance* 27 (9): 1859–78. September.

Kroszner, R. S. 1999. Can the financial markets privately regulate risk? The development of derivatives clearinghouses and recent over-the-counter innovations. Part 2: The role of central banks in money and payments systems. *Journal of Money, Credit and Banking* 31 (3): 596–618. August.

Kroszner, R. S. (Governor, Federal Reserve Bank of Chicago). 2006. Central counterparty clearing: history, innovation, and regulation. European Central Bank and Federal Reserve Bank of Chicago Joint Conference on Issues related to Central Counterparty Clearing, Frankfurt. April 3.

Kuan, J. W., and S. F. Diamond. 2006. Ringing the bell on the NYSE: Might a nonprofit stock exchange have been efficient? bepress Legal Series Paper 1451, Santa Clara University School of Law. July 13.

Kwong, K.-C. 2002. Remarks. Press release by CEO of HKEx. July 31.

Kyodo News International. 2005. Murakami fund sells entire stake in OSE operator. Osaka. December 29.

Lackritz, M. E. (President, SIA). 2005. Testimony before the Committee on Banking, Housing and Urban Affairs. US Senate Hearing on "Regulation NMS and recent market developments." May 18.

Ladekarl, J. F. 2000. Electronic trading in the case of Denmark. In *Futuro de la negociación de valores*, pp. 61–81. San José, Costa Rica: Superintendencia General de Valores (SUGEVAL).

Lamb, A. 2004. Speech. ISSA, Wolfsburg, Switzerland. June 17.

Lambert, E. 2008. Bearpit: inside the world's biggest financial exchange. *Forbes.com.* January.

Langevoort, D. C. 2000. The human nature of corporate boards: law, norms and the unintended consequences of independence and accountability. Georgetown University Law Center, 2000 Working Paper Series, Business, Economics, and Regulatory Law, Working Paper No. 241402. September 8.

LCH.Clearnet. 2003. Creating the central counterparty of choice.

———. 2005a. Report and consolidated financial statements 2004.

———. 2005b. Interim accounts. July 30.

———. 2005c. Clearing of transactions executed on MTS Italy, use of Cassa di Compensazione e Garanzia ("CC&G") as an allied clearing house. Instruction I.3-2, Notice No. 2005-0106. July 18.

———. 2006a. Competition in EU securities trading and post-trading, issues paper—response by LCH.Clearnet Group Ltd. June 30.

———. 2006b. LCH.Clearnet rationalises IT strategy. Press release. July 21.

———. 2006c. Report and consolidated financial statements.

———. 2007. LCH.Clearnet and Euronext announce repurchase by LCH.Clearnet of shares held by Euronext to more closely align customer and shareholder interests. Press release. March 12.

———. 2009a. LCH.Clearnet to launch Eurozone clearing of credit default swaps. Paris. February 13.

———. 2009b. LCH.Clearnet Ltd introduces 1p clearing fees on EquityClear. London. May 5.

———. 2009c. BATS Europe appoints LCH.Clearnet to clear UK and Swiss stocks. London. May 5.

———. 2009d. LCH.Clearnet signs MOU with Chi-X Europe to offer CCP services. London. May 6.

———. 2009e. LCH.Clearnet to clear for NYSE Arca Europe. London. May 6.

———. 2009f. LCH.Clearnet to clear for Turquoise. London. May 7.

———. 2009g. LCH.Clearnet signs MOU to launch clearing in cooperation with EMCF. London. May 20.

———. 2009h. LCH.Clearnet SA introduces €0.05 clearing fees on cash equity markets. Paris. September 15.

Lee, C. 2002. Remarks at the government press conference on market consultation relating to listing eligibility. July 28.

Lee, C., and M. Ready. 1991. Inferring trade direction from intraday data. *Journal of Finance* 46 (2): 733–46.

Lee, R. 1998. *What Is an Exchange? The Automation, Management and Regulation of Financial Markets.* Oxford: Oxford University Press.

———. 2000. London should sell at the highest price. *Euromoney*: 34. June.

———. 2001. Central counter-parties and the stock exchange industry. Oxford Finance Group, prepared for the International Federation of Stock Exchanges (FIBV). January 25.

———. 2002a. Capital markets that benefit investors: a survey of the evidence on fragmentation, internalisation and market transparency. Prepared by Oxford Finance Group for the Association of Private Client Investment Managers and Stockbrokers/European Association of Securities Dealers, British Bankers Association, Danish Securities Dealers Association, Futures and Options Association, International Primary Market Association, International Securities Market Association, International Swaps and Derivatives Association, London Investment Banking Association, Swedish Securities Dealers Association, and The Bond Market Association. September 30.

———. 2002b. The future of Securities Exchanges. In *Brookings-Wharton Papers on Financial Services 2002.* Edited by R. E. Litan and R. Herring, pp. 1–33. Washington, D.C.: Brookings Institution.

———. 2002c. Corporatisation of exchanges and central counterparties: the dark side will come. In *Handbook of World Stock, Derivative and Commodity Exchanges.* London: Mondo Visione.

———. 2003a. A poor deal for Europe's market users. *Financial Times.* September 2.

———. 2003b. Changing market structures, demutualization and the future of securities trading. In *The Future of Domestic Capital Markets in Developing Countries.* Edited by R. E. Litan, M. Pomerleano, and V. Sundararajan, pp. 283–303. Washington, D.C.: Brookings Institution. Chap. 10.

———. 2003c. Report on governance and block trading on the Macedonian stock exchange: international experience, domestic analysis and recommendations. USAID Contract No: PCE-I-00-99-00008-00, submitted to USAID/Skopje by Deloitte Touche Tohmatsu Emerging Markets, Ltd., Macedonia Financial Sector Strengthening Project, Report No. 2003-12. October 31.

———. 2007. Never mind the economics. *The Banker*: 50–51. January.

———. 2009. *The Governance of Financial Market Infrastructure Institutions.* Oxford Finance Group.

Leinonen, H. 2003. Restructuring securities systems processing—a blue print proposal for real-time/t+0 processing. Bank of Finland Discussion Papers 6/3/2003. July.

Leinonen, H., and K. Soramäki. 2003. Simulating interbank payment and securities settlement mechanisms with the BoF-PSS2 simulator. Research Department, Bank of Finland Discussion Paper 23-2003. October 1.

Levine, D. S. 2007. Secrecy and unaccountability: trade secrets in our public infrastructure. *Florida Law Review* 59: 135–93.

Levine, M. E., and J. L. Forrence. 1990. Regulatory capture, public interest, and the public agenda: toward a synthesis. *Journal of Law, Economics, & Organization* 6: 167–98. Special issue: papers from the Organization of Political Institutions conference.

Levrau, A., and L.A.A. Van den Berghe. 2007. Identifying key determinants of effective boards of directors. Universiteit Gent, Faculteit Economie en Bedrijfskunde, Working Paper 2007/447. January.

Lim, J. Y., and C. G. Pascual. Undated. The detrimental role of biased policies: framework and case studies. The Political Economy of Corruption. Transparent and Accountable Governance. Study 3.

Linciano, N., G. Siciliano, and G. Trovatore. 2005. The clearing and settlement industry: structure, competition and regulatory issues. Quaderni de Finanza: Studi e Ricerche. CONSOB, N. 58. May.

Lipton, D. 1983. The SEC or the exchanges: Who should do what and when? A proposal to allocate regulatory responsibilities for securities markets. *University of California Davis Law Review* 16: 527–72, Spring.

Lloyd-Smith, J. 2000. Brokers demand more detail on iX regulation. *The Independent*. August 22.

Lo Giudice, Salvatore. 2007. Settlement internalization: the production and distribution of services in the (clearing and) settlement industry. *Journal of Financial Transformation* 20: 127–41.

London Economics. 2005. Securities trading, clearing, central counterparties and securities settlement in EU 25—an overview of current arrangements. Report commissioned by the Competition Directorate General of the European Commission. June.

London Investment Banking Association (UK), French Association of Investment Firms, Italian Association of Financial Intermediaries, French Banking Federation, and Swedish Securities Dealers Association. 2005. Statement of principles to be applied to the consolidation of stock exchange and infrastructure providers in Europe. February 3.

London Stock Exchange. 2002a. A practical guide to listing.

———. 2002b. Clearing and settlement in Europe: response to the first report of the Giovannini Group. February 7.

———. 2006. London Stock Exchange agrees terms with SIS x-clear to offer customers choice of clearing provider. News release. May 24.

———. 2007a. NASDAQ Stock Market, Inc. Final offers lapsed. RNS number: 0668R. February 12.

———. 2007b. QIA invests in London Stock Exchange. Press release 18/07. September 20.

———. 2008. London Stock Exchange group to promote dual CCP model for London market. Press release 27/08. September 24.

Lorsch, J. W., and E. MacIver. 1989. *Pawns or Potentates: The Reality of America's Corporate Boards.* Boston: Harvard Business School Press.

Loss, L., and J. Seligman. 1990. *Securities Regulation.* Boston: Little, Brown & Company. Vol. 6, 3rd ed.

Low, C. K. 2004. A framework for the delisting of penny stocks in Hong Kong. *North Carolina Journal of International Law and Commercial Regulation* 30 (1): 76–120, Fall.

Lublin, J. S. 2003. Where was the NYSE board? *Wall Street Journal.* September 11.

Mace, M. 1971. *Directors: Myth and Reality.* Boston: Harvard Business School Press.

Macey, J. R., and D. D. Haddock. 1985. Shirking at the Securities and Exchange Commission: the failure of the national market system. *University of Illinois Law Review* 2: 315–62.

Macey, J. R., and M. O'Hara. 1999a. Globalization, exchange governance, and the future of exchanges. In *Brookings-Wharton Papers on Financial Services 1999*. Edited by R. E. Litan and A. M. Santomero, pp. 1–23. Washington, D.C.: Brookings Institution.

———. 1999b. Regulating exchanges and alternative trading systems: a law and economics perspective. *Journal of Legal Studies* 28 (1): 17–54. January.

———. 2002. The economics of stock exchange listing fees and listing requirements. *Journal of Financial Intermediation* 11 (3): 297–319. July.

———. 2005. From markets to venues: securities regulation in an evolving world. *Stanford Law Review* 58 (2): 563–600. November.

Macey, J. R., M. O'Hara, and D. Pompilio. 2005. Down and out in the stock market: the law and finance of the delisting process. Working paper. April.

Madhavan, A. 2000. Market microstructure: a survey. *Journal of Financial Markets* 3 (3): 205–58.

Magnusson, N., and W. McSheehy. 2007. Dubai to buy stakes in Nasdaq, LSE; strikes OMX deal. Bloomberg. September 20.

Maguire, F. 2001a. Virt-x shelves central counterparty. *Financial News Online.* September 24.

———. 2001b. Clearing houses join forces. *Financial News Online.* August 6.

Mahoney, P. G. 1997. The exchange as regulator. *Virginia Law Review* 83 (7): 1453–1500. October.

———. 2001. The political economy of the Securities Act of 1933. *Journal of Legal Studies* 30 (1): 1-31. January.

———. 2003. Public and private rule making in securities markets. Policy Analysis No. 498, Cato Project on Corporate Governance, Audit, and Tax Reform. November 13.

Malkamäki, M. 1999. Are there economies of scale in stock exchange activities? Bank of Finland Discussion Papers 2/2003. March 31.

Malkamäki, M., and J. Topi. 1999. Strategic challenges for exchanges and securities settlement. Bank of Finland Discussion Papers, Research Dept. No. 21/99. December 31.

Manifest. 2006. Standards and guidance: no single approach to clearing and settlement to be imposed. *Governance News.* August 28.

Mann, B. 2003. "We didn't know" is no excuse. *The Motley Fool. www.fool.com.* September 17.

Marcus, S. 2000. Financial Sector Assessment Program: feedback from governments and lessons from the program. Presentation to Senior Banking Supervisors from Emerging Market Economies. October 16.

MarketWatch. (Chris Oliver). 2009. Tokyo Stock Exchange shelves IPO. March 24.

Markham, J. W. 1987. *The History of Commodity Futures Trading and Its Regulation.* New York: Praeger.

———. 2003. Super regulator: a comparative analysis of securities and derivatives regulation in the United States, the United Kingdom and Japan. *Brooklyn Journal of International Law* 28 (2): 319–410.

Markman, N. A. 2002. Regulation of a demutualized derivatives exchange (United States). In *Demutualization of Stock Exchanges: Problems, Solutions and Case Studies*. Edited by S. Akhtar. Asian Development Bank. Chap. 10.

Marley, T. (Vice President and Legal and Corporate Secretary, CDS). 2005. Letter to Cindy Petlock, manager, Market Regulation, Ontario Securities Commission. *Ontario Securities Commission Bulletin* 28: 3483, 3485. March 10.

Martin, W. M., Jr. 1971. The securities markets: a report with recommendations. Submitted to the Board of Governors of the New York Stock Exchange. August 5.

Mayhew, S., and V. Mihov. 2004. How do exchanges select stocks for option listing? *Journal of Finance* 59 (1): 447–71. February.

McCarthy, C. (Chairman, FSA). 2007. Financial regulation: myth and reality. British American Business London Insight Series and Financial Services Forum. Speech. February 13.

McCue, A. 2006. Failed IT project costs clearing house €47m: LCH.Clearnet system "not economically or technically viable". *www.silicon.com*. July 25.

McGhie, T. 2007. Nasdaq in talks over its LSE stake. *Financial Mail*. September 16.

McPartland, J. (Financial Markets Adviser). 2002. Open architecture clearing. *Futures Industry Magazine* Outlook 03: 18-23. March.

———. 2005. Clearing and settlement demystified. *Chicago Fed Letter*, Essays on Issues, No. 210. January.

McTague, R. 2006. Panelists at AEI forum say SEC rule thwarts deregulation of market data. *Securities Regulation and Law Report (BNA)* 38: 610. April 10.

Mendiola, A., and M. O'Hara. 2004. Taking stock in stock markets: the changing governance of exchanges. Working paper, Johnson Graduate School of Management, Cornell University. March.

Miller, S. S. 1985. Self-regulation of the securities markets: a critical examination. *Washington and Lee Law Review* 42: 853–87.

Millman, G. J. 2002. ECN: A new force in the stock markets? (Global Securities). *Financial Executive*. May 1.

Millstein, I. M., and P. W. MacAvoy. 1998. The active board of directors and performance of the large publicly traded corporation. *Columbia Law Review* 98 (5): 1283–1322. June.

Milne, A. 2004. Competition and the rationalisation of European securities clearing and settlement. Working paper, Cass Business School. July.

———. 2005a. Standard setting, interoperability, and competition in securities settlement systems. June.

———. 2005b. Standard setting and competition in securities settlement. Bank of Finland Research Discussion Papers 23.

Mistry, H. B. 2007. Battle of the regulators: Is the U.S. system of securities regulation better provided for than that which operates in the United Kingdom? *Journal of International Financial Markets* 4: 137–42.

Mitchell, L. E. 2005. Structural holes, CEOs, and informational monopolies: the missing link in corporate governance. *Brooklyn Law Review* 70 (4): 1313–68. Summer.

Moiseiwitsch, J. 2003. The twilight regulator. *CFO Asia*. March.

Moloney, N. 2008. *EC Securities Regulation*. Oxford: Oxford University Press. 2nd ed.

Moore, J. 2000. Brokers fear raw deal on merger—Deutsche Börse. *The Times*. May 11.

Morck, R. 2004. Behavioral finance in corporate governance—independent directors and non-executive chairs. Harvard Institute of Economic Research, Discussion Paper No. 2037. May.

Morgan, B., and K. Yeung. 2007. *An Introduction to Law and Regulation: Text and Materials*. Cambridge: Cambridge University Press.

Moser, J. T. 1994. What is multilateral clearing and who cares? *Chicago Fed Letter* 87. November.

———. 1998. Contracting innovations and the evolution of clearing and settlement methods at futures exchanges. Federal Reserve Bank of Chicago Working Paper No. 1998–26.

Moskow, M. H. (President and CEO, Federal Reserve Bank of Chicago). 2006. Public policy and central counterparty clearing. *Economic Perspectives* 4Q: 46–50. Federal Reserve Bank of Chicago.

Moteff, J., and P. Parfomak. 2004. Critical infrastructure and key assets: definition and identification. Congressional Research Service, Resources, Science, and Industry Division. October 1.

Muth, M., and L. Donaldson. 1998. Stewardship theory and board structure: a contingency approach. *Corporate Governance* 6 (1): 5–28. January.

Nagy, D. M. 2005. Playing peekaboo with constitutional law: the PCAOB and its public/private status. *Notre Dame Law Review* 80 (3): 975–1071.

Na-Ranong, K. (CEO, Stock Exchange of Thailand). 2002. Demutualization. Regional Seminar on Non-Bank Financial Institution in East Asia: How Can NBFIs Play a Greater Role in a Bank-Based Economy? September 5.

NASDAQ. 2005. Letter to SEC "Re: Proposed Rulemaking on SRO Governance (File No. S7-39-04); Concept Release Concerning Self-Regulation (File No. S7-40-04)." Edward S. Knight, Executive Vice President and General Counsel. March 8.

———. 2006. Announcement in response to public rejection by LSE. March 10.

———. 2007a. NASDAQ with Borse Dubai and OMX takes leadership to create a unique global exchange platform. Press release. September 20.

———. 2007b. NASDAQ obtains clearance from the Committee on Foreign Investment in the United States. Press release. December 31.

NASDAQ OMX. 2008. NASDAQ OMX Announces its intent to launch the NASDAQ Clearing Corporation. Equity Trader Alert No. 2008–116. October. 8.

NASDAQ OMX, EMCF, EuroCCP, and SIX x-clear. 2009. NASDAQ OMX announces timeline for competitive central counterparty clearing in Nordics. EMCF, EuroCCP and SIX x-clear agree on January 29th 2010 timeline for CCP interoperability on NASDAQ OMX Nordic markets. June 12.

National Association of Securities Dealers. 1995. Report of the NASD Select Committee on Structure and Governance to the NASD Board of Governors. September 15.

National Council on Public Works Improvement (US). 1988. Fragile foundations: a report on America's public works. Final Report to the President and Congress. Washington, D.C. February.

National Economic Research Associates. 2001. The role of market definition in monopoly and dominance inquiries. Economic Discussion Paper 2, Prepared for the Office of Fair Trading, OFT342. July.

New York Stock Exchange. 2003a. NYSE board to implement committee's recommendations to strengthen governance of exchange. Press release. June 5.

———. 2003b. NYSE announces new contract for Dick Grasso through May 2007. August 27.

———. 2006. Annual report 2005, form 10-K.

New York Stock Exchange LLC. 2007. Second amended and restated operating agreement of New York Stock Exchange LLC. April 4.

Niels, G., F. Barnes, and R. van Dijk. 2003. Unclear and unsettled: the debate on competition in the clearing and settlement of securities trades. *European Competition Law Review* 24 (12): 634–39.

Norman, P. 2007. *Plumbers and Visionaries: Securities Settlement and Europe's Financial Market.* Chichester: John Wiley & Sons.

NYSE Group. 2006. Prospectus. May 4.

Nystedt, J. 2004. Derivative market competition: OTC markets versus organized derivative exchanges. IMF Working Paper WP/04/61. April.

O'Hara, M. 2004. Searching for a new center: U.S. securities markets in transition. *Federal Reserve Bank of Atlanta Economic Review* 89 (4): 37–52. 4th quarter.

Oesterle, D. A., D. A. Winslow, and S. C. Anderson. 1992. The New York Stock Exchange and its outmoded specialist system: Can the exchange innovate to survive? *Journal of Corporation Law* 17: 223–311. Winter.

Office of Fair Trading. 2003. Statement on LCH.Clearnet merger. August 11.

———. 2004a. Market definition: understanding competition law. Competition Law Guideline OFT403. December.

———. 2004b. Assessment of market power: understanding competition law. Competition Law Guideline OFT415. December.

———. 2007. OFT clears NASDAQ's bid for the London Stock Exchange. Press release 10/07. January 18.

Ogus, A. 2000. Self-regulation. In *Encyclopedia of Law and Economics.* Vol. 1: *The History and Methodology of Law and Economics.* Edited by B. Bouckaert and G. De Geest. Cheltenham: Edward Elgar. Chap. 9400.

Oliver, J. J. (President & CEO, Investment Dealers Association of Canada). 2005. Reforming self-regulatory organizations: the impact on financial intermediaries and financial markets. ICSA 2005 Annual Meeting, Lugano, Switzerland. May 3.

Ontario Securities Commission. 2000a. OSC examination of the corporate governance and organizational structure of the Investment Dealers Association of Canada and review of the 1999 Member Regulation Self-Assessment. July.

———. 2000b. In the Matter of the Securities Act, R.S.O. 1990, Chapter S. 21, As Amended (The "Act") and In the Matter of the Toronto Stock Exchange Inc. (TSE) 23 O.S.C.B. 2495. Panel: David Brown, Howard I. Wetston. April 3.

Organisation for Economic Co-operation and Development. 2004. OECD principles of corporate governance.

———. 2005. OECD guidelines on corporate governance of state-owned enterprises.

Osaki, S. 2005. The implications of a recent attempt to acquire shares in Osaka Securities Exchange. *Nomura Capital Market Review* 8 (4): 2–12. Winter.

Osborne, G. 2006. The way to prevent American regulatory creep. *Financial Times*. October 12.

Oxford Economic Research Associates. 2004. Review of the impact of the Financial Services and Markets Act 2000 on competition. Stage 1: sifting methodology. Prepared for Office of Fair Trading, OFT 714. March.

Packel, I. 1970. *The Law of the Organization and Operation of Cooperatives.* Philadelphia: Joint Committee on Continuing Legal Education of the American Law Institute and the American Bar Association. 4th ed.

Pagano, M. 1989. Trading volume and asset liquidity. *Quarterly Journal of Economics* 104 (2): 255–74. April.

Pagano, M., and A. J. Padilla. 2005. The economics of cash trading: an overview. LECG—a report for Euronext. May 4.

Pagano, M., O. Randl, A. A. Röell, and J. Zechner. 2001. What makes stock exchanges succeed? Evidence from cross-listing decisions. *European Economic Review* 45 (4–6): 770–82. May.

Peake, J., and M. Mendelson. 1994. "Intermediaries or investors"—Whose market is it anyway? *Journal of Corporation Law* 19: 443. Spring.

Pearson, W. 2002. Demutualization of exchanges—the conflicts of interest (Hong Kong). In *Demutualization of Stock Exchanges: Problems, Solutions and Case Studies*. Edited by S. Akhtar. Asian Development Bank. Chap. 5.

Pellervo (Confederation of Finnish Cooperatives). 2000. Corporate governance and management control in cooperatives. November.

Perrin, S. 2006. Nasdaq bid raises Sarbox fears. www.financialdirector.co.uk. March 30.

Peston, R. 2007. LSE: fight for independence. *BBC Blog*. February 1.

Petrella, G. 2009. Securities markets regulation and competition across trading venues in Europe and United States. Working paper, Catholic University, Milan. January 13.

Pfeffer, J., and G. R. Salancik. 1978. *The External Control of Organizations: A Resource Dependence Perspective*. New York: Harper & Row.

Pirrong, C. 2000. A theory of financial exchange organization. *Journal of Law and Economics* 43 (2): 437–71. October.

———. 2005. Bund for glory, or it's a long way to tip a market. Working paper, University of Houston. March 8.

———. 2007a. The industrial organization of execution, clearing and settlement in financial markets. Working paper, Bauer College of Business, University of Houston. October 9.

———. 2007b. Color me skeptical. The professor @ 8:57 am. http://streetwiseprofessor.com/?m=200705. May 24.

Pistor, K., D. M. Berkowitz, and J.-F. Richard. 1999. Economic development, legality and the transplant effect. November.

Pitofsky, R., D. Patterson, and J. Hooks. 2002. The essential facilities doctrine under U.S. antitrust law. *Antitrust Law Journal* 70: 443–62.

Porter, P. K., and G. W. Scully. 1987. Economic efficiency in cooperatives. *Journal of Law and Economics* 30 (2): 489–512. October.

Posner, E. 2006. The new transatlantic regulatory relations in financial services. 1st Annual GARNET Conference on Global Financial and Monetary Governance, the EU and Emerging Market Economies. September.

Prentice, R. A. 2002. Whither securities regulation? Some behavioral observations regarding proposals for its future. *Duke Law Journal* 51 (5): 1397–1511. March.

———. 2005. Regulatory competition in securities law: a dream (that should be) deferred. *Ohio State Law Journal* 66 (6): 1155–1230.

———. 2006. The inevitability of a strong SEC. *Cornell Law Review* 91 (4): 775–840. May.

Pritchard, A. C. 2003. Self-regulation and securities markets. *Regulation* 26 (1): 32–39. Spring.

Quinn, J. 2007. Nasdaq cosies up to Turquoise banks. *Telegraph*. February 2.

Rajan, R. G., and L. Zingales. 2001. The great reversals: the politics of financial development in the twentieth century. NBER Working Paper No. 8178.

Ramos, S. B. 2006. Why do stock exchanges demutualize and go public? Swiss Finance Institute, Research Paper Series No. 06–10.

Ramphal, N. R. 2007. The role of public and private litigation in the enforcement of securities laws in the United States. Dissertation, Pardee Rand Graduate School. August.

Ranson, A. 2005. Euronext N.V.: the fight for LIFFE. *Arthur W. Page Society Journal*: 18–29. Case Study Competition in Corporate Communications.

Reece, M. 2001. Infrastructure organizations and IPOs. *Journal of Financial Transformation* 2: 106–7. August.

Reiffen, D., and M. Robe. 2007. Ownership structure and enforcement incentives at self-regulatory financial exchanges. Working paper, CFTC & Kogod School of Business, American University. May 31.

Reiser, D. B. 2007. Director independence in the independent sector. *Fordham Law Review* 76 (2): 795–832.

Reuters. 1999. Cedel, Deutsche Boerse create clearing giant. May 14.

———. 2000a. Tokyo bourse talks with NYSE, others on global market. June 7.

———. 2000b. Euronext seen launching bid for LSE. September 11.

———. 2001. Nationality of buyer unimportant in LIFFE. October 20.

———. 2004. Grasso refusing to return NYSE payout. February 27.

———. 2007. Markets watchdog urges Russian exchanges to merge. 11:06 pm. February 6.

———. 2008. Grasso case "over" as court dismisses claims. July 1.

Review Committee on the Canadian Depository for Securities. 1974. Report. September.

Rochet, J.-C., and J. Tirole. 2003. Platform competition in two-sided markets. *Journal of the European Economic Association* 1 (4): 990–1029. June.

———. 2005. Two-sided markets: a progress report. Working paper. November 29.

Rodrigues, U. 2007. The fetishization of independence. University of Georgia Law School, UGA Legal Studies Research Paper No. 07-007. March.

Roe, M. 2003. Legal origins and modern stock markets. CIFRA TI finance seminars. September 27.

———. 2005. Delaware's politics. *Harvard Law Review* 118 (8): 2491–2543. June.

Romano, R. 1998. Empowering investors: a market approach to securities regulation. *Yale Law Journal* 107: 2359–2430.

Rosenstein, S., and J. G. Wyatt. 1997. Inside directors, board effectiveness, and shareholder wealth. *Journal of Financial Economics* 44 (2): 229–48. May.

Rubin, B. L., and C. J. Cannon. 2006. The house that the regulators built (revisited): an analysis of whether respondents should litigate against NASD. *Securities Regulation & Law Report* 38 (19): 810–17. May 8.

Russo, D., T. L. Hart, M. C. Malaguti, and C. Papathanassiou. 2004. Governance of securities clearing and settlement systems. European Central Bank, Occasional Paper Series No. 21. October.

Russo, D., T. L. Hart, and A. Schönenberger. 2002. The evolution of clearing and central counterparty services for exchange-traded derivatives in the United States and Europe: a comparison. European Central Bank Occasional Paper No. 5. September.

Russo, T. A., and W.K.S. Wang. 1972. The structure of the securities market—past and future. *Fordham Law Review* 41: 1–42.

Sale, H. 2006. Federal fiduciary duties for directors. Law and Economics Workshop, University of California, Berkeley, Paper 7.

Salman, T. K. (Chairman, Investment Dealers Association of Canada). 2003. Self-regulation works best by putting the public interest first. Annual Meeting & Conference, St. Andrew's by-the-Sea, New Brunswick. June 23.

Schaper, T. 2009. Organizing Equity Exchanges. Goethe-University Frankfurt, efinancelab, Discussion Paper 22/2009. 15th Americas Conference on Information Systems, San Francisco. August 6.

Schlag, P. 2007. The de-differentiation problem. University of Colorado Law School, Working Paper no. 07-09, Legal Studies Research Paper series. August 6.

Schmiedel, H. 2001. Technological development and concentration of stock exchanges in Europe. Bank of Finland Discussion Paper No. 21. August 10.

Schmiedel, H., M. Malkamäki, and J. Tarkka. 2006. Economies of scale and technological development in securities depository and settlement systems. *Journal of Banking and Finance* 30 (6): 1783–1806.

Schmiedel, H., and A. Schönenberger. 2005. Integration of securities market infrastructures in the euro area. European Central Bank Occasional Paper Series No. 33. July.

Schooner, H. M., and M. Taylor. 2003. United Kingdom and United States responses to the regulatory challenges of modern financial markets. *Texas International Law Journal* 38 (2): 317–46. Spring.

Schrader, L. F. 1989. Equity capital and restructuring of cooperatives as investor-oriented firms. *Journal of Agricultural Cooperation* 4: 41–53. July.

Schwarcz, S. L. 2008. Systemic risk. *Georgetown Law Journal* 97 (1): 193–249.

Schwartz, R. A., and M. S. Pagano. 2005. On exchange consolidation and competition. A comment letter to the Competition Commission in connection with the London Stock Exchange inquiry. May 31.

Scott, C. 2004. Regulation in the age of governance: the rise of the post-regulatory state. In *The Politics of Regulation: Institutions and Regulatory Reforms for the Age of Governance*. Edited by J. Jordana and D. Levi-Faur, pp. 145–74. Cheltenham: Edward Elgar. Also National Europe Centre Paper No. 100, Australian National University. June 6, 2003.

Securities and Exchange Board of India. 2003. Corporatisation and demutualisation of stock exchanges in India. SMD/POLICY/Cir No. 3/03. January 30.

———. 2005. Order under section 4B(6) read with section 4B(7) of the Securities Contracts (Regulation) Act, 1956 in the matter of the BSE (corporatisation and demutualisation) scheme, 2005. Mumbai F. No. SEBI/MRD/40967/2005. May 20.

Securities and Exchange Commission. 1980. Regulation of clearing agencies. (Standards release.) Release No. 16900. June 17.

———. 1988. Intermarket Clearing Corporation—Order granting temporary registration as a clearing agency. Release No. 26154. October 3.

———. 1989a. Order granting Delta Government Options Corporation temporary registration as a clearing agency. Release No. 26450. January 12.

———. 1989b. Order granting the Participants Trust Company temporary registration as a clearing agency. Release No. 26671. March 28.

———. 1996. Report pursuant to section 21(a) of the Securities Exchange Act of 1934 regarding the NASD and the NASDAQ market. Release No. 37542. August 8.

———. 1998a. Self-regulatory organizations; Emerging Markets Clearing Corporation; order granting temporary registration as a clearing agency. Release No. 39661. February 13.

———. 1998b. Regulation of exchanges and alternative trading systems. Release No. 40760. December 8.

———. 2004a. Self-regulatory organizations; order approving proposed rule change and amendment No. 1 thereto and notice of filing and order granting accelerated approval to amendments No. 2 and 3 to proposed rule change by the Boston Stock Exchange, Inc. relating to the creation of the Boston Options Exchange Regulation, LLC. Release No. 49065. January 13.

———. 2004b. Self-regulatory organizations; Philadelphia Stock Exchange, Inc.; order approving proposed rule change and notice of filing and order granting accelerated approval of amendment No. 3 thereto relating to the demutualization of the Philadelphia Stock Exchange, Inc. Release No. 49098. January 16.

———. 2004c Self-regulatory organizations; Pacific Exchange, Inc.; order approving proposed rule change and notice of filing and order granting accelerated approval of amendment No. 1 thereto relating to the demutualization of the Pacific Exchange, Inc. Release No. 49718. May 17.

———. 2004d Self-regulatory organizations; order approving proposed rule change and amendment nos. 1, 2, and 3 thereto and notice of filing and order granting accelerated approval to amendment nos. 4 and 6 to the proposed rule change by the American Stock Exchange LLC relating to the National Association of Securities Dealers, Inc.'s sale of its interest in the American Stock

Exchange LLC to the Amex Membership Corporation. Release No. 50927. December 23.

———. 2004e. Fair administration and governance of self-regulatory organizations; disclosure and regulatory reporting by self-regulatory organizations; recordkeeping requirements for self-regulatory organizations; ownership and voting limitations for members of self-regulatory organizations; ownership reporting requirements for members of self-regulatory organizations; listing and trading of affiliated securities by a self-regulatory organization. Release No. 50699. November 18.

———. 2004f. Concept release concerning self-regulation. Release No. 50700. November 18.

———. 2005. In the Matter of the New York Stock Exchange, Inc., Respondent: Order instituting public administrative proceedings pursuant to Section 19(h)1 and 21C of the Securities Exchange Act of 1934, making findings, ordering compliance with undertakings, and imposing a censure and a cease-and-desist order. Release No. 51524. April 12.

Securities and Exchange Commission, Division of Market Regulation. 1994. Market 2000: an examination of current equity market developments. January.

Securities and Exchange Commission of Pakistan, Expert Committee. 2004. Demutualization and integration/transformation of stock exchanges. Report. September 2.

Securities and Futures Commission. 2002a. Quality of markets and the case for more effective delisting mechanism. Corporate Finance Division and Research Department. Press release. July 25.

———. 2002b. Quality of markets and the case for more effective delisting mechanism. *SFC Quarterly Bulletin*. Corporate Finance Division and Research Department. Summer.

Securities Industry Association. 2003. Re-inventing self-regulation. White paper for the Securities Industry Association (05/01/2000). Updated by SIA staff. October 14.

———. 2005. Letter to SEC re SRO governance and transparency proposal—file No. S7-39-03, SRO concept release—file No. S7-40-04. From Marc Lackritz, President. March 9.

Sedo, K. J. 1987. Cooperative mergers and consolidations: a consideration of the legal and tax issues. *North Dakota Law Review* 63: 377-403.

Seifert, W. 2001. Managing growth in the securities process chain. *Finance Foundation News* 1: 7–29. October.

Seligman, J. 2003. *The Transformation of Wall Street: A History of the Securities and Exchange Commission and Modern Corporate Finance*. New York: Aspen Publishers. 3rd ed.

———. 2004. Cautious evolution or perennial irresolution: stock market self-regulation during the first seventy years of the Securities and Exchange Commission. *Business Lawyer* 59 (4): 1347–87. August.

Serifsoy, B. 2007. Stock exchange business models and their operative performance—empirical evidence. *Journal of Banking and Finance* 31 (10): 2978–3012. October.

———. 2008. Demutualization, outsider ownership, and stock exchange performance—empirical evidence. *Economics of Governance* 9 (4): 305–39. October.

Shah, A., and S. Thomas. 2000. David and Goliath: displacing a primary market. *Journal of Global Financial Markets* 1 (1): 14–23. Spring.

———. 2001. Policy issues in the Indian securities market. Working paper. July 13.

Shaw, L. 2006. Overview of corporate governance issues for co-operatives. Discussion paper, Commissioned by the Global Corporate Governance Forum. November.

Shin, D. undated. Die "Essential-Facilities"-Doktrin im europäischen Kartellrecht. Dissertion zur Erlangung des Grades eines Doktors der Rechte des Fachbereichs Rechts- und Wirtschaftswissenschaften der Johannes Gutenberg-Universität Mainz.

Shivdasani, A., and D. Yermack. 1999. CEO involvement in the selection of new board members: an empirical analysis. *Journal of Finance* 54 (5): 1829–53. October.

Shy, O. 2001. *The Economics of Network Industries*. Cambridge: Cambridge University Press.

SIS x-Clear. 2006. Competition in EU clearing services. Letter to EU Commission, Sean Greenaway. June 26.

———. 2008. SIX x-clear introduces a new pricing model and reduces its prices. December 5.

———. 2009a. EuroCCP and SIX x-clear sign agreement on interoperability—Turquoise first platform to benefit. London. May 7.

———. 2009b. SIX x-clear Ltd to provide competitive clearing for QUOTE MTF. Zurich. August 24.

SIX x-clear and European Multilateral Clearing Facility. 2009. EMCF and SIX x-clear forge link in triumph for interoperability. London. February 3.

Squam Lake Working Group on Financial Regulation. 2009. Credit default swaps, clearinghouses, and exchanges. Working paper. July.

State Street. 2006. Response to DG Internal Market "Draft working document on post-trading" and DG Competition "Issues paper—competition in EU securities trading and post-trading". June 30.

Steil, B. 1996. Equity trading I: the evolution of European trading systems. In *The European Equity Markets: The State of the Union and an Agenda for the Millennium*. Edited by B. Steil ECMI & RIIA. Chap. 1.

———. 2001. Creating securities markets in developing countries: a new approach for the age of automated trading. *International Finance* 4 (2): 257–78. Summer.

———. 2002a. Changes in the ownership and governance of securities exchanges: causes and consequences. In *Brookings-Wharton Papers on Financial Services 2002*. Edited by R. E. Litan and R. Herring, pp. 61–82. Washington, D.C.: Brookings Institution.

———. 2002b. Building a transatlantic securities market. Council on Foreign Relations. December.

———. 2003. Comment letter on NYSE governance to Messrs. H. Carl McCall and Leon Panetta, co-chairs, Special Committee on Governance of the NYSE. July 1.

———. 2005. Europe's securities markets need new plumbing. *Financial Times*. August 11.

———. 2007. Turquoise promise: to unclog European trading. *Financial Times*. May 8.

Strickberger, M. 2002. EuroCCP closes; a victim to low-trading activity. *Operations Management*. September 16.

Stuchfield, N. (Managing Director, Stuchfield Consultancy). 2005. Is exchange liquidity contestable? In *Handbook of World Stock, Derivative and Commodity Exchanges*. London: Mondo Visione.

Sundaramurthy, C., and M. Lewis. 2003. Control and collaboration: paradoxes of governance. *Academy of Management Review* 28 (3): 397–415.

Sunday Telegraph. 2001. LSE in talks with LIFFE on forming an alliance. May 27.

Sunday Times. 2001a. Garban will bid for Liffe. June 3.

———. 2001b. Euronext to bid for LIFFE in competition with LSE. September 30.

Sutcliffe, C., J. Board, and S. Wells. 2002. *Transparency and Fragmentation: Financial Market Regulation in a Dynamic Environment*. Basingstoke: Palgrave Macmillan.

Swan MP, the Hon. Wayne, Treasurer (Australia) & Hon. Chris Bowen MP, Minister for Human Services, Minister for Financial Services, Superannuation and Corporate Law (Australia). 2009. Reforms to the Supervision of Australia's Financial Markets. Joint media release. August 24.

SWX, SIS x-clear, and LCH.Clearnet. 2006. SWX central counterparty service—service overview. News release. April.

Sydney Futures Exchange. 2000. Information memorandum. June 19.

Tafara, E., and R. J. Peterson. 2007. A blueprint for cross-border access to U.S. investors: a new international framework. *Harvard International Law Journal* 48 (1): 31–68. Winter.

Tapking, J., and J. Yang. 2004. Horizontal and vertical integration in securities trading and settlement. European Central Bank, Working Paper Series, No. 387. August.

Temple Lang, J. 1994. Defining legitimate competition: companies' duties to supply competitors, and access to essential facilities. *Fordham International Law Journal* 18, 437–524.

———. 2005. The application of the essential facility doctrine to intellectual property rights under European competition law, Antitrust and Patent Copyright. In *Antitrust, Patents, and Copyright: EU and US Perspectives*. Edited by F. Lévêque and H. Shelanski. Cheltenham, UK: Edward Elgar. Chap. 3.

Tessler, J. 2006. TARGET2: prospects and challenges for the clearing and settlement of securities. *Euro Finance Week*. November 9.

Thain, J. 2004. The quest for the right balance. *Wall Street Journal*, A14. December 21.

Thomas Murray. 1999. *Thomas Murray CSD Guide*. Thomas Murray Publications.

Thomson Reuters. 2009. Thomson Reuters addresses equity market liquidity fragmentation and price competition in Japan. Jul 21.

Tiner, J. (CEO, FSA). 2006. Keynote address at the enforcement law conference. June 16.

Tonello, M. 2006. Revisiting stock market short-termism. Corporate/Investor Summit Series, The Conference Board Research Report No. R-1386-06-RR. April.

Toronto Stock Exchange. 2006. TSX Group: history at a glance. Media release. August 15.

Trade News, The. 2007. Chi-X ATS starts clearing and settling European equities trades. April 16.

———. 2009a. Regulatory concerns halt LCH's interoperability deals. October 27.

Trade News, The. 2009b. Nasdaq OMX abandons US CCP plans. October 30.

Treptow, F. 2006. *The Economics of Demutualization: An Empirical Analysis of the Securities Exchange Industry.* Munich: Deutscher Universitäts-Verlag. Innovation und Entrepreneurship. Gabler Edition Wissenschaft.

Trombly, M. 2007. Asia report: competition looms. *Waters Magazine.* July 1.

Tumpel-Gugerell, G. (Member, Executive Board of the ECB). 2006. TARGET2-securities: from vision to reality. The eurosystem's contribution to an integrated securities market. EU Commission's Conference on the EU's New Regime for Clearing and Settlement in Europe, Brussels. Speech. November 30.

———. 2007. TARGET2-Securities: a big win for European integration. *Journal of Financial Transformation* dinner, London. Speech. September 27.

Turnbull, S. 2000. The competitive advantages of stakeholder mutuals. International Institute for Self-Governance; University of Sydney, Department of Government and International Relations. September 20.

Turney, J. 2005. Defining the limits of the EU essential facilities doctrine on intellectual property rights: the primacy of securing optimal innovation. *Northwestern Journal of Technology and Intellectual Property* 3 (2): 179–202. Spring.

U.S. Department of Justice. 2007. Statement of the Department of Justice Antitrust Division on its decision to close its investigation of Chicago Mercantile Exchange Holdings Inc.'s acquisition of CBOT Holdings Inc: Investigation finds that combination not likely to substantially reduce competition. June 11.

———. 2008. Comments on "Review of the regulatory structure associated with financial institutions," Department of the Treasury TREAS-DO-2007-0018 (17/10/2007). January 31.

U.S. Senate. 1975. Senate Report No. 94-75 (1975) accompanying S. 249, 94th Congress, 1st Session.

U.S. Senate Subcommittee on Securities, Committee on Banking Housing and Urban Affairs. 1973. Securities industry study. S. Rep. No. 13, 93d Cong., 1st Sess. April 6.

U.S. Treasury. 2009. Administration's regulatory reform agenda reaches new milestone: final piece of legislative language delivered to Capitol Hill. Press Release TG-261. August 11.

Van Cauwenberge, S. 2003. New structure for clearing and settlement systems in the EU. *Financial Stability Review, National Bank of Belgium*: 83–104.

Van Cayseele, P. 2004. Competition and the organisation of the clearing and settlement industry. Discussion paper, C.E.S., K. U. Leuven.

Van Cayseele, P., and C. Wuyts. 2005. Cost efficiency in the European securities settlement and safekeeping industry. Working paper, K. U. Leuven, Department of Economics, and Universiteit van Amsterdam. July 18.

Vaughan, R., and R. Pollard. 1984. *Rebuilding America*. Vol. 1: *Planning and Managing Public Works in the 1980s*. Washington, D.C.: Council of State Planning Agencies.

Venkataraman, K. 2001. Automated versus floor trading—an analysis of execution costs on the Paris and New York exchanges. *Journal of Finance* 56 (4): 1445–85.

virt-x. 2003. virt-x, LCH and SIS x-clear launch first pan-European CCP structure. Media release. May 6.

———. 2005. LSE merger inquiry—new remedy option—interoperable central counterparties. Letter to Competition Commission. London. VTX-MCO-COR-20050425/E. September 13.

virt-x, SIS x-clear, and LCH.Clearnet. 2004. virt-x central counterparty service—members' service description. The cross-border exchange. May.

Voth, H.-J. 2005. Competition from OTC cash equity trading and the pricing behaviour of stock exchanges. Submission to Competition Commission regarding potential takeover of London Stock Exchange by Deutsche Börse and Euronext.

Waller, S. W., and B. M. Frischmann. 2006. Essential facilities, infrastructure and open access. Working Paper. November 2.

———. 2007. The essential nature of infrastructure or the infrastructural nature of essential facilities. Working Paper. February 6.

Walsh, F. 2006a. Furse to meet Nasdaq chief after share swoop. *The Guardian*. April 13.

———. 2006b. LSE rejects £2.7bn Nasdaq bid. *The Guardian*. November 20.

Walther, B. R. 1997. Investor sophistication and market earnings expectations. *Journal of Accounting Research* 35 (2): 157–79. Autumn.

Waters magazine. 2006. Clearing the air. Waters Profile. February 1.

Webb, D. M. 2002. The delisting fiasco. http://webb-site.com/articles/delisting.asp. July 29.

Weber, B. W. 2006. Adoption of electronic trading at the international securities exchange. *Decision Support Systems* 41: 728–46.

White, B. 2003. Grasso handpicked pay panel—structure at NYSE called unusual. *Washington Post*. September 12.

Williamson, O. E. 1975. *Markets and Hierarchies: Analysis and Antitrust Implications*. New York: Free Press.

———. 1979. Transaction-cost economics: the governance of contractual relations. *Journal of Law and Economics* 22 (2): 233–61. October.

———. 1985. *The Economic Institutions of Capitalism*. New York: Free Press.

———. 1990. The firm as a nexus of treaties: an introduction. In *The Firm as a Nexus of Treaties*. Edited by M. Aoki, B. Gustafson, and O. E. Williamson. London: Sage.

———. 1996. *The Mechanisms of Governance*. Oxford: Oxford University Press.

World Bank and International Monetary Fund. 2005. *Financial Sector Assessment: A Handbook*. Washington, DC.

World Bank, Independent Evaluation Group. 2006. Financial Sector Assessment Program: IEG review of the joint World Bank and IMF initiative.

World Federation of Exchanges. 2005. Regulation of markets survey 2004. With the collaboration of Roberta S. Karmel. January.

———. 2006. Cost and revenue survey 2005. September.

———. 2008. 2007 Cost and revenue survey. December.

Wright, W. 2000. Unease over iX voting structure. *Financial News*. July 24.

———. 2001. Euroclear lobbies Cedel shareholders. *Financial News*. May 28.

———. 2006. A step forward in clearing. *Financial News*. July 10.

Xu, C., and K. Pistor. 2005. Enforcement failure under incomplete law: theory and evidence from financial market regulation. Working paper, London School of Economics and Columbia Law School. December.

Yartey, C. A., and C. K. Adjasi. 2007. Stock market development in sub-Saharan Africa: critical issues and challenges. IMF Working Paper, African Department WP/07/209. August.

Yiu, E. 2002. Stock exchange chief says he will stand down next April. *South China Morning Post*. November 14.

Zenina, Z. A. 2001. Case study: merger of the London and Frankfurt Stock Exchanges. Harvard Law School, International Finance Seminar. May 14.

Zhang, Y. (President & CEO, Shenzhen Stock Exchange). 2001. The PRC securities markets: an overview of its regulatory capability and efficiency. Conference on Financial Sector Reform in China. September 11–13.

Contributors

JAMES J. ANGEL IS associate professor of Finance at Georgetown University. He studies the structure, operation, and regulation of financial markets with a special interest in short selling, and has visited over 50 exchanges around the world. He is also a former Chair of the NASDAQ Economic Advisory Board, and is a member of the boards of directors of DirectEdge Stock Exchanges. He holds a B.S. from Caltech, an M.B.A. from Harvard, and a Ph.D. from UC Berkeley, and is a CFA.

BRANDON BECKER is Executive Vice President and Chief Legal Officer at TIAA-CREF. Previously, he was a Partner at WilmerHale and Chair of its Broker-Dealer Group. Brandon worked at the SEC from 1978 to 1996, where he served as Director, Division of Market Regulation. He holds a B.A. (University of Minnesota), a J.D. (University of San Diego School of Law), and an LL.M. (Columbia Law School).

SONYA BRANCH is a Senior Director, heading up the Markets & Projects/Series and Public Markets Group, and a member of the Senior Management Team, at the Office of Fair Trading, United Kingdom. She was previously an Antitrust Partner at the global law firm Clifford Chance, and in this position had key client relationships with a number of global companies, including Barclays and Citigroup.

JOHN CARSON is Managing Director of Compliax Consulting, and a capital markets expert with extensive international experience in the operation and regulation of capital markets. Formerly a senior executive of the Toronto Stock Exchange, his recent major projects concern the organization and operations of SROs, international trends in regulatory structure, and the evolution of exchanges.

ANDREA M. CORCORAN is Founder and Principal of Align International LLC, a financial regulatory consultancy. She is currently also Adjunct Professor at Georgetown Law Center, Chair of the Securities Advisory Board of the Toronto Centre, and member of the Committee of European Securities Regulators Consultative Panel. She previously held several senior positions at the US Commodity Futures Trading Commission, and chaired the IOSCO Implementation Task Force. She twice received the highest award for US government service.

JENNIFER ELLIOTT is a Senior Financial Sector Expert in the Monetary and Capital Markets Department of the IMF. where she evaluates securities regulatory systems and recommends reforms. She has also been legal counsel at the Ontario Securities Commission, legal counsel in Member Regulation at the Investment Dealers Association of Canada, and legal counsel at the Toronto Stock Exchange.

ALLEN FERRELL is the Greenfield Professor of Securities Law, Harvard Law School. He has written widely in the areas of securities law and corporate governance.

He received his J.D. from Harvard Law School and his Ph.D. in economics from MIT. He is also a faculty associate at the Kennedy School of Government and a member of the board of economic advisors to FINRA.

ANDREAS M. FLECKNER is a Senior Research Fellow at the Max Planck Institute for Comparative and International Private Law, Hamburg, Germany, and a Lecturer at Bucerius Law School. He has a Ph.D. from Regensburg, an LL.M. from Harvard, and is an attorney-at-law (New York).

STAVROS GADINIS is an assistant professor at UC Berkeley Law School. His research examines how international competition for financial services shapes regulatory policy, and how regulators enforce securities laws. Recent articles include "The Politics of Competition in International Financial Regulation" (*Harvard International Law Journal*) and "Markets as Regulators: A Survey" (with Howell Jackson) (*Southern California Law Review*).

MARK GRIFFITHS is Competition Counsel for the Absa Group, one of Africa's largest banks. Prior to his appointment, he was an associate in the EU and Competition practice of Clifford Chance (London office). He also previously worked for the European Commission as well as being specialist legal advisor to the House of Lords EU Select Committee.

GEOFFREY HORTON is an economist, consultant, and former industry regulator. He was the first utility regulator in Northern Ireland, a director at the Office of Fair Trading, Director of Regulation in electricity in Britain, Senior Economic Adviser in the UK Department of Energy, and a Treasury economist. He is now a consultant in regulatory economics in many industries and jurisdictions.

PAMELA HUGHES is a senior partner in the Securities Group at Blake, Cassels & Graydon LLP, Toronto, Canada. Her practice focuses on international corporate finance and mergers and acquisitions transactions and advice regarding capital market regulation. She was formerly Director of the Capital Markets/International Markets Branch of the Ontario Securities Commission, and the primary negotiator of the multijurisdictional disclosure system between Canada and the United States.

HOWELL E. JACKSON is the James S. Reid, Jr., Professor of Law at Harvard Law School. His research interests include financial regulation and international securities markets.

HUW JONES has been a reporter for 14 years with Reuters news agency in New York, London, and Brussels. He has written extensively about Wall Street, US derivatives exchanges, the emergence of a pan-European stock market, exchange consolidation, and EU financial policymaking. He is joint author of *European Equity Investor: Markets, Companies and Culture.*

CALLY JORDAN is an associate professor of Law at the University of Melbourne and visiting professor at Duke University Law School. She teaches courses on international finance and capital markets regulation and is an expert on comparative aspects of corporate law and finance. She spent several years at the World Bank and practiced with the New York office of Cleary, Gottlieb, Steen & Hamilton.

Roberta S. Karmel is Centennial Professor of Law and Codirector of the Dennis J. Block Center for the Study of International Business Law at Brooklyn Law School. She is a former commissioner of the Securities and Exchange Commission.

Chee Keong Low is an Advocate and Solicitor of the High Court of Malaya and an Associate Professor in Corporate Law at the Chinese University of Hong Kong. He is also a member of the Listing Committee of the Stock Exchange of Hong Kong and a member of the Financial Reporting Review Panel in Hong Kong and served as a member of the Listing Committee of the Stock Exchange of Hong Kong from May 2006 to July 2010.

Alistair Milne is Reader in Banking and Finance at Cass Business School, London, and a visiting scholar at the Research Department of the Bank of Finland. Previously he was economic adviser at the Bank of England; lecturer in economics at the University of Surrey, research fellow at London Business School, and a macroeconomist working for HM Treasury and for the Government of Malawi. He holds a Ph.D. from the London School of Economics.

Sadakazu Osaki is Head of Research, Center for Strategic Management and Innovation, Nomura Research Institute, and Visiting Professor, University of Tokyo Law School. He specializes in the regulation of capital markets. His English publications include *Insider Trading: Global Developments and Analysis* (2009 joint) and *Selected Legal Issues of E-Commerce* (2002). He received an LL.M. with Distinction (London University and Edinburgh University) and an LL.B. (Tokyo University).

Onenne Partsch is a lawyer registered with the Brussels and Luxembourg bars. She works on both domestic and international issues for a range of clients including both private and public institutions, in developed and developing countries. She worked previously for Clearstream International, the Central Bank of Luxembourg, and the European Central Bank. She holds a law degree from Liege (1995) and an LL.M. from Harvard Law School (1998).

Alix Prentice is Special Counsel in the London office Financial Services Department of Cadwalader, Wickersham & Taft LLP. Previously she was Counsel in the London and New York offices of WilmerHale, and also worked in the General Counsel's office of the UK Financial Services Authority.

Duo Qin is Senior Lecturer at Queen Mary, University of London. She specializes in applied econometrics, empirical finance, international economics, emerging markets, and macroeconomic modeling.

Reinhard H. Schmidt has been Wilhelm Merton Professor of International Banking and Finance at Goethe-Universität in Frankfurt, Germany, since 1991. Before that, he was a professor of finance at the Universities of Goettingen and Trier and Georgetown University in Washington, DC. His recent research work focuses on comparative financial systems and corporate governance. He is the author or editor of 23 books and more than 150 articles in academic journals and books.

BARIS SERIFSOY works for UBS AG in London. He was previously a research assistant at the Finance Department of the Goethe University Frankfurt for four years, which he spent in part as a visiting scholar at the Wharton School. During this period he published a series of articles on the economics of the stock exchange industry. He obtained his Ph.D. in 2006.

HERBIE SKEETE is the founder of Mondo Visione, the leading source of insight and knowledge about the world's exchanges and trading venues. He also organizes the Mondo Visione Exchange Forum. He edits the industry-standard *Handbook of World Stock, Derivative and Commodity Exchanges*, as well as *World Exchanges: Global Industry Outlook and Investment Analysis* and the newsletter *Trading Places*.

CATHERINE WADDAMS is Director of the interdisciplinary ESRC Centre for Competition Policy and Professor in Norwich Business School at the University of East Anglia. Her research has focused on the energy sector and the effects of privatization, regulation, and market opening, particularly their distributional impacts and the role of consumers. She was a part-time member of the UK Competition Commission from 2001 to 2009.

CHERIE WELDON is Special Counsel at Wilmer Cutler Pickering Hale and Dorr LLP. She advises clients on a variety of issues related to exchanges, clearinghouses and broker-dealers, with a focus on market structure questions. She has a B.A. in Mathematics from Williams College and a J.D. from Yale Law School.

STEPHEN WELLS is a Senior Research Fellow at the ICMA Centre Henley Business School, University of Reading, and an independent consultant on financial markets. He has conducted developmental studies for many markets, particularly in developing Asia. He has also undertaken empirical studies of developments in the UK equity and bond markets as well as cross-border studies of world stock markets.

Index